Literary Taste, Culture and Mass Communication

Volume 10

AUTHORSHIP

Literary Taste, Culture and Mass Communication

Volume 10

AUTHORSHIP

edited by

Peter Davison/Rolf Meyersohn/Edward Shils

CHADWYCK-HEALEY CAMBRIDGE
SOMERSET HOUSE TEANECK, NJ

© Chadwyck-Healey Ltd 1978

Chadwyck-Healey Ltd
20 Newmarket Road
Cambridge CB5 8DT
ISBN 0 85964 045 0

Somerset House
417 Maitland Avenue
Teaneck, NJ 07666
ISBN 0 914146 53 X

Library of Congress Cataloging in Publication Data
Main entry under title:

Authorship

(Literary taste, culture and mass communication;
v. 10)
Bibliography: p.
1. Authorship — Addresses, essays, lectures.
2. Authors — Addresses, essays, lectures. I. Series

AC1.L79 vol. 10 [PN151] 808'.02   77-90619

British Library Cataloguing in Publication Data

Literary taste, culture and mass communication.
Vol. 10: Authorship

1. Arts and society — Addresses, essays lectures.
I. Davison, Peter II. Meyersohn, Rolf
III. Shils, Edward Albert IV. Authorship

700   NX180.S6

Printed in England

Contents

Introduction

Volumes 10 and 11 are devoted to authorship. Volume 11 is concerned
exclusively with the writer and politics (although shading into an analytical
study of radio and film as propaganda in one instance), whereas this volume is
concerned with a variety of other aspects of authorship, from 'Why I Write',
via the economics of writing and the sociology of authorship, to the fate of
writers. It will be noted that these volumes contain a majority of contributions
by established authors — there are twenty-one authors, beginning with John
Betjeman and concluding with Dylan Thomas, in *Horizon*'s questionnaire on
the 'Cost of Letters', alone. Some of the contributions are quite slight and,
indeed, there is even a touch of facetiousness — or is it desperation? — in
some of the replies to *Horizon*'s questionnaire. Thus, the little piece from *The
Author* of 1909 is not offered as a detailed analysis of authorship in the
market place, nor of the philosophy of decadence, but as a *cri de coeur* of the
position in which the author finds himself betwixt the claims of art and
economics. What it is hoped that these contributions will do is suggest anew
the circumstances in which the creative writer must work, touching on the
author's motivation, social relationships, economic vulnerability, and his or
her creative processes.

Orwell is refreshingly free of humbug in analyzing his motives for
writing (as he himself puts it, it is humbug to pretend that 'sheer egoism' is
not one of the motives for writing — 'and a strong one', p. 5). But he also
tellingly expresses his joy in 'mere words' and, in the process, gives by
implication a far better justification for old-spelling editions than I have ever
heard advanced by bibliographers (p. 6)!

Jacques Barzun is, after over a quarter-of-a-century, also refreshing in
dashing cold water over the too-loose association of artist and society.

> Society taken in the lump does not systematically reject or divorce
> the artist. It is for the most part unaware that any marriage or
> engagement has taken place . . . All the nonsense written and
> spoken about the blessed unity of the thirteenth century, is sheer
> illusion and *sehnsucht* — a mirage, and as such dangerous, because
> it leads away from real cases (p. 15).

He is also sharply aware of the grave social consequences of the work that
attempts to be a near-masterpiece but fails and falls 'into facsimile' (p. 24).

Storm Jameson is also represented in this series by a contribution made
in 1937 to *Fact*, reprinted in volume 11. In this volume she is concerned
with the novel 'in a galloping decline', the author elbowed out by radio and

television. It is easy to point to the little piece reprinted from *The Author* in 1909, on 'The Decadence of the Novel' and, pondering on developments between 1909 and 1956, and since 1956, to assume that Storm Jameson and the anonymous author of 1909 were in error. The novel survived after 1909 long enough for Storm Jameson to fear its going under to radio and television. Yet after another twenty years, it has hardly done that. If their worst fears have fortunately not been fully realised, their voices were an essential part of the process of adaptation to new technical and social structures. Thus, whilst sympathising with Storm Jameson's understandable response to the analysis of a scene from *Hamlet* by computer as a 'solemn frivolity' (p. 37), we can be warned against an instrument 'endowed by human ingenuity with inhuman powers' (p. 37) but simultaneously be grateful for, at the least, the concordance-compiling capacity of the computer.

Richard Altick's statistical analysis shows very clearly how 'solid' middle-class most authors were until two or three decades ago and how they inevitably had to adapt to a growing readership of a different social class and with different aspirations (pp. 60—61). 'The genuinely dedicated literary artist, however, found himself in a predicament that has deep reverberations in our own time' (p. 61). Is this the real problem — or was it merely the coming of radio and television that so affected the craft of writing? Altick might usefully be contrasted with Hawkins's radio interview of George Orwell on the proletarian writer, which concludes this volume.

Philip Thody's defence of the literary critic stands midway between the concerns of volume 6, *The Sociology of Literature* and volume 12 (under 'Reviewing'), but it is included here because of the way it suggests how, from a critic's point of view, 'an author's work can reflect the basic social conflicts and problems of the society in which he lives' (p. 76). (Professor Thody, incidentally, has given on film a brilliant insight into how to lecture by demonstrating with devastating effect and wit how not to lecture.)

The next two articles, by Catharine Patrick and Roger L. Brown are concerned with the process of creativity. It is unlikely that any analysis of how creativity works will convince everyone, but the attempt to understand the creative process is perennial. Catharine Patrick had, a little earlier, written a monograph on creativity in poets (see Further Reading), but as the paper reprinted here is also concerned with the pictorial interpretation of poetry, it was thought it might have a double interest. Brown is concerned with the creative process in writing for the popular arts and although he can reasonably argue that this 'task itself can only be tackled in the same way that the writer's task has always had to be tackled' (p. 129), the pressures of the market-place may surely be seen differently by the writer — as *The Author* of 1909 suggests. Dale Warren's light-hearted account of the working habits of authors offers an ironist's response to the process of creativity.

The first of the two short articles on psychoanalysis and literature suggests that psychoanalysis will give the novelist greater insight into the motivation of his characters and enable the reader to distinguish more readily 'between serious and "true" fiction and fiction that is only catering to wish-fulfilling dreams' (p. 152). The second argues that literature can be used to study personality — of authors and 'human personality in general'. William Barrett looks again, post-Freud, at the supposed similarity of madness and inspiration.

The place of the author in the community and the pressures of the community upon authors are the concern of the next four contributions. Douglas Goldring's bitter plea for a revolution to free the English writer from the 'Stagnation, intrigue, snobbery, log-rolling, deadness' that marked for him the London literary scene — a revolution akin to that he found in the Germany of 1919 where, he says, the intellect was set free and 'the imagination of the artist (was) liberated from bondage' (p. 187) — follows. His response to the London of his time will not seem particularly dated, but the fresh winds he found in the Berlin of 1919 must inevitably strike us very differently when juxtaposed with what Charles Morgan has to say, writing just after the war that was to follow (and see Further Reading to volume 11 for the reference to Kurt Tucholsky's *Deutschland über alles*). Morgan is particularly interesting when he contrasts the open-mindedness of Victorian literary criticism — e.g. the response to Mrs Humphry Ward's *Robert Elsmere*, 1888 (which centres upon a young minister of religion's loss of faith) — with the authoritarianism of even great writers and critics (his example is Yeats) between the wars. Stephen Spender (two of whose articles appear in volume 11), writing in 1945, discusses the conflict between the power necessary to solve the problems of the post-war world and freedom, especially as it affects the writer. He points to two directions which literary movements might take: 'personalism' (which he associates with England and America), and a tendency in European literature in which authors 'create an ideal above politics, which political movements should seek to interpret in action' (p. 227).

The remaining articles, except Goldring's poem and the very last contribution, are concerned with the economics of authorship. Vytautas Kavolis (whose article on 'Political Dynamics and Artistic Creativity' begins volume 11) offers a sociological account of the effect of economic pressures on creativity. This is followed by a series of twenty-one responses to a short questionnaire on 'the cost of letters' (and it is ironic that a journal largely devoted to creativity should have circulated such a questionnaire in the light of Dale Warren's account of Rex Beach's response to questioning — see [Warren] pp. 138–139. Relative values of money in different periods and circumstances are very misleading, but it might be useful to compare the £500 a year that Alex Comfort lived on in the mid-1940s with the 'average' pay in the United Kingdom of something like seven times that amount in 1978. Geoffrey Wagner points to the problem faced by the minority writer (despite what he says, not, perhaps, peculiar to 1953), and Elmer Rice, one of the twentieth century's most innovatory dramatists, and James T. Farrell consider briefly and at greater length respectively the effects of industrialization

and commercialization on authors. Farrell cuts through the distinction
between high and low culture and points to the danger of 'commercial culture'.
He sees the possibility for cultural growth in post-war America and realises
how significant will be the role that writers might play. And one can reiterate
that their significance is not only in writing itself but in ever bringing before
their fellow authors and the general public the dangers to writing — to
authorship as such. Creative writers represented in this and volume 11 can
justly claim to have been well to the fore in being vigilant to the dangers
facing creativity, even if, (and perhaps chiefly because) economic necessity
quickened their response to the circumstances of publication. James Farrell's
article was also issued as a pamphlet and two more of his contributions are
to be found in volumes 11 and 12. His article is followed by a
tabulation of the fate of 'first novelists' in the decade just before and during
the 1939—45 War, drawn up by Alice Hackett.

A different facet of the problem posed for the author by increasing
commercialization and mechanization is prophetically presented by the
publisher, Geoffrey Faber, writing in 1936. His concern, twenty years before
the advent of the long-playing record was that the book should find a way of
exploiting the new media, rather than that author and publisher should adopt
a siege mentality and assume the inevitability of the operation of Gresham's
Law with the advent of mass media. How right has proved his prophecy now
that recorded novels are available on cassette in supermarkets:

> The commercial 'talking-book' is bound to come. Already there
> are 'talking-books' for the blind — ordinary gramophone records,
> each of which will run for twenty-five minutes. The time must
> arrive when it will be in the power of the ordinary citizen to put
> a record on his gramophone and sit down to listen to it for half-
> an-hour. Only — it may not be a gramophone at all. There are
> several other sound-reproducing mechanisms in the process of
> being invented or perfected (p. 371).

He goes on to describe an 'optical' gramophone, using paper tape, sold for
the price of a cinema ticket (pp. 371—372). As with anxieties that have not
been fully realised, the importance of Faber's prophecy is not its accuracy,
but his lively response to the problems faced by books and authors, and,
perhaps, his hopefulness.

The volume concludes with a radio discussion with George Orwell, to
which reference has already been made, and this is preceded by a poem by
Douglas Goldring published in 1920. I confess that the inclusion of these
verses is something of an indulgence on my part, and it is not even as if the
volume is wholly without verse (see Orwell's 'Why I Write', pp. 6—7). But
Goldring, wittily and charmingly, expresses an author's dilemma of a kind
different from those which are chiefly our concern when considering 'the
sociology of authorship', the community and the writer, economics and
psychoanalysis. We speak readily of the relationship of the author to his age,

his time, his group, his society — but see Jacques Barzun, (pp. 14–15). Yet it is easy to forget that all these may pass and leave an author feeling stranded. Literary tastes change and, in so doing, pass by the authors who gave them effect.

PETER DAVISON

Further Reading

There are some thirteen columns devoted to Authorship in the *New Cambridge Bibliography of English Literature*, iv, 1900—1950 (cols 61—74) and these include sections on how to write and market various kinds of literature, patronage, literary agents, relations with publishers and editors, and the author and politics. Publishers' archives are now being made available on microfilm by Chadwyck-Healey Ltd, Cambridge (the publishers of this series). Amongst the archives so far made available are those of the Cambridge University Press, 1696—1902; Longman, 1794—1914; Elkin Matthews, 1811—1938; Richard Bentley & Son, 1829—1898; Routledge, 1853—1902; Kegan Paul, Trench, Trübner and Henry S. King, 1853—1912; Swan Sonnenschein, 1878—1911; George Allen, 1893—1915; and Grant Richards, 1897—1948. A full review outlining the significance of this project was contributed by Professor Bernhard Fabian to *Börsenblatt für den Deutschen Buchhandel*, 5, 36 (1978).

Compared to the large amount of attention paid to distinctions between high and low cultures, the processes of communication, and the effects of mass media upon audiences and literature, relatively little attention has been paid to the author and the sociology of authorship. Thus, in the first of the Mass Culture readers, Rosenberg and White's collection bearing that title (1957), only one of nearly fifty contributions was specifically devoted to creativity: Herbert J. Gans's 'The Creator-Audience Relationship in the Mass Media: an analysis of movie making'. This, though interested in the creators (defined as 'the producers, directors, writers, actors and others whose decisions and actions create the movie', p. 315), is particularly concerned with the image the creators have of the audience: 'For analytical purposes this *audience image* can be isolated from the creative process as a whole' (p. 315; Gans is well aware that 'the audience' can be the creator himself, incidentally). There is no question that Gans is right, of course. I well remember how Robert Morley's play, *Edward My Son*, was not deemed by M.G.M. in 1948 to have an appropriate ending. What suited Morley — or his image of a London West End audience? — was not considered appropriate for a mass cinema audience. So a different ending was written for the film script — and a third ending actually filmed — but only for distribution in Britain. *That* ending was not considered by M.G.M. to be suitable for an American audience and the cast and sets were later re-assembled at great expense to make a fourth ending which the company thought right for its image of an American audience.

Malcolm Bradbury, a successful novelist as well as an academic and literary critic, does not neglect authorship in his *The Social Context of Modern English Literature* (Oxford 1971). Part Three is devoted to 'The Writer Today' and has illuminating chapters on 'The Place of the Artist in Liberal Society', 'Who Our Writers Are', and 'How Our Writers Live'. Bradbury, incidentally, is concerned with other matters appropriate to this series, having two chapters on 'Communications': 'The Climate of Literary Culture and the Literary Periodcial' and 'The Institutions of Literary Culture: the book and the media'; and a chapter called 'High and Mass Culture'. Like Findlater, Bradbury has also written on 'What are Authors Worth?' (*New Society*, 1965). Diana Laurenson's contribution to her and Alan Swingewood's *The Sociology of Literature* (London 1972) is devoted to 'The Writer and Society'. She discusses 'Origins of Authorship and Patronage'; 'The Professionalization of the Writer'; and 'The Writer in the Present Century'. See also Storm Jameson's *The Writer's Situation* (1947).

Richard Findlater wrote a second pamphlet for the Society of Authors in addition to the one reproduced in this volume. It is entitled *The Bookwriters, Who Are They?* (1966). He also contributed 'The Writer Considered as a Wage-Earner' to the *Times Literary Supplement*, 24 July 1969. J.W. Saunders's *The Profession of English Letters* (London 1964) covers a long period of authorship but reaches into the twentieth century. See also John Gross, *The Rise and Fall of the Man of Letters, English Literary Life since 1800* (London 1969), the Epilogue to which is included in volume 5, and Van Wyck Books, *The Writer in America* (New York 1953).

Catherine Patrick's monograph, 'Creative Thought in Poets', *Archives of Psychology*, no. 178 (1935) is mentioned in the Introduction. *Perspectives* 9 (1954) was devoted to a symposium on 'The Creative Artist and his Audience', with contributions by Saul Bellow on literature (arguing that people no longer respond as once they did to forms of reality); Robinson Jeffers on poetry; Robert Motherwell on painting (who argues that without an ethical conscience a painter is only a decorator); and Roger Sessions on music. Martin Turnell's and Charles Glicksberg's articles reprinted in volume 6 are also relevant to this volume.

Donald Davies has a provocative piece in *Twentieth Century* 155 (1954), 540–546, asking 'Is there a London Literary Racket?' He concludes that there isn't, but that there is a charmed circle of reviewers, third-programme mandarins, and editors, from whom those outside are estranged.

Finally, several of Allen Tate's articles reprinted in his *Essays of Four Decades* (1970) are well worth reading in the context of this volume. I have in mind 'The Profession of Letters in the South' (1935); 'The New Provincialism' (1945); 'The Man of Letters in the Modern World' (1952) – but see his Preface, reprinted in *Essays of Four Decades* written to the collection of essays bearing that title; and especially 'To Whom is the Poet Responsible?' (1950–51).

PETER DAVISON

Literary Taste, Culture and Mass Communication

Why I Write
George Orwell

from

Collected Essays, Journalism and Letters of George Orwell, vol. 1, Sonia Orwell and Ian Angus (eds.). Secker and Warburg, London, 1968.

1. Why I Write

From a very early age, perhaps the age of five or six, I knew that when I grew up I should be a writer. Between the ages of about seventeen and twenty-four I tried to abandon this idea, but I did so with the consciousness that I was outraging my true nature and that sooner or later I should have to settle down and write books.

I was the middle child of three, but there was a gap of five years on either side, and I barely saw my father before I was eight. For this and other reasons I was somewhat lonely, and I soon developed disagreeable mannerisms which made me unpopular throughout my schooldays. I had the lonely child's habit of making up stories and holding conversations with imaginary persons, and I think from the very start my literary ambitions were mixed up with the feeling of being isolated and undervalued. I knew that I had a facility with words and a power of facing unpleasant facts, and I felt that this created a sort of private world in which I could get my own back for my failure in everyday life. Nevertheless the volume of serious—i.e. seriously intended—writing which I produced all through my childhood and boyhood would not amount to half a dozen pages. I wrote my first poem at the age of four or five, my mother taking it down to dictation. I cannot remember anything about it except that it was about a tiger and the tiger had "chair-like teeth"—a good enough phrase, but I fancy the poem was a plagiarism of Blake's "Tiger, Tiger". At eleven, when the war of 1914–18 broke out, I wrote a patriotic poem which was printed in the local newspaper, as was another, two years later, on the death of Kitchener. From time to time, when I was a bit older, I wrote bad and usually unfinished "nature poems" in the Georgian style. I also, about twice, attempted a short story which was a ghastly failure. That was the total of the would-be serious work that I actually set down on paper during all those years.

However, throughout this time I did in a sense engage in literary activities. To begin with there was the made-to-order stuff which I produced quickly, easily and without much pleasure to myself. Apart from school work, I wrote *vers d'occasion*, semi-comic poems which I could turn out at what now seems to me astonishing speed —at fourteen I wrote a whole rhyming play, in imitation of Aristophanes, in about a week—and helped to edit school magazines, both printed and in manuscript. These magazines were the most pitiful burlesque stuff that you could imagine, and I took far less trouble with them than I now would with the cheapest journalism. But side by side with all this, for fifteen years or more, I was carrying out a literary exercise of a quite different kind: this was the making up of a continuous "story" about myself, a sort of diary existing only in the mind. I believe this is a common habit of children and adolescents. As a very small child I used to imagine that I was, say, Robin Hood, and picture myself as the hero of thrilling adventures, but quite soon my "story" ceased to be narcissistic in a crude way and became more and more a mere description of what I was doing and the things I saw. For minutes at a time this kind of thing would be running through my head: "He pushed the door open and entered the room. A yellow beam of sunlight, filtering through the muslin curtains, slanted on to the table, where a matchbox, half open, lay beside the inkpot, With his right hand in his pocket he moved across to the window. Down in the street a tortoiseshell cat was chasing a dead leaf," etc etc. This habit continued till I was about twenty-five, right through my non-literary years. Although I had to search, and did search, for the right words, I seemed to be making this descriptive effort almost against my will, under a kind of compulsion from outside. The "story" must, I suppose, have reflected the styles of the various writers I admired at different ages, but so far as I remember it always had the same meticulous descriptive quality.

When I was about sixteen I suddenly discovered the joy of mere words, i.e. the sounds and associations of words. The lines from *Paradise Lost*,

> So hee with difficulty and labour hard
> Moved on: with difficulty and labour hee,

which do not now seem to me so very wonderful, sent shivers down my backbone; and the spelling "hee" for "he" was an added pleasure. As for the need to describe things, I knew all about it already. So it is clear what kind of books I wanted to write, in so far as I could be said to want to write books at that time. I wanted to write enormous naturalistic novels with unhappy endings, full of detailed descriptions and arresting similes, and also full of purple passages in which words were used partly for the sake of their sound. And in fact my first completed novel, *Burmese Days*, which I wrote when I was thirty but projected much earlier, is rather that kind of book.

I give all this background information because I do not think one can assess a writer's motives without knowing something of his early development. His subject matter will be determined by the age he lives in—at least this is true in tumultuous, revolutionary ages like our own—but before he ever begins to write he will have acquired an emotional attitude from which he will never completely escape. It is his job, no doubt, to discipline his temperament and avoid getting stuck at some immature stage, or in some perverse mood: but if he escapes from his early influences altogether, he will have killed his impulse to write. Putting aside the need to earn a living, I think there are four great motives for writing, at any rate for writing prose. They exist in different degrees in every writer, and in any one writer the proportions will vary from time to time, according to the atmosphere in which he is living. They are:

1. Sheer egoism. Desire to seem clever, to be talked about, to be remembered after death, to get your own back on grown-ups who snubbed you in childhood, etc etc. It is humbug to pretend that this is not a motive, and a strong one. Writers share this characteristic with scientists, artists, politicians, lawyers, soldiers, successful businessmen—in short, with the whole top crust of humanity. The great mass of human beings are not acutely selfish. After the age of about thirty they abandon individual ambition—in many cases, indeed, they almost abandon the sense of being individuals at all—and live chiefly for others, or are simply smothered under drudgery. But there is also the minority of gifted, wilful people who are determined to live their own lives to the end, and writers belong in this class. Serious writers, I should say, are on the whole more vain and self-centred than journalists, though less interested in money.

2. Aesthetic enthusiasm. Perception of beauty in the external world, or, on the other hand, in words and their right arrangement. Pleasure in the impact of one sound on another, in the firmness of good prose or the rhythm of a good story. Desire to share an experience which one feels is valuable and ought not to be missed. The aesthetic motive is very feeble in a lot of writers, but even a

pamphleteer or a writer of textbooks will have pet words and phrases which appeal to him for non-utilitarian reasons; or he may feel strongly about typography, width of margins, etc. Above the level of a railway guide, no book is quite free from aesthetic considerations.

3. Historical impulse. Desire to see things as they are, to find out true facts and store them up for the use of posterity.

4. Political purpose—using the word "political" in the widest possible sense. Desire to push the world in a certain direction, to alter other people's idea of the kind of society that they should strive after. Once again, no book is genuinely free from political bias. The opinion that art should have nothing to do with politics is itself a political attitude.

It can be seen how these various impulses must war against one another, and how they must fluctuate from person to person and from time to time. By nature—taking your "nature" to be the state you have attained when you are first adult—I am a person in whom the first three motives would outweigh the fourth. In a peaceful age I might have written ornate or merely descriptive books, and might have remained almost unaware of my political loyalties. As it is I have been forced into becoming a sort of pamphleteer. First I spent five years in an unsuitable profession (the Indian Imperial Police, in Burma), and then I underwent poverty and the sense of failure. This increased my natural hatred of authority and made me for the first time fully aware of the existence of the working classes, and the job in Burma had given me some understanding of the nature of imperialism: but these experiences were not enough to give me an accurate political orientation. Then came Hitler, the Spanish civil war, etc. By the end of 1935 I had still failed to reach a firm decision. I remember a little poem that I wrote at that date, expressing my dilemma:

> A happy vicar I might have been
> Two hundred years ago,
> To preach upon eternal doom
> And watch my walnuts grow;
>
> But born, alas, in an evil time,
> I missed that pleasant haven,
> For the hair has grown on my upper lip
> And the clergy are all clean-shaven.

And later still the times were good,
We were so easy to please,
We rocked our troubled thoughts to sleep
On the bosoms of the trees.

All ignorant we dared to own
The joys we now dissemble;
The greenfinch on the apple bough
Could make my enemies tremble.

But girls' bellies and apricots,
Roach in a shaded stream,
Horses, ducks in flight at dawn,
All these are a dream.

It is forbidden to dream again;
We maim our joys or hide them;
Horses are made of chromium steel
And little fat men shall ride them.

I am the worm who never turned,
The eunuch without a harem;
Between the priest and the commissar
I walk like Eugene Aram;

And the commissar is telling my fortune
While the radio plays,
But the priest has promised an Austin Seven,
For Duggie always pays.

I dreamed I dwelt in marble halls,
And woke to find it true;
I wasn't born for an age like this;
Was Smith? Was Jones? Were you?[1]

The Spanish war and other events in 1936–37 turned the scale and thereafter I knew where I stood. Every line of serious work that I have written since 1936 has been written, directly or indirectly, *against* totalitarianism and *for* democratic Socialism, as I understand it. It seems to me nonsense, in a period like our own, to think that one can avoid writing of such subjects. Everyone writes of them in

---

[1] This poem first appeared in the *Adelphi*, December 1936.

one guise or another. It is simply a question of which side one takes and what approach one follows. And the more one is conscious of one's political bias, the more chance one has of acting politically without sacrificing one's aesthetic and intellectual integrity.

What I have most wanted to do throughout the past ten years is to make political writing into an art. My starting point is always a feeling of partisanship, a sense of injustice. When I sit down to write a book, I do not say to myself, "I am going to produce a work of art." I write it because there is some lie that I want to expose, some fact to which I want to draw attention, and my initial concern is to get a hearing. But I could not do the work of writing a book, or even a long magazine article, if it were not also an aesthetic experience. Anyone who cares to examine my work will see that even when it is downright propaganda it contains much that a full-time politician would consider irrelevant. I am not able, and I do not want, completely to abandon the world-view that I acquired in childhood. So long as I remain alive and well I shall continue to feel strongly about prose style, to love the surface of the earth, and to take pleasure in solid objects and scraps of useless information. It is no use trying to suppress that side of myself. The job is to reconcile my ingrained likes and dislikes with the essentially public, non-individual activities that this age forces on all of us.

It is not easy. It raises problems of construction and of language, and it raises in a new way the problem of truthfulness. Let me give just one example of the cruder kind of difficulty that arises. My book about the Spanish civil war, *Homage to Catalonia*, is, of course, a frankly political book, but in the main it is written with a certain detachment and regard for form. I did try very hard in it to tell the whole truth without violating my literary instincts. But among other things it contains a long chapter, full of newspaper quotations and the like, defending the Trotskyists who were accused of plotting with Franco. Clearly such a chapter, which after a year or two would lose its interest for any ordinary reader, must ruin the book. A critic whom I respect read me a lecture about it. "Why did you put in all that stuff?" he said. "You've turned what might have been a good book into journalism." What he said was true, but I could not have done otherwise. I happened to know, what very few people in England had been allowed to know, that innocent men were being falsely accused. If I had not been angry about that I should never have written the book.

In one form or another this problem comes up again. The problem of language is subtler and would take too long to discuss. I will only say that of late years I have tried to write less picturesquely and more exactly. In any case I find that by the time you have perfected any style of writing, you have always outgrown it. *Animal Farm* was the first book in which I tried, with full consciousness of what I was doing, to fuse political purpose and artistic purpose into one whole. I have not written a novel for seven years, but I hope to write another fairly soon. It is bound to be a failure, every book is a failure, but I know with some clarity what kind of book I want to write.

Looking back through the last page or two, I see that I have made it appear as though my motives in writing were wholly public-spirited. I don't want to leave that as the final impression. All writers are vain, selfish and lazy, and at the very bottom of their motives there lies a mystery. Writing a book is a horrible, exhausting struggle, like a long bout of some painful illness. One would never undertake such a thing if one were not driven on by some demon whom one can neither resist nor understand. For all one knows that demon is simply the same instinct that makes a baby squall for attention. And yet it is also true that one can write nothing readable unless one constantly struggles to efface one's own personality. Good prose is like a window pane. I cannot say with certainty which of my motives are the strongest, but I know which of them deserve to be followed. And looking back through my work, I see that it is invariably where I lacked a *political* purpose that I wrote lifeless books and was betrayed into purple passages, sentences without meaning, decorative adjectives and humbug generally.

Gangrel [No. 4, Summer], 1946; SJ; EYE; OR; CE.

Artist Against Society: Some Articles of War
Jacques Barzun

from

Partisan Review, vol. 19, no. 1, 1952.

Jacques Barzun

ARTIST AGAINST SOCIETY:
SOME ARTICLES OF WAR*

There are at least three reasons why, in spite of all that
has been said and written on the subject, we must keep discussing
the question of Artist and Society, especially in the United States.
One reason is that from all sides, in all the arts, government support is
being clamored for. A second is that industrial society (whether
capitalist or socialist) is, or is said to be, inimical to the production
of great art. The third is that the characteristic art of our century—
so-called modern art—is, or is said to be peculiarly obscure and
charmless—hence *insupportable* as well as unrepresentative.

And then there is the outward reason arising from all of these,
which is that hardly a week passes without some explicit complaint
being uttered about the present situation of the arts. The observer
soon finds that this miscellaneous literature of protest makes use of
set terms, and appeals with the aid of historical platitudes to well-
rehearsed feelings about art and social life. In short, an established
public opinion exists on the subject, corresponding to emotions whose
importance is quite simply that they affect the people most closely
concerned with art.

In a time of self-conscious and self-righteous purposes, it is
perhaps inevitable that we should try to fill the gap between hope
and fulfillment by means of clichés, comparisons, and complaints.
But it may also be true that part of the despair is due to our circling
around among ill-considered notions which arouse contradictory feelings and leave us dissatisfied as well as exhausted. We start, for
example, with the axiom that art, in and of itself, is a good thing.
Not necessarily true but—agreed. Then we are reminded that art is a

*This essay is drawn from the Northwestern University Centennial Lecture
delivered by the author at Evanston, Illinois, on April 16, 1951.

costly undertaking, which society should in some way regularly support. Granted. Therefore the artist has a duty to society. But of course we don't want to dictate his style or his opinions—the results of totalitarian practice are too fresh in our minds and all too clear. At the same time, ours being a democratic country, the people should get what they like—especially if their taxes pay for it—and they don't seem to like high art. It follows that the really great artist finds no support, and feels alienated from his society, divorced—and without alimony. Now since in our conscious moments we admire only great artists, and as they are all alienated, we are forced to conclude that art has never been so little honored as now. This is because America is materialistic, everyone seeking coarse pleasures with automobiles and iceboxes. Now in the thirteenth century, when men had a common faith, why——

And so it goes, from plausibility to plausibility without once touching the earth. Consider the vagueness—and the vulgarity—of that fundamental phrase, "the artist and his society." What lies behind this personification and this possessiveness? "Herman Melville and *his* society." "*Our* society and *its* artists." The implication seems to be that these are two contracting parties, who in a healthy state would live together on terms of amiable give-and-take. Society above all would give and would take. Herman Melville should have had readers *and* royalties, and in return the American society of 1865 should have been "expressed," embalmed, apotheosized, by Melville.

But who composes this "society" and how is its contract with any one artist, who is necessarily self-appointed, to be drawn up and enforced? Again, what is the exact meaning of the artist's "expressing" his society? To illustrate once more with novelists, it is clear that what Proust and Henry James are praised for is damning "their" society; they are cheered for depicting its fatal illness and elaborately jumping upon the corpse. It is true that they also lived rather comfortably out of *its* pocket; but that did not disarm their enmity— surely a curious relation for contracting parties under the rule of give-and-take.

Is it not obvious that innumerable confusions hide behind the phrase which sets up artist and society as two sovereigns in compulsory alliance, and prescribes their conduct in the language of claim and counterclaim? To question this is not to imply that an artist has no claim upon his contemporaries, but merely to bring out the absurdity of embodying the complexities of the case in the possessive adjective, no matter which way it points. As long as we use it, the danger is that the indignation we feel about the lot of the artist will be misdirected; it will be the indignation of cheap melodrama, which contrasts the artist-hero pursuing truth with the villain society pursuing the Almighty Dollar. The fact is that the artist is a part of the society we incriminate, and if we wish to improve his lot, he must have dollars too.

Society taken in the lump does not systematically reject or divorce the artist. It is for the most part unaware that any marriage or engagement has taken place. Society possesses no single mind and will, and we must not impute one for the mere satisfaction of casting blame; any more than we must fancy, for the pleasure of praise, a society with the mind and will of a cultivated art-collector. All the nonsense written and spoken about the blessed unity of the thirteenth century, or about the Greeks being "a people of artists," is sheer illusion and *sehnsucht*—a mirage, and as such dangerous, because it leads away from real oases.

In other words, any serious discussion of art and society must clearly conceive the two things whose relation it treats of, and it must refine upon each conception as required. Society at large exists to secure the simplest needs of man—food, clothing, shelter—and the overwhelming majority of men in every known society have been, and continue to be, so beset by the hardships of maintaining and perpetuating their kind that art for them does not exist. It is perfectly proper that they should feel so. Life, as the ancients said, comes first, then philosophy. Life first and then art. This is not a matter of taste. It is a necessity, and it turns out on examination that this necessity in all its aspects is the very subject matter of art. That is why we dare to take pleasure in the spectacle of Henry James or Proust or Melville pitting his mind and hardening his will against the works of man and God, against society or the universe: we respond because we feel at once the primacy of life and the clutch of necessity. In Paradise or Utopia there is no need of art because there reality is synonymous with perfect design.

Now an imperfect society must be in part prosperous before it can spend any large sum on maintaining its design-makers whom we call artists. One has to say "in part prosperous" because history affords no example of any great society prosperous throughout. The past is one vast scarcity economy, and all the mighty historical movements, from the expansion of Rome to the expansion of Europe and America, have mainly been plundering expeditions to remedy the niggardliness of Nature or the economic failure of man. So that if we survey what may be termed the alimentary history of art in the West, the fact that stands out is that with a few (and perhaps misleading) exceptions, art has always led a hand-to-mouth existence. It has had to find the few nutritious pockets of a social system that could hardly maintain government without going bankrupt, and that never succeeded in truly organizing material life.

To put it differently, art and artists have invariably had to seek out the temporary holders of power and wealth, the Elite. On its side, this variable class—again with a few individual exceptions—has never supported art from motives of pure generosity, nor has it ever regarded the artist as a man on a level with its own members. The reasoning that we now take for granted, that art is "a good thing," a regular product among other goods which a self-respecting nation must produce, is of recent origin. The traditional motives for support have been such as we should now consider irrevelant, or at least secondary: ritual and religious motives—celebrating the ancient City or propagating the law, the gospels, and the glory of God; civic rivalry and collective self-advertisement in the later Middle Ages; political and dynastic motives in royal establishments and their appurtenances; sheer ostentation and conspicuous consumption in princely or bourgeois households since the Renaissance; personal snobbery and commercial profit within the last two hundred years, when the idea of Art as a good-in-itself has gradually taken shape.

It is worth dwelling on this point that at no time within the 2,500 years of Western history has art been financed for the intrinsic reasons now proposed to our century. Yet we know that despite this fact Western art has been remarkably abundant, varied, indomitable, profound, inspiriting—one is tempted to say god-like. It has defied the dead hand of authority, circumvented policing, and escaped the suicide of anarchy; it has sprouted in all the likely and unlikely places, and overcome what must have looked like the laws of Nature itself—

in Gothic architecture, in polyphonic music and equal-tempered harmony, in repeated victories over the barbarism of vernacular tongues, and not less in the continuity of its hold on a part of the population whose very habits of eminence and wastefulness made them heedless, stupid, or proud.

As regard these last, the vicissitudes of the great artists at grips with the rulers of the earth need but a word to be recalled. Everyone knows about Mozart's treatment by the Archbishop of Salzburg, the complaints of Michelangelo and Cellini about the Popes, the tussles of Poussin or Dr. Johnson with their respective patrons, Louis XIV and Lord Chesterfield; the encounters of Dante, and Tasso, and Cimarosa with the forces of the state. Again, one need only allude to other recurrent evils such as Puritanism, censorship, cabals, popular vandalism, and even the dangers of having powerful friends. After all, the clearest fact in the biography of Phidias is that he died in prison for having committed masterpieces on money which his patron Pericles had misappropriated to beautify Athens. One direct utterance from an embattled artist will typify the artist's struggle with adversity: here is what Bach tells an old friend in 1728 about his post of cantor at Leipzig:

I find that the duties are by far not so agreeable as they were originally described to me; and that quite a few of the bonuses attached to the post have been withdrawn; that the cost of living is very high here; and that the authorities are rather strangely hostile to music, that I have to live with the powers that be in a state of almost constant struggle; that envy prevails and vexations are numerous; [hence] I find myself, so help me God, compelled to seek my fortune elsewhere. If Your Excellency knows of any suitable position, I should be deeply obliged for your help and recommendation in securing it; in exchange for which I can promise full satisfaction in the discharge of duty.

My salary here is 700 *thalers,* and when there are more burials than usual, the added fees raise this proportionately higher. But whenever the air is a little more healthful, the loss is great. Last year the fees for common burials showed a deficit of 100 *thalers.* With 400 *thalers* I could support myself in Thuringia more comfortably than here with twice that amount, for the cost of living in Leipzig is exorbitant.

Taking only the great masters is of course misleading. The energy of the genius generally enables him to survive. But art does not live by geniuses alone, and in every age and in every art we read the pathetic story of a vast "Grub Street," which until recently was considered not only normal but comic—witness Pope's *Dunciad*.

All these considerations irresistibly suggest that we are flatly wrong when we speak of our modern "materialistic" civilization as doing less for art and caring less for artists than previous epochs. Here too one need do no more than catalogue the institutions concerned today with giving art its due—the foundations, institutes, museums, and universities; the prizes, the travel funds and the training scholarships; the theaters, galleries, orchestral societies, book publishers, radio stations, magazines, and newspapers; the guilds, unions, and civic associations; the government councils, ministries or committees; the national and local collections, the libraries, and in some countries the bureaucracies which deal exclusively or partially with the fine arts—all these represent a sum of energy, brains, and capital which would make any earlier culture gape with envy.

And apropos of earlier cultures it must be said categorically that the familiar piece of cant which contrasts the United States—that well-known materialistic nation—with Europe, that haven of disinterestedness and pure art, is sheer nonsense and mischievous falsehood. Not only does the United States spend a very respectable amount of money on cultural enterprises, including the fine arts; not only does it produce, disseminate, and organize more actively than any other nation the substance of culture, not only does it *worry* about Art with a capital "A," but it shows at the same time a spirit of fair play, or open-mindedness, a love of diversity and of youthful talents absolutely unknown to the Old World. The reason it can do so is of course that its resources are relatively greater, like its territory.

In contrast with this, the reason that the material life of culture in Europe is so bitterly bad is that resources are small and that their concentration in the hands of government at the capital gives rise to a series of gang wars for the capture of the spoils. Let no one pretend that European artists care nothing about money, titles, and honors. It is not so. Even the artist who starts as a free lance and whose temperament *is* disinterested finds himself compelled by centralization to compete for the kind of reward which will enable him to carry on his work. Needless to say, these European facts, combined with the dangers of bureaucracy in matters of the mind, constitute the chief reasons for warning American artists against the lure of government support of the arts.

Many artists and their well-wishers will retort that my bird's-eye view of the facts ignores the desperate plight of culture at the present time. I shall be told that the various endowments and agencies just enumerated do not suffice, and that artists actually suffer want and lack of recognition. This is why modern democratic society, when it is taken as the equivalent of the rich patron, is approached and assailed on behalf of the artist; the vision of plenty haunts the generous mind as always, but with the added poignancy that for the first time in history we think technology will yield the means if we only learn how to manage the technology.

This is the point where the particular desires of the advocates of art branch off from the general desire of the majority. Since the new abundance springs from the soil of industrial democracy, it goes with the ideals of fair distribution, equal opportunities, and deliberate choice of social ends, as opposed to the good old catch-as-catch-can. This means, among other things, that the elite no longer rules. There is no elite, it has dissolved into the great mass, even though the number of cultivated persons who compose it has probably increased. But their weight is now negligible. It is not simply our new ideal but also our practical life that compels us to hold it negligible. Take the familiar instance of the literary periodical. A public of five or even ten thousand readers will not support a magazine. Why not? Because, first, the costs of printing are high—they are hitched to our high standard of living for workmen; and second, because the income from small-range advertising is low—it follows the standard set by the mass distribution of mass-produced goods. The small magazine must therefore be subsidized; but even with a subsidy it will certainly not influence the mind of the nation. Too many other things are going on for it to be heard. Consequently we sigh for the days when a British Quarterly could sway the universe by virtue of its grip on a few hundred readers. What has happened is that the total number of people who count, or *who must be counted*—it now comes to the same thing—has so enormously increased that the tastes of ten thousand are to the total what the tastes of a single man would have been to the entire elite in the year 1800. We now sacrifice the minority as formerly it sacrificed the majority.

The artistic problem is thus intertwined with the great, the overriding problem of the mass age—the problem of numbers. A huge increase in the number of people, in the number of activities and possibilities, of desires and satisfactions, is the great new fact. It—and not any greater wallowing in sensuality—is what makes us complain of intellectual decadence. It—and not any falling away from a common controlling faith—produces our sense of helpless confusion. For the world has always been confused and decadent, but the number of humans on the planet has never been so great, their individual weight has never before been presumed equal each to each, and the consciousness of chaos has never been re-echoed from so many minds simultaneously, to become a burden added on top of the fact itself.

In the domain of culture we are never allowed to forget these numerical facts and democratic assumptions. It was only a short time ago that the proposed deferment of college students aroused angry protests, led by the presidents of Harvard and Princeton. The words "privilege," "caste," "elite" were freely used to indicate the abominations that would ensue if intellectual occupations set apart for a few months an admittedly valuable group of the nation's youth. Yet at the very same time we are not allowed to disregard the masses' "right" to culture, even though they may scorn it. We are committed to nursing the possible germ of interest or talent in much the way that we keep working over a drowned man. We educate, we encourage, we expose, and there is undoubtedly a large if not a great harvest of intellect and love of art. Who can remain unmoved on hearing that in one great university of the Middle West some two thousand students have taken up painting? Here again we seem to outdo at one bound any previous achievement of the kind, and even to be recovering one of the natural functions of art, which is to give enjoyment to the maker.

But when we speak of art and artists we still tend to mean professional art, the high art of the bourgeois epoch since the Renaissance, and we continue to force that interpretation upon the young. They espouse it, and the result is an enormous number of people who paint, write, and compose with professional skill; then a larger group who wish to do these things and who toil in the vain hope of learning the elusive secret. And around them all a still wider circle of teachers, critics, historians, managers, administrators, and connoisseurs of art.

The tastes and opinions, and even more, the decisions made by the members of these groups do somehow influence the public's choice. It is not an assured influence, for the outer public is fluid, miscellaneous, and distant from those who originate or distribute works of art. Yet, though scattered and anonymous, this smaller democracy within the large is none the less the true "society" we should speak of when we speak of art; the behavior of these groups is what we must study if we want to reform art's social conditions. We must acknowledge—to advance but one generality—that this indeterminate crowd, precisely because it is not an elite, allows a wide diversity, both of tastes and of motives, for taking cognizance of art. At one extreme are the young of college age who use the very latest art as a protection against the ideas of their family and the horrors of the world. At the other extreme are the amiable suburbanites who will buy a reproduction of Van Gogh's sunflowers when the interior decorator has got around to pushing what he thinks is modern art. In between is a regular gradation of groups marked by endless differences of interest and income. No wonder that the artist who is living and working today, and for whom Van Gogh is an old master, does not know which of his fellow men he is addressing, nor who will support him. No wonder that after rebuffs and commercial unsuccess he comes to believe that democracy as such is inimical to art.

But this is a hasty judgment. A spontaneous diversity of tastes, a "federal" system as regards museums, libraries, orchestras, an absence of official standards, must in the long run prove inherently superior to the system of centralization and monopoly which older cultures have usually developed.[1] Moreover an *industrial* democracy provides unlimited opportunities for the use of art in daily life. Everything from the design and decoration of factories to the

1. By the latest count there are 659 symphonic societies in the United States. Compare this many-sided opportunity, actual or potential, with that afforded by the centralized nations of Europe, with their two or three orchestras at the capital, the rest being in fact and in reputation beneath notice.

packaging of goods is a chance for the artist, and no one can deny that since 1900 the common objects and common sights of our urban life have improved artistically beyond the most sanguine expectation. Even advertising—that obsessive and stupefying mythology of our marketing system—has learned the rudiments of art and has unconsciously advanced public taste by very competently aping modern creative techniques.

It is easy enough to pooh-pooh these results and call the means sordid; it shows nice feeling to wish that all our artists could be supernaturally fed, by Elijah's ravens or the spirit of the Medici. But we may ask what is the next step to be taken if we are to oppose commerce and its bourgeois institutions? Do we abolish copyright and go back to the sweatshop system of publishing? Do theatrical companies revert to guarding jealously the scripts of their plays? Does the painter live on your bounty, as a household retainer in the kitchen of your three-room apartment? The mere posing of these questions is enough to show that turning back is impossible. The earlier modes of patronage belong to a narrow and lopsided economic system, based on agrarian and monarchical ideas that we cannot recapture, save in Mr. T. S. Eliot's utopia—a utopia which, to the unbeglamoured eye, is simply a chromolithograph of England under the first Georges.

This does not mean that Mr. Eliot's grievance against the present state of culture is groundless, any more than is the demand for government support of art. The two complaints are interlocking: one states that commercialism lowers public taste and makes it harder for good works to find their audience; the other, that existing agencies are not equal to absorbing and paying for all the good work that is being done. Hence the government must act as a sort of high-minded purchasing agent for a heedless or misguided nation.

For my part, I have not the slightest objection to the use of public funds to make up certain deficits in the finances of going concerns—orchestras and theaters, museums and libraries, whose traditions are set and whose management remains in private hands. But any initiative or any participation in the conduct of the fine arts is another matter. For it raises the delicate and sometimes sinister questions of quality, tastes, genres, and vested interests. Here *the* artist crumbles into several pieces as "society" did before: government will not be dealing with *the* artist of our dreams, but with a miscellaneous lot of citizens working at the arts. Perhaps a democratic state dare not classify them, but we must, at least in the abstract.

Beginning at the bottom, we may describe the largest group of successful producers as tradesmen, meaning both the artists who work for industry, advertising, and mass media, and the artists of greater pretensions who nevertheless exercise their craft for the million—such as writers of popular fiction or of bestsellers in any field. The supposed harm done by these tradesmen seems to me quite imaginary, and the argument against, let us say, popular literature, is actually an argument against mankind as it has been through the ages. Already in Horace's day, the complaint was that the superficial and flashy crowded out the good; and certainly since the invention of printing the law of publishing has been that good books *tend* to bring no profits until long after the author's death. Yet this slow reversal of opinion does take place and it implies a rather feeble attachment to cheap literature. Who can remember the bestsellers of ten years ago? Who re-reads them or recommends them to his friends? They vanish like last year's autumn leaves, and without even making us nostalgic.

The reason we are so distressed today by low forms of art is, let me repeat, that the consumers of it are numerous and audible. But there is no warrant for assuming that today these lower forms displace higher forms to any greater extent than in the past. In the year when *Moby-Dick* was being ridiculed in the best English journals as "Bedlam literature," Mrs. Caroline Norton's *Stuart of Dunleath* was the subject of general conversation. Until the vogue of *St. Elmo* (never out of print since 1861) had somewhat abated, we could not even be aware of *Moby-Dick*. Our mistake, when we grow despondent, is to compare the more and more neatly sorted-out past with an unkempt present-day, and to conclude that the world's current mess of infatuations will be eternal.

The class of art above the bestseller is harder to characterize. It is a more than average product which can reach a merit just short of greatness. As such it often finds response, circulation, and reward in its own day, and it is of the utmost importance for culture that it should. For these are the sort of works which prepare the mind for the highest reaches, works which sustain the spirit of both the choice public and the artistic circles when the tides of falseness and vulgarity are, as they must be, periodically at the flood. Unfortunately, such works are not published every week nor every month, and moreover they come surrounded, and sometimes entirely obscured, by a quantity of other works which resemble them closely without being a real thing. These are the works that attempt to be the near-masterpiece but fail and fall into facsimile. This particular substitution of an imitation for the genuine work of art occurs without any intent to deceive and through no failure of will, but rather owing to a flaw of nature which is for the author its own conclusive punishment.

But the social consequences may be very grave. For although it is true that the inevitable second-rate help to maintain continuity in artistic concerns, they and their works perpetuate many abuses. To begin with, they tend to multiply their kind, and it is from them that we hear an ever louder outcry about the plight of art in general. They report quite truthfully on the difficulty of getting published, exhibited, produced, or performed. They are right in saying that art does not keep its man. But while we applaud them for reminding us of neglected genius, we must deplore their evident unawareness that they are talking not of genius but of themselves.

And surely their direct role in the economy of art is not easy to justify. Their works afford neither the simple entertainment of popular art nor the lasting pleasures of fine work. Meanwhile, the insidious worthlessness of their middling productions subtly corrupts the public deep down in the soul, as is proved by the fact that geniuses usually come into their own only after displacing some pseudo-artist whom contemporaries called great. We may be most conscious of this in painting because we have the word "academic" to denote that appalling competence which so readily outshines true art. But the trick succeeds in every art, until the day when the glamour suddenly pales and the new generation wonders how "taste," "the best taste," could admire such patent emptiness. One answer is: the emptiness helped make the work a playground for familiar feelings; the fraudulent sincerity and skill was the snare which caught both artist and public. So it remains a question whether such practitioners can claim our sympathy in the name of their devoted but luckless striving. Formerly the question would not have arisen at all, because their lesser numbers would have led unpretentious lives as craftsmen. Today, the crafts having succumbed to the machine, these men must be Shakespeare or nothing.

Yet one ought not to decide their fate too hastily, even in thought. We must grant that since these pseudo-artists are usually good citizens and hard workers, since their imitation is unconscious and may serve an educational purpose by diluting the strong doses of originality they find in others, thus preparing the public stomach for coming great works; finally, since we must grant that it is seldom easy to tell at a glance who is a genius, who a carrier of tradition, and who an empty academic—for all these reasons, this fat cushion of mediocrities in all the arts is entitled to its central place in our scheme of things. But there is no reason why they or anyone else should feel that their competitive position is unjust and intolerable. Exactly as the entertainers must compete for trade, the mediocre, who turn art into a profession, must compete for the managerial posts of artistic big business. Why should this type of practitioner be favored over the lawyer or the engineer? Why subsidies or a guaranteed monopoly? The only claim strong enough to upset the normal order is the claim of genius. But this is precisely the claim that is hardest to validate and that professional mediocrity is almost the last to recognize. Their record in history should make them modest, though they never are, and it is they who, in any government Bureau of Fine Arts, will hold, for themselves and their friends, the monopoly of supplying the nation with artifacts that might have passed for new fifty years ago.

Certainly any plea on behalf of this group must take into account the existing freedom which is already their unique privilege. No man can install an electric light plug, or give legal advice, or pull teeth without suitable training and the testing of his acquirements; but whoever wants to practice, teach, or criticize the arts need ask no one's permission—a freedom still further enhanced by the cheapness of the equipment and materials for setting up in the business. Add the possibilities of combining a career in pseudo-art with one in commercial or popular art and you need not wonder that the cultural market is flooded with an amount of high-finish low-quality goods which no detergent but Time can rid us of.

Unfortunately, with the last and highest category of artist—the genius—the test of time comes too late. For when alive he will probably defy recognition by signs. Either he resembles ordinary men too much for our storybook minds, or he gives so few proofs of worldly judgment that it is hard to credit him with any capacity whatever, or again the mixture in him of talent and folly, or talent and turpitude, discourages further inquiry.

It is safer to go to the work than to the man. But the work, the masterpiece, presents difficulties of its own, the chief of which is that it usually does not correspond to any established taste, however sophisticated, and hence is literally of no use. In effect, no one really wants a masterpiece, there is no demand for it, which is why it ultimately signifies an addition to our riches. The only desire for it at first is in the breast of the maker and it is for this that he is called a creator. After a while we see that he belongs to a tradition, that he has forged the next link in a chain, but this hindsight takes a great deal of effort, and often requires the removal of the rubbish that stood between the masterpiece and the world, namely the rubbish of pseudo-art representing as real a world departed.

When the world and the new work are confronted, they are seen to bear a likeness, but as in a good portrait the implied comment is not flattering. We may think today that Dante was a true seer and that we should have been glad to meet him. But it is more likely that we would have thought him too angry and egotistical to be quite sound on Church and State. His remarks on the late Pope, his gossip about his friends, his naming himself as the sixth great poet of the world—the man's bad taste is writ in his own hand. And such parts of the poem as are not disgusting are dull. Here and there a fine image, to be sure, or a brief scene but—no, not a masterpiece, a labored monster: to change this view at large took roughly five hundred years.

Now why should the highest art bear one or both of these stigmata, incomprehensibility and offensiveness? Why is the great artist at loggerheads with society? The answer is implied in the adjective great, which being interpreted means searching, thorough, outspoken, final. These are qualities commonly praised, but their effect when added together in a fixed utterance can only be expressed in one word: terrifying. Masterpieces are terrifying because they call into question all the conveniencies by which we live. Nor is this limited to the declarative art of literature. When Rembrandt turned from flattering portraits of Dutch burghers to deeper studies of the human face, he lost his clientele and his reputation; for his technique had altered, and what it became was in itself sufficient to send shudders through any Dutchman. What do we hear of the first reception of Beethoven's symphonies? That the music is grandiose, no doubt, but very upsetting. As for the later quartets, they must be mad, for otherwise *we* are mad.

We must not fail to notice and to admit it is the *art* and not the opinions of the artist that causes this unsettling and makes the work truly subversive. *Moby-Dick,* for example, says little directly that could shock an American of a hundred years ago. But coming after the pleasant dreamland of the same author's *Typee* and *Omoo,* it tastes bitter and virtually fails. A dozen years after *Moby-Dick,* Melville's entire yearly sale of ten of his books amounts to three hundred copies.

Yet it is through such failures that the great artist momentarily regenerates the world; it is by acts of aggression such as Rembrandt's and Melville's that the crust of dead thought and feeling is broken up and room made for the fresh impulse.

The question remains whether something deliberate can be done to gear the power of the great artist to our expensive social machinery for art—the institutions that profess themselves ready to exploit him nobly for the nation's good. Can the great artist not be fed and praised without being tamed out of his genius? Certainly, but not by an institution, whether it be competitive fellowships for projects, or a term on some charming campus as captive Poet for pet undergraduates. Still less can he work as one of the daisy-chain gang in some ideal retreat for gestating artists. In all these situations, he will pleasantly stifle. He will be somebody's man, without even being able to resent the slavery.

The simple solution is that the genius should be born to an independent income. But this is less and less likely under our increasing egalitarian collectivism. And this in turn means that the remaining sources of funded wealth—the foundations, the corporations, the universities, as well as the few private patrons—must adopt policies which will truly bestow independence. So far, they seem not to have given this a thought. They naturally find it hard to go against current practice, which is to exact a quid pro quo for anything paid out. Yet it is a solemn fact that their only hope of achieving results is: not to hunt them down. Let the millionaire endow an artist chosen by lot. Let the foundations award lump sums without applications, interviews, or progress reports, and without seeking for their list of fellows the advertising value of well-known names. If the government enters the field, as it must in connection with public building, let the worker's output be bought as a speculation, not as supplies. Give a man a ceiling to paint, and don't come back till he is through and has gone. This system—or lack of system—may seem wasteful, prodigal, insane, but the truth is, if you want art—great art—you must pay for it; and if you pay for it, you must not go about spending the wealth of the Indies with the manners of Manchester.

No need to be afraid that this lavishness will ever justify the charge of criminal generosity: no artist will grow as rich on it as any simple racketeer or businessman holding a war contract. No need even to fear that you will be doing something new. The principle proposed is only a generalization from old practice wherever it has been truly successful—in Greece, the Middle Ages, the Renaissance or modern times. The only institutional alternative is Bertrand Russell's old notion of "the vagabond wage" to be provided—again without strings—by a benevolent state. But it lies far, far in the future of unpractical politics.

So much for bread, which is only one requisite. What spiritual food does the great artist need in order to make his duel with society something more than a personal brawl? Here, as society reassumes its role in the productions of genius, we find in our end our beginning—plus a moral, if not a conclusion. American criticism has for many years been asking why our great artists are so short-winded. They make a fine start and then stop, kill their talents or themselves. These days we probably think first of Scott Fitzgerald, and we say that perhaps he expected too much from life and not enough from himself. Certainly he had no guidance except that which came from selfish outsiders bent on exploiting him. This is another way of saying that when an American discovers in himself gifts of a certain kind, he has no traditional recipes for nurturing them. He is the first in his family to think about such things, and he does not suspect that the departed great could be his vocational family. He does not study the right things. He simply follows the path to acceptance that seems to be opening out before him. Being a good fellow, blithely uneducated, a democrat at heart, he is neither wild enough nor self-controlled enough to forge and temper his soul; and at the first strain it bends and cracks.

The ultimate cause is that in modern democracies—European as well as American—the tendency is not to accumulate experience on such tragic matters, to thicken it by concentration, and transmit it, strong and bitter, to those who can stomach strength and bitterness. The tendency is all the other way—to spread it and make it bland. And the reason is social: We keep initiating new groups to the enjoyment of life, which includes a ticket to some cultural lessons. In effect we are constantly teaching; we use our artists, whether in the university or not, as day-by-day teachers rather than as mighty condensers of life's experience. We spend them in small change, for every decade brings a new wave of eager virgin minds to whom once again the first rudiments have to be given.

We institutionalize this process and have gone so far that for the first time in history higher education includes contemporary art and literature in its curriculum. What a loss under an apparent gain, robbing the young as it does of intellectual adventures, of the difficulties of choice, and of the exclusive possession of new idioms! We go still farther and hope that by dint of cultivating the great works of the past and the fine things of the present, original greatness will spring up just where we are digging. We forget that art comes not out of culture but out of life, that it springs not out of the formed but out of the unformed. We forget that if the masterpiece terrifies, it is because we feel in it the terrible grip of life and not the gentle hands of the museum curator.

To be sure, we need gentleness and culture, and it is not wise to gaze upon the Furies except now and then. Our cultivated consciousness about art remains touching and right, for in our situation we can do nothing better than to be intelligent. But consciousness bears good fruit only when time has somewhat submerged it, when our painful effort of thought has become easy habit, or still better, instinct. And it cannot help but be so with our endeavors to improve and multiply American art. To say this is not to suggest that we desist from the fight for culture, or give up what brings us pleasure, but simply to plead for patience and soberness. Let us not press so hard for results, for geometrical adjustments of artist to situation and situation to art. Let us not have too many theories—even historical ones—but rather empirical judgment and the nerve to seize happy chances. Above all, let us keep amid our incorrigible good deeds a little capacity for wonder and surprise. For art is not just "a good thing" among other good things. It stands with the supreme goods, next to life, analogous though unlike; and it shares with life that which must put it forever beyond our mere industry or our mere acceptance—namely the secret of incarnation.

The Writer in Contemporary Society
Storm Jameson

from

The American Scholar, vol. 35, no. 1, Winter 1965—66.

The Writer in Contemporary Society

STORM JAMESON

IN DECEMBER LAST YEAR, that nervously alert voice of English letters, the *Times Literary Supplement,* compared the precarious situation of the arts in the twentieth century to the survival, only as a luxury, of the horse.

They also have been made redundant by technological progress, and the first task of criticism ought to be to discover how this came about and what precisely has replaced them. So far most of those who practise and write about the arts have been reluctant to face this situation frankly, partly because they have the excuse that novels—even thrillers—are not yet actually written by computers, but mainly because no class of people is enthusiastic about writing its own obituary. . .

We are being invited, *sans façon,* to attend the deathbed, if not yet the funeral, of all arts that depend on an individual hand and brain. The novelist is the humblest of the named victims of progress, but the chart of his critical condition will apply, with inessential differences, to every form of imaginative writing. Moreover, an illness is most easily studied in its advanced stages, and not even the most self-complacent of novelists will pretend that today the novel is better than an interesting invalid.

Since the death of Proust, the novels that matter very much would fit into a small bookcase, in which room will have to be found for *Ulysses* and *Finnegans Wake,* although these two latterday epics, far from injecting new energy into the novel, led it into the splendid but airless museum reserved for works that require endless explanation. Joyce strained the resources of language in *Ulysses* to a limit he could overstep only by breaking language down and reshaping it to convey a highly subjective and eccentric vision of reality. In *Finnegans Wake,* the one major work of fiction

✪ STORM JAMESON, the English novelist, is author most recently of *The Road from the Monument* and *The Blind Heart.* Among her other books are *The Green Man, The Hidden River* and *The Writer's Situation, and Other Essays.*

that more or less obeys Mallarmé's dictum that the world exists to be made into a book, he handles words much as an abstract painter uses line and color, to embody a reality intelligible only in reference to the workings of the writer's mind, not by its relation to the objective world—of which other minds are part. His method is the antithesis of surrealism: he uses immense intellectual ingenuity—consciously—to distort the structure of language, bending logic to make a hare of logic. This particular revolt against the pinchbeck rhetoric and devitalizing clichés of a mass civilization has never been pushed farther. Like a great cairn, *Finnegans Wake* marks the end of a road. Reflecting coldly, I believe that Joyce did literature a disservice by the skill, persistence, courage, with which he toiled at the dismembering of language, one of the thin walls humanity has built up over centuries against its own brutal and destructive impulses. Against the very impulse that, in a few days in August 1944, destroyed all the great libraries of Warsaw. With one half my mind I admire Joyce as the bold experimenter; the other half sees him as the nihilist, the antihumanist, the atomizer of meaning.

A really lively art can support any number of violent rebels, and even any number of clever charlatans and drugged self-dupes. If these were all it ailed, the novel would not be in a galloping decline. It is declining in every sense. In the mass of ephemeral novels published every year, a small number of works by serious writers compete for attention; a few of these live out the year, the rest die quickly of neglect, and there is no resurrection morning. The figures for the last five years show a steady turning away from fiction to biography, history, popular science, political affairs, in short to what an innocent reading public thinks of as truth. The number of nonfiction books rises every year. To complete the picture of a modern sweated industry, note that very few novelists earn, by their novels, more than the wage of a junior clerk, and must supplement it by any means their ingenuity suggests.

Apologists for the failing health of fiction are apt to blame the complexity of the world, so appalling as to crush the energy even of a Tolstoi. A respectable excuse and, I think, a superficial one. No great novelist of the past ever did attempt a total picture: Tolstoi himself offered only a vivid intimation of the whole. I am convinced that none of the difficulties that dismay the imaginative writer when he looks about him was past prayer until they were increased, immeasurably, by technical developments. If the arts really have been made redundant, are on the point of becoming, like the horse, a rare survival, it is the new mediums of communication—radio and television and, on a different level, in a subtler way, the development of the computer—that are the effective cause. These sacred monsters cannot replace the individual artist, but they can displace him, can elbow him out of the market and deflect him from his proper business. And to a noticeable degree they are doing so.

The truth is that the threat to the novel is one aspect of a profound change in the structure itself of society. We are living on the frontiers of an age in which the printed book is being overtaken by the new electronic mediums very much as the handwritten manuscript was overtaken by the invention of print. The process is only beginning and will probably never be total, but already those of us to whom it has not occurred to think that literacy can rest on anything but the habit of private reading are as out-of-date as a medieval scholar who disliked the look of a printed page and clung to his parchments. A wireless talk means little to me until I have read it in print. Television wearies me by forcing me to attend to it with the ear I use for external noises and an eye unused to sudden shifts of focus. My nervous system rejects a forced involvement with the nervous systems of millions of my contemporaries. It rebels against the—to me—demoralizing pressure of information thrust on it from all sides. No doubt I could train myself to take in by ear more than I do. But that is not the point. Nor is it the point that nine-tenths of the entertainment and instruction offered is of the crudest and shoddiest. It is plainly not because miracles of technology are used to disseminate rubbish that they are the serious novelist's enemies: he has always—since the onset of semiliteracy—had to keep his head above the flood of trash. The new mediums are his enemies *because they exist*. Because they are creating mental habits that are not simply unlike, but directly opposed to the habits of a man who sits down to take part in a dialogue with the writer of the book in his hand. The point, the crucial point, is the incessant flow of sounds and images into millions of eyes and ears, and the instantaneous appearance to them of events taking place anywhere in the world. Radio and television speak to the mass man, to a mass that is learning new habits with the docile facility of a circus pony, and we attend to them as, in the days before newspapers, villagers attended to the town crier. Or, if we do not attend, we are deliberately holding ourselves aloof, trying stubbornly to keep the habits of a past age, trying to erase the electronic factor from our lives, to retreat into an artificial oasis of silence, an invisible monastery. It can be done, but at a psychological cost not everyone is willing to pay.

Whether the benefits of living in one vast mechanically begotten community will outweigh the loss of privacy and separateness is not my concern. I am concerned with the possible disappearance, or four-fifths eclipse, in such a world, of the imaginative writer, novelist, poet, who is only able to share his deepest and subtlest experience of life with as many of his fellows as are prepared to wait patiently for him to unfold it at length, with the strictest honesty of which he is capable. An effort he will never be able to make through the public mediums of the electronic age. Never.

Nor is this the whole story. The devaluation of the written word begun, with the potent help of Early Bird, by loudspeaker and television screen, is obvious, measurable and just might be remedied. The psychological effect of the computer, of machines that extend the human brain as massively as television and radio extend our eyes, ears and nervous systems, is ambiguous, incalculable and infinitely more disturbing. To the individual writer, there is something obscurely menacing about a machine complex enough to solve problems of its own devising, to learn through its own mistakes. Sheepishly and irrationally he resents and is overawed by it. His sense of being in some way threatened is not attached to anything the computer does that actually affects him. Even what seems to, even translation by computer, is of less importance to the imaginative writer than to the student of semantics. Obviously, as the machines are further developed and as we deepen our understanding of linguistics, the usefulness of autonomous translation will increase. But no writer believes that the computer can be programmed to imitate completely the way our minds use language. A first-class human translator draws subconsciously on a vast hinterland of ambiguities of sense and sensation. The process is one of unimaginable delicacy. But why speculate on the intellectual and artistic bankruptcy that would be implied by an attempt to transfer to an electronic brain this particular aspect of consciousness?

I am skeptical, too, about the value of computer technique in literary criticism. Certainly it can save time and routine drudgery in research: what I mistrust is its use, merely because it is there, on work the living mind can do better. Or on work of no literary value. On such solemn frivolities as the recent use, in the English department of an American university, of a computer to search for the themes in Act 2, Scene 1, of *Hamlet*. The time spent programming the machine would have been a great deal more intelligently spent searching for them by the light of reason and critical sensibility. And when an English scientist assures me that in the foreseeable future computers will be used to paint pictures and write poems, I am politely certain that her knowledge of what goes on in the mind of painter and poet is laughably crude. The slow and infinitely complex process of *improvisation* that is great literature can be mimed by a machine, but not conceived by it, not given breath. There are two sorts of possible communication. There is the communication of information, which television in one way and the computer in others can deliver with incomparable speed and efficiency. And there is the communication of a profound insight into the human condition. I am sure, in the marrow of my writer's bones, that this will not be provided by even the most advanced machines.

Nevertheless I think of the computer and its yet unrealized potentialities with discomfort and an equivocal sense of being spiritually diminished. And this is not, not in any degree, started up by puerile nonsense about computer poetry and paintings. Its roots are deeper—in an impotent and less than half-conscious resentment of the god in the machine. A man-made god, but overwhelmingly powerful. Endowed by human ingenuity with inhuman powers.

An inhuman power—one felt as inhuman—breeds submission, apathy, boredom or rebellion. The literary rebel who can imagine no other way of outwitting it will turn nihilist. You can see this happening at the moment in the novel, on two levels. On the sophisticated level of the *nouveau roman,* and in the growth, or irruption into daylight, of the pornographic novel. The first is an urbane, highly intellectual and fragile growth. Its most self-explanatory practitioner, Alain Robbe-Grillet, sees human beings as a kaleidoscope of moods, and communication between them little more coherent than a conversation on crossed telephone wires; to pass judgment on their acts, thoughts, feelings, is sense-less or impossible. This irrational philosophy lays an ax to the roots of any intelligible vision of reality, so that by an ironical paradox the New Novelists devalue man, rob him of his identity, as fatally as does the most menacing product of technology.

At a first glance it seems absurd to see the writers of the newest erotic or pornographic novel as part of the revolt against a civiliza-tion in which machines are felt to be more than a match for men. But these doctrinal works, from *Lady Chatterley's Lover* down-ward, a long way down, to William Burroughs' *Naked Lunch,* are treated seriously as literature—not only by their authors. (These—since writers write in the hope of being read—no doubt see them *also* as a chance to be heard above the roar of a million television sets.) Critics are prone to see them as "a gesture of lib-eration, intellectual and moral." I don't suggest that these critics are out of their minds; I suggest that they are the innocent dupes of an *ad hoc* critical theory which lays down that all dimensions of human experience are equally worth a writer's devoting energy and brains to explore them. All without exception. This is worse than silly, it is sentimental or hysterical. Clinically reported acts of sex are of interest, no doubt, to an ignorant adolescent, if such exists. What is infinitely more interesting, revealing, and a great deal more difficult, is to discover and give a lucid account of the emotions involved, their strength, effect, circumstances, the slow corrosion of Anna Karenina's life by her passion for Vronski, not the method she used to avoid pregnancy. Sexual emotion is the most complex of human impulses, the great fugue of existence;

hunger, ambition, parenthood, the controlled ferocities of artist and scientist, can at any time, in any man or woman, elbow it aside; none of them equals it in complexity and range of force. What puzzles me—and fills me with real doubts of their competence—is the reverent attitude of so many critics to the anything but genial insistence in a novel on familiar details of sex and excretion. Are they afraid of being thought timid, or of missing a vogue? Or only indulging in what the French call *la blague sérieuse*, prepared to drop the poor pornographer the moment the wind changes. No matter. What does matter is that the extreme example, so far, of the school, the novels of William Burroughs, greeted by reviewers and generously befuddled fellow-writers as "one of our greatest living novelists," are a sharp reminder that a counterrevolution is as likely to get out of hand as any form of social violence. It goes far beyond the obligatory clinical scenes, to turn on and destroy the human instincts themselves. What is baffling is that there are intelligent people willing to accept as literature the efforts of a writer so disgusted by his physical humanity that he labors to make it dull and disgusting to a reader. They would be better employed trying to decide why he hates himself. He is rebelling, yes. It is easy to see against what. But for what? If the author of *Naked Lunch* had wished to cut off at their source the sensual springs of life, could he have devised a surer way? An attack on conventions—which can be gay and salutary and life-giving—begins to shock me when it becomes an attack on our self-respect and decent self-love. The roots joining a literature of self-contempt and self-hatred to the worlds of Belsen and Auschwitz run underground, but they run.

And it is all futile. The electronic age is with us for good. We can't, as writers, go back to a pretechnical age, to an image of man as Homer or Dante or Turgenev saw him. The problem for the writer, as for the man in the street, is not how to escape from the machine, but how he can be free in relation to the machine. And here I am at a loss. I do not believe that the mediums of mass communication can ever be used to transmit the imaginative vision of a new Proust, a new Kafka, a new Tolstoi. It is inevitable that, for a mass audience, emotive language will always have to be thinned down, robbed of the utmost delicacy, the utmost subtlety, of which a good writer is capable. Language is memory and metaphor, it stores up the experience of the race and translates it into another form. The distinction drawn between speech and writing is, at the deepest level—that is, at an Atlantic depth below the possibilities of wireless—empty. Behind the written word, there is an oral tradition; the echoes go back to the child hearing his mother's voice saying *bread* or *sleep*. The most intimate meanings of an English word elude the inner ear of a man born to use another tongue. And it is on this deepest sense of language that poetry and precise subtle prose call. We learned, some few centuries ago, to translate the printed word back into these buried subtleties of sound and sense, to send them through the eye to the inner remembering ear of a reader who is attending not only to the words but to their endless echoes in his own experience. This same reader may, as scientist or scholar, draw on the prodigious memory of an electronic brain. He knows, or he should, that there are memories on which he cannot draw except in the age-old communion of one man speaking to another, without haste, in solitude. The gap between what the writer means and what he is able to say can only be closed in silence, in the silence during which the attentive eye sees and the attentive brain hears the word on the page.

One thing is certain. The serious writer's situation is more difficult than it was only two decades ago. With long practice we might, in time, have learned to use the radio to hear all the subtlety of which words are capable. I don't believe this, but it is conceivable. But now that the picture of an event can be flashed across the globe in the moment it happens, not only are we forced to endure an assault on all our senses at once, but we endure it in a world reduced to one pair of ears, one pair of eyes straining to catch the image as it flies, like children watching an airplane. At this primitive level of communication there is no place for the writer to act as interpreter or to answer the questions the television audience does not ask: What does my life mean? What is real? What is the value of a single human being? Questions the great novelists thought themselves competent and compelled to answer.

What it comes down to is simple and awful. The shock tactics of the pedantic immoralists, the Mailers and Burroughses, are self-defeating: the first scream startles, the tenth bores. The serious novelist has one vital resource, one only, in his effort to make himself heard above the strident electronic voices. That is, to create in depth, to uncover with more and more lucidity his total response to experience, to squeeze into words more meanings than can be broadcast or televised or put into a computer. What this involves for him is so exacting that few care to look it in the face. He will be forced—if he is to survive as a novelist, and not merely as an overwhelmed spectator of the modern world, or a clever amusing startling anything-you-like literary haberdasher, with a weather eye on his new powerful competitors—to write fewer novels. Far fewer. Which will be good for his soul although not, if he hoped to live by them, for his belly.

As a serious-minded novelist who has made a living by writing far too much, I say that the habit of writing to pay the bills is deplorable, pitiable, foolhardy—choose your own term. This was always true. It is a hundredfold truer now, when your craftsman writer is in competition with machines that can outbid him in diversity of entertainment on every level but the highest. In the near future there will be no level wholly free for him *except* the highest, no unoccupied place for a whole-time novelist but the one that can only be filled by a master, able to answer the questions, about birth, death, love, ambition, cruelty, that will be no use putting to the most carefully programmed computer or hoping to hear answered in the television studio for the flapping ears of a million listeners.

What the embryo novelist ought to be told is: Earn your living in any way that does not draw on your imagination, your respect for words, and write your novel slowly, over unlimited time, enriching it by what you learn as you go. Be prepared to wait ten years to produce your *summa mundi,* your vision of human nature caught between the furies of its instincts and the pitiless dynamics of society, your quintessential report from the depths. You need not even be a great innovator. If you can only say what you have to say in a new form, however outrageously revolutionary, do so. And if you prefer the traditional forms, use them as you like. But look to your tools. Words that have been poured out in torrents of cheap print, or by a million reverberating machines, become meaningless. When too much is said too quickly, by men or machines, or by men using machines, the danger of slipping into jargon is hideously easy; your perpetual task, today, tomorrow, forever, is the sharpening of language into a more and more precise and flexible instrument, as far removed as possible from the automatic response, the empty abstraction, the flabby half-exact phrase.

I am talking, need I say, about a writer who is the equal in his field of Einstein in his. You don't expect an Einstein to make a statement of his findings every twelvemonth. Why expect it of a novelist worth reading?

I was born suspicious of dogma. But I am dogmatically sure that the spread of automation into one field of human activity after another desperately needs a powerful human counterbalance. Lacking it, the cancer of dehumanization and boredom is going to spread and spread. In a world on the way to becoming one vast tribal encampment, hemmed in by the compulsions of collectivity, drugged by the torrent of information and entertainment pouring from the ever-open jaws of radio and television, we need as never before the slower and more lasting stimulus of solitary reading.

We are in danger of becoming exiles in our world, dwarfed by the great machines and the great buildings in which we do not worship. But we are not to be saved by any and every sort of writing. It was never more necessary than it is today for the writer to look cruelty in its face—if he is mature enough, clearheaded and sanely sensuous enough to do it without shuddering or wallowing or exploiting it for effect, or becoming hysterical and screaming at the top of his voice. We shall never grasp in its final terror and grandeur the reality of, let's say, Auschwitz, until it has been fused in the imagination of an unborn Dostoevski. The agony of Lear, the death of Antigone, the end of Mother Courage, are terrible— and exalting and exciting because they convince us that a few men and women can endure anything. The indecencies of *Naked Lunch* are enervating, clumsy and unpardonably boring.

We feel rightly that *Undertones of War* is worth a great deal more than most modern novels. But do we feel that it is worth more than *War and Peace?* We prefer actuality to let's pretend, but do we prefer it to a work in which the characters are the vehicles of an otherwise unimpartable self-knowledge, images of a reality that cannot get itself said in any other or easier form? What may very well not survive, killed by technological progress, is the merely good novel. What remains a vital necessity are the few great novels, written and to be written, that—in a sense below and above anthropology and archaeology—are human history.

Do I seem to regard the electromagnetic discoveries which have revolutionized our world, especially the computer, as antihuman in some mystical way? I don't. There is nothing intrinsically antihuman about a device that allows knowledge to be stored in a form that makes it easily accessible to scholars, scientists, and students of linguistics. (Provided they don't use it to suffocate us with more doctoral treatises.) "There is a place for everything when everything is in its place." A place for that extension of our brain and senses which is the computer and Early Bird, and a place for the one-to-one communion in which we come face-to-face with ourselves. Neither our dead nor our unborn can reach us by any but this single living channel, this naïvely human miracle.

The Sociology of Authorship. The Social Origins, Education and Occupations of 1,100 British Writers, 1800–1935
Richard D. Altick

from

Bulletin of The New York Public Library, vol. 66, no. 6, 1962.

The Sociology of Authorship

The Social Origins, Education and Occupations of 1,100 British Writers, 1800–1935

By Richard D. Altick

The Ohio State University

IN HIS recent book, *The Long Revolution* (London 1961), Raymond Williams points out what every student of the relations between literature and society has long known: "We argue a good deal about the effects on literature of the social origins of writers, their kind of education, their ways of getting a living, and the kinds of audience they expect and get. Theoretical questions, often very difficult, are of course involved in this argument, but the most obvious difficulty is the lack of any outline of facts by which some of the theoretical principles could be tested" (p 230). Williams then presents "an outline of such facts based on a standard list, . . . the index of the *Oxford Introduction to English Literature*, and with the *Dictionary of National Biography* as main authority." In all, he analyzes the social origins, education, and non-literary occupations of about 350 writers born between 1470 and 1920.

For no period of English literary and cultural history is the need for such information more urgent than the epoch beginning about 1800 and covering roughly four generations: the age when readers of books and periodicals came to be reckoned no longer in tens of thousands but instead in millions. During it, the role of literature in the nation's total culture was profoundly altered, and writers became the suppliers of a valuable commercial product. It was the long age immediately preceding our own, in which the problems of so-called mass culture and the plight of the author in a mass-culture society have attained both crucial and heatedly controversial significance.

We know that the dramatic change in the nature of the English reading audience in the nineteenth and the early twentieth centuries wrought a veritable revolution in popular and semi-popular literature. Was there an accompanying change in the class origins and other relevant aspects of the life histories of the people who made the nation's literature? A number of years ago I supervised the gathering of a mass of data which was intended to help answer this question and thus illuminate one of the innumerable dark spots that make the theorizing of the sociologists of literature less well informed than it should be. The appearance of Williams' analysis of a relatively small number of writers — 163 from the years 1780–1930 — offers a fitting moment to put into print the results of this much more comprehensive survey of British authorship in a limited period.[1]

The material to be presented in this article relates to the lives of 1,100 British and Irish writers, born between 1750 and 1909, whose reputations were established between 1800 and 1935. For the nineteenth century, the authors studied were those listed in the following sections of the *Cambridge Bibliography of English Literature*, Volume III: Section 2 ("The Poetry"), Section 3 ("Prose Fiction"), Section 4 ("The Drama"), and Section 5 ("Critical and Miscellaneous Prose"). These sections are broken down chronologically into three subdivisions, marked "Early Nineteenth Century," "Mid-Nineteenth Century," and "Later Nineteenth Century" in the case of the major figures, and into corresponding periods ("1800–1835," "1835–1870," and "1870–1900") in that of the minor ones. Forty-two writers were added from the section devoted to "Anglo-Irish Literature." Since the chronological divisions are merely convenient designations of the *floruit* era for each author, a certain amount of approximation is bound to diminish the statistical rigor of our proceedings. But in a study of this kind, arbitrary groupings are inevitable, as Williams' own use of even longer periods — half-centuries — suggests; and at all events, the tripartite division of the nineteenth century is useful for the study of broad trends.

The three periods, 1800–1835, 1835–1870, and 1870–1900, will be designated as I, II, and III respectively. In order to continue the analysis as close to the present as the availability of standard lists of modern authors permits, I have added a fourth period (IV), which reaches from 1900 to 1935. The authors examined for this epoch were drawn from Millett's *Contemporary British Literature* (New York 1935), supplemented with a large selection from Kunitz and Haycraft's *Twentieth Century Authors* (New York 1942). The twenty-three authors who are listed in both *CBEL* and Millett were assigned to Period III (late nineteenth century) rather than IV (early twentieth) in conformity with the view of the *CBEL*'s editor that they had begun to produce their significant work before the end of the nineteenth century. Writers whose family background and the major part of whose education were non-British (e.g. Joseph Conrad and Katherine Mansfield) were excluded, as were those on whom no relevant data were obtained.

---

[1] The demanding task of compiling the data for the nineteenth century was discharged by Mrs Phyllis Koehnline and Mrs Delane Morgan. To them, and to Professor James F. Fullington, at the time chairman of the Department of English at the Ohio State University, who made their research assistance available to me, I am deeply grateful. I owe an equal debt to my wife, Helen Altick, who extended the study into the twentieth century. For the statistical analysis and the commentary, I must assume sole responsibility.

In the categories from which the list of nineteenth-century writers was drawn, the *CBEL* has entries for 849 men and women. For 112 of these, however, no biographical information was found in the two principal sources consulted, the *Dictionary of National Biography* and Allibone's *Critical Dictionary of English Literature.*[2] Thus the net number of nineteenth-century authors on whom some relevant data were available was 737. The early twentieth-century writers on whom information was obtained totaled 363.

Any discussion of authorship and its social bearings which confines itself to the celebrated names and neglects the journeymen inevitably has its limitations. Concentration on the élite is less culpable, to be sure, when the reading public itself is composed chiefly of the intelligent, well-educated minority. But when the audience for the printed word has a broader base, as it has had in the past century and a half, the study of the people who produced its reading matter must be similarly broadened. We must keep always in mind the fact that, just as the public for sub-literature has dwarfed the one which reads what we prefer to call genuine literature, so the suppliers of sub-literature have also become far more numerous. These second- and third-rate authors are as meaningful for cultural analysis, in a period when the audience for their wares was swelling year by year, as the first-rate ones are for the pre-democratic centuries of reading.

The present compilation has the advantage of including a much wider range of literary producers than Williams'. Far from being limited to those whose fame is preserved in the standard histories of English literature, it gathers into its net, as a glance through the names in the preliminary pages of the *CBEL*'s Volume III will show, hundreds of writers of importance — or popularity — in their own day, whose celebrity has proved ephemeral. In fact, the tabulations that follow include all but the very lowest stratum of hacks, who are not commemorated in the *CBEL* or any other reference work.[3]

---

[2] Had a copy of that extremely scarce work been available when the data were being assembled, Frederic Boase's *Modern English Biography* (Truro, etc 1892–1921) would doubtless have reduced somewhat the number of authors who died after 1850 and on whom the requisite data were not obtained. I might add, for the benefit of scholars and librarians who have often been frustrated by the inaccessibility of Boase, that the work is now obtainable in a Xerox reprint.

[3] In the first chapter of his *New Trends in Education in the Eighteenth Century* (London 1951), Nicholas Hans analyzes the social origins and education of 3,500 "men of national repute," born between 1685 and 1785, who have places in the *Dictionary of National Biography.* Unfortunately he does not treat authors in a distinct category, and so far as I know there is — apart from Williams' brief passage in *The Long Revolution* (p 234–36) — no study of eighteenth-century authors comparable to the one I am here presenting of later generations. My colleague William Charvat has called my attention to a somewhat similar survey of American authors: Edwin Leavitt Clarke's *American Men of Letters: Their Nature and Nurture* ([Columbia University] Studies in History, Economics, and Public Law, LXXII, Number 1 [1916]).

Who, then, made up the British author-class, and what shifts were there in its composition from Wordsworth's time to Dylan Thomas'? Our data allow us to examine four aspects of the problem: the proportion of men to women, the social origins of writers, their educations, and their extra-literary occupations.

In all periods the proportion of women writers to men remained fairly constant. The range of less than six percentage points is insignificant in terms of the numbers involved:

Period	I	II	III	IV
		(Total entries in *CBEL*, including those on whom no other data were found)		(All writers in Millett, plus selection from Kunitz and Haycraft)
Males	223	256	206	283
Females	59 (*20.9%*)	49 (*16.1%*)	56 (*21.4%*)	80 (*22.0%*)
Total	282	305	262	363

Clearly the broadening opportunities in the field of letters had little effect on women during the nineteenth century, because of the inadequate educational provisions and the persisting prejudice against careers for females. The woman's place in the home was not at the writing desk. Even so, from the 1880s onward the distribution shown in figures obtained from sources that imply literary value judgments is markedly different from that derived from the coldly objective census returns. The former does not reflect the impact that the late Victorian and Edwardian "emancipation" of women had on the profession of authorship as on so many other aspects of society. The latter, on the other hand (see footnote 7), reveals a slow but uninterrupted increase in the number of women who counted themselves professional writers, from 8% of the total in 1881 to 16.6% in 1931. In the nineteenth century, female writers were either strictly amateurs, who would never have dreamed of enrolling themselves in the census returns as professional authors, or women who, like Mrs Trollope and Mrs Oliphant, were forced by circumstances to support themselves and their relatives by the pen. In the twentieth, as the census figures show, journalism enlisted the talents of more and more women, as editors and contributors to popular periodicals — at no cost to their respectability and often with considerable financial success. The increasing percentage of "working" women writers, however, had no effect on that of women who attained a certain reference-book status in the profession.

But a much more important topic on which statistical analysis can help shed light is this: Were the gradual disintegration of the old social structure and the increasing social mobility of the period after 1800 responsible for a greater democratizing of the profession of letters? Put in another way, to what extent, if at all, did men and women of humble origin enter a profession that had hitherto, as a general rule, been closed to them? While the occupation of the father is not always an accurate indication of social position, it is the best guide we have, and the nineteenth century, and to hardly less an extent the twentieth, set great store by it. The divisions adopted here, while inescapably arbitrary, reflect prevailing nineteenth-century standards. The fathers of both male and female authors are included in this tabulation:

Period	I	II	III	IV	TOTAL I/IV
Upper Class					
Nobleman	12	10	5	8	
Baronet, knight, squire	6	5	5	--	
Gentleman	8	11	3	16	
Total	26	26	13	24	89
Percentage	*12.7%*	*11.3%*	*7.9%*	*10.0%*	*10.6%*
Middle Class					
Upper division					
Merchant, shipowner	31	15	17	5	
Banker, broker	5	10	3	5	
Middle division					
Arts and professions:					
Physician	6	12	7	13	
Journalist, writer, scholar	6	15	9	14	
Tutor, schoolmaster, professor	9	11	8	29	
Clergyman	18	39	31	36	
Solicitor, barrister, law-court official	11	25	18	21	
Gov't official, civil servant, diplomat	9	14	5	13	
Composer, painter, engraver, actor, architect, theatre manager	15	12	5	11	
	} 74	} 128	} 83	} 137	
Manufacturer, shipbuilder	9	6	2	5	
Engineer	--	--	4	4	
Dock owner	--	1	2	1	
Farmer (mainly yeoman)	15	8	8	4	
Builder	--	2	2	1	
Officer in army, navy, merchant marine	9	13	9	16	
Workhouse master, estate agent, auctioneer, club manager	1	2	--	3	
Miscellaneous businessman (incl commercial traveller, insurance agent)	--	--	--	11	
Irish politician	--	--	--	2	
Jewish ritual orator, social worker	--	--	--	2	

MIDDLE CLASS, *continued*

Lower division

Tradesman	17	9	12	4	
Artisan	7	9	5	2	
Domestic servant	2	--	--	--	
Riding master, carrier, book-keeper	2	--	1	--	
TOTAL	172	203	148	202	725
Percentage	83.9%	87.8%	90.3%	84.2%	86.3%

LOWER CLASS

Laborers of all descriptions	7	2	3	14	26
Percentage	3.4%	.9%	1.8%	5.8%	3.1%

Thus for the four periods as a whole, of 840 authors whose fathers' occupation and social status have been identified, 10.6% were born into the nobility and gentry, 86.3% into the middle class, and only 3.1% into the working class. The percentages would be slightly altered, of course, were we to translate a few wealthy merchants, bankers, and the like to the upper class and, by an equally permissible exercise of discretion, to demote some small tradesmen and artisans to the lower, or working, class. The Victorians were never sure to which station of life people in such occupations belonged. But even if adjustments of this sort were made, the great majority of English writers from 1800 to our day could still be said to have come from the middle class. Yet, according to a rule of thumb favored by writers on social and economic topics throughout the nineteenth century, the upper and middle classes together constituted only about a quarter of the total population.[4] All but 3% of the writers, in other words, came from a numerically minor portion of the people. The chief reason is that the schooling available to children of the working classes (75% or more of the population) was so meagre and ineffectual that the odds against a working-class child's becoming a writer, or for that matter the practitioner of any other art or humane discipline, were overwhelming. That this remained true long after the Forster Act of 1870 spread, and subsequent laws made compulsory, the benefits of elementary education is proved by the fact that only fourteen out of 240 writers of the period 1900–1935 had working-class origins; and the number would be even smaller if

4 See, for example, P[atrick] Colquhoun, *A Treatise on the Wealth, Power, and Resources of the British Empire* (London 1814) 106–107; G. D. H. Cole and Raymond Postgate, *The Common People, 1746–1938* (London 1938) 70, and the 1947 edition of the same book, p 63; O. F. Christie, *The Transition from Aristocracy 1832–1867* (London 1927) 66–71; and Leone Levi, *Wages and Earnings of the Working Classes* (London 1885) 25.

Irish writers were eliminated from the list. Thus, whatever progress British popular education has made in the past sixty or seventy years, the results, as I shall have occasion to note below, have only just begun to be evident in the increase of writers with proletarian backgrounds.

Several other points of interest may be observed in connection with the preceding table. In spite of the widely discussed decline in the cultural authority of the upper class during the nineteenth century — its degeneration into Carlyle's "idle dilettantes" and Arnold's "barbarians" — the percentage of writers it produced remained fairly constant. A more perceptible decline is that in the number of writers who came from the aristocracy of wealth (merchants, shipowners, bankers, brokers): thirty-six in Period I, twenty-five in Period II, twenty in Period III, and only ten in Period IV. At the same time, notwithstanding its immense numerical growth, the commercial portion of the middle class never bred more than a handful of writers. In Period I, there were seventeen; in II, nine; in III, twelve; and in IV (if we lump "tradesmen" and "miscellaneous business men" together), fifteen. Throughout the era studied, by far the largest proportion of writers came from the professional and artistic grades of the middle class. Indeed, of the total of 840 writers represented, 422, or almost exactly half, were children of physicians, teachers, lawyers, government officials, and persons associated with the various arts; and in every period writers whose fathers were clergymen outnumbered the children of men in any other single profession. Thus the assumption that the professional and artistic classes tend to perpetuate themselves seems well supported. Literary ambitions, it appears, were more likely to be nurtured in a social group traditionally favorable to literature than one — such as the commercial class — whose members had only recently begun to have books about them.

Some information was found on the schooling of 946 authors of both sexes (197 in Period I, 233 in Period II, 186 in Period III, 330 in Period IV). For the men, the figures are as follows:

PERIOD	I	II	III	IV
Little or no schooling	20 (11.3%)	13 (5.9%)	7 (4.1%)	19 (7.2%)
Education ended on secondary level	64 (36.2%)	62 (27.9%)	43 (25.0%)	54 (20.5%)
Education continued into university or comparable institution	93 (52.5%)	147 (66.2%)	122 (70.9%)	191 (72.3%)
TOTAL	177	222	172	264

The records afford little definite information on where our authors received their elementary education. On only a few writers, in each of the first three periods, are such data forthcoming:

Period	I	II	III
"Self-educated"	5	8	2
Educated at home	11	17	13
Charity, parish, burgh or private school	22	15	10

If specific evidence were available on the early schooling of all the authors under study, it is unlikely that the proportions suggested by the above figures would hold good. The fact that a writer was "self-educated" was so noteworthy as to call for mention in even the briefest biographical sketch, whereas in the middle class from which the great majority of authors came, some amount of formal education could reasonably be assumed. Probably, therefore, the majority of nineteenth-century writers received their early education in parish, burgh, or private venture school. (Few authors attended the charity schools of the National or British and Foreign School Society, because these draw their pupils almost exclusively from the working class. Similarly, only a small handful of twentieth-century authors were products of the board and council schools that sprang up after 1870.) Throughout the first two thirds of the nineteenth century, of course, a number of prospective writers were taught the rudiments by parents, governesses, or tutors. But this practice virtually ceased, except on the highest social level or in special circumstances, notably illness, when school attendance was made compulsory.

The biographical sources are much more specific on the matter of secondary education:

Period	I	II	III	IV
Grammar schools				
The nine "ancient" ones:				
Eton	11	18	9	19
Harrow	9	6	7	6
Rugby	2	5	2	9
Shrewsbury	--	2	2	3
Winchester	2	3	1	5
Westminster	7	3	--	3
Charterhouse	3	4	--	5
St Paul's	2	--	2	6
Merchant Taylors	--	3	2	2
TOTAL	36	44	25	58

Grammar schools, *continued*

Nineteenth-century foundations

King's College School (1829)	--	4	3	--
University College School (1833)	1	2	2	--
Cheltenham (1841)	--	1	4	2
Marlborough (1843)	--	1	3	6
Edinburgh High School	3	6	--	--
Other (local) grammar schools	36	41	37	95
TOTAL OF ALL GRAMMAR SCHOOLS	76	99	74	161
Dissenting academies	10	7	12	3
Edinburgh Academy	--	2	2	2
Private venture schools	58	61	45	8
"Privately educated" (by tutor)	9	23	12	15
Catholic schools (especially Stonyhurst)	4	2	8	8
Foreign schools	5	9	9	6
Miscellaneous (teacher training schools, Birkbeck Institute, etc)	--	--	--	12

Perhaps the most interesting set of trends to be noted here is the changing relative importance, as seed-beds of literary talent, of the three major types of secondary schools: the old-established "public" (national grammar) schools, the lesser (local) grammar schools — both endowed and proprietary — and the private venture schools, many of which offered an education modelled after that of the grammar schools while others specialized in a non-classical, "modern" curriculum. In Period I, of all writers who had gone to some kind of grammar school, nearly half (thirty-six out of seventy-six) had been to one or another of the public schools.[5] This proportion then decreased to forty-four out of 99 in Period II, twenty-five out of seventy-four in Period III, and only fifty-eight out of 161 in Period IV. In the latter part of the Victorian era, therefore, the rehabilitated endowed and proprietary grammar schools overshadowed the ancient public schools as producers of literary men. This marked change may be interpreted in either of two ways: as a more positive evidence of the decline in cultural authority of the top social classes, whose schools these traditionally had been, or as evidence that the upper- and upper-middle-class talents which formerly had been nourished almost exclusively in the great public schools, were now more widely distributed among the nation's grammar schools.

Unquestionably the growing importance of the less famous schools was due to the educational reforms inspired by the Taunton Commission inquiry

[5] The apparent supremacy of Eton as a nourisher of literary talent is to some extent a statistical illusion. In the past two centuries the school has always had at least twice as many students as any of its rivals.

of 1864–68, which exposed the decay into which numerous schools on old foundations had fallen. Their reëmergence as reputable institutions of learning is probably the reason why the private venture schools so prominent in the educational histories of nineteenth-century writers — and in their fiction: both Mr Creakle's and Mr Squeers' establishments belonged to the type — virtually disappeared as an educational force by the end of the century. They had been set up in the first place to supply the needs of the enlarging middle class, needs which were most inadequately met by the ancient public schools and their hundreds of local satellites. When the grammar school system was revitalized, above all by the gradual modernization of the curriculum, the private schools, good, bad, and indifferent, to which many scores of nineteenth-century writers had gone, passed into eclipse.

It will be observed, incidentally, that at no time did the dissenting academies, which had had so conspicuous a role in eighteenth-century English education, produce many men of letters. They were characteristically more utilitarian in their educational philosophy than the grammar schools and many of the private schools; their boys were trained for commercial, not literary, careers. The secondary education of the great majority of English authors was classical in spirit and substance. Whatever its virtues and defects (and it was of course bitterly attacked throughout the utilitarian-minded nineteenth century) it played no small part in determining the ideas, attitudes and even the literary style of the epoch's writers, and through them, in turn, the opinions and tastes of their millions of readers.

As for higher education, we have already seen a steady increase in the percentage of literary men who attended a university or other post-secondary school, from 52.5% in Period I to 72.3% in Period IV. Analyzed in more detail, this was the pattern:

PERIOD	I	II	III	IV	TOTAL I/IV
Oxford	33	40	58	78	209
Cambridge	22	45	25	51	143
London (i. e. King's College, University College)	--	14	7	8	
Edinburgh	8	18	9	4	
Trinity College, Dublin	13	10	6	5	
Glasgow	9	5	8	3	
Other universities	2	1	1	13	
Art schools (especially Slade)	3	11	6	10	
Miscellaneous (including Woolwich, Sandhurst, medical college)	3	3	2	19	

In all but one period (and the reason for this mild reversal of form is not apparent) Oxford held a substantial edge over Cambridge in the number of former undergraduates engaged in letters. Its over-all superiority of 209 to 143 conforms to the tradition that Oxford is the seat of the humanities and Cambridge that of the sciences. (One wonders if a similar analysis of the educational careers of 1,100 nineteenth-century scientists would support the belief.[6]) Although no strict count was made, the single Oxford college to which the greatest number of future writers belonged unquestionably was Balliol; its Cambridge counterpart was Trinity. The rise of provincial universities in the late Victorian era and the early twentieth century is reflected in the number of writers in Period IV who went to universities other than Oxford and Cambridge — a trend which is being accelerated in the present "redbrick" era. Somewhat puzzling, however, is the discovery that the two early teaching colleges of London University (University College, opened 1828, and King's, 1831) contributed twice as many writers to England in the generation immediately after their founding than in either of the subsequent epochs.

Much less information is available on the schooling of the women authors than of the men. In each of the three nineteenth-century periods, approximately ten or eleven women writers were specifically reported to have received their education at home, and the same number to have had formal schooling on both the elementary and secondary levels. In Period III, in addition, seven had gone on to some kind of advanced study — an indication of the slow progress of higher education for women. However, among the sixty-six women writers of the early twentieth century on whom educational data were found, the pattern is notably different. Twenty-five were educated at home; but thirty-seven attended private secondary schools in England, in addition to a few who "finished" on the continent. The single institution that produced more than two writers was Cheltenham Ladies' College, five of whose alumna are included in our list. In view of Cheltenham's distinction as a pioneer in late Victorian education for girls, this is pleasantly appropriate. Probably the most noteworthy feature in the educational histories of women writers in Period IV is the fact that twenty-five studied in higher institutions — among them seven at London University, six at Somerville College, Oxford, and three at Cambridge (two at Newnham, one at Girton). Thus the typical twentieth-century woman author, unlike her predecessors in the generations of Harriet Martineau and Ouida, brought to her profession a

---

[6] Hans's figures (op cit, p 32) on seventeenth- and eighteenth-century scientists do, but only by a narrow margin. One hundred and twenty-five scientists went to Cambridge, 116 to Oxford.

considerable amount of formal education, and of education that in general was more liberal than had been possible under Victorian conditions.

Our final concern is with the degree to which the authors studied constituted a true *profession* of letters. How many earned their livelihood exclusively or chiefly as writers, how many wrote as a sideline to some other occupation, and how many had independent incomes? In the nature of the case, no clear-cut answers are possible. The biographical sources are unsatisfactory on the subject of a man's private income, and the occupational restlessness and versatility of many, if not most, nineteenth-century writers defeat the categorizer. An author who at one time or another followed as many as half a dozen non-literary vocations cannot easily be identified as a professional writer, nor is classification simplified when an author pursued another career simultaneously with his literary one.

Between 1800 and 1935 the number of professional writers — men and women, that is, who derived their chief if not their sole livelihood from the pen — steadily grew. According to Sir Walter Besant, "it was estimated that in 1836 there were no fewer than four thousand persons living by literary work. Most of them, of course, must have been simple publishers' hacks. But seven hundred of them in London were journalists. At the present day [1888] there are said to be in London alone fourteen thousand men and women who live by writing. And of this number I should think that thirteen thousand are in some way or other connected with journalism." [7] Certainly it is true that with the widening of the reading audience and the intensified commercialization of literature, it became increasingly possible to make a living

---

[7] *Fifty Years Ago* (new edition, London 1892) 176–177. Besant's figures, to put it mildly, lack substantiation. The official census returns for England and Wales throw only a fitful and dubious light on the number of persons who regarded themselves as professional writers. In the 1841 census, the first to include detailed occupational breakdowns, 167 persons were entered as authors and 459 as newspaper editors, proprietors, and reporters. In 1851, 2,671 "authors" were counted (but the fact that 123 of them were under twenty years of age is a measure of the seriousness with which we should regard all these figures!). In 1861, 1,673 men and women were included under the heading "author, editor, writer." In 1871 the classification was monstrously enlarged by the inclusion of "students" among "authors" and other "literary persons," with the result that the total was 139,143. For the next six decades the classifications were fairly consistent, although in the last two (1921, 1931) the limitation to England and Wales was removed and figures for all of Great Britain used instead:

	MALE	FEMALE	TOTAL
1881: Authors, editors, journalists, reporters, shorthand writers	5,644	467 [8%]	6,111
1891: Authors, editors, journalists, reporters	7,485	787 [9%]	8,272
1901: Authors, editors, journalists, reporters	9,811	1,249 [11%]	11,060
1911: Authors, editors, journalists, reporters	12,030	1,756 [13%]	13,786
1921: Authors, editors, journalists, publicists	12,240	2,166 [15%]	14,406
1931: Authors, editors, journalists, publicists	17,190	3,409 [17%]	20,599

For locating this information in the Parliamentary Papers, I am indebted to Miss Eleanor Devlin of the Reference Department of the Ohio State University Library.

by the pen. Journalism, as distinct from book-writing, was the principal support of numerous writers in each of our four periods. A very conservative count, including only those who for a considerable period of their lives were editors, reporters, and staff members of newspapers, magazines, and reviews, shows that seventeen authors were professional journalists in Period I, forty in Period II, twenty-seven in Period III, and thirty-seven in Period IV. If we were to take into account those who frequently contributed to periodicals but were usually not salaried employees, the number of authors connected with journalism would be much larger for each period, and probably would represent a larger proportion of the whole for each successive period.

These are the main extra-literary professions of our authors:

Period	I	II	III	IV
Clergyman	29	38	16	3
Practicing solicitor or barrister	5	10	2	4
Government official, civil servant, diplomat	17	27	17	13
Artist, architect, musician, actor	11	21	10	13
Teacher, professor	4	17	25	37
Practicing physician	5	10	2	4

The church, the arts, and government obviously were the three institutions which helped subsidize the production of literature in the nineteenth century. It is noteworthy that after reaching a peak of influence in the middle of the century, the church declined into insignificance as a habitat of writers, at least of belles lettres, in the twentieth century; and simultaneously the academic profession, to which few poets, novelists, critics, or dramatists belonged in the earlier decades of the nineteenth century, grew in importance through the succeeding periods. The law, government service, and the arts had a more or less steady role in the support of literature in all four periods.

In addition to the authors who were also medical practitioners or lawyers for a substantial part of their lives, a number entered literature with some training in these professions:

Period	I	II	III	IV
Read law but never practiced	14	27	14	9
Studied medicine but never practiced	2	4	4	3

Literature has often been a profession to which a man turned after discovering himself unsuited for some other. The traffic flow in the other direction has been at least as heavy, but of it we have no record.

In every period there were, of course, numerous men whose workaday occupations, either before or during their literary careers, were remote from literature and the other learned or artistic professions. We find, for example, a dozen or two bankers, manufacturers, insurance agents, and other kinds of businessmen; a scattering of army and navy officers, nearly all of whom retired before beginning to write; a few engineers; clerks of various descriptions, accountants, commercial travelers. And in every period, too, we find record of some authors who were artisans or common laborers. Among our nineteenth-century writers are two miners, five weavers, two shoemakers, two peddlers, a shepherd, a railroad platelayer, a cooper, an upholsterer, a millwright, two stonemasons, a calico printer, a wool sorter, a silk miller, a basketmaker, a wood turner, and a reed maker. Their appearance in literary annals reminds us that an occasional, highly exceptional member of the working classes could and did find his way into print. Few if any contributed much to literature, but the drama of their struggle against adversity won them a fair amount of publicity and prestige in their own time.

Nevertheless, the self-made writer of working-class background has until recently been the sport, the anomaly, of the literary scene. But the post-war reforms by which workers' children are given a somewhat better chance for secondary and university education promise within a decade or two to substantially alter the class-distribution of writers. The present prominence of young authors like Colin Wilson (son of a boot-and-shoe machine operator, himself a former laborer, mortuary attendant, café waiter, and junior tax collector), Alan Sillitoe (son of a bicycle-factory worker, himself a former mill-hand and lathe operator), Brendan Behan (the slum-bred scion of a family of housepainters), Arnold Wesker (ex-kitchenhand), and Harold Pinter (son of an East End tailor) is clearly not a mere recrudescence of the sentimental interest in self-made authors — shepherds and milkmaids — that was a minor symptom of early nineteenth-century romanticism. It is, on the contrary, an augury.

But that is a matter for the future, and our concern here is with the past. The predominant conclusion we are forced to reach through a review of our data is that from the beginning of the nineteenth century down to the dawn of the Welfare State, the readers of Great Britain have been supplied by authors the great majority of whom have sprung from the "solid" middle class. They have, for the most part, had whatever intellectual advantages the formal education of their time offered them; and socially and politically they have, with conspicuous exceptions that come immediately to mind, been in sympathy with the attitudes of their class and era.

Between 1800 and 1935, therefore, the author-class remained relatively constant in its makeup; but the reader-class did not. As literacy and leisure increased, and cheap production of books, magazines, and newspapers made the printed word infinitely more accessible than ever before in British history, the essence of the literary situation was no longer, as it had been ever since Caxton's time, a dialogue of equals — well educated, socially superior writers addressing well educated, socially superior readers. Instead, most nineteenth-century writers found themselves in the unprecedented position of having to adapt their techniques and messages to the limited capacities and special expectations of a newly formed mass audience. This literary lag, this lengthening discrepancy between an author-class that was slow to mirror the social changes of the time and a reader-class that was in a state of constant flux and expansion, had all kinds of ramifications. The circumstance that the multitude of new readers were ill educated and only half literate posed a staggering problem of communication.[8] But to attempt to solve it was eminently worthwhile, since the middle-class domination of the press made possible the spreading and (hopefully) the perpetuation of the middle-class ethos and of middle-class literary taste. The genuinely dedicated literary artist, however, found himself in a predicament that has deep reverberations in our own time. To what extent was he obliged, as a member of his age's ruling class and supported, sometimes handsomely, by the pounds and shillings of his cultural inferiors, to debase his art, either for the sake of sheer intelligibility or for the more specific one of imparting desirable social, political, moral, and aesthetic attitudes? Amidst all the complaint, then and now, that the advent of a huge new audience meant the corrupting of literary tastes, it might be pertinent to inquire who did the corrupting.

Such generalizations as I have made from the data assembled in the preceding pages have, I think, their validity and value. Others will occur to everyone who has read this far. But a social profile of British authorship in a given epoch provides only a first tentative step toward a solution of the manifold riddles that have been posed since the problem of author-audience relationship became a subject of impassioned debate. These, we can say (granting that we need to collect much more information about them), were the people who *wrote*; what about the equally important people who *read*? Before we can go much farther into the cultural and literary implications of the data we possess on authors, we need a comparable analysis, or, actually,

[8] Volumes of valuable analysis are waiting to be written on this crucial topic. James Sutherland's pages on the intellectual equipment and literary experience the eighteenth-century poet assumed his reader to possess (*A Preface to Eighteenth Century Poetry* [Oxford 1948] Chapter III) suggest what should be done, on a much larger scale, for the nineteenth century.

a whole series or complex of analyses, of the quantitative growth, social composition, and above all the tastes of the public for whom our 1,100 authors wrote over the course of a century and a third. In my book *The English Common Reader* (Chicago 1957) I attempted a preliminary exploration of the social history of the nineteenth-century reading public, though deliberately and explicitly disclaiming any concern with its tastes. There have subsequently been a very few discussions of the latter topic, among them Margaret Dalziel's *Popular Fiction a Hundred Years Ago* (London 1957). But we simply cannot talk intelligently about the interaction of social and literary processes in any age, including the present one, without having more facts — and, I venture to add, without divesting ourselves of our preconceptions and violent prejudices.

Reviewing Williams' *The Long Revolution* in the *Universities Quarterly* (September 1961), A. H. Gomme observed that "a more secure sense of history might have resulted in rather more progress and rather less iteration." The remark might well be applied to the whole record, to date, of the literature-and-culture controversy. The abundance of sociological double-talk, which even past masters of the art have found oppressive in Williams' book, has not satisfactorily concealed the paucity of information. If we are to get anywhere with such topics as the many-faceted one of the relationship between author and audience, we will somehow have to bring ourselves to vacate the steamy arena of speculation, theory, and tendentiousness, and move to a platform supported by at least a few concrete blocks of historical evidence. In a debate as important and complicated as this one is, it is always useful to have some dependable facts, however prosaic, to refer to. The foregoing essay in statistical analysis is offered as a modest step toward that most desirable goal.

The Sociology of Literary Creativity : a Literary Critic's View
Philip Thody

from

International Social Science Journal, vol. XX, no. 3.

The sociology of literary creativity :
a literary critic's view

Philip Thody

If all writers—with the possible exception of the lyric poet[1]—write in order to be read, then the role of the literary critic is first and foremost that of an intermediary. He writes in order that other people may read better, and thus enable what Matthias Waltz and G. N. Pospelov[2] present as the essentially social function of literature to be more fully realized. His purpose is fulfilled when the reader makes a remark such as: 'Ah yes, now I see why the hero acted as he did', or 'Yes, now I see why this poem had to be written in lines of ten syllables', or 'Yes, now I see why I was more moved by what happened to X than by what Y said about himself'. The literary critic could, in fact, take as his guide those words which Browning put into the mouth of Fra Lippi when, in his discussion of the visual arts, he made the painter say:

1. See Alphonse Daudet, discussing the poet Mistral and quoting Montaigne, 'Souvienne-vous de celuy à qui, comme on demandait à quoi faire il se peinoit si fort en un art qui ne pouvoit venir à la cognoissance de guère de gens, "J'en ay assez de peu, répondict-il. J'en ay assez d'un. J'en ay assez de pas un".' *Lettres de mon moulin, Le Poète Mistral*, Ed. Lemerre, p. 155.
2. *International Social Science Journal*, Vol. XIX, No. 4, 1967.

We're made so that we love
First when we see them painted, things we have passed
Perhaps a hundred times nor cared to see;
And so they are better, painted—better to us,
Which is the same thing. Art was given for that;
God uses us to help each other so,
Lending our minds out.

The literary critic is the man who, lending his mind out, points to things that might otherwise be missed. His purpose is essentially revelatory. He helps communication to take place.

Before he begins to write, however, he makes two presuppositions. He assumes, to begin with, that both the writer and the average reader can in some way benefit from his intervention, and this assumption is, in turn, based on the presupposition that he has some special knowledge, skill or sensitivity that entitles him thus to play the honest broker. As far as the literature of the past is concerned, this presupposition is fairly easy to justify. If the critic is also a philologist, then he can help the modern spectator of *Othello* to understand more of the complexities and ambiguities of the play by pointing to the different meanings which the word 'honest' had in seventeenth-century English. If he is a historian, he can offer a fuller understanding of *Gulliver's Travels* by analysing in detail the extent to which a book which seems, on first reading, to be a kind of fairy story is in fact a savage political satire. And, if he is versed in anthropology or psychoanalysis, he can offer the average reader some valuable new insights into plays such as *Hamlet, Oedipus Rex* and *Antigone*. If he is concerned with modern literature, his presumption to intervene may at first sight seem less justifiable, since his historical and philological knowledge will not be fundamentally different from that of the ordinary person. Nevertheless, it is not difficult to imagine a critic who has read the whole of Sartre's work being able to show *Les Séquestrés d'Altona* in a different and more interesting light by pointing to the similarity between its plot and that of *Les Mains Sales,* or bringing out an important but often neglected aspect of the play by comparing its treatment of the theme of fatherhood with Sartre's attitude towards the same subject in *Les Mots*. As long as the end achieved is a fuller understanding or a greater appreciation of the work under discussion, the critic may use any kind of knowledge he likes. Indeed, he may not even use knowledge in a general sense at all. The critic of poetry, for example, the man who helps us to appreciate the verbal beauty and intellectual complexity of a sonnet by Mallarmé or Ronsard, is not necessarily called upon even to make a special appeal to his knowledge of language. He may simply be someone with a keen ear for music, a sharp sense of poetic rhythm, and an appreciation of verbal harmony which he has trained and improved and refined by a careful reading of many other poems. All these skills and all these forms of knowledge can and should be relevant to the task which the critic has undertaken: that of helping the reader to understand the writer, that of helping the writer to communicate with his public.

This view of criticism as essentially revelatory does not, of course, exclude many of the functions which critics have taken it upon themselves to perform in the past. It does not, for example, deny all value and relevance to the approach of a Sainte-Beuve. It may well be helpful to a reader to know something of an author's life, and the person who has just read *L'Étranger*, for example, will see the book in a different and perhaps more comprehensive light when he learns that Camus, like Meursault, was born in Algeria, that at one time he worked in an office, and that all he knew of his father was the latter's physical detestation of the institution of capital punishment. Nor does this concept of the critic's role, however, deny that there can be a work of art which is better treated in isolation from what we know of its creator's life, looked upon as a 'Calme bloc ici-bas chu d'un désastre obscur', and analysed without reference to its origins. The literary critic can still use his sensitivity, his increased awareness of language, his knowledge of other works, to interpret, to analyse, to elucidate, to explain. Similarly, without in any way being unfaithful to his main function, he can still perform the more traditional function of formulating value judgements. It is a help to a clearer view of Dickens's achievement in *Great Expectations*, for example, to learn that *Oliver Twist*, another novel that deals with crime and childhood, is rightly considered to be a less mature and complex work, infused with a peculiarly nineteenth-century sentimentality that is absent from the later novel.

The literary critic who is seeking, as Miss Helen Gardner puts it, 'to display the work in a manner which will enable it to exert its own power',[1] is led, inevitably, to adopt an essentially eclectic approach. All is grist that comes to his mill: the findings of the social historian, the intuitions of the psycho-analyst, the discoveries of the anthropologist, the methods of the sociologist, the exact knowledge of the linguist or grammarian. There is only one attitude that he eschews: that of the censor who, basing his views on ready-made artistic, religious or political concepts, roundly declares such and such a work to be good or bad because it either fits or fails to fit some Procrustes' bed of unchanging and unchangeable aesthetic or ideological doctrines. The literary critic does not judge by rule—indeed, except on very rare occasions, he does not judge at all. He explains, interprets, elucidates, compares, analyses and suggests. If, after his explanations and analyses, he does not like what he finds, it is his duty to say so. But he begins with the intention of widening, not of narrowing, his reader's area of experience, of increasing our awareness of the richness of a work of art, not of showing why it is inadequate or unsatisfying.

The literary critic's attitude towards sociology is, in this definition of his role, analogous to that which the physician adopts towards the histologist,

---

1. *The Business of Criticism*, Oxford, Clarendon Press, 1959, p. 17.

the microbiologist, the medical statistician or the bacteriologist. He seeks, that is to say, to improve his performance in his own general field of activity by appealing to the results obtained in other more specific disciplines. He does not want to replace these disciplines, or to be replaced by their practitioners. He has his own job to do, and is always on the look-out for new and interesting tools or techniques; nor does he intend to change his job or to take on somebody else's. He cannot, without being unfaithful to his calling, allow himself to be absorbed into some general inquiry concerning the relationship between the author and society. This is more properly the province of the sociologist, and he is not even, *qua* critic, particularly interested in the problem of literary creativity as such. His concern is with the finished product, with the novel or poem as printed, with the play as performed.

It is interesting to learn something of the different stages through which a novel such as *A la recherche du temps perdu* passed before it was published in what we now think of as its definitive form, and valuable to know something of the social, intellectual and spiritual atmosphere in which writers such as Pascal or Racine were brought up. But the information which the specialist in literary genesis, in sociology or in the history of ideas, may offer to the literary critic in no way obliges the latter to adopt a particular attitude towards a work of art. If the critic says, for example, that parts of *La Fugitive* are boring and repetitive, or, on the contrary, that the middle sections of Proust's novel gain immensely from the presence of Monsieur de Charlus, this is because he is reporting honestly, for the benefit of his readers, on what he has felt, and is inviting them, by comparing their experience and reactions with his own, to increase their appreciation of Proust's work. He is not saying that, because the author did not have time to revise them before final publication, certain portions of the work are boring, or that other sections are interesting just because the author wrote them under the influence of obsessions he had earlier suppressed. Such considerations can only be in the nature of *post-facto* explanations, confirming an original opinion that has already been formed for a variety of aesthetic reasons. Similarly, while they may enable this judgement to be seen in a different and possibly fuller light, they do not in any way determine the judgement which is made. The sociologist may demonstrate, by his analysis of a work of art, that its social implications are disagreeable and reactionary, but this does not then oblige the critic to denounce it as bad art—any more than the discovery that its social implications were impeccably moral and progressive would compel him to declare it excellent.

With some important modifications, these remarks apply particularly to Lucien Goldmann's study of Pascal and Racine in *The Hidden God*. There is certainly convincing evidence for relating the *Pensées* to the general world view of extremist Jansenism, and for interpreting certain plays by Racine in the light of what we know of the conflicts and negotiations between the Jansenists and the Crown during the period when Racine was writing them. It is impossible to read the *Pensées* without being constantly struck by the very great differences between the arguments which Pascal puts forward in this text and the approach which he adopted in the *Provinciales*, and yet, before Goldmann wrote his book, these differences were either ignored or else 'explained away' in a rather unsatisfactory manner. Since *The Hidden God*, however, we can both appreciate these differences more fully and see how they came into being, and Goldmann's work on Pascal is, in this respect, almost a model of what the sociologist can offer the literary critic: it shows him how to read a text in a more satisfying and comprehensive way. Yet for all its merits, Goldmann's approach does not invalidate the literary critic's claim to be pursuing an independent intellectual discipline in its own right, and one which can be supplemented by the findings of sociology but not supplanted by them. The critic still has to integrate these findings into his over-all assessment of the work. Moreover, the primarily philosophical and sociological approach adopted in *The Hidden God* is not entirely free from a certain number of ambiguities which carry with them the danger of misleading literary judgements. In the sections on Racine, in particular, there are some unjustified preconceptions which lead to an artificially narrow view of the nature of tragedy and thus to bad literary criticism.

At first sight, there is something rather strange in Goldmann's insistence, both in *The Hidden God* and in his article, 'The Sociology of Literature: Status and Problems of Method', that we should take as our starting point 'the text, the whole of the text and nothing but the text'.[1] Any literary critic who did not do so would put himself out of court from the very beginning, and the need which Goldmann feels to stress this truism is a sad reflection on those interpretations of Pascal and Racine that he has read. His insistence does, however, draw attention to another truism whose existence is perhaps more relevant to his approach: both Pascal's *Pensées* and Racine's tragedies existed as works of literature in their own right before Goldmann showed them to have 'the structural categories . . . which . . . corresponded strictly to the structure of thought of the extremist Jansenist group'.[2] But if no one before Goldmann had pointed to these structural categories or formulated what seems to be the law that 'the significance of the work, in so far as it is a literary work, is always of the same character, namely, a coherent universe within which the events occur and the psychology of the characters is situated and within the coherent expression of which the stylistic automatisms of the writer are incorporated',[3] can we therefore infer that no one, before 1956, had done more than catch a glimpse of the true achievement of Pascal and Racine? This would be an absurd contention, and Goldmann nowhere suggests that he is trying to put it forward. He nevertheless comes close to suggesting that Pascal and Racine are great writers because they gave coherent expression to the world view of the extremist thinkers of Jansenism, and that their mastery of language, the range and power of their minds, the acuity of their psychology, and the many other qualities which

1. *International Social Science Journal*, loc. cit., p. 498.
2. ibid., p. 504.
3. ibid., p. 508.

critics have found in them in the past and still find in them today, are either irrelevant epiphenomena or else directly attributable to the coherence of the vision they express.

The point of view of the literary critic is bound to be different. He is fully prepared to see that Pascal and Racine give a peculiarly accurate expression to the ideology which the *noblesse de robe* embraced at a particular moment in its history, and to recognize that this gives them considerable importance for the historian. Similarly, he is quite happy to accept the fact that Pascal anticipated certain features of the dialectical thought more fully developed in Hegel and in Marx, and to agree that this gives him great significance both for the historian of ideas and for any philosopher writing at the present day. But these achievements, for the literary critic, are like the successive leaves which Peer Gynt peels off the onion in his attempt to discover its essence. As Peer Gynt discovers, this essence lies nowhere but in the complex relationship between the individual leaves; it cannot be said to lie in any one individual leaf, however important this may seem when looked at from a particular point of view.

There is then, to change the metaphor, no *open sesame* which the sociologist can whisper to the literary critic and thereby enable him to solve the problems with which the interpretation and analysis of any particular literary text may confront him. Neither will a sociological approach help him to fulfil what T. S. Eliot called 'the rudiment of criticism': 'the ability to choose a good poem and reject a bad poem; and . . . its ability to select a good *new* poem, to respond properly to a new situation'.[1] It may enable him to understand one aspect of a new poem or of an accepted masterpiece, but it will not do more than this. The final aesthetic synthesis will still have to be made. Of course, if we are asking the question: 'What did Pascal really mean?', and if we are assuming that Pascal is first and foremost a philosopher or a theological thinker, then Goldmann's approach is quite invaluable. We can see much more clearly what an author really meant— or, to put it in terms which Goldmann would probably find more satisfactory, what the objective meaning of his work really is—when we see him in relationship to the world view of the social group from which he sprang. But the question of an author's meaning is only one of the questions which the literary critic asks, in the same way as 'What is the normal incidence of this disease?' or 'What are the principal features of the histological analysis?' are only some of the questions asked by a physician in his attempt to arrive at a correct diagnosis. It is certainly essential to understand that Pascal's was a coherent attitude, but this is only a starting point. The literary critic still has to elucidate what this attitude was, examine the various devices which Pascal used in order to communicate it to his reader, evaluate it by reference to those attitudes adopted by other thinkers, and explain why so many other people have found it penetrating or profound.

It is true that Goldmann does not, either in *The Hidden God* or in his

---

1. *The Use of Poetry and the Use of Criticism*, London, Faber and Faber, 1933, p. 18.

article, 'The Sociology of Literature: Status, Problems and Methods', restrict himself merely to showing the relationship between the structure of the Jansenist world vision and the work of Pascal and Racine. Indeed, when he writes that 'a literary work is seen to be all the more valuable and more important according as this tension (between sensible multiplicity and richness and, on the other hand, the unity which organizes this multiplicity into a coherent whole) is both stronger and more effectively overcome, that is to say, according as the sensible richness and multiplicity of its universe are greater and as that richness is more rigorously organized, and constitutes a structural unity',[1] he does seem to be offering a fruitful aesthetic approach to literature, and thus coming closer to the central aims of literary criticism. It is, therefore, rather disappointing to discover, on reading those chapters in *The Hidden God* which deal with a writer whose work is undoubtedly more literary than philosophical, that the definition of tragedy which Goldmann takes from Lukàcs leads him to discuss both Racine's plays and the general nature of tragedy in a rather one-sided manner.

Briefly expressed, the view of tragedy put forward in *The Hidden God* is that tragic characters are those whose greatness lies precisely in the fact that they refuse the world and this life. They are possessed by an impossible demand for the absolute and for purity, and recognize that the nature of reality is such that they can satisfy this demand only by an attitude of compromise which their very essence prevents them from adopting. As soon as the possibility of success is envisaged, the play ceases to be a tragedy, and Goldmann refuses the title of 'tragedy' to *Bajazet*, *Mithridate* and *Iphigénie* on the grounds that the central characters in these plays do at some point come close to success through a readiness to compromise with the world. He also maintains that neither *Esther* nor *Athalie* are tragedies, and prefers to call them, because of the direct intervention of God in history which characterizes their plot, 'sacred dramas'. There are, in his view, only four plays by Racine that can legitimately be called tragedies: *Andromaque*, *Britannicus*, *Bérénice* and *Phèdre*; and even within them, he argues, the genuinely tragic characters are not always those to whom critics in the past have accorded most importance: in *Britannicus*, for example, the tragic character is Junie, not Néron, Britannicus or Agrippine, and neither Thésée nor Hippolyte are, in his view, in any way entitled to be considered as tragic characters; even Andromaque, he maintains, temporarily ceases to be tragic when she adopts the subterfuge that will enable her to ensure Astyanax's protection by marrying Pyrrhus and then killing herself.

In some ways, of course, this is a perceptive and rewarding way of looking at Racine's plays. Just as the chapters in *The Hidden God* which dealt with Pascal showed that we were right to look upon the *Provinciales* and the *Pensées* as representing different world views, so the pages on Racine underline the mistake of looking at all his tragedies as if they were the same kind of play. There are obvious differences between the structure of *Andromaque*

---

1. *International Social Science Journal*, loc. cit., p. 514.

and that of *Iphigénie*, for example, just as there are similarities between *Andromaque* and *Phèdre*, and it is useful for the critic to have these differences explained and analysed.

In its treatment of Racine, as in its analysis of Pascal, *The Hidden God* does offer the literary critic the possibility of looking at a work of art in a new, stimulating and rewarding light, of seeing relationships and similarities hitherto ignored, and of appreciating distinctions not fully made before. Where it is less satisfactory, however, is in giving the impression that the definition of tragedy culled from Lukàcs is the only one which is either aesthetically or intellectually valid. Aristotle may well not be telling the whole truth when he says that a tragedy inspires 'terror and pity', but when characters such as Néron, Agrippine, Oreste, Hermione or Thésée have had this effect on generations of spectators, it is a little hasty, to say the least, to adopt a definition of tragedy which refuses to consider them as anything but 'wild beasts'.[1] Bradley may not have been entirely right to see the tragic hero in Shakespeare's plays as the man who, like Macbeth, Hamlet, Othello or Mark Anthony, finds all his noble characteristics ruined by the action of just one defect.[2] Nevertheless, Bradley's views provide a sufficiently rewarding way of looking at one of the greatest tragic playwrights of all times that again it is unwise to define a tragedy without ever referring to what he says. For none of Shakespeare's plays contains a character who tries to 'live in accordance with the principle of all or nothing',[3] or who is torn apart, as in *Andromaque*, by two equally valid but contradictory demands, and yet no one can seriously deny that *Hamlet, King Lear, Othello, Macbeth*, and *Anthony and Cleopatra* are tragedies, or that they can, at least initially, be fruitfully studied within Bradleyan or Aristotelian terms. If the literary critic has to choose between his experience of seeing or reading Shakespeare and the rigid and exclusive definition of tragedy which Goldmann adopts from Lukàcs, then he would be denying the whole nature of his calling if he did not prefer the first. The great objection to fixed and unchanging categories is that they prevent communication from taking place. They deny the very essence of the critic's calling.

We have not yet had a sufficiently long experience of the application of sociological methods to literary problems to decide whether or not Goldmann's reintroduction of Procrustes' bed is merely an accident, or whether it reflects some genuine weakness in the sociological approach. If sociology is going to be applied to literature in the way suggested in parts of *The Hidden God*, then a certain amount of excessive schematization would seem to be inevitable, and Matthias Waltz's assumption that 'love poetry is a means of solving problems of group life'[4] scarcely suggests that sociologically inspired studies of John Donne or Charles Baudelaire will be very fruitful from a literary point of view. They may, of course, tell us a very great deal

1. The term used in *Le Dieu Caché* is 'fauves'.
2. See A. W. Bradley, *Shakespearian Tragedy*, London, Macmillan, 1904.
3. *International Social Science Journal*, loc. cit., p. 523.
4. ibid., p. 613.

about the relationship between the writer and society in seventeenth-century England or nineteenth-century France; they may provide invaluable insights as to why Baudelaire found it essential to deride the *bourgeois* or to deny the possibility of sexual happiness; they may tell us a great deal about the situation of the clergy at a crucial period in the history of the Church of England or about the wider problem of the relationship between religion and eroticism; they may also enable us to form hypotheses about the changes that come over the actual form of poetry as well as over the organization of society, and no one would deny that all these are legitimate fields of inquiry both for the sociologist himself and for the literary man. But if sociology is to be, in one of its manifestations at least, a tool which the literary critic can use to evaluate and interpret works of art, it will have to do away with rigid concepts and accept the fact that Kipling's recognition that there are:

> Nine and sixty ways of constructing tribal lays
> And every single one of them is right

has an important corollary: no key fits every door.

Yet even though there can be no fixed rules for the application of sociology to literary criticism, it is possible to indicate certain areas in which the sociological approach has already given particularly fortunate results in the literary field. First and foremost, of course, come those writers who have used sociological concepts to analyse works belonging only marginally to what is normally classified as 'literature': George Orwell in his essays on boys' papers, comic postcards, or *No Orchids for Miss Blandish*;[1] Boileau and Narcéjac in their study of the violent detective novel, *La Fin d'un bluff*;[2] Kingsley Amis on James Bond or on science fiction in *New Maps of Hell*;[3] Richard Usborne on the works of John Buchan, Sapper and Dornford Yates in *Clubland Heroes*;[4] and, of course, Umberto Eco on Eugène Sue.[5]

It does seem to be the case that works which are popular rather than intellectual in their appeal and which do not really qualify as 'literature' are best suited to a primarily sociological analysis. Both their social inspiration and their social implications are much closer to the surface than can ever be the case in more finished works of art. There, everything is more completely fused together and all the implications are so deeply embedded in the complex structure of the work that a primarily sociological approach reveals much less of its over-all value or significance. It is relatively easy for Orwell, for example, to show that *No Orchids for Miss Blandish* reflects a falling off in the general moral standards of society, while the Raffles books, in contrast, show

---

1. See *Critical Essays*, London, Secker and Warburg, 1946.
2. See *La Fin d'un bluff. Essai sur le roman noir américain*, Paris, Le Portulan, 1949.
3. Published by Gollancz, London, 1961 and 1966 respectively.
4. *Clubland Heroes. A nostalgic study of some of the recurrent characters in the romantic fiction of Dornford Yates, John Buchan and Sapper*, London, Constable, 1953.
5. *International Social Science Journal*, op. cit., p. 551-69.

a world where the concept of 'the gentleman' is still valid,[1] and it is not difficult for Boileau and Narcéjac to argue that the work of Peter Cheyney, when contrasted with that of Agatha Christie, mirrors a world in which ruthless action has taken the place of cold calculation and where the mind is therefore given less importance than the body. It is, however, more difficult to say anything quite so simple or quite so obviously true about the social implications of Dickens' or Stendhal's novels, precisely because Dickens and Stendhal seem, for the most part, to have been very aware of the society around them, and to have commented on it in a much more subtle and self-conscious way. It is fascinating to learn something of the social group with which Stendhal was most frequently in contact while writing his novels; but it is less certain that this knowledge can tell us why *Le Rouge et le Noir* is a good novel or whether Julien Sorel acts consistently or not when he tries to shoot Madame de Rênal.

The most impressive and original feature of Goldmann's work is that he does apply sociology to authors who are aesthetically significant—Racine and Pascal in the seventeenth century, Malraux in the twentieth—and that he does say something interesting about them as writers. Whether his methods can be applied to other and equally significant authors remains to be seen. In the meantime, however, it may be helpful in conclusion to mention an essay which is concerned with an aesthetically significant author, and which does use, if not sociological concepts, then at least historical ones, in order to illuminate certain moral and aesthetic features of the work under discussion: the chapter on Graham Greene's *The Heart of the Matter* in Donat O'Donnell's *Maria Cross*.[2]

The chapter is entitled 'The Anatomy of Pity' and contains a brilliant dissection of the ambiguities and uncertainties both in the actual behaviour of Scobie, the main character in the novel, and in Graham Greene's presentation of this behaviour to the reader. Pity, concludes Donat O'Donnell, is the main inspiration for Scobie's actions, and he points out that this pity also shows itself in the way Graham Greene wrote the novel, in its 'intellectual dishonesty, its ellipses of approximation and selective omissions, as well as in its fragmention of character'.[3] This, in itself, is a perceptive piece of criticism, but it is not until the next stage in O'Donnell's analysis that the introduction of historical or sociological considerations changes his essay into an example of how such considerations can really illuminate a work of art and enable the critic to see it in a fuller and richer light. *The Heart of the Matter*, he argues in the very last section of his essay, is a novel where 'the sense of history is present but, according to the classical mode, compressed into the personal relationships of a few people'.[4] Though not 'a neat ballet with each movement corresponding to a stage in the decay of monopoly

1. See *Critical Essays*, analysis of *No Orchids for Miss Blandish*.
2. Published by Chatto and Windus, London, 1953. The chapter on Graham Greene is on p. 63-91.
3. op. cit., p. 88.
4. ibid., p. 88.

capitalism',[1] it can be read as a dramatization in fictional terms of the various contradictions which characterize a declining imperialism: Scobie sees all his relationships on the model of those between a father and his children, as did the imperialist powers in their time of supremacy; but, like them, he can help those whom he pretends to love only by killing himself. He 'cannot keep the emotional commitments he has incurred, any more than the imperial powers can meet their financial liabilities'; but he nevertheless becomes an accomplice in the murder of his native servant, just as the *rentier* class in the 1930s was an accomplice in the murders committed by Fascism. And, although O'Donnell does not specifically say so, there is no doubt that the intense appeal which the novel makes is linked to the expression which it gives to the contradictory situation both of its author and of its present-day readers. Greene, like all writers in a society which has lost its historical self-confidence but still retains some of its old ethical imperatives, cannot but reflect this contradiction, consciously or unconsciously, in what he writes. And his readers, whether they agree with the political implications of what he writes or not, cannot fail to respond to this dramatization of their own historical situation.

This essay thus provides an example of how sociological considerations can help the literary critic in his work. After he has seen how *The Heart of the Matter*, without in any way setting out to be a conscious denunciation of colonialism, nevertheless reflects imperialism at a particular stage in its decay, and shows the curious and multiple effects of this decay in people's private lives and apparently individual moral concerns, he appreciates Graham Greene's achievement more fully. The critic gets more out of the novel, and, since his task is to help other people to read better, he is more capable of performing it.

This, however, does not imply that the same line of approach would be valid for every novel that makes an impact on a modern reader. Neither does it imply that we should deliberately set out, first and foremost, to see what the sociological or historical content of a work of fiction really is, and it is highly significant, in this respect, that O'Donnell did not begin with a primarily sociological aim in mind. He was writing about the 'imaginative patterns' which the work of certain Catholic writers revealed, and his general intention was in fact to show something about the nature of criticism: that, as he illustrated by a quotation from G. K. Chesterton, its essential object was to say things about an author's work whose existence the author himself did not suspect, but which, when revealed, 'would make him jump out of his boots'.[2] This remark has curious analogies with Goldmann's insistence that it frequently happens that an author's 'desire for aesthetic unity makes him write a work of which the over-all structure, translated by the critic into conceptual language, constitutes a vision that is different from and even the opposite of his thought and his convictions and the intentions which

1. ibid., p. 90.
2. Preface of *Maria Cross*, p. viii.

prompted him when he composed the work',[1] and illustrates how different lines of inquiry in literary matters can, apparently by sheer accident, occasionally converge. For O'Donnell is a Catholic and Goldmann a Marxist, and their intellectual approach and presuppositions are widely different in many other ways. Nevertheless, in the conclusions which they reach about different literary works, they do agree in quite a remarkable manner on at least one point: that either consciously or subconsciously, an author's work can reflect the basic social conflicts and problems of the society in which he lives.

Truths, however, are often more important when we stumble across them than when find them at the end of a diligent search. Of a young man about to embark for a trip to England, Taine asked that most significant of all philosophical questions: 'Et quelle hypothèse allez-vous vérifier là-bas?' If we approach a work of art looking for sociological implications, we shall certainly find them whether they are there or not. This is the danger against which both the sociologist and the literary critic should constantly guard themselves, and they must always bear in mind the fact that although there may be a certain structure in Racine's tragic universe, this does not necessarily mean that it explains everything in Racine or that it will be at all helpful in studying Shakespeare. If a sociological analysis of the work of Eugène Sue helps us to understand more of his appeal in the past and his relevance to the future, we must not assume that a similar analysis will be as relevant and valid when applied to Henry James. Just because Aldous Huxley's portraits of Utopias and anti-Utopias reveal certain aspects of a particular class mentality,[2] we should not leap to the conclusion that a study of George Orwell's *1984* will do the same. And even if the sociologist did discover a model capable of explaining how societies worked and how literary works came into being, this would still only be marginally relevant to the literary critic's task of explaining, elucidating and revealing.

1. *International Social Science Journal*, loc. cit., p. 497.
2. See T. Adorno's work on Aldous Huxley, mentioned by J. Leenhardt, *International Social Science Journal*, loc. cit., p. 525.

Creative Thought in Artists
Catharine Patrick

from

Journal of Psychology, 4, 1937.

CREATIVE THOUGHT IN ARTISTS*[1]

Columbia University

CATHARINE PATRICK

THE LITERATURE

The problem is to study as directly as possible the process of creative thought in sketching pictures. Artists have consented to sketch pictures under experimental conditions, and for purposes of comparison non-artists have also performed the task of drawing under the same conditions.

Galli (3) obtained reports from various artists and writers concerning their general methods of working. At the time of inspiration the idea appears suddenly in the mind of the artist or inventor, without his seeking it. Often it comes as a brilliant flash, a new idea, without any evident reason, from an atmosphere more or less subconscious. It does not appear through the power of attention. The composer often works in such a feverish state that the hand cannot keep up with the thought. The new idea does not come from chance, but is developed from associations and knowledge. The work of art is not complete at the time of inspiration, but there must be revision and criticism.

Bahle (1) reports an experiment on the source and nature of ideas and inspiration in musical creation. He sent poems to thirty composers with the request that they compose music about one of them and write a report of how they did it. He used the questionnaire method and the reports of the different composers are cited. One composer said that the inspiration was best compared to the appearance of the spirit in an occult seance after everything was prepared. Another stated that "he always had the feeling that the idea is outside of time and space, that it was generated in the background of his feelings and thoughts, and that it was not native." The "sudden

*Received in the Editorial Office on February 12, 1937, and published immediately at Provincetown, Massachusetts.

[1]The author is indebted to Prof. R. S. Woodworth for a careful reading of the manuscript; and to Miss I. M. Kibbey, Mr. V. Ellis, Mr. Niequist, Mrs. J. Hone, Mr. J. Martelli, Mr. W. Elfedt, Mr. A. Ketcham, Mr. L. Richmond, Miss M. Hammond, and other artists for their cooperation.

idea" is characterized by the independent appearance of a clear structure with a consciousness of unfamiliarity. It is like an abstract pattern which relates itself to the content. The characteristics of the "sudden idea" are its fitness for the problem at hand, its capacity for expansion, and its vitality, freshness, and originality.

In a previous study by the present author (5) creative thought in poets was studied. The poets composed poems, talking aloud during the process. An analysis of the reports shows that there are four stages of creative thought, preparation, incubation, illumination, and revision or verification. In that study the history of the concept of incubation is brought out.

SELECTION OF SUBJECTS

One hundred subjects took part in this experiment and were divided into two groups, an "experimental group" of 50 artists and a "control group" of the same number of non-artists.

The terms "experimental" and "control groups" are not strictly correct as applied to our procedure. At the outset, the experimental factor was conceived to be "previous practise in making pictures," and the question was what difference this experimental factor would make in the process of drawing a sketch. Our "control group" can be thought of as furnishing a norm. The work amounts to a comparison between two groups.

The experimental group was composed only of artists of ability, whose work has appeared in the better exhibits. They have shown their work abroad in foreign countries as France, Great Britain, Italy, Switzerland, Holland, Egypt, Finland, and Denmark, and in the larger cities of the United States as New York, Chicago, Boston, San Francisco, Philadelphia, St. Louis, Cleveland, Los Angeles, St. Paul, Kansas City, Denver, Minneapolis, Washington, Cincinnati, and others. Their work has been exhibited in the Royal Academy, London; the Paris Salon; the Arteneum in Finland; the Spring Salon, Denmark; the Chicago Art Museum; The International Water Color Show; the Brooklyn Art Museum; the Carnegie Institute; the St. Louis Museum of Art; the Artists' National Exhibit; the Cleveland Art Museum; the National Academy of Design; the Vose Galleries, Boston; the New York Water Color Society; the

Feragil Galleries, New York; the Colorado Art Academy; and other places.

The control group was composed of 50 persons who were not doing any art work and had never done any, except possibly as school assignments. If they had only done a little art work at school ten or twenty years ago and had not done any since, it was considered that the effect of such small training would be negligible. A variety of occupations was represented. There were psychology students, secretaries, teachers, economists, biologists, nurses, engineers, lawyers, librarians, and home-makers.

Several cities and various sections of the country were represented in the selection of subjects for both groups. One of the cities was in the middle west, another in the east, and a third in the south.

The two groups were equated on the basis of the vocabulary test taken from the Thorndike CAVD Intelligence Test. This measure of vocabulary ability was the closest one to intelligence that could be obtained, for it would have been impossible to get the cooperation of artists in taking a regular intelligence test. Since there is a high correlation between vocabulary and intelligence tests, it was thought that this would give a good index of general ability. The list was composed of 200 items taken from levels M, N, O, P, Q, Forms 2-5, making 40 items at each level. The score was the number of items answered correctly in the total list. The groups were then equated by matching the distribution of scores for the two groups (Figure 1). The average for both groups is 102 and the median 100.

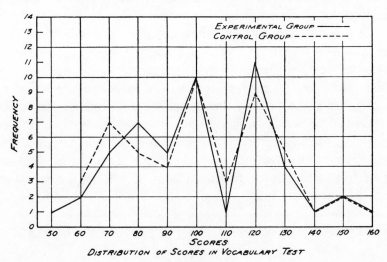

DISTRIBUTION OF SCORES IN VOCABULARY TEST

FIGURE 1

Twenty-one of the artists were men as compared with 23 of the controls. The groups were thus approximately equated as to the distribution of the sexes.

The groups were approximately equated as to age. The ages could only be estimated, for no direct information was available on that point. The average estimated age for the experimental group was 34 years as compared with 29 for the controls, a difference of 5 years. The median was 30 for the artists compared with 30 years for the controls. We did not think it was necessary to have the distribution of ages exactly the same in both groups, for all of the subjects were mature adults. It has been shown that vocabulary ability does not change much after reaching maturity until old age.

The subjects were all of the white race. Thus the two groups were equated in sex, age, and race, and in vocabulary ability, which is closely related to intelligence. They differed in that the experimental group was composed of artists of ability, while the control group was composed of those who had not done art work, except to a negligible degree. The differences that have come out in this experiment can be attributed to the greater ability of the artists to create pictures.

PROCEDURE

For this type of experiment it was necessary to have an individual interview with each subject. The experimenter made a personal call on each artist at his or her studio or home. It was thought that the artist would be able to create a picture more naturally there than in a laboratory where the situation is more or less artificial. Almost all of the interviews were held in the afternoon, which was found to be the most convenient time for the subjects.

The first part of the interview consisted of a preliminary conversation, the chief purpose of which was to enable the artist to become accustomed to talking aloud, while the experimenter recorded what he said in shorthand.[2] Also it served the purpose of getting some of the information for the questionnaire on methods of work. The nature of this conversation varied from person to person, and its duration from fifteen minutes to an hour, depending on whether the artist talked more or less at ease.

---

[2]Claparede (2) has described a similar method for the study of thought processes.

When the artist had become accustomed to the situation, he was presented with a poem and asked to draw a picture about it or whatever it suggested. The poem was a selection from Milton's "L'Allegro" and was chosen because of the variety of images which it contained. The selection follows:

> Sometime walking, not unseen,
> By hedge-row elms, on hillocks green,
> Right against the eastern gate
> Where the great Sun begins his state
> Robed in flames and amber light,
> The clouds in thousand liveries dight;
> While the ploughman, near at hand,
> Whistles o'er the furrow'd land,
> And the milkmaid singeth blithe,
> And the mower whets his scythe,
> And every shepherd tells his tale
> Under the hawthorne in the dale.
> Straight mine eyes hath caught new pleasures
> Whilst the landscape round it measures;
> Russet lawns, and fallows gray,
> Where the nibbling flocks do stray;
> Mountains, on whose barren breast
> The laboring clouds do often rest;
> Meadows trim with daisies pied,
> Shallow brooks, and rivers wide;
> Towers and battlements it sees
> Bosom'd high in tufted trees,
> Where perhaps some Beauty lies,
> The Cynosure of neighboring eyes . . .
>   These delights if thou canst give,
> Mirth, with thee I mean to live.

The artist was given a drawing pad and pencil. He was presented with this poem and given the following instructions:

> Draw a picture about this poem, any phase of it, or anything that you happen to feel like as you read it. Say anything that happens to come to your mind as you think of it before you begin to draw, no matter how irrelevant it may seem. Take all the time that you want and draw it at your leisure, for there is no time limit. The chief thing is to talk aloud constantly from the minute I present the poem, for I want to get everything you happen to think of, no matter how irrelevant it may

seem. Talk about anything you want to as you think about the poem, and then eventually, when you feel like it, draw the picture. The pictures will all be treated anonymously, and no one will know them. Take all the time you want, for there is no time limit.

The experimenter was seated a little distance from the subject, either at his side or behind him, depending on circumstances of furniture arrangement. The experimenter recorded in shorthand everything that the subject said and drew. He noted every line that was sketched and the order in which the objects were formed. The time was recorded in five minute intervals, but great care was taken to conceal that fact from the subject, for one of the chief conditions of the experiment was the absence of haste.

A record was kept of everything that was spoken and drawn from the moment of presenting the poem until the subject announced that the picture was finished, and needed no more revision. The subject was then asked the remaining questions on the questionnaire about methods of work, which he had not answered in the preliminary conversation. The questionnaire consisted of the following questions:

1. Do you usually complete the essential structure of a picture at one sitting?

2. When you get ready to make a picture do you incubate it a while first? If so, describe the process of incubation to me. How long does it usually last? What are its characteristics?

3. Was the method of making a picture under the conditions of this experiment fairly representative of your usual method of working?

4. When you sketch a picture, do you do it in a warm, stirred-up emotional state or in a cold, detached, objective state?

5. Do some parts of a picture seem to draw themselves and come more automatically and spontaneously than other parts of the same picture?

6. Do you revise your work much?

7. Do you have regular hours for your art work?

8. What different kinds of art work do you do?

9. Do you consider your art work a vocation or an avocation?

10. Do you consider your art work an important source of funds?

The questionnaire was given orally, but care was taken to ask the questions in the same form each time. After this information had been obtained, the subject was given the vocabulary test from the Thorndike CAVD Intelligence Test.

After the interview, the shorthand report was typed as soon as possible, while the details of the experiment were still fresh in the mind of the experimenter. The complete report contained everything that the subject had said from the moment of the presentation of the poem until the picture was finished, with the passage of time indicated in five-minute intervals.

Each of the 100 subjects, both control and experimental, was given a private interview in the manner described. The procedure for the two groups was the same, except that the control subjects were not given the questionnaire about their usual habits of work.

Statistical Results

(a). *Stages of Creative Thought*. Since previous work along this line has shown four stages of creative thinking, namely, preparation, incubation, illumination, and revision, we decided to see what evidence there was for them in the reports of the two groups. Instead of arbitrarily classifying the data under this outline, each protocol was divided into four equal quarters on the basis of the total time consumed, to see what evidence there was for the stages in each quarter.

First a subject's report was analyzed for the number of *thought changes* occurring in each quarter, and the number was converted into a percentage of the total number occurring in the report. For the purpose of objectivity, a thought change was considered to be any modification of thought, which was sufficient to cause it to form a new sentence. Three-fourths of the thought changes for both groups occur in the first quarter, which is evidence of the period of preparation, when associations are shifting.

The number of *general shapes of objects* that were drawn for the first time in each quarter was found and the percentages calculated. Over two-thirds of the objects were drawn for the first time in the second and third quarters, with over 40 per cent in the second quarter, which is evidence of the period of illumination.

The number of *instances of revision* were found for each quarter and the percentages calculated. An instance of revision might take the form of shading an object to clarify it, the addition of detail, or the critical surveying of the picture as a whole. The instances of revision, as so defined, were counted, and the average percentages are given in Table 1. Over three-fourths of the instances of revision occurred in the third and fourth quarters, with over 40 per cent in the last quarter.

Another way of showing the same relations was to take the num-

TABLE 1

Average Percent of Thought Changes, General Shapes First Drawn, and Revisions for Each Quarter

Group	Quarters			
	1	2	3	4
Thought Changes				
E	80	15	3	2
C	76	16	4	4
General Shapes Drawn For First Time				
E	20	42	29	9
C	12	44	32	12
Revisions				
E	3	17	34	46
C	2	21	35	42

TABLE 2

Percent of Subjects Showing "Most" Instances in Each Quarter

Group	Quarters			
	1	2	3	4
Thought Changes				
E	98	2	0	0
C	92	8	0	0
General Shapes Drawn for First Time				
E	19	46	30	5
C	10	60	25	5
Revisions				
E	2	13	28	57
C	0	17	30	53

ber of subjects showing the most instances of each type in each quarter. Thus 98 per cent of the artists had the most numerous thought changes in the first quarter and 2 per cent in the second quarter. The per cents are given in Table 2.

Each report was then analyzed for the amount of time spent in the period of thought changes, or unorganized thought, and this amount of time was reduced to a per cent of the subject's total time. The same thing was done for the amount of time spent in the first drawing of shapes of objects, or organized thought, and for the time spent in revising. The average per cents for both groups are given in Table 3. They do not add up to one hundred, for there is over-lapping of the stages. Thus, for example, the time for organized thought was measured from the time the first object was drawn until

TABLE 3

TOTAL TIME SPENT EACH STAGE

Group	Unorganized	Organized	Revision
E	6 min. (31%)	7 min. (37%)	12 min. (63%)
C	5 min. (30%)	8 min. (47%)	11 min. (64%)

the last one was, even though revision had already begun. The groups were also compared to see the differences in the absolute amount of time which was spent on the different stages.

The presence of incubation was shown if an idea occurred early in the report, recurred one or more times, the subject meanwhile talking of other things, and at last appeared as the chief topic of the picture. The per cent of subjects in each group, who showed such evidence of incubation, is given in Table 4. Since this evidence of

TABLE 4

PRESENCE OF INCUBATION

Group	Sure	Uncertain
E	84%	16%
C	86%	14%

incubation is present in over four-fifths of the cases of both groups, we conclude that incubation is one of the stages of this type of thought. It does not differentiate the artists from the non-artists, but is apparently characteristic of the process of creative thinking.

(*b*). *Speed of Composition.* The average amount of time required for the drawing of the pictures was about the same, being 19 minutes for the artists and 17 minutes for the controls.

The controls draw more objects and more different kinds of objects in their pictures than the artists and the difference is reliable (Table 5).

When the total time is divided by the number of objects drawn

TABLE 5

OBJECTS DRAWN IN PICTURES

	Experimental Av.	Sigma Av.	Control Av.	Sigma Av.	D/ Sigma Diff.
Number	9.8	.8	14.	1.17	3.00
Different Kinds	4.9	.35	6.6	.16	4.5

by each subject, the average speed is seen to be 1.9 minutes per object for the artists as compared with 1.18 minutes per object for the controls.

The diagram, Figure 2, shows the distribution of scores for total time consumed.

(*c*). *Manner of Handling Material.* The percentages of each

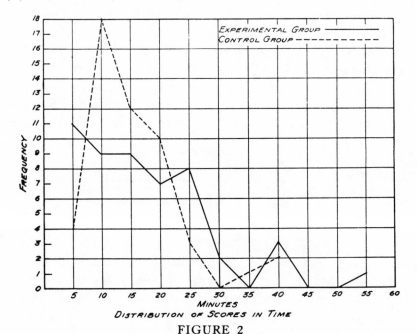

FIGURE 2

group who employed different methods of handling the material **were**
found as given in Table 6. About the same number began **their**

TABLE 6

Manner of Handling Material	% of Experimental	% of Control
Drawing Background first	48	54
Drawing Foreground first	52	46
Draw Right Side First	18	14
Draw Left Side First	42	56
Draw Center First	28	24
Draw Upper Center First	12	6
Draw Lower Center First	0	0
More Objects Left Side	44	54
More Objects Right Side	56	46
"Center of Interest" Left Side	20	28
"Center of Interest" Right Side	48	**44**
"Center of Interest" Middle	32	28
Human Figure Emphasized	68	32

Techniques of Art

	% of Experimental	% of Control
Good Perspective	91	34
Forms Well Developed	78	10
Composition Present	88	4
Black-White Shading Present	82	30
Used Shadows	46	4
All Areas Filled	50	14
Poorly Bounded Areas	36	70
"Center of Interest" Empty	14	42
Balance Lacking	8	28

Topics Sketched

	% of Experimental	% of Control
Topics In Poem	52	70
Topics Not In Poem	48	30
Landscape	70	90
Topics besides Landscapes	30	10

pictures by drawing the background first as the foreground. **Most**
of the subjects of both groups begin their drawings on the left side,
and the upper and left parts of a picture are developed before the
lower and right parts. In the completed picture, however, both
sides are equally developed in the number of objects in each. The
"center of interest" is more often placed on the right. Although
there were more human figures in the pictures of the controls (there
being totals of 66 and 34 respectively) yet when the artists employed
the human form they more frequently emphasized it, due probably

to their greater ability to sketch it. The average number of objects, besides clouds, above a middle line, which divided the picture into upper and lower halves, was 2.3 for the artists and 3.4 for the controls. Twenty-six per cent of the non-artists discarded an idea, which they might have used for a picture, because of inability to depict it as compared with 8 per cent of the artists.

(d). *Techniques of Art.* More artists had good perspective in their pictures and well-developed forms, which showed solidarity and three dimensions. A larger proportion had good composition, made use of black-white shading, and indicated the shadows of objects. More of them had all the areas of the pictures filled, with fewer poorly-bounded areas. One of the techniques of art is that objects should be placed in that part of the picture where the "center of interest" is located, which the controls neglected to do. More of them also failed to show balance in their pictures. As indicated in a previous diagram, the control subject draws more different kinds of objects and employs more varied details than the artist who tends to select and eliminate them.

(e). *Analysis of Data For the Different Topics Treated in the Pictures.* A larger percentage of artists drew pictures about topics not mentioned in the poem, as seen in Table 6. Although the poem was generally represented by a landscape, more of the artists drew other objects, indicating a greater diversity of approach. The data were classified according to the subject matter of each picture taken as a whole: i.e., the chief idea which the artist intended to convey. The artists did more of the topics shown in Table 7.

TABLE 7

Group	Mood	Shepherd	Trees	Flowers	Clown Head
E	20%	6%	16%	4%	2%
C	6%	2%	6%	2%	0%

The two groups did the same in the topics shown in Table 8.

TABLE 8

Group	Mountain and Hills	Plowman	Pasture	Milkmaid	Sun
E	10%	14%	4%	6%	10%
C	10%	10%	4%	4%	8%

The controls did more of the topics presented in Table 9.

TABLE 9

Group	Groups of Working People	House	Lake	Castle	Gate	Wayfarer
E	0%	2%	2%	4%	0%	0%
C	18%	10%	4%	8%	4%	4%

As a whole, it can be said that the controls depict more often the practical features of everyday life, as houses and working people, while the artists deal more with the less practical as moods, shepherds, and trees.

The various objects which appeared in the pictures were classified into those which were mentioned in the poem and those which were not. The percentage of each group which depicted each object was found. We will consider first the objects mentioned in the poem. The controls drew more of the objects shown in Table 10.

TABLE 10

Group	Daisies	Gate	Milkmaid	Mower	Plowman	Streams	Sun
E	6	2	4	2	24	14	24
C	22	6	26	10	36	20	44

The two groups drew about the same number of the objects shown in Table 11.

TABLE 11

Group	Castle	Clouds	Mountains	Trees	Sheep	Wanderer
E	14	66	50	82	20	18
C	12	70	56	80	24	14

The only objects which the artists drew more were shepherds, the percentages being: Experimental 12, Control 8.

When the controls drew sheep they frequently omitted the shepherd. In interpreting these percentages we must bear in mind that the controls drew a greater total number of objects and would be expected to draw more of each kind. They did so except in the case of the shepherd, an object foreign to the daily life of most of the subjects.

We will consider now the objects not mentioned in the poem. The artists drew more of the objects shown in Table 12.

TABLE 12

Group	Knight	Church	Sun-God	Clown Head	Mailbox	Conventional Flowers
E	2	2	2	2	2	2
C	0	0	0	0	0	0

Both groups drew about the same number of the objects shown in Table 13.

TABLE 13

Group	Fence	Lake	Boats	Flags	Hats
E	18	8	4	2	2
C	20	10	6	2	2

The controls drew more of the objects shown in Table 14.

TABLE 14

Group	House	Road	Chickens	Hollyhocks	Fish Line	Automobile	Pump	Birds
E	10	16	0	0	0	0	0	6
C	30	28	2	2	4	2	2	12

In those cases where the percentages run higher than 2 (for such a small percentage represents merely the variation of a single object) we find that both groups did about the same on fences, lakes, and boats, and the controls more roads and birds. More of the controls drew objects not mentioned in the poem as expected from the fact that the controls drew a greater number of objects. We find that the non-artists in their deviations depict more practical objects of everyday life.

(f). *Merit of Pictures Drawn.* The finished pictures were judged by three artists, according to the standards of artistic merit (Figure 3). They rated them on a scale from 0 to 100. The pictures of the artists and controls were shuffled all together and no names visible. The judges gave each picture a grade and the average grade was found for each group. All three judges gave a reliable difference between the averge score for the artists and that for the

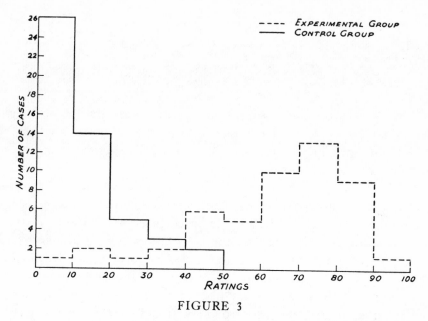

FIGURE 3

controls as seen in Table 15. The same result was found by two non-artist psychology students who also acted as judges.

TABLE 15

Raters	Experimental Group Av. Rating	S. D. Av.	Control Group Av. Rating	S. D. Av.	D/ S. D. Diff.
	Artist Raters				
Rater A	77.7	3.5	12	1.4	16.8
Rater B	62	3.41	17.4	2.27	11.6
Rater C	48.5	3.6	12	2.5	8.1
	Non-Artist Raters				
Rater X	79.6	2.3	32	2.21	14.9
Rater Y	76.2	2.7	28.4	2.8	12.6

The numerical value of the average score given to the pictures of each group is not so important, for the numbers are purely arbitrary, and any values might have been used. The important thing is the reliable difference between the average scores of artists and controls. Further evidence of the merit of the artists' product in the experimental conditions will be presented later.

The correlations between the ratings of the three artist judges was found, and also that between the two non-artist judges (Table 16).

TABLE 16

Group	A and B	B and C	C and A	X and Y
E	r .69 PEr .05	r .42 PEr .08	r .26 PEr .09	r .89 PEr .02
C	r .35 PEr .08	r .17 PEr .09	r .41 PEr .08	r .52 PEr .07

The correlations between the non-artist raters tend to be higher than those between the artist raters. For the raters as a whole, the correlations are higher for the pictures of the artists than for the pictures of the controls.

(*g*). *The Relationship of Merit to Other Variables.* The ratings of the artists were combined and correlated with time consumed and number of objects drawn. The coefficient of biserial distribution was found with other measures as seen in the following table. There is a slight tendency for the better pictures to be drawn more slowly. There is no relation between merit and the number of objects sketched, the selection of topics in the poem for subject matter, and whether or not the background was drawn first in the picture. In the artist group the ratings are higher in those pictures where the human figure is emphasized, but in the control group the ratings are higher where the human figure is not made important in the picture (Table 17).

TABLE 17

RELATION OF MERIT TO OTHER VARIABLES

Variable	Experimental Group		Control Group	
	r	PEr	r	PEr
Total Time For Drawing Objects	.13	.09	.30	.09
Number of Objects	.17	.09	.02	.10
Poem or Not Poem	—.002	.10	—.02	.10
Background Drawn First	.01	.10	—.05	.09
Human Figure Emphasized	.33	.08	—.36	.08

(*h.*) *Testimony from the Questionnaire.* In addition to the analysis of the manner in which the pictures were drawn, we have the data of the questionnaire:

a. Eighty-two per cent said that the method of sketching in this experiment was fairly representative of their usual method of work; 14 per cent stated that they very seldom, if ever, used pencil; 4 per cent said that they usually sketched from life instead of from imagination, as this experiment required.

b. Seventy-six per cent usually incubate the general idea of what they are going to depict a while before they sketch it; 18 per cent sometimes incubate it; 6 per cent said that they usually sketch a picture on the spur of the moment of whatever they happen to see before them; 36 per cent incubate an idea a short time as several days or less, while 34 per cent said that the period often lasted weeks or months. Several asserted it occasionally extended over years. The period of incubation not only varies from person to person, but also in the same person.

c. All the artists, with one exception, agree that they sketch the essential structure at one sitting.

d. Seventy-six per cent said that parts of a picture would come more spontaneously than other parts; 24 per cent said that did not occur, and that all parts of a given picture were generally of the same difficulty.

e. They agree, with the exception of two artists, that they do not change the chief structure in revision. A third of the artists stated that they touch up their pictures quite a bit.

f. Eighty-two per cent sketch in a warm emotional state; 18 per cent work in a cold, detached objective state.

g. Fifty-eight per cent considered art work their chief source of income, while 42 per cent depended mainly on other sources.

h. Two-thirds of the artists considered art a vocation, and one-third an avocation.

i. The artists worked in various types of art besides pencil sketches. Often the same artist would engage in several kinds. The number participating in the different types is as follows: oil 70 per cent; water color 56 per cent; pastel and charcoal 40 per cent; etching 10 per cent; woodcuts 10 per cent; lithography 10 per cent; sculpture 10 per cent; batticks 4 per cent; marionettes 4 per cent.

j. Seventy-two per cent do not have regular hours for work, 28 per cent have regular hours.

DISCUSSION

(*a*). *Stages of Thought.* As we examine the results of this experiment we find evidence of four stages of thought, to which we shall apply the terms *preparation, incubation, illumination,* and *verification.* Helmholtz (4) had used the first three terms, and Wallas (7) and Poincare (6) used all four.

In order to investigate the first one, *preparation,* when the subject is receiving various ideas, we have measured the number of thought changes that occur in each quarter. We find that three-fourths of the thought changes occur in the first quarter for both groups. This substantiates the theory that there first comes a period of preparation.

To present evidence that this leads to *incubation,* or the second stage, we have noted those cases in which the idea of the poem appeared earlier in the report, after which the subject talked of various things, and then this original idea reappeared as the subject of the poem. This is the fact in four-fifths of the cases in both groups. Our data are in accord with the hypothesis that preparation leads to incubation.

The stage of *illumination,* in making a picture, would be the period at which the general shapes of the objects were first sketched. For both groups we find that the general shapes of three-fourths of the objects were first sketched in the second and third quarters, with more in the second. This bears out the statement that illumination or formulation of thought follows preparation and incubation.

The fourth stage, *verification* or revision, is easily identified. We find that three-fourths of the instances of revision occur in the third and fourth quarters, with more in the last quarter, in both groups. Revision thus constitutes the final stage.

We will now discuss the characteristics of these four stages of thought more in detail. First comes *preparation,* when the subject is assembling or receiving new ideas. During this time the associations shift rapidly. Preparation is a time when the creative thinker is receiving or gathering his raw material.

Incubation follows preparation, although it may accompany it. We quote below some of the statements regarding incubation which were obtained from the artists by aid of our questionnaire:

> "I almost always carry an idea around a while in my mind before I start to work. It keeps coming back several times while I am doing other things, and I can work it out later. Sometimes I lose it if I don't work on it. In coming back it changes, and sometimes improves as it comes back. If I don't grab it I may get something different."
>
> "I incubate an idea for periods of two or three weeks. It may be for a month or more when I am not working on it. I think now of making a picture of Coconut Grove as it used to look, and I have been incubating that two years. Then I get

to feel like I want to paint. I keep vaguely thinking of something like it to do. I am thinking now of a still life. This afternoon I may start on it. The idea recurs while I am doing other things, as I have thought of a still life for two or three weeks now. I think of the roundness of the fruit, and shapes against the glass bottle. It recurs in color, so when I am ready to paint I know what I want to do and do it very rapidly. A complicated thing becomes simple by thinking about it. I noticed a tree and did not think about it and before I knew it, I had all sorts of information for making it."

"I usually carry an idea around in my mind. I see the picture completely in my mind before I paint. It recurs from time to time and lasts a couple of weeks. I know the color scheme before I start and get a model to fit that."

"I incubate a planned thing and other types of pictures more than a landscape, which I see. I draw a landscape from life but do not incubate it. I find a thing to interpret not as seen but as the effect of light, etc. One must put over to the observer what one sees. Often I incubate an idea and it keeps recurring, as I saw children in the north end of town and the idea stayed with me until painted a while later."

"I incubate an idea, as color and movement might interest me. It lasts a week only. It grows more intense till finished."

"I often carry an idea around for several weeks before I make a picture though sometimes longer. I got ideas in Santa Fe last summer to do now. The ideas recur from time to time while I am occupied with other things."

From the data of the questionnaire, we find that the artists generally incubate an idea, which may be accompanied by a feeling. It is often only partly formulated into what would constitute a mental picture and is but vaguely expressed. Most of them gave the report that incubation consisted of an idea which kept recurring over a period of time ranging from a few minutes to several years.

From the data of the questionnaire and reports obtained under the conditions of this experiment incubation can be defined as follows: A mood or idea is being incubated when it involuntarily repeats itself with more or less modification during a period when the subject is also thinking of other topics. According to Poincare (6) this modification is due to the working of the subconscious mind. Helmholtz (4) states that the modification is due to the overcoming of fatigue and the handling of material better. Similarly

Woodworth (8) writes that "in the preparatory period the necessary cues have been assembled along with much irrelevant material, which is an interference." With lapse of time when the individual makes a fresh attack the whole matter is clear.

Illumination follows incubation. This is seen from the data of the questionnaire where the idea is incubated before it is sketched. The essential structure is completed at one sitting although it may be revised later. In the period of illumination, when the artist first sketches a picture, he is generally in an emotional state. On the other hand, there are a fifth of the artists who state that they very rarely sketch a picture with an emotional feeling. They usually work in a cold, detached, objective state. Thus an artist is often emotionally stirred up at the time of sketching a picture, but it is not necessary or essential that he be so.

While most of them say that portions of a picture generally come more spontaneously and automatically than other parts, yet a fourth of them assert that there is no difference between the parts, which occur with the same difficulty. Thus illumination occurs when the idea, which has been incubating, becomes definitely related to a specific goal. It is the period when a picture is first sketched.

The idea, which is obtained in illumination, must be elaborated and revised during the last stage of *verification*. We find that this stage occurs in almost all of the pictures drawn in this experiment. Although there is revision, the essential structure is seldom changed.

These four stages, which can be distinguished in creative thought, may overlap. Incubation often occurs along with preparation, and revision may begin during the period of illumination. In the stage of preparation, while the subject is still receiving new ideas, one idea may be incubated and recur from time to time. Also revision of objects may start before all of them are sketched.

We will now present one or two of the reports actually obtained from the artists in this experiment to illustrate the stages of thought.

In the following protocol there is first the period of *preparation,* when associations are shifting. *Incubation* is brought out. Early in the report the artist mentions the plowman set in a landscape with mountains in back. He then turns to other topics and talks of various details in the poem as daisies. He says that he also thinks of brooks; that the towers and battlements might be used; that the whole thing is bathed in mood because it is the sunrise type of thing.

He proceeds to read it over and gets the idea of the plowman again and the various other images as milkmaid, mower, shepherd, mountains, brooks, towers and such. The idea of the plowman recurs and is made the subject of the picture. This recurrence is typical of incubation. *Illumination* is seen in the first drawing of the general shapes of the objects. The final stage of revision and verification follows. It is seen, for instance, in the making of the details of the plowman's body and the horse. Thus the four stages are brought out. See Figure 4 for the picture which was sketched by this artist.

FIGURE 4

SUBJECT *A*

"This is Milton."
"Where the great sun begins his state
Robed in flames and amber light is very nice."
"Of course I immediately think of the whole thing in color. The color note strikes me."

"The existence of the plowman takes form set in a landscape with mountains in back."

"There are various details in the poem as daisies."

"I think also of brooks and rivers flowing along."

"There are towers and battlements that might be used. They might be used for an illustration."

"The whole thing is bathed in mood because it is the sunrise type of thing."

"I don't know what to draw. I might use any one of several things."

"One time I drew a picture from the breast of a horse I saw in New York and the head of one I saw in Santa Fe. It made a composite."

"I will read the poem over again."

> Sometime walking, not unseen,
> By hedge-row elms, on hillocks green,
> Right against the eastern gate
> Where the great Sun begins his state
> Robed in flames and amber light,
> The clouds in thousand liveries dight,
> While the ploughman, near at hand,
> Whistles o'er the furrow'd land,
> And the milkmaid singeth blithe,
> And the mower whets his scythe,
> And every shepherd tells his tale
> Under the hawthorne in the dale.
> Straight mine eye hath caught the pleasures
> Whilst the landscape round it measures;
> Russet lawns and fallows gray,
> Where the nibbling flocks do stray;
> Mountains, on whose barren breast
> The laboring clouds do often rest;
> Meadows trim with daisies pied,
> Shallow brooks and river wide;
> Towers and battlements it sees
> Bosom'd high in tufted trees,
> Where perhaps some Beauty lies,
> The Cynosure of neighboring eyes . . .
>   These delights if thou canst give,
> Mirth, with thee I mean to live.

"I think of all the different images mentioned in the poem."

5 *min.*

"I will draw the plowman"—
    Draws frame.
1. Draws head of plowman.
2. Draws body of plowman.
3. Draws horse.

Details of plowman's body.
Details of horse.
Details of plowman's body.
Details of body of horse.
Details of head of horse.
Shades foreground.

4. Draws hill behind.
Erases nearly all the hill behind and plowman and horse.
Makes details of arms of plowman.

5. Draws plow.
Details of plowman's body.
Details of head of plowman.
Details of body and head of horse.
Details of plowman's head.

10 *min.*

Details of leg of horse.
Erase head of horse.
Details of body of plowman.
Details of plow seat.
Details of plowman's leg.
Details of plowman's body.
Details of body of horse.
Details of legs of horse.
Details of head of horse.
Details of hills.
Details of foreground.
Details of hill.
Erase hills.
Erase part of plowman and horse.
Details of foreground.
Draws frame.
Details of plowman's seat.
Details of body of plowman.
Details of head of plowman.
Details of hill behind.
Details of body of horse.
Details of legs of horse.
Details of head of horse.
Details of legs of horse.

15 *min.*

Details of head of horse.
Details of ears of horse.
Details of tail of horse.

6. Draws rein of horse.
   Details of hill behind.
   Details of cross lines of reins.
   Shades hill behind.
   Shades face of horse.
   Shades body of horse.
   Shades foreground.
   Shades hill in background.
   Shades face of plowman.
   Shades top of sky.
   Shades foreground.
   Details of tail of horse.
   Details of rein of horse.
   Shades hill.
   Shades foreground.
   Draws cross line.
   Details of plowman's body
   Details of body of horse.
   Details of head of horse.
   Shades body of horse.

20 min.

Shades plowman's body.
Shades foreground.
Shades hills.
Shades hills left.
Shades foreground left.
Shades middle foreground.
Shades head of horse.
Details of body of horse.
Shades sky.
Details of rein of horse.
Details of hill.

23 min.

(*b*). *The Pictures of This Experiment Representative of Usual Work.* The pictures which the artists drew under the conditions of this experiment were representative of their usual work. This is brought out by the following facts:

In the first place, from the data of the questionnaire, it is seen that the artists in general agreed that the method of sketching under these experimental conditions was characteristic of their usual methods of work. Eighty-two per cent said that it was fairly representative of their usual manner of sketching; 4 per cent said that they always worked from life instead of imagination; 14 per cent said that they very seldom, if ever used a pencil. Thus four-fifths of the artists assert that there is no essential difference between the pictures, which they sketched under the conditions of this experiment, and the pictures which they usually make. This is important evidence indicating that the method of sketching pictures under the conditions of the experiment was representative of that which they usually employ. The features of creative thought brought out by the data of this experiment can be said to be characteristic of the creative thought which the artists in general experience.

In the second place, three artists rated the pictures according to artistic standards. All of the judges found a reliable difference between the average quality of the work done by the artists and that done by the controls. We conclude that, under the conditions of this experiment, the artists sketched pictures which had higher artistic values than the non-artists did, which corresponds to the facts of daily life.

In the third place, several of the artists volunteered to sign their work, although they were told that the conditions of the experiment required that all the pictures be treated anonymously. They evidently considered the method of sketching under experimental conditions representative of their usual manner of working.

In the fourth place, when we compare other pictures of the same artists with the pictures which they sketched in this experiment, we find that they are done in the same characteristic manner. The two pictures in Figure 5 were both done by the same artist, the first under experimental conditions, the second under her usual circumstances of working. Another artist drew the sketches seen in Figure 6, one during the experiment, and one under usual conditions.

From these four lines of evidence we may conclude that the creative process demonstrated in this experiment is typical of the creative process which the artists experience in their usual work.

(c). *Differences and Similarities between the Groups.* We will now compare the results of the group of artists with those of the non-artists. In the first place, in regard to those features in which they are alike, we find that the reports of the controls also reveal the four stages of thought. We have already presented the report of an

FIGURE 5

artist to illustrate this point, and will now quote one of the protocols of the non-artists. The four stages are represented in this report also.

In the accompanying report first comes *preparation. Incubation* is present. Early in the report the subject speaks of a gate with the sun shining on it. She then turns to other topics and mentions the clouds, that she sees many colors and that she sees farm people, naming them, as the plowman, milkmaid, mower. A part of the poem is re-read, and she speaks of mountains with clouds close to them. She also talks of a brook surrounded by trees and a peaceful, quiet atmosphere. The original idea of the gate returns and is made the chief subject matter of the picture. This recurrence is typical of incubation. The third stage of *illumination* follows, with

FIGURE 6

the general shapes of the objects first drawn in the order indicated. Revision follows, as seen in the making of the details of the gate or looking over the picture as a whole. See Figure 4 for the picture which this control subject drew.

SUBJECT *B*

"Isn't that a sunset?"

"I have just been reading Milton."

"Well I see a farm."

"There is a fence and gate and sun shining on gate."

"There are clouds."

"I see many colors."

"I see farm people."

"I see a plowman who could be used as an illustration."

"There is a milkmaid, of whom I might draw a picture."

"There is a mower sharpening his scythe. He could be used."

"*Russet lawns and fallows gray*
Where the nibbling flocks do stray give a picture of flocks."

"In the background there are mountains with clouds close to mountains."

"Over in the distance is a brook surrounded by trees."

"There is a peaceful quiet atmosphere."

5 min.

"I will draw a gate."

1. Draws line of left post.

2. Draws line of right post.

3. Draws upper curve of gate.

    Details of panels of gate.

    Details of latch of gate.

4. Draws clouds.

"Can't make the sun shine through."

    Details of panels.

    Details of latch.

"Gate ought to be attached to fence."

"Where should I have fence?"

5. Draws fence left.

    Extends fence right.

"Hard to make fence."

    Details of fence left.

    Details of fence right.

"I would put a cow around but don't draw cows."

"I would put it back over here by tree."

6. Draws tree left.

"Can't draw tree or palm tree."

7. Draws cow by tree.

    Details of fence.

8. Draws grass.

"Russet lawn."

"One sees through a gate."

"Gate has hinge."

    Details of hinges.

"Ought to be a walk to gate."

9. Draws a walk.

    Details of grass.

    Details of fence.

    Details of gate.

"This is terrible."

    Details of foreground line.

        Looks over all.

10. Draws lake.

10 min.

Details of lake.
Details of trees by lake.
Works on trees by lake.
Details of lake.
Details of tree by lake.
Details of shore of lake.
Details of grass by lake.
Details of clouds.
Details of grass by tree left.
Details of grass in foreground.
Details of fence.
Details of gate.
Details of gate panels.
Details of grass by gate.
"I can't draw."
     Looks over all of picture.
Details of tree left.
"This is bad."
"I can't draw."
Details of tree left.
Details of grass by tree left.
Details of clouds.
Details of gate.
     Looks over all of picture.
"I would like to draw cow well."
"I would like to have cow resting under a tree."
Details of horns of cow.
Details of legs of cow.
"Looks like a pig."
"This is funny."
Details of tail of cow.
"Looks like a rat."
Details of cow.
Details of legs of cow.
15 min.
Details of tail of cow.
Details of legs of cow.
Details of head of cow.
Details of grass by tree left.
Details of grass by trees right.
     Makes waves in lake.
Details of waves of water.
Details of grass right.

> Details of trees by lake.
> > Looks over all of picture.
> Details of fence.

17 *min.*

A few of the pictures of the controls equaled the quality of the work of the artists. The extent of this overlapping is shown in the histogram Figue 3. The ratings in this diagram are the averages of the three artist ratings for each picture.

The protocols that have been presented illustrate the first point of likeness, in that the work of both artists and non-artists shows the four stages of thought. There are several other respects in which the groups are alike.

We find practically no difference between the groups in the average amount of time taken to draw the pictures. The artists produce a better quality of work than the non-artists, but they do it in the same time. The number of minutes that is spent on each of the three stages is practically the same, with more on revision than on preparation and illumination.

Half of each group drew the background first and half the foreground. Most of the subjects of both groups begin their drawings on the left side, probably due to the fact that most of them have the habit of writing from left to right and are right-handed. The next in preference is the center. The upper and left parts of a picture are developed before the lower and right parts. Although the left side of the picture is usually drawn first, both sides contain the same number of objects at the end. The "center of interest" is developed on the right as a rule.

We will now consider the differences between the groups.

The non-artists draw more objects in their pictures. The average speed is seen to be slower (as measured in minutes per object) for the artists than for the controls. This is to be expected, since the two groups consume the same amount of time, yet the controls draw more things. They tend to put more objects in the upper half of the picture than the experimental group did, which is related to the fact that they have less sense of balance and composition.

The controls drew twice as many human figures. However, when the artist did use the human form he emphasized it and made it an important part of the picture much more often, probably due to his greater talent in drawing it. This is also brought out by the fact that in the artist group those pictures in which the human form is emphasized have the higher ratings, while in the control group the higher ratings are found where it is not emphasized.

Many more of the controls discarded ideas which they would like to have drawn because poor technique prevented them from expressing themselves as freely.

The fact that the artists tend to be dominated more by the conventions of art is brought out from the data of this experiment. They follow the techniques of art more closely as seen in their more frequent use of perspective, shading, shadows, balance, and the development of forms. The artist builds up the "center of interest" more, has better composition, and fewer vacant and poorly integrated areas. He selects and eliminates a variety of detail as the control does not.

The artists interpreted the poem differently than the controls and had a different range of associations, as seen in the objects which they drew. We will note first the kind of a topic, which was chosen as subject matter for the picture as a whole, and then proceed to analyze the different objects within a picture.

Although the poem was generally represented by a landscape, yet it could be portrayed by drawings of single human figures or other objects, as some people did. Many more of the artists drew objects besides the landscape, as the subject matter of pictures, than of the controls, indicating a greater diversity of approach among the artists. When we analyze the different topics chosen as subject matter for the pictures we find that the artists attempted to portray the subjective element, as a mood, more often. Also they did trees, flowers, and shepherds more frequently. As a whole, it can be said that the controls depict the practical features of everyday life, as houses, gates, and working people, while the artists deal more with the less practical, as moods, shepherds, trees, and flowers.

If we turn now to the various kinds of objects drawn within the pictures we find certain differences between the groups. Since the controls sketched more objects in general, it is to be expected that they would draw more of each kind. It is significant then that the only objects which the artists drew more of were shepherds, which are objects quite removed from practical, daily life. The controls drew more streams, daisies, suns, milkmaids, mowers, plowmen, and gates, which are practical features of everyday life.

The fact that the artists have a wider imagination is also brought out by the fact that they tend to go further from the picture than the controls. Only half of the artists drew pictures about the poem as compared with three-fourths of the controls. The work of the artist has more significance and meaning and possesses a unity which is lacking in that of the non-artist.

COMPARISON OF ARTISTS AND POETS

A previous experiment, similar to this one, was performed on poets.[3] The method was the same, except that the poet was shown a picture of a landscape and asked to write a poem about it. He similarly talked aloud all the time that he was doing it, and the experimenter recorded all that was said in shorthand.

We will now compare the results of the two experiments in those respects where such a comparison is possible.

In the first place, we find that both poets and artists, as well as the two control groups, all exhibit the four stages of thought. Over half of the thought changes of all groups occur in the first quarter of the process, indicating that there is first a stage of preparation, when associations are shifting.

The second stage, incubation, is present in all four groups. It is found in over two-thirds of the cases of each.

The third stage, illumination, is likewise found in all four groups. In writing poetry, it is found in the first formulation of lines. In drawing pictures, as pointed out above, it is present when the general shapes of objects are first drawn. In all four groups, we find that over two-thirds of the first writing of lines or drawing of objects occurs in the second and third quarters, which indicates that illumination follows preparation and incubation.

The fourth stage, revision or verification, appears in all four groups. An instance of revision for a poet would be changing a word or line to extend the meaning, the partial or total re-reading of the poem, and changing words or lines to fit the meter. For all

---

[3] The average scores on the *CAVD* Vocabulary Test for the poets and their controls were 128 and 127 respectively, while those for the artists and their controls were 102 and 102. This difference between the groups is probably not important in interpreting the comparisons between the groups.

four groups, over three-fourths of the instances of revision occur in the third and fourth quarters with most in the last quarter, which indicates revision follows the other three stages.

When the data are treated a little differently using the percentage of subjects showing "most" instances in each quarter, we find the same results. About three-fourths of the subjects of all four groups show most thought changes in the first quarter, about three-fourths show most instances which indicate illumination in the second and third quarters, and over half show most instances which indicate revision in the last quarter.

The four groups can be compared on the average percentage of the total time spent on each stage. All of the groups spent about a third of the total time on the period of thought changes, or unorganized thought. The period of organized thought is when lines are first formulated or general shapes of objects are first drawn. We find that both artists and poets spent slightly less time on this than their respective controls. The artists spent about the same amount of time on revision as their controls, while the poets spent slightly less.

If we compare the average absolute amount of time spent on each stage we find no difference between the two groups writing poems, in the period of unorganized thought, but the artists spend slightly more time than their controls. In the period of organized thought, the poets and artists spend slightly less time on this than their respective controls. In revision the poets spend slightly less time than their controls, while the artists spend slightly more. It must be remembered that these differences, which have been mentioned, are very slight and not in any sense reliable. We can summarize by saying that all four groups spend about the same amount of time on the periods of unorganized and organized thought, and considerably more on revision. As has been mentioned before, these stages overlap to some extent.

When we compare the average total amount of time required for these experiments we find that both groups writing poetry consumed 21 minutes. In the drawing of pictures, the artists required 19 minutes and the controls 17. While the drawing of pictures requires slightly less than the writing of poetry, all four groups are seen to have consumed about the same amount of time. This is the more interesting when we consider that the instructions stressed the condition of unlimited time. As a matter of fact we find wide individual variations, but the averages between the groups are about the same.

The groups can be compared for the percentage of each who drew a picture or wrote a poem about the stimulus which was presented. The stimulus for the poets was a picture, for the artists a poem. Only about half as many of the poets wrote about the stimulus presented as of their controls. Both of the groups skilled in creative work show greater imagination and a wider range of associations than the two control groups who lack those types of ability. Within the group of all those writing poems no relation was found between the ratings of merit and whether or not they followed the stimulus. The same was true of the people drawing pictures.

We can compare the groups in a general way in regard to the topics drawn and written about. The poets emphasized the philosophical and supernatural more, and wrote less of ordinary animals and people than the controls. The artist or poet does not limit himself as much to the ordinary features of daily life as the control subject does.

If we compare the results of the questionnaire, which were very much the same for the artists and poets, we find certain similarities and differences.

In the first place, three-fourths of both artists and poets assert that they generally experience incubation in doing their work. In both groups it may last several minutes, or extend several days, weeks, months, or even years. It varies from person to person and also within the same individual from time to time.

In the period of illumination the poets agree that they produce the essential structure at one sitting, as the artists did. Four-fifths of the artists and poets assert that they draw or write in a warm emotional state, while a fifth of each group say that they do it in a cold, detached objective state. An emotional reaction often accompanies the making of poems or pictures, but it is not a necessary condition to the actual production of creative work. Ninety per cent of the poets assert that parts of a poem or picture come more spontaneously and automatically than other parts, as most of the artists stated.

In the stage of revision artists and poets agree that they don't change the essential structure.

About four-fifths of the poets said that they wrote poems in a fairly representative manner in the experiment, and the artists said the same thing about making pictures.

One-fourth of the artists have regular hours for work as compared with 7 per cent of the poets. Two-thirds of the artists state that art is their vocation, while only 44 per cent of the poets make such a claim for poetry. About half of the artists are dependent on their art work while only a fifth of the poets rely on their poetry for income. This difference in the statements may be due partly to the fact that under the category art work a single artist may engage in several kinds, while the poet is referring to only one type of writing.

In both experiments, the samples of work done under experimental conditions were rated. We find that there are wider and more reliable differences between the artists and their controls than between the poets and their respective controls. This difference between the results of the two experiments may be due to a variety of causes. It may be that the average subject has more ability to make poems than to draw pictures, or that technique counts for more in drawing than in composing a poem.

In both studies the ratings of the different judges were correlated with each other. We find about the same amount of agreement between the judges in the two cases. For the subjects writing poems, the correlations between the raters run a little higher for the control group than for the experimental. For those drawing pictures, on the other hand, the correlations are higher for the group with ability than for the control without that ability. This result may indicate that the standards of judging good art are more clear-cut than those of good poetry, although various other factors may be operating to produce the result.

For both poets and artists the correlations between ratings and time consumed were higher for the control than for the experimental groups. There is a closer relation between the time consumed and the merit of the product for the unskilled than for the skilled subject. However, the relationship between time and merit was not very marked in any case.

The following paragraph contains some of the experimenter's general observations of poets and artists. There is no statistical evidence here, but merely the general impressions derived from interviewing over two hundred subjects.

There was no evidence of a poetic or artistic physical type. Various physiques and kinds of facial features were represented and different shades of eye and hair color. Various types of personalities were present with the usual distribution of extroverts and introverts. With the exception of two or three individuals there was no greater occurrence of emotional reactions among them than among their respective controls. One would not say that poetic or artistic ability is associated with an ill-adjusted personality. Probably the artists had spent more time in formal education and directed study than the poets, who had worked as much in unsupervised study. Both artists and poets had probably spent considerably more time in unsupervised study than many (not all by any means) of the controls in their own respective fields. The poet writes at home in his study alone, while the artist works in his studio, which is apt to be located in the same building with other studios and permits more interchange of ideas while working. At the beginning of the interviews all four groups seemed to have difficulty in deciding on an idea and getting oriented. When an idea had once been decided upon, it was executed with more completeness and precision by the artists and poets than by the controls. The stage of illumination occurred more as a unit for the skilled group, with less interruption by revision, while the non-talented person often appeared to experience difficulty in finishing the thought.

SUMMARY

1. This experiment on artists reveals four stages of creative thought, namely, *preparation, incubation, illumination,* and *verification.* Preparation is the period when associations are shifting rapidly and the subject is receiving new ideas. Incubation is the spontaneous recurrence from time to time of a mood or idea with more or less modification, while the subject is thinking of other topics. It may range from a few minutes to several years. We find that it occurs in miniature within the experimental period, and on a broader scale in the regular work of the artists. Illumination occurs when the mood or idea, which has been incubating, is sketched for the first time. An emotional reaction is frequently present, although not necessarily, and parts of a picture often seem to come

automatically and spontaneously. Verification or revision is the last stage. These stages may overlap with each other, as incubation may occur with preparation, and revision may start before all the objects have been sketched.

2. The method which the artists employed in drawing pictures in this experiment was characteristic of their usual method of work. On the questionnaire, four-fifths of the artists said that the method of sketching in this experiment was fairly representative of the way in which they usually worked. In this experiment the artists drew pictures of greater artistic value than those of the controls. In several cases the artists volunteered to sign their work, which shows that they considered the work done in this experiment of the usual standard. When the pictures, which were sketched in this experiment, are compared to other pictures of the same artists, they are found to be done in the same characteristic styles.

3. Although the individuals in both groups vary in almost every respect, certain similarities and differences exist between the groups. The general course of thought is about the same in the two groups in certain respects. Half of each group drew the background first and half the foreground. There is no relation between the merit of the picture and whether the background or foreground is drawn first. Most of the subjects begin their drawings on the left side of the picture. The upper and left parts are sketched before the lower and right parts. The same number of objects is eventually drawn on the right side as on the left. The "center of interest" is more frequently developed on the right.

4. Certain differences exist between the results of the control and experimental groups. The non-artists draw more objects than the artists, on the average. There is no appreciable correlation within the groups between the number of objects and the rated merit of the picture. The controls also draw more different kinds of objects. They tend to put more in the upper half of the picture. Although the controls drew the human figure more often than the artists, yet when the latter used it, they more often emphasized it and made it an important part of the picture. In the artist group the pictures in which the human figure was emphasized tended to be of better merit, while in the control group those in which it was less important rated higher. The artists are less hampered in the expression of their ideas by lack of ability to depict what they wish. The artist

makes more use of artistic techniques, such as perspective, shading, shadow, balance, and the development of forms. He builds up the "center of interest" more, has better composition, and fewer vacant and poorly integrated areas. He selects and eliminates a variety of detail as the control does not. The artist goes further from the poem in the selection of topics for his picture. He deviates more from the practical features of everyday life, and oftener introduces objects besides the landscape as the subject matter. The work of the artist has more significance and meaning and possesses a unity which is lacking in that of the unskilled person.

5. This experiment may be compared with a previous experiment on poets in certain respects. The artist, poet, and two control groups all show the four stages of thought. All four groups spend about the same amount of time on the periods of unorganized and organized thought and considerably more on revision. The two groups writing poems required about the same average time for the experiment as the two groups drawing pictures. In the selection of topics for their work both poets and artists are less limited by the practical features of everyday life than the controls. Most of the artists and poets considered the work done under the conditions of the experiment fairly representative of their usual work. With the subjects drawing pictures there were wider differences in the merit of the product between the trained and untrained groups than with the subjects writing poems. More of the artists have regular hours for work, consider it a vocation, and depend on it for income than of the poets. In both studies there was about the same amount of agreement among the judges who rated the work. The agreement was slightly higher for the control than for the experimental group in the case of the poems, while the reverse was true of the pictures. In either study the relationship between time and merit was not very marked, but it was higher for the untrained subjects.

REFERENCES

1. BAHLE, J. Einfall und Inspiration im musikalischen Schaffen. *Arch. f. d. ges. Psychol.,* 1934, **90**, 495-503.

2. CLAPAREDE, E. La Genese de l'Hopotheses. *Arch. de Psychol.,* 1934, **24**, 69-70.

3. GALLI, E. La conscienza nella formazione dell'opera d'arte. *Riv. di psicol.,* 1932, **27**, 107-114; 185-193; 275-284.

4. HELMHOLTZ, H. VON Vortrage und Reden. 5th Aufl. Braunschweig f. Vieweg. u. Sohn, 1896, **1**, p. 15.

5. PATRICK, C. Creative Thought in Poets. *Arch. of Psychol.,* 1935, No. 178. Pp. 74.

6. POINCARE, H. Science et Methode. Paris: Flammarion, 1908. Pp. 314.

7. WALLAS, G. The art of thought. New York: Harcourt Brace, 1921. Pp. 314.

8. WOODWORTH, R. S. Psychology. (3rd ed.). New York: Holt. 1934. Pp. 540.

Columbia University
New York City

The Creative Process in the Popular Arts
Roger L. Brown

from

International Social Science Journal, vol. XX, no. 4.

The creative process in the popular arts

Roger L. Brown

It is generally agreed that the development of the mass media of communication since 1900 has brought about radical changes in the cultural life of advanced, industrialized societies. Similarly, most social historians would agree that the growing importance of the forms of popular culture disseminated via the mass media has hastened the final demise of many folk cultures, and perhaps, too, of those local autonomous cultures which developed in the nineteenth century among the working classes of great cities. Serious discord and dissension arise concerning the effects of popular culture on the 'serious', 'high' or 'fine' arts. And when critics consider the *quality* of the newer forms of popular culture, the views expressed rapidly become polarized and apparently irreconcilable. No doubt this is partly due to the very vagueness of the concepts employed, and to the fact that the majority of them—the Bauers' 'mass culture', for example, or Shils' trichotomy of 'superior', 'mediocre' and 'brutal' cultural levels—are often used at the same time as both heuristic tools and as evaluative labels.[1]

Various rejoinders have been made to the laments of the more pessimistic critics. Toffler and Berelson seek to produce data which indicate that the amount of serious art produced and enjoyed is already very considerable and is on the increase.[2] The Bauers argue that the pessimism of the critics can be accounted for by the fact that the critics themselves are elitist intellectuals occupying somewhat marginal positions in society, though this attempt at a 'sociology of knowledge' analysis of the situation has itself been attacked.[3] An alternative line of inquiry seems to be offered by

1. See: Raymond A. Bauer and Alice H. Bauer, 'America, Mass Society and Mass Media', *The Journal of Social Issues*, Vol. 16, No. 3, 1960, p. 3-66; and Edward Shils, 'Mass Society and its Culture', in: Norman Jacobs (ed.), *Culture for the Millions*, New York, 1961. The Bauers paper does attempt a critical examination of the term 'mass culture', but the authors may be charged with confusing it with 'mass society'.
2. See: Alvin Toffler, *The Culture Consumers*, New York, 1964; and Bernard Berelson, 'In the Presence of Culture...', *Public Opinion Quarterly*, Vol. 28, No. 1, 1964, p. 1-12. These reports deal only with the situation in the United States.
3. See: Lewis A. Coser, 'Comments on Bauer and Bauer', *The Journal of Social Issues*, Vol. 16, No. 3, 1960, p. 78-84.

an examination of the manner in which contemporary popular culture is produced, and of the creative personnel involved. The approach is in fact suggested by the number of available critical characterizations of popular culture which make some direct or implicit reference to this phase of the cultural process. Thus van den Haag, for example, suggests that 'unlike any other type of culture, popular culture—a full-fledged style of living with a distinct pattern of feeling, thinking, believing and acting—was made possible and in the end necessary by mass production'.[1] Fiedler argues that 'the articles of popular culture are made, not to be treasured, but to be thrown away. . . . The sort of conspicuous waste once reserved for an élite is now available to anyone . . .',[2] while Arendt, too, posits an essential similarity between popular culture and more tangible products: 'The wares offered by the entertainment industry are indeed consumed by society just as are any other consumer goods'.[3] It is perhaps unnecessary to stress that these remarks, notably the last two, not only suggest *descriptions* of popular culture and the way it is produced, but implicitly condemn product and process at the same time.

In brief, then, it has been frequently argued that popular culture is bound to be of inferior quality because of the manner in which it is characteristically produced: but this proposition deserves considerably greater scrutiny than it usually receives. Many of the agencies which produce popular culture are rightly referred to as industries if judged by the scale of their operations, the technologies they employ, and the way they are organized. But the real question to be asked is the extent to which industrial techniques are applied to the actual creative process.[4] In as far as they are engaged in what Williams has referred to as the 'multiple dissemination' of works of popular art,[5] the responsible agencies—publishing houses, film studios, record companies and (to a limited extent) broadcasting organizations—do make use of industrial mass production techniques. Indeed, these techniques provide the only means by which standard copies of products can be sent quickly and cheaply to vast markets. Printing, the oldest of the mass media, has always been a mass-production industry in this sense: the press makes it possible to run off a virtually limitless edition of the same sheet from one forme of type. In the cinema industry, many exhibition copies of the same film can be made from the one master negative, just as many copies of a record can be pressed from the same mould. As far as the broadcasting media are concerned, the situation is different, since a modulated carrier wave is itself the technical basis of dissemination,

1. Ralph Ross and Ernest van den Haag, *The Fabric of Society*, New York, 1957, p. 167.
2. Leslie A. Fiedler, 'The Middle against Both Ends', in: Bernard Rosenberg and David M. White (eds.), *Mass Culture*, New York, 1957, p. 539.
3. Hannah Arendt, 'Society and Culture', in: Norman Jacobs (ed.), op. cit., p. 48.
4. An extended discussion of the topic is provided by Edgar Morin, *L'esprit du temps*, Paris, 1962, chapter 2, 'L'industrie culturelle'. The present paper is much indebted to this analysis of the situation.
5. The term serves to underline the fact that the media are, as technical devices, essentially neutral.

but, of course, broadcasting itself sprang from the projected development of a receiver-manufacturing industry. However, the fact that mass production techniques (and the bureaucratic, formal organizations that go with them) play a vital role in the circulation of works of popular art need not necessarily have any effect on the quality of what is produced or on the way in which creative artists go about their business.[1] Yet it is often assumed that the creative process in the world of the popular arts is itself organized in ways closely analogous to those demanded by the technologies of mass dissemination and the sheer size of the producing corporations.

The tendency to blur the line between the creative and disseminatory activities of popular culture agencies is seen clearly enough in Coser's account: 'The industries engaged in the production of mass culture share basic characteristics with other mass production industries. In both, the process of production involves a highly developed division of labour and the hierarchical co-ordination of many specialized activities. In these industries no worker, no matter how highly placed in the organizational structure, has individual control over a particular product. The product emerges from the co-ordinated efforts of the whole production team, and it is therefore difficult for an individual producer to specify clearly his particular contribution.'[2]

Coser is here, of course, leading up to a discussion of the place of the writer within the Hollywood film industry, and it may be that this description fitted the major Hollywood studios fairly accurately in their heyday before the advent of television. But it would serve rather less adequately today as a characterization of the *production* sector of the American film industry, given the recent rise of a number of smaller, essentially *ad hoc* production companies. Indeed, it is worth suggesting that our thinking about the way popular culture is produced has been far too highly coloured by the state of affairs prevailing in the film industry of one particular country at one stage of its development.[3]

One of the arguments implicit in Coser's description merits particular attention. By saying that the mass culture industries are marked by 'the hierarchical co-ordination of many specialized activities', the idea is planted that formal organizations of this sort are inherently inimical to the creation of worth-while works of art.

It would, however, in fact be misleading to suggest that the production of works of art within the framework of complex, and possibly bureaucratic organizations necessarily means that the works themselves will lack artistic merit. The world's great opera and ballet companies are themselves large organizations within which the division of labc ~ is carried quite as far as within one of the major Hollywood film companies. Yet there are,

1. The point is discussed more fully by Richard Hoggart, 'Mass Communications in Britain', in: Boris Ford (ed.), *The Modern Age*, Harmondsworth, 1961, p. 448.
2. Lewis A. Coser, *Men of Ideas*, New York, 1965, p. 325.
3. There is a considerable literature on the topic. See, in particular: Hortense Powdermaker, *Hollywood the Dream Factory*, New York, 1950; and Leo Rosten, *Hollywood*, New York, 1941.

of course, differences (including differences in cultural 'level') between what is produced by an opera or ballet company and the type of film we associate with Hollywood, particularly in the era prior to television, and the reasons for these are not hard to find. In the first place, the *policies* of the institution concerned are of major importance in determining what the end product shall be like. In the case of the opera or ballet company, the major aim is to present the best possible performances of established and new works in the relevant media. In the case of the film companies, the overriding objective was commercial, particularly following the Depression, when Hollywood studios came and more under the control of financial and banking interests. The policy differences between these two types of artistic agencies would inevitably be reflected in the role assigned to the musical director or choreographer in the case of the opera or ballet company as against the less commanding role assigned to the film director. But it would seem just as possible to give effective control to an artistic director within a complex organization as it is to give effective control to an accountant. The same type of structure can lend itself to a wide range of objectives.[1]

Again, on the basis of the foregoing account, it might be assumed that the mass culture industries approached their creative problems in a completely rational way, and applied the full range of cost-conscious business techniques to the task of turning out a stream of new products. However, from Powdermaker's account of the way in which a major Hollywood studio went about the task of producing a shooting script it seems to have been approached in an extremely disorganized fashion, while the techniques employed to pre-cost a production were far less sophisticated than those one would expect to be applied in a normal manufacturing industry.[2] It is interesting, too, that the very looseness of the formal structure seems to have allowed studio heads, producers and directors a good deal of scope for the expression of their 'artistic' temperaments.

Of course, the technologies of the newer media—film and television—do call into being a whole new range of craft skills (those of lighting technicians, cameraman, scenery crews, and so on) and the individuals filling these roles do have to be organized and managed if the job is to be done at all. But the same set of skills can bring to birth a *Potemkin* or a *Kane*, or alternatively a 'B' Western. The type of organization may be dictated by the technology of the medium, but the artistic quality of the finished product will have a great deal more to do with the ability of those performing the major creative functions and with the general sociocultural milieu.[3] It must also be admitted, however, that an organized team of technicians is an instrument that lends itself very readily to the assembly-

1. An interesting collection of essays on the problem of encouraging creativity within various types of formal organization is contained in Gary A. Steiner (ed.), *The Creative Organization*, Chicago, 1965.
2 Powdermaker, op cit., especially chapter 8, 'Assembling the Script'.
3. A recent attempt to develop a theoretical account of how particular cycles of films came to be made is contained in George A. Huaco, *The Sociology of Film Art*, New York, 1965.

line fabrication of highly stereotyped artistic works. The drama and comedy series which currently dominate American network television and fill a considerable proportion of the programme time of the television services in other countries, are produced in just this fashion, many by offshoots of the original Hollywood 'Big Five'. It is worth asking about the conditions which lead to this highly mechanized use of production resources, and raising a query about its implications for the quality of the end product.

The mass media of communication are commonly said to have a voracious appetite for new material, but of course this state of affairs is partially the media's own responsibility. Particularly with those media closely involved in, and heavily dependent on, consumer advertising, novelty is at a premium and becomes a major selling point. The style of the short stories or programmes within which the advertisements are embedded can be rendered effectively obsolescent merely by the introduction of new fashions. More important, the economics of the media make a constant supply of new work a necessity. A magazine retains its audience and stays in business by offering something new each week or each month, while the paperback-book industry depends on a complex distribution network and the display of a wide range of titles at the point of sale. Despite market research, public taste is only crudely predictable, so that a large number of new products must be released annually if an adequate number of best-sellers is to emerge. The products of a broadcasting company are in the obvious sense inherently evanescent, and in competitive situations there is little inducement to revise materials which have been stored on tape or film. In all the media nowadays some new work of popular art reaches its entire potential market if not instantaneously, then within a period of days or weeks. Multiple dissemination itself means that the production agencies face a chronic shortage of new artistic material.

The usual answer to this problem, of course, has been to re-use the same, basic artistic elements again and again, refurbishing and re-combining them so as to lend the newer versions the required appearance of novelty. An author sitting down to write a short story for a particular women's magazine will have at his disposal a number of stock characters, dramatic situations, locales and ways of resolving the plot. The creative task now becomes that of fitting these elements together (no doubt with the addition of some genuinely new components) into a satisfactory *gestalt*. The possibilities are perhaps rather similar to those offered the architect by a set of standardized, modular constructional components, or available to the technician in control of a car assembly line, where a range of chassis, engines and bodies can be combined together into a number of distinct models. Saleability may also, of course, be more easily guaranteed if story elements already tested in the market are employed. Today, television series and serials probably embody the principle in its most obvious form, though film westerns and some of the longer sequences of detective novels also illustrate it. Naturally enough, critics of popular culture have condemned the end results of these replaceable-part operations as inevitably lifeless and stereotyped.[1]

It is, however, all too easy to import value judgements into the discussion in clandestine fashion. By saying that the plots of film westerns or of television series tend to be 'stereotyped', a negative note is struck immediately. However, the fact that a number of the necessary elements are provided for the writer when he comes to prepare the script for a new film or new programme may potentially be an artistic advantage. In one sense, the creative task is made simpler, since a number of constraints are already present: but this may allow the writer to concentrate more on the remaining tasks. Again, over time, it may be possible to explore all the permutations and combinations which the elements provided permit, and to discover which are artistically effective and which failures. Perhaps the position of the mass media artist working with already provided artistic elements is not so dissimilar in this respect to that of many hundreds of 'serious' artists who have worked within established traditions in the past. Most artists, in fact, make use of established formulae, whether it is the structure of the Elizabethan sonnet, drawing in perspective, the sonata form, or the twelve-tone scale. Of course, art does have a history, and the great landmarks of art were set by those artists who put traditional forms to radically new uses, or legitimated significant departures from established technique. But even the innovative genius builds on what has gone before: *Hamlet* is a Revenge Play, as well as being much more than that, while *Measure for Measure* is in part a Morality Play, as well as being many times more complex than its mediaeval forerunners. At a much lower level, film westerns such as *Shane* or *High Noon* make use of an established genre as well as going beyond it to make new comments and explore new human perplexities. Popular culture has its traditions, just as much as the 'high' arts: it is the way that the tradition is used which is all-important, not the fact that a tradition exists. And the popular work which explores beyond the bounds of the tradition perhaps gains force from the very tension set up between the conventions and the departures from it.

If the popular culture disseminated via the media of mass communication *does* tend towards standardization and sameness, this may spring from factors other than the assembly-line methods resorted to by particular media at particular times. Popular culture agencies which are in competition for the same audience, whether the competition springs from attempts to increase advertising revenue, by maximizing 'guaranteed sales', or from some other source, will inevitably tend to ape each other. A magazine that manages to boost sales by means of a novel content formula quickly finds its rivals producing their own versions of the same material; and the same holds true with competing television channels. In fact, increasing the number of popular cultural agencies does not necessarily mean that a

5. An interesting analysis of stereotypes is given in T. W. Adorno, 'Television and the Patterns of Mass Culture', *Quarterly of Film, Radio and Television*, Vol. 8, 1954, p. 213-35.

wider range of products becomes available: just the opposite may happen; but this has more to do with the over-all structure of the industry than with the tactics adopted by one firm to cope with a threatened famine of artistic material.

But what are the consequences of the way popular culture is produced as far as the creative individuals involved are concerned? How does being a performing or creative artist within cultural industry differ from playing the equivalent role within the world of the 'high' arts?

Unfortunately, all too little research has been conducted into the beliefs and motivations of media personnel, and only a very small fraction of what published research does exist is concerned with specifically artistic and creative workers.[1] As with descriptions of the way the creative process is organized, however, a number of generalizations about these matters are current in the critical literature and themselves deserve similar scrutiny.

It has, for example, often been suggested that working in the popular culture industries places considerable strain on the truly creative individual. Critics of popular culture argue that agencies which produce this type of output necessarily adopt an instrumental orientation towards works of popular art, while the creative personnel employed regard their task as essentially expressive.[2] Yet it can surely be argued that many creators of 'high' art in the past have demonstrated a combination of instrumental and expressive motivations. The audiences to be expected at the Globe, and later the Blackfriars, are reflected in Shakespearian drama; and Shakespeare was a working dramatist with shares in the company he wrote for. Again, much of the finest of Baroque music was written on commission, and composers' careers depended on the satisfaction of clients. Going further back in time, accounts of the extent to which many artists of the Italian Renaissance were answerable to the whims of chronically indecisive patrons suggest that the existence of instrumental and essentially extra-artistic pressures do not necessarily inhibit creative activity. In the case of popular art, the way in which managers, administrators and financiers view their audiences seems more important than the mere fact that relatively very large audiences are required to make the enterprise viable.[3]

Along the same line, it has been implied that the poor quality of 'mass' culture is due to the fact that the writers and artists responsible are characteristically forced to work under severe time pressures in order to meet

1. Researchers have experienced considerable difficulty in gaining access to the mass media institutions. Artistic personnel in particular may be unsympathetic to research, since it comes to be perceived as something which might replace their own artistic judgement of what will be artistically and otherwise successful. This attitude is, of course, particularly related to market research, but then this is what 'research' means for many media personnel.
2. There is a danger in this field of making over-confident assumptions about the artist's orientation to his work and to the larger society. The idea that art is 'expressive' dates largely from the Romantic period. See also, in this connexion, Cesar Graña, *Bohemian versus Bourgeois*, New York, 1964.
3. For an attempt to characterize the major types of mass media system, see: Raymond Williams, *Communications*, Harmondsworth, 1962, p. 88-96.

deadlines determined by the rational organization of marketing operations. But many acknowledged works of art have been produced during very brief, intense periods of activity (music perhaps provides the best examples). as well as under pressure from patrons. Sir Walter Scott produced his later novels in a vain race to repay enormous debts, while Dickens produced novels which still receive critical attention against deadlines determined by serial publication. Given these sorts of examples, it seems very hazardous to claim that the best artistic work is produced only at a certain pace and under an exactly specifiable set of conditions.

Related to the idea of an inevitable clash between instrumental and expressive orientations is the notion that popular artists are necessarily alienated from their work. Again, this warrants careful examination. Marx pointed out that the industrial employee merely sells his labour in the market and has no control over the finished products on which he performs some limited and intermediate operation, arguing that the inevitable result is alienation. The adequacy of this analysis has, of course, been challenged in the case of mass production industry itself; its applicability to popular culture agencies also needs questioning. In the first place, too, much has probably been made of the idea that the popular artist necessarily lacks effective control over what he creates. There appear to be two arguments here: first, that the institution rather than the individual decides what is to be produced; second, that a radical division of labour within cultural industry results in a fragmentation of creative responsibility.

On the first point, it seems likely that many popular artists successfully internalize the aims of the industry they work for, so that it becomes meaningless to speak of an unwilling compliance with external constraints. Perhaps artists who have never considered the possibility of working elsewhere than in a popular cultural agency are most likely to internalize the institution's aims, but this is again properly a subject for empirical research, and not a question to be settled by *a priori* speculation. In his *Men of Ideas*, Coser entitles the chapter most relevant to this discussion 'Intellectuals in the Mass Culture Industries'.[1] But this rather begs the question. Surely, too little is known about the recruitment patterns of creative personnel in the popular culture industries for us to assume that such people are necessarily members of the intelligentsia, with all the characteristics (both in terms of ability and in terms of critical detachment from social institutions) which that term connotes.

Further, although there undoubtedly are cases on record of serious artists being drawn into working within the 'mass' culture industries and experiencing considerable tension and alienation, this is perhaps not the point within a society at which feelings of alienation on the part of the artist characteristically arise today. Nash has suggested, on the basis of a social-psychological study of some two dozen 'serious' American composers, that these artists (some of whom, it is true, wrote film music) felt marginal

1. Coser, *Men of Ideas*, chapter 24.

to contemporary American society.[1] The suggested sources of their feelings of alienation include the fact that society at large regards their work with little interest, provides few opportunities for it to be performed, and hence offers little in the way of financial reward. It can indeed be argued that it is the 'serious' rather than the popular artist who is likely to feel alienated from modern society: the public for the serious artist is relatively small, while that for the popular arts is, by definition, enormous.[2] Alienation may stem just as much from the value which society in general places on a given type of expertise as from the frustrations of the work situation.

But the contention that the popular artist feels alienated from his work because he is only partially responsible for the finished product again invites specification of the particular circumstances when this is likely to occur, and in which media. In television, and particularly in films, the way in which a programme or new feature is made is necessarily complex, involving as suggested a wide range of technical and craft skills; and given these types of organization it is no doubt easier to take final control out of the hands of the producer or director. The very large capital investment often involved in one production may also predispose senior managers to play a virtually continuous role within the production process. Even here, however, the achieved status of the producer or director and the policies of the broadcasting organization or film company can make a considerable difference. And in other media the situation may be quite different.

Indeed, the actual working conditions of many writers who currently turn out novels and stories with a popular audience in mind are inevitably little different from those we traditionally associate with the craft. The authors of stories destined for popular magazines, particularly women's magazines, are mainly freelances, so that they are not in a strict sense members of the formal organizations of the publishing house. While their own abilities and the audience they are working for determine the complexity, originality and artistic value of what they write, the task itself can only be tackled in the same way that the writer's task has always had to be tackled. Whether the finished product is to be a great and innovatory novel or a short story for some 'slick' or 'pulp' magazine, there is no escape from the pen or typewriter and the stack of blank sheets. The writer is in virtually complete control of the process (subject to editorial suggestion and the necessity to revise, constraints which may also be present in the case of the 'serious' novelist); and there seems little reason for the writer to become alienated from his work on account of the way the production process itself is organized. Indeed, such testimony as is available from popular writers of fiction suggests just the opposite: they claim to derive a considerable degree of personal satisfaction from the work they do.[3] The division of

1. Dennison Nash, 'The Alienated Composer', in: Robert N. Wilson (ed.)., *The Arts in Society*, Englewood Cliffs, 1964.
2. But see the works referred to in footnote 2, page 613.
3. In this connexion, the replies to Mrs. Leavis's survey of successful popular writers are worth studying. See: Q. D. Leavis, *Fiction and the Reading Public*, London, 1932, particularly chapter 3, 'Author and Reader'.

labour may be carried a long way in the publishing house itself (and, of course, in the printing plant) but this may affect the specifically creative personnel very little.[1]

So far as the newer media are concerned, empirical researchers might well set themselves the task of analysing the situational factors affecting the degree of control which creative individuals can exercise over the finished product. As suggested above, there are clear and obvious differences between media (notably perhaps between the print media and the others); but there are probably also important variations within a particular medium. A record of impressive successes at the box office, or a *succès d'estime* with one's colleagues, no doubt provides an artist with considerable bargaining power, currency he can cash for an extra measure of control over what he produces. An analysis of the biographies of creative personnel in different media might well furnish material for a more subtle analysis of this career variable.

It seems possible, too, that the effects of a progressive division of labour within society may in one way bear more heavily on the 'serious' artist than on the popular. Nash has suggested that the lack of a feeling of genuine musical community in the United States at the present time is due to a number of factors which serve to distance the composer from his audience.[2] The fact that the mass media of communication now provide one of the major channels through which music is disseminated is put forward as one reason, but Nash places greater stress on the fact that roles within the musical world have now become intensively specialized, so that the composer is seldom the performer, while those filling the specialized roles of entrepreneur, critic and teacher have important parts to play in structuring his relations with the consuming public. If we argue that it is important for the serious composer to feel in close touch with his audience (particularly when his position in society is highly marginal), then the proliferation of middlemen may be more damaging for the 'high' than the popular arts. Again, the critic is considerably less important as far as the popular arts are concerned, than in respect of the serious arts. It may be traditional for the theatre-going public to read (and take notice of) reviews of new plays on Broadway or in the West End: it is far less characteristic of the general cinema-going public to take equally serious notice of film reviews. What Gans has termed the 'creator-audience relationship' may present few problems for the successful popular artist, while for the more *avant garde* composer or writer it can prove a constant source of unease.[3]

Yet even if it is admitted that the degree to which popular artists feel alienated from their work has probably been exaggerated, there are other possible sources of strain for creative personnel. Since only a small percentage

---

1. Becoming a free-lance writer, of course, and hence moving quite outside the immediate control of editors, is often regarded as a mark of achievement.
2. Nash, op. cit.
3. Herbert J. Gans, 'The Creator-Audience Relationship in the Mass Media: an Analysis of Movie Making', in: Bernard Rosenberg and David M. White (eds.), op. cit,

of those who serve some form of artistic apprenticeship are able to earn an adequate living from 'high' art, the agencies responsible for the production of popular works are likely to contain a number of individuals who feel that they are functioning at a lower level than their abilities justify. Their more successful peers may still serve as an important comparative reference group, and consequent feelings of relative deprivation may engender chronic dissatisfaction: but again there is all too little empirical evidence about the existence and location of individuals of this type. Further, a number of alternative reference groups exist for the popular artist. The esteem of colleagues may come to be the most sought-after reward, while the camaraderie of the work situation (in films and television particularly) may effectively insulate an artist from those other worlds to which he once aspired.

Even so, there no doubt still exist artists who feel that they are prostituting themselves by working within the domain of popular culture; yet Gans has suggested that even this situation may have its positively functional aspects: 'Much of our popular culture is produced by creators whose personal tastes are "higher" than those of their audiences. Although this relationship breeds problems of role, morale, and product quality, it may also provide the creator with enough emotional distance between himself and the audience to permit him to create for an audience of so many different publics.'[1] Here again, however, there are differences between the media: while the cinema industry has so far moved only a short distance in the direction of catering to the tastes of specialized audiences, social differentiation (in terms of leisure—and life-styles particularly) is increasingly reflected in the output of the magazine industry.[2]

When minorities become large enough to constitute markets worth catering to, the popular artist is given new inducements to specialize in a particular type of work. A writer may specialize not merely in short-story writing, but in the construction of romantic stories designed to appeal to women from a particular socio-economic background. So although the writer is in charge of turning out the story, and the division-of-labour principle is not applied to the creative task in the sense of fragmenting it, still the writer may have little chance to widen his or her scope. And it is possible to find examples of a similar degree of specialization within the performing arts, notably in the 'pop' music world, where a particular singer becomes identified with a characteristic type of song and style of presentation. Indeed, the product differentiation which springs from marketing considerations itself provides a spur towards creative specialization; and the expertise which springs from successful specialization may itself be a source of status and the ground in which a minor sort of professionalism may flourish.

1. ibid.
2. Some discussion of the current range of British periodicals is given in David Holbrook, 'Magazines', in: Denys Thompson (ed.), *Discrimination and Popular Culture*, Harmondsworth, 1964. Holbrook regards the highly specialized periodicals as the most worth while.

But even if some allowance is made for the particular creative possibilities provided by situations in which the raw materials are largely 'given', it can still be argued that constraints of this type are inimical to true creativity, rather than supportive of it. Yet the inbuilt 'dynamic obsolescence' of much popular culture,[1] the search for novelty, and the institutional need for product differentiation all mean that a considerable premium is placed on the invention or discovery of essentially new formulae, which will be progressively re-worked in their turn until themselves supplanted. It may be at this point in the creative cycle that a particular, and no doubt limited sort of originality reaps its highest rewards. More generally, the fact that tastes change (or are changed) means that the popular culture industries cannot reduce their operations to the level where automatons become adequate replacements for human beings.

Specialization, whether or not this is accompanied by fragmentation of the creative task, loss of control, or psychic withdrawal, is in fact one manifestation of a broader trend. In terms of style, medium, intended audience, level of seriousness and degree of innovation, the range of artistic products available today is far wider than a hundred years ago. Perhaps it is not surprising that social critics have tended to react to this situation by setting up a simple set of categories which furnish both a means of bringing order out of chaos, and the starting point for a hostile critique of most sorts of majority culture. To date, such schemata have perhaps been accepted too readily. By looking at the differences between media, by searching for similarities and differences between the work and working conditions of popular and other artists, and by studying the various constraints imposed by technology, marketing economics and institutional policy, it may be possible to arrive at a less rigid analysis.

1. This phrase is made a key term in Vance Packard, *The Waste Makers*, New York, 1960.

Roger L. Brown is a research officer at the Centre for Mass Communication Research, University of Leicester, England. He was formerly a staff member of the Institute for Communications Research at the University of Illinois. He is the author of Wilhelm von Humboldt's Conception of Linguistic Relativity *(1967).*

On the Working Habits of Authors
Dale Warren

from

The Bookman, New York, vol. 70, no. 6, 1930.

ON THE WORKING HABITS OF AUTHORS

by Dale Warren

I HAVE in mind a picture I once saw of a man and a woman sitting in wicker basket-chairs in a garden. Lilac or jasmine or something of the kind forms a leafy background and a closely clipped lawn stretches out before them. The man is wearing white flannels and a tweed coat. His legs are crossed in an attitude of happy indifference and his freshly lighted cigar gives him the air of one who is comfortably settled for a late afternoon siesta. A setter lies contentedly at his feet. With a pillow at her back, the woman leans slightly forward in her chair. She has a pencil in her hand and holds a notebook in her lap.

The woman in the cool summer dress is Winifred Tolton, and the man in the white flannels is E. Phillips Oppenheim. The scene is somewhere on the Riviera and the occupation in which these two are indulging requires but a slight effort of the imagination. For those who know Mr. Oppenheim have heard him describe his unique method of work, and readers of his novel, *The Mystery Road*, may remember its dedication: "To Winifred Tolton, the most wonderful secretary and dearest friend of my life".

Contrast this picture with the traditional conception of "an author at work". Where are the flat-topped desk and the student lamp, the rickety typewriter and the graying dawn? Where are the piles of discarded manuscript and the nervous fingers that tear the hair? Where the dictionary and the pot of black coffee, the thesaurus and the bottle of synthetic gin?

For all I know, Mr. Oppenheim started writing in just such a way. I can easily imagine him as a desperate youth in London some forty years ago, striving against odds to gain a foothold with *False Evidence, A Monk of Creta*, and other earlier books long ago forgotten. But even so, the lean years are now buried under an avalanche of opulent decades and the key fits securely into the golden lock. The combination works; and there he sits, corpulent and prosperous, in the garden of his French villa, endlessly dictating, turning out three novels a year. Not even after the hundredth was finished did he call a halt, for fear of developing what he calls mental indigestion. The unwritten stories, crowding for space in his mind, could not be dissuaded from effervescing.

The strange thing about Mr. Oppenheim's plots is that he never knows how they will develop. He gets an idea of two main characters—the man (he is the main thing) and the woman (very secondary). These two elements, together with his first chapter, constitute his preparation. Then he lives with his characters for a while, eats with them, walks with them, plays golf with them. Finally they begin to act according to their own wills and at that point he lets them go, to work out their several destinies by themselves. He "simply pulls the strings". He does not work from a synopsis because if he did so he says the result would be so stilted that he could never expect to have another reader. His characters would resent this false note and kick over the traces.

Mr. Oppenheim has so arranged his life that half of his time is devoted to his writing and the other half divided between exercise and sport, visits to London, and travel. "Many a time, earlier in life," he says, "when I used to write my stories with my own hand, I have found that my ideas would come so much faster than my fingers could work that I have prayed for some more speedy method of transmission. My present method of dictating to a secretary is not only an immense relief, but it enables me to turn out far more work than would be possible by any other means. I find my best time for writing is in the morning, from about 9:30 until 1 o'clock. Unfortunately, however, my scheme for the day is complicated by the fact that this is also the time during which I play golf. So I have schooled myself into an artificial preference for working between the hours of four and seven in the evening."

While Oppenheim is hooking and slicing (for who does not?) from one sand-trap to another, John Galsworthy is doing his best work, maintaining that his imagination is most alert in the morning. Then during the hours between tea and dinner, while Oppenheim is dictating in the basket-chair, Galsworthy revises what he has written before lunch. Revision, to the creator of the Forsytes, is not a satisfied perusal which consists of adding a comma here and a colon there, because he revises his manuscript again and again and corrects both his first and second typewritten copies several times. He works in every place and in every weather—in his study, on the train, and best of all in the sun. After dinner he never works, for fear it will rob him of well-earned sleep.

Anne Douglas Sedgwick does not care for sport. Neither does she dine out with the frequency of Galsworthy. Yet she is sorely beset by temptation. Birds are her hobby, at least so she confided to Esther Forbes, and when she is seated at her table conveniently placed before a large open window she gazes for long moments, when she should be working, at the birds disporting themselves in her rose garden. Frequently the author of *Dark Hester*, *Tante* and *The Little French Girl* forgets all about what she is writing and lets her imagination run away with her. "I sometimes wonder," she says, "when I watch a fly-catcher hovering with upstretched wings, if any Pavlova can offer such an exquisite spectacle, and listening to the delicate melody of the willow-warbler, dropping among the leaves like a tiny chain of crystals, I have thought that jazz itself was dated. Why not sit down and look about with a pair of field-glasses and listen for an hour or two? If we are rewarded only by the bubbling song of the chaffinch or the sight of the wren, slipping in and out of the hawthorne hedge, we shall have gathered a fresher sense of the value of peace and solitude."

Peace and solitude indeed! How could one who has found them be guilty of either shallow thought or discordant prose?

Miss Sedgwick's preference for a table at which to work is not shared by another English novelist, Maud Diver, who began scribbling many years ago when she was a girl in India. Mrs. Diver admits two trivial idiosyncrasies, one of which is writing on her knee in an armchair. The other is her insistence that the chair be out of doors regardless of the weather. It may be a foolish fancy, but she shares to the full the Indian belief that "something living must watch a man at work, if he wants to come near perfection". She wakes up before six, makes her own early tea and starts writing at once, always in pencil and never on a typewriter. When she is "on a book" she writes nearly all day. She says that she is a poor starter but a good stayer and that her novels, in spite of their unusual length, are polished and pruned to the best of her ability.

Osbert Burdett, biographer of Gladstone, Coventry Patmore and the Brownings, is another writer who abhors a typewriter, declaring that the click of the keys can be heard in the style of all who use one. Fatigue, paradoxically, is the most effective stimulant under which he can work. Edgar Wallace has long since graduated from the ranks of those who must decide between pencil, typewriter, or secretary because he has discovered the efficacy of the dictaphone and through this agency is said to be able to acquit himself of sixteen thousand words a day. Some time ago, James Boyd tried to introduce this labor-saving device into America and posed for a picture demonstrating its use, but I seriously doubt if the custom has come to stay.

A battered old Remington on which he has pounded out several million words does quite nicely for Valentine Williams, the mystery-story writer, who likewise shares Mr. Oppenheim's fondness for the Riviera. When I last heard from him it was installed in an abandoned kiosk which he had discovered so close to the edge of a high cliff above the Mediterranean that if he split an infinitive one half would fall down into the deep blue sea. The kiosk serves as an ideal work-room, for Williams is one of those who can do better work in one hour without interruption than in three hours with one interruption. Virgin paper is piled on one side of the Remington and on the other are sheets of completed manuscript. At the back is a row of pipes, a tin of tobacco, a box of cigarettes, a large ash-tray, a bit of paper or the back of an old envelope on which he jots down ideas and snatches of dialogue which come into his mind as he writes.

Roland Pertwee also needs quiet while he works and has evidently found it in his London home in Drayton Gardens. "The study where I write," he says, "opens its windows on a fig tree and is delightfully quiet in contrast to its predecessors. The other, which I was forced to flee, overlooked the parade ground of Wellington Barracks whence all day long came the clatter of arms and accoutrements and the inspiring music of fife and drum. Sometimes, in fact often,

young soldiers learned to play the bugle under my window—a difficult art and one that in practice makes all other arts impossible." Pertwee, I venture say, would have had great sympathy for the luckless Fanny Burney who, finding no peace in the house, was said to have retreated to a cabin at the end of her stepmother's garden at King's Lynn, only to be driven back again by the vigorous and frequently reiterated oaths of the sailors which drifted up to her innocent ears from the river below. Sarah Orne Jewett fared more successfully on her literary excursions, since she had the wisdom, if we can judge from her *Country of the Pointed Firs*, to select a remote country schoolhouse during the summer months while it was deserted by teachers and pupils.

The question of how or where a person shall write seems to lend itself to an amazing variety of answers. Think of the blind Milton dictating to his daughters. Think of Emily Dickinson and her little slips of paper. Think of Proust writing in bed in a cork-lined room in Paris. Think of Amy Lowell writing all night in Brookline with only an open fire, a cat and a box of cigars for company. Think of Trader Horn telling his story to Ethelreda Lewis in South Africa.

Struthers and Katharine Burt each have a separate study in their house in Southern Pines, and the home of the Hamilton Gibbses must be fitted up with two writing rooms. Esther Forbes writes best in her sister's farmhouse in western Massachusetts and Phyllis Bottome in a châlet in the Austrian Tyrol, surrounded by her dogs. Blair Niles works in a scrap of a room in New York, hung with pictures of Devil's Island. Louis Bromfield writes in Paris or on the Riviera, and Scott Fitzgerald wherever he is at the time. Henry Beston prefers his "Fo'cs'le" on Cape Cod. Tarkington writes in a bathrobe. Julia Peterkin goes day after day to a cabin on her plantation in South Carolina and finds that ideas flow most freely when it is too hot to breathe. Demetra Vaka thinks out all her plots lying flat on her back on a couch in a shaded room. Dorothy Cottrell takes a machine in her automobile out into the Australian wilderness. Gina Lombroso, the wife of the historian, Ferrero, also uses a portable. When I was staying with them in Italy I was awakened soon after it was light by a vigorous clicking outside the window, and there she was at work on her *Soul of Woman* under a fruit tree in the courtyard.

Warwick Deeping shares with Anne Douglas Sedgwick an interest in nature, as certain of his novels would indicate, and lives in a historic English house, the gardens of which were originally built for Mrs. Siddons. He begins work about seven o'clock in the morning and after a cup of tea sits down at his desk and lights a briar pipe. He is another longhand artist. Absolute quiet is his chief requirement and his wishes are so far respected that on one occasion it is recounted that a servant girl slipped off a pair of squeaky boots before passing his door.

If photographs tell the true story, Viña Delmar writes with a child on her lap, and someone else (I can't think who) with a parrot on his shoulder. Rosita Forbes and Elinor Mordaunt, if my memory is correct, write in Arabian deserts, on Chinese rivers, in Oriental bazaars and now and then on camel-back. Morris Gordin, the one-time Communist, wrote a book on cigarette papers and smuggled it out of Russia in his shoes. Emanie Sachs has a secret studio and no one knows where it is except her chauffeur, who brings out her lunch in a dinner pail. Samuel Merwin used to have a hidden room somewhere in Boston, but possessed neither a chauffeur nor a dinner pail.

A friend of mine once wrote a book on settlement work while commuting by boat from New York to Sea Bright, New Jersey. Another used to do most of his work in the subway. A third had to give up writing because his wife said he was getting unbearable. A fourth began a novel when he had the grippe but never had a chance to finish it because the attack apparently rendered him immune.

Martha Ostenso does no writing until the afternoon; her housework keeps her busy in the morning. The amount she can do in one day depends on how well she can concentrate. Some days it is three thousand words, some days three hundred. On others she writes nothing that she cares to keep. She deplores the habit of taking tea or coffee to whip up a tired brain. *Wild Geese* was begun during an illness in the course of which she thought some form of occupational therapy was necessary. The story itself was written in six weeks, but it had been growing in her mind for four years. "After I got up," she says, "I rented a typewriter for a month and rewrote the manuscript. I had to do it in the one month because I could not afford to keep the typewriter any longer." Stranger yet is the case of Margaret Ayer Barnes, the younger sister of Janet Fairbank. She broke her back in an automobile accident in France and during her convalescence dictated some stories to her nurse and corrected them in bed. When they came out in book form after magazine publication she dedicated the volume (in a spirit of utterly charming forgiveness) to *Saint Christophe, Patron des Voyageurs,* as she had been given, in the interests of safety, a medal reputedly blessed by him just before she started on the trip.

One of the best ways to find out what you want to know about a particular author is to send him a list of questions with an accompanying threat if he fails to answer them. This method was lately used to great advantage on Rex Beach by Ruth Raphael of Harpers. Although Miss Raphael's enthusiasm is such that she easily jotted down a hundred or more, I shall limit myself to the first ten, also giving Mr. Beach's far from evasive replies:

Q. Where do you write?
A. Wherever I happen to be.

Q. What hours do you prefer for writing?
A. Mornings. Evenings are good. Afternoons terrible.

Q. Do you smoke while writing?
A. Always and invariably. No smoke, no write.

Q. What are your working clothes?
A. I have never tried a dinner coat or running pants.

Q. Do you find alcohol or other stimulant helpful in promoting ideas or their expression?
A. Ruinous.

Q. Do you ever dictate?
A. Never. I've been married for years and am out of the habit.

Q. Do you keep a notebook? For ideas? For phrases?
A. I've often tried but never succeeded.

Q. After finishing a story how long do you wait before beginning another?
A. As long as my wife will let me.

Q. What are the people in your household forbidden to do while you are working?
A. Discharge pistols. Yell "Fire!" Cook cabbage.

It seems that ever since childhood Wanda Fraiken Neff has been a frightful consumer of ink and paper and that, to stave off bankruptcy, her mother started her writing on paper bags and old envelopes. Lately she has acquired the habit of using the backs of galley proofs with the disadvantage, however, that neither she nor her husband get books published fast enough to supply her demand. Scraps of paper are always at her hand in the kitchen, or beside the davenport, for some of her best thoughts come while she is cooking dinner or trying to take a nap. Sophia Cleugh once told me that her idea of heaven would be to go to prison with a typewriter and several reams of paper. Certainly an advanced case of *scribendi cacoethes* and what a far cry from Norman Douglas, who writes only as a last resort, with great reluctance, groaning and protesting! Possibly the happy medium is struck by Fannie Hurst, who laments: "I'm not happy when I'm writing, but I'm more unhappy when I'm not".
At one time when I was spending some

weeks at a country inn, Hugh MacNair Kahler was living in the rooms directly above mine. One morning the colored maid came in to make the bed before I felt any desire to get up, and the bright idea came to me of suggesting that she take her dustpan and brush to Mr. Kahler's suite and return to mine when she had finished. "Oh, no!" she answered. "Don't you hear him walking around? Well, that means he's writing and I'm not supposed to disturb him when I hear him walking up and down." Surely enough his measured tread was clearly audible, and in the interests of Mr. Kahler and the *Saturday Evening Post* I hastily arose and started to shave. Homer Croy, I am told, always takes off his shoes before he starts to work, not for fear of disturbing a possible sleeper below, but by way of resisting the temptation to get up and take a stroll.
Writing now and then takes the form of a seasonal occupation, just like haying or delivering ice. Hugh Walpole never writes at all during the London season, firmly believing in one thing at a time. John Buchan does most of his work when he can retire to his home in Scotland, so pressing are the demands of Parliament when it is in session. John Erskine and other professors quite naturally look to the summer months as a gift from the gods.
Edna Bryner goes each fall to a camp in the Adirondacks and works like mad, actually typing each one of her drafts herself instead of passing them on to a stenographer. Bill Hart wrote his autobiography with the stub of a pencil about two inches long so that it would fit into his vest pocket when he was not working. John W. Vandercook summers in New York and says: "I rise punctually at eleven, hurry through breakfast and go to lunch at the Players' Club fifty feet from my door. There I will prolong that function as long as is decent and about an hour after that point, then I will walk fifty feet back and, the day's exercise done, I will sit at a typewriter, moan, make gutteral noises in the

throat, gaze solemnly at the wall, cross out sentence after sentence, throw away reams of stuff, smoke too much, welcome correspondence as a blessed interruption, and try to finish by next spring the book that my publishers confidently hope to issue this fall".

Maristan Chapman detests the slavery of writing and puts no faith in inspiration. "I may hope for inspiration," she said in an interview, "but I can't count on it." To her, writing is an eight-hour day, six days a week, just like any other job. She does a great deal of revision on her first drafts and despises what she calls the superficiality and the artificiality of the artistic pretence. "If there is anyone alive who actually likes to write short stories," affirms Wilbur Daniel Steele, "either he's a queer one or else they aren't very good stories. There is a time when a tale is a fine and beautiful creature, a masterpiece without flaw, a drama calculated to move one beyond any drama yet written by man; and that is just before you sit down to write it." The truth is Mr. Steele would much rather lay bricks.

Fannie Hurst writes six hours a day, because a shorter period would leave her with practically a blank page at the end of a workday. As it is, the bulk of her day's work is accomplished in the last hour. It takes her from one and a half to two years to write a novel and from six to eight weeks to complete a short story. She regards her method of induction into the creative mood as a bit mundane. Regardless of the night before, her morning begins about 7:30. A walk in Central Park with her dogs. Breakfast. Letters. Reluctance to unhood her veteran typewriter. The excuse of letters to be answered. Telephone calls to be made. A session with her cook. Finally, the round, black hour of nine; with slow and dragging feet she goes to her desk.

As many of Miss Hurst's characters are remembered long after the events which surround them are forgotten, it is interesting to learn that her people invariably precede their plots. The character, she says, sits in the center like an immense spider weaving a web. Strangely enough, Fannie Hurst has never written a story from life. The impulse to do a certain type of story comes and she depends more upon her intuition to lead her through than upon concrete knowledge of a subject. Very often she finds that a character from an environment about which she knows very little emerges the most convincingly. "In the last analysis, methods are not important any more than the number of eyes that used to go blind in weaving a queen's coronation robe. The glory of the fabric is the thing, and the author's eyes, and how he uses them, are his lonely and eternal concern."

The insatiable curiosity of the public is nowhere more evident than where authors are involved. Let a man, or a woman, publish a novel and he must be prepared to state how long it took him to finish it, describe his writing accessories, confess his literary sins and paint an accurate picture of himself in the throes of composition. The public must be told, as Archibald MacLeish bewails, that W. B. Yeats shaves in camel's milk, if indeed that happens to be the case. By contrast, Henry Ford, Mussolini and Lindbergh are comparatively safe. They are asked what leads to success, what is the meaning of Fascism, what makes an airship fly, but no one gives a damn what time they get up in the morning, what they wear to work, or how they like their jobs. Their private and more intimate personal habits are largely their own concern. But authors have grown callous and even if their books are their own the same cannot be said of their souls. What? Where? When? Why? is the everlasting rapid fire and there is no escape. But it certainly pays to be quick on the answering trigger, and my vote for the prize goes to Stephen Vincent Benét, who was recently greeted by a ship reporter just as he was docking from Europe. Asked the reporter: "Well, Mr. Benét, how did it feel to write *John Brown's Body?*" Answered Mr. Benét: "Just about like giving birth to a grand piano".

Psychoanalysis and Creative Literature
Llewellyn Jones

from

English Journal, vol. 23, no. 6, 1934.

PSYCHOANALYSIS AND CREATIVE LITERATURE

LLEWELLYN JONES

The name, if not the work, of Freud is known to all of us, and we are aware when we read such contemporary works as Eugene O'Neill's *Mourning Becomes Electra* that Freud, whether at first hand or indirectly, had something to do with the title as well as the motivation of the play. Few of us realize, however, the complexity of the relationships between psychoanalysis, art, and criticism. The present paper can only hint at them, and give a few scattered examples of how the new psychology affects art and the relation of the critic and reader to the artist.

At first blush the relationship of psychoanalysis to art seems a hostile one. Freud strips away the last vestige of that easy romanticism which made the artist a man apart—of finer clay than ordinary humanity. Freud equates him to the neurotic. That sounds like a new version of Max Nordau's short-lived theory of the artist as "degenerate," but it is not. For Freud, the word "neurotic" has no such connotation. We are all neurotic in so far as we have conflicts, repressed desires, which we deal with as best we may: by sublimation, by acting out, by flight from the world. So instead of saying the artist is a neurotic, Freud would prefer to say that the neurotic is an unsuccessful and purely individual artist. The artist sublimates his conflicts into works which appeal to us because our conflicts find sublimation in them. The neurotic, lacking the technique of art and the social sense of the artist, makes up a private work of art appreciable only by himself. And I may say, in passing, that Freud no longer deals with the "libido" and its desires alone. He has also analyzed that power we call "conscience" and shown us that it is just as "real" and as powerful as are the unconscious urges.

Meanwhile, one does not have to be a Freudian to recognize the unconscious. Without Freud we might still have had those "stream of consciousness novels"—reaching at least a little below the level of consciousness—of which Marcel Proust's *Remembrance of Things Past* (about ten volumes in the English translation), Dorothy Richardson's *Pilgrimage*, and James Joyce's *Ulysses* are the outstanding examples.

At least we should have had two of them, for Proust, according to his French critics, had not read Freud when he began his monumental work, having learned about the unconscious from his distant kinsman, Henri Bergson.

Dorothy Richardson was enabled to write the adventures of her heroine Miriam from the vantage-point of Miriam's own inner life because she herself has a rare faculty of "total recall." Mr. H. G. Wells once told the writer that one of the scenes in Miriam's life is an afternoon tea at which Mr. and Mrs. Wells were present—if, indeed, I remember aright, Mrs. Wells was the hostess. The story came out some years later, and Mrs. Wells remarked that Miss Richardson had remembered every guest in detail, all the "decor": one of her characters was given a purple dress where the original had worn a green one, but that was the only error. *Ulysses*, on the other hand, was written after Joyce had studied Freudian psychology. And in a greater degree than either Miss Richardson or Proust, Joyce relinquished the censor's control of his material in order to give us all sorts of infantile associations and symbols.

Indeed, in Joyce we pass from the mere stream-of-consciousness novel to the specifically Freudian novel. The difference is between exhibiting a freely running stream and exhibiting one that is dammed up.

For if Freud did not discover the unconscious he did discover the fact that in all of us the unconscious is dammed up at every point where its free running would interfere with our success in life—fulfilling "ego demands"—and conscience.

But the demands of the libido are inexorable. Held back from overt expression, they express themselves in fantasy. From idle day-dreaming to hysterical insanities is one line of their expression. It is an individualistic line, satisfactory only to the man who travels along it.

The other line of fantasy production is that of art. It differs from day-dreaming in that it is social: the fantasy is so normal, as one may say, that it fits into the fantasy world of all of us. Also, it is controlled by the rational mind: the real artist is never a split personality. Indeed fantasy may not invade the content of his work at all. The fantasy element in painting, for example, may be a sublimation of an infantile form of sexuality which has, in earlier life, expressed itself in a love of daubing, of playing with mud pies. On the other hand, what is known as "oral infantile sexuality," when sublimated, gives us the artist who plays with words: the oral erogenous zone—first stimulated at the maternal breast—is still active but with a sublimated activity. The content of the works of these two exemplars may be severely realistic and rational.

The reader may easily imagine, therefore, that those critics who have hastily rushed in to judge all works of art as if they were dreams, to be interpreted by Freudian symbolism, have outdared the angels. If, in a lyric poet, image after image comes up which has a definitely symbolic character, we may suspect this or that. But we must remember that an image in poetry is not of necessity a symbolic expression in the Freudian sense. When Yeats, for example, in a number of poems uses the figure of the rose:

> Red rose, proud rose, sad rose of all my days!
> Rose, of all roses, Rose of all the world!

we must not imagine that we can refer to the index of Freud's *Interpretation of Dreams* and find out some particular "suppressed desire" of which the rose is a symbol. In the first place, that is not how it is done anyway; and in the second place, the rose to Yeats is a symbol in another sense of the word—it is the rose of the Rosicrucian order: that is to say, it is not a Freudian symbol at all but a metaphor, used by him for its intellectual significance.

On the other hand, the preoccupation of Edgar Allan Poe with symbols of death, with pale and dying (and even with dead) women, is not a literary exploitation of any set of metaphors, but the expression of himself. Here we can check the poetry with the life of its writer. Poe's attractions were all to women already sealed by death. His mother died when he was a month under three years of age; Mrs. Allan, his foster-mother, whom he loved, died when he was a youth. Jane Stith Stanard, to whom he wrote,

> Helen, thy beauty is to me . . . .

died soon after he had met her.

Then he married Virginia Clemm, already with the aspect of death on her face. Poe himself, before he was twenty, was aware of this, and wrote the following lines:

> I could not love except where Death
> Was mingling his with Beauty's breath,
> Or Hymen, Time, and Destiny,
> Were stalking between her and me.

But later he deleted them from his published work: probably their self-revelation frightened him or could no longer be borne by him.

Criticism of Poe has ranged all the way from the early stupidities and slanders of Griswold, to partial comprehension in our own country, and more complete comprehension abroad. What will undoubtedly be for our generation and longer the definitive book on Poe has just been published in France. *Edgar Poe: Étude Psychoanalytique* (2 vols.), by the Princess Marie Bonaparte, is a detailed and thoroughly documented study of Poe's life and work. It is an excellent example of the psychoanalytic method of literary criticism. No attempt is made in it to solve the ultimate problem of genius. But the thesis is laid down that every motif in Poe's work—as in every other artist's—every image used, is, if we have enough biographical and psychological evidence, explicable and inevitable. Lacking this evidence on one crucial point, the Princess Marie asks us to make one assumption: that the infant Edgar (aged 2 years and 11 months) last saw his mother as she lay dying and just after her death. That the child should, before Mrs. Allan took him away, be brought to see his dead mother is a natural enough assumption. If we make it, Poe's subsequent relations to women in life and his treatment of love in his work become more than merely intelligible: they make a rigidly logical pattern. His loves were but re-enactions of his first love: for a mother that was dead. As the Princess Marie Bonaparte says, in an apologetic aside, it may even weary the reader to consider the cycle of stories that includes *Berenice, Morella, Ligeia, The Fall of the House of Usher, Leonora, The Oval Portrait, The Assignation,* and *Metzengerstein:*

Avant de poursuivre cette macabre revue des héroïnes poesques, il me faut m'excuser de la monotonie du thème. C'est toujours et encore le même tableau manifeste: une femme ideale qui dépérit, qui meurt, mais qui n'est pourtant pas vraiment morte, et reste vivante d'un éclat surnaturel, putride et éthéré à la fois. C'est encore et toujours le même thème latente: l'agonie et la morte de la jeune actrice Elizabeth Arnold, reproduites par delà les années par l'agonie et la morte proche de la petite Virginia.

In the fanciful landscape stories the critic sees another cycle of mother-reminiscences, and in other tales the unconscious expression of the revolt against the father, who for Poe was not his own father but John Allan.

The reader may object that, Poe being confessedly abnormal, a method of interpretation seemingly applicable to his poetry would not necessarily be applicable to the poetry of other artists.

Let us look, then, at the work of a living American poet, Robinson Jeffers. Apart from an early work which attracted little attention, his first significant—and long—poem was "Tamar" published in 1924, followed by "Roan Stallion," "The Women at Point Sur," "Cawdor," "Dear Judas," etc.

The locale of most of the longer poems is rural California, but we may feel more or less certain that the actions and thoughts of the characters are not typical of the inhabitants of that state. One of Mr. Jeffers' most typical themes is that of incest; although in Tamar and one or two other poems there are so many other sexual aberrations thrown in that even the moralistically-minded reader will not be unduly shocked by the incest.

The poet himself has explained to the writer of a "portrait" of him—*Robinson Jeffers: A Portrait,* by Louis Adamic (University of Washington Chapbooks)—that in his poetry incest is used consciously as a symbol (a symbol, that is, not in the Freudian sense, but meaning a metaphor or allegory). To quote him:

. . . . Incest is symbolized as racial introversion—man regarding man exclusively—founding his values, desires, his pictures of the universe, all on his own humanity.

Jeffers, as is well known, lives apart from humanity, and revolts at the idea of close human contact, of "humanitarianism." But, unfortunately, we are "members of one another" and the religious humanists will be shocked to find that, in the mind of this poet, their aim is one that can only be symbolized under the figure of "the primal crime"—which, according to Freud, is a crime of which all humanity has been guilty in the unconscious mind.

But we know that the springs of art are deeper than the conscious mind; and any psychologist would say that Jeffers' own explanation of his figure of speech is a rationalization. Indeed, to Jeffers' own mind his figure of speech for introversion may appear an apt one. It would hardly appear so to the neutral observer. Its suitability to him must be dictated by unconscious motives. And in order to understand his poetry fundamentally we should have to know those motives.

For appreciation of his poetry in the ordinary sense, however, we do not have to know them. Shakespeare's *Hamlet* has been appreciated by thousands who did not understand Hamlet's motivation. For more than two centuries impatient critics have exclaimed, "If Hamlet was told to kill his uncle, and meant to do so, why did he delay so much?" But in seeing the play we forgot that question: we were moved by and accepted the play. The psychoanalytic explanation of the delay and of our acceptance of it is that Hamlet, unconsciously in love with his own mother, hates her infidelity to his father and her second marriage—that is, her withdrawing from him of her motherhood—even more than he hates his uncle's crime. It is this hatred he is expressing when, for no sufficient reason in the conscious realm, he spurns Ophelia. He cannot hate his uncle with this same single-mindedness, for he has a fellowship of guilt with him. His uncle has only done successfully and overtly what he has desired to do in his unconscious. The whole chain of motivation has been worked out by Ernest Jones in an essay, "A Psycho-Analytic Study of 'Hamlet' " in his *Essays in Applied Psycho-Analysis*.

"But what did Shakespeare know about Freud?" is the instant objection. Dr. Jones answers that consciously, of course, he knew nothing about Freud. But that Hamlet (as indeed most critics admit) is a self-portrait. And that in writing the play Shakespeare expressed both unconscious workings of his own mind and conscious experiences. Frank Harris has suggested, for instance, that Shakespeare in this play identified Hamlet's mother with his own unfaithful Mary Fitton. And we, when we see the play, are moved by it because we, too, unconsciously have felt the same strains and stresses in our own emotional relationships. The play "gets under our skins" in part without the mediation of the critical intellect.

Again I turn from a dead to a living author. Shakespeare was a genius and wrote from his heart—or his unconscious. When your dramatist knows his Freud to begin with, however, he complicates the critical problem. Eugene O'Neill in *Strange Interlude* and in *Mourning Becomes Electra* has used a great deal of Freudian material but with a difference. It seems to be done self-consciously and coldly. One feels that the work is fabricated rather than felt—especially in *Mourning Becomes Electra*. Here O'Neill has paralleled the old Greek tragedy in modern terms. But he has been so anxious to have us understand the transposition that he exaggerates throughout. As Ludwig Lewisohn points out in his *Expression in America*—a history of American literature written in psychoanalytic terms—the incest-wish is an unconscious wish. And in 1865 people had not even been told they possessed such a thing. When, therefore, Mrs. Mannon says to her daughter, "You've tried to become the wife of your father and the mother of Orin" she was talking quite a few years ahead of herself. The spectator of the play will have noticed, too, how in the later acts the daughter identifies herself with her mother by beginning to wear the same color and cut of clothing: it is a little bit too obvious and gross for the mechanism of "identification" which it is intended to express. But the stage, perhaps, is a medium which forbids too great a subtlety.

Nor must we forget that O'Neill was writing a play in which he had to make Freudian motivation visible to people who had never read Freud. As popular knowledge of the Freudian mechanisms grows, dramatists and novelists will be able to take more for granted in their work in this new field.

For a new field has been opened up. In the past the realm of dream and fantasy was, for the novelist, a fantastic realm. Lewis Carroll would have laughed at any attempt to explain *Alice In Won-*

derland in rational terms. If, in addition to "pure art," there has been any ulterior aim in exploiting either dream or fantasy, it has been that of allegory or the didactic. That is notably true of James Branch Cabell's books from *Jurgen* to the just published *Smirt*. Mr. Cabell calls his work romance, but it is not that. It is the allegory, not even disguised, of a pessimist and a victim of boredom. All Mr. Cabell's romantic heroes find that romantic love is ruined by marriage, and that marriage domesticates them and unfits them for romantic love. And so, Mr. Cabell, in his essays which explain his fictional intensions (see *Straws and Prayer-books*), tells his readers that life is a boring business, that drink and illicit love as diversions have uncomfortable consequences, and that they had better confine their love-affairs to women who are safely dead, like Helen of Troy, but who live in the pages of writers of belles-lettres. And in the meantime wives have their place: there are always buttons to be sewed on.

Since Freud, however, the dream and fantasy in general have taken on another function in the hands of the writer of fiction. As they are a part of us and as much "determined" and symptomatic as are our very deeds, they may be used realistically. The best example of this use of the dream with which I am acquainted is *Czardas* by Jeno Heltai (English translation published by Houghton Mifflin). Heltai, it is not without significance, lives in Budapest, which was also the home of the late Sandor Ferenczi, who, as a pioneer worker in psychoanalysis, ranks perhaps only second to Freud himself. And the foremost Hungarian novelist undoubtedly knew his fellow-townsman. The title of the work is the name of a Magyar dance, and the dance here is that of fantastic images through the dreams of an aviator from Budapest, who has lost an arm in the war and is sent home free from further military service. His nerves as well as his arm have been injured and he dreams of a blind man whose cane taps on the floor as he seeks him, with evil intent. But another dream consoles him, that of a porcelain statue of a beautiful woman who speaks comforting words to him. Home in Budapest, his old friends gone or forgetting him, he seeks to find the realities behind these dreams.

This, of course, cannot be done without analytic aid, but the author has the march of events take the place of an analyst, and our hero is at length able to reconstruct his past. Into his mouth, by the way, the author places a suggestive expression of what may be called the philosophy of living that is implicit in the new psychology. It is a warning against letting the happenings of life split our personality, a plea that we be integrated and true to all that is within us:

O mortals, how can you live like that? With the indifference of strangers you pass by what was yesterday, and you have forgotten what happened to you ten, twenty, thirty years ago. You do not try to assemble the fragments of your life so as to keep it whole and present all the time. You do not pick up the broken threads of the past to link minutes to hours, hours to years, and years to youth.

How can you exist without desiring to hold in yourselves forever the thoughts that have passed through your mind? Can one really live without seeing himself at one and the same time child and old man, happy and unhappy, good and bad, living and dead? Is one really alive if he limits his life to a single time, and lives for that time alone, instead of living everywhere a life eternal and without end . . . . ?

People often ask if the day of the realistic novel is over and if we are going back to romance. The sophisticated reader who knows that every overt action in life has also a basis in the unconscious and a relation to conscience will never be content again with the objective realism (in intention, that is, for no fiction was ever purely objective) of Bennett and Dreiser. But then he will not be satisfied with romance of the costume and sword school.

The novelist of the future, I imagine, will have to know his Freud or else write autobiographically, as so many beginning novelists do. Of course, if he is a genius he may see, as Dostoevsky did, much that the Freudian arrives at by analysis. But the merely realistic novelist will have to watch his step. He cannot, as Willa Cather did in *The Lost Lady*, have a lout of a boy put out a bird's eyes: just to show us that he was innately cruel. In a conversation with me some years ago the late Harvey O'Higgins, who wrote short stories and a novel based on Freudian findings, pointed that out as a "howler." An ordinarily cruel person would not perform that action but only a person with a definite kind of complex headed in a definitely indicated mental direction. And this was not the case.

The actual exploitation of psychoanalysis for plot material will not, however, give us the significant fiction of the future: that sort of thing cannot compete with real cases for significance, and appeals only to the curious. The value for literature of the new discipline will be in the greater insight which it gives the novelist into motivation and in the aid it will give the reader in distinguishing between serious and "true" fiction and fiction that is only a catering to wish-fulfilling dreams.

And while the new discipline may discourage the minor novelist who comes under its sway from overvaluing his own psychic situations, it will not, in our time, penetrate so deeply into the soul that we need fear that our geniuses may analyze away their creative gifts.

———————

Literature as a Resource in Personality Study: Theory and
Methods
Harold Grier McCurdy

from

Journal of Aesthetics and Art Criticism, 8, 1949.

LITERATURE AS A RESOURCE IN PERSONALITY STUDY: THEORY AND METHODS

HAROLD GRIER McCURDY*

Since Freud's psychoanalytic note on *Hamlet*[1] and his observations on the kinship between dream and literary fiction[2], numerous studies have appeared guided by the principle that the literary work of imagination (novel, poem, drama) is in some degree an objectification or projection of the author's personality. Most of these studies have been concerned with probing into individual dark corners or with adding a little colorful embroidery to some previously expressed theory; on the whole, they have not been concerned with the problem of method, nor with the general theory of artistic creation. In particular, there has been no resolute effort to employ fictional literature as a special means of investigating personality, after the manner of a physicist, let us say, studying the structure of various materials by means of radiations. Provided that the notion of a projection of the personality into the literary work can be accepted as a serious and meaningful one for psychology, and provided that methods adequate to the material and the theory can be worked out, it is at once obvious that fictional literature would afford a nearly inexhaustible resource for personality study, and one which has the very great advantage of being available to workers everywhere and over long periods of time.

Now, what do we find when we begin to investigate the relations between literary works and their authors? First of all, we see that the author draws more or less directly upon his environment for the content of his work—the scenery, the incidents, the personal qualities of his characters. To be sure, it is often not so much the contemporaneous as some earlier environment, particularly that of childhood, to which he is thus indebted. Assimilation of the external world to the point of literary usefulness seems to require a lapse of time. In the second place, we see that there is a consistency in a series of works by a given author, sometimes very conspicuous, both in the style of writing and in the themes which are dealt with. Some authors appear to tell the same story in book after book. Others, the great creators, tell several stories and intertwine them in complicated ways. The presence of persistent themes of this sort in the fantasies of non-literary people has been emphasized by Henry Murray and his co-workers.[3] The similar individual consistency of series of dreams has been brought out in many psychoanalytic studies, and recently Calvin Hall has been exploring the matter statistically.[4]

The author of fiction, then, appears to convey into his work (as the dreamer into his dream) his experience of the world as selected and colored and strongly

---

* Paper presented at the annual meeting of the American Society for Aesthetics in Cambridge, Mass., September 4, 1948.

[1] In *The Interpretation of Dreams*.
[2] "Der Dichter und das Phantasieren," *Gesammelte Schriften*, X.
[3] *Explorations in Personality*, 1938.
[4] "Frequencies in certain categories of manifest content and their stability in a long dream series." *American Psychologist*, July, 1948, p. 274.

shaped by his own particular nature. It is from this point of view that analysis of literary work is simultaneously analysis of the personality which produced it.[5]

The simplest kind of analysis, and perhaps the most important, is the extraction and comparison of the themes or plots. But this is something which can be done at various levels of abstraction. The more complex the work, the farther away must one stand in order to see clear and simple contours. The vastness and richness of Shakespeare's dramas, for instance, produce such an impression of universality that to many critics he has seemed to transcend human comprehension altogether. "Others abide our question: thou art free, Outtopping knowledge." In a simpler case, such as that of the novelist D. H. Lawrence, the task is easier. In novel after novel Lawrence presents a conflict going on between characters who are literally and metaphorically dark and others who are literally and metaphorically light; between those in whom the animal impulses, particularly the sexual ones, are strong and mystically valued, and those in whom they are weak or culturally suppressed; and, in the course of time, the dark sexual characters rise from a defeated to a victorious position in the complex of relationships successively explored. Here is a clear, persistent theme, undergoing a fairly clear one-way change. Without knowing more, we can conclude that the presence of the dark and the light characters and the conflict between them stand for something important in Lawrence's personality. If we go to Lawrence's biography, we find a dark passionate father and a blond ambitious brother, idealized by the mother, who serve as prototypes for the dark and light characters of the novels; and, at that level of analysis, we should infer from the novels that a change of attitude toward the father and brother and what they ethically meant must have taken place in Lawrence as he grew older—a guess which is borne out by the statements of the biographers.[6]

Here it should be interjected that any theme or character-type persistently occurring should, theoretically, be counted as an important feature of the author's personality, whether or not it is traceable to historical circumstances known to the biographers. To illustrate with a minor instance: In a recent study[7] of the novels of the Brontë sisters, I found that a number of inferences regarding Charlotte's family and her relations with it, as made from analysis of the novels, were verified biographically; but while it was correctly inferred that she had a brother whom she both admired and disliked, the further inference, also possible, that this brother was older than herself was not true. In retrospect, it might be argued that the representation of the brother-figures of the novels as older than the ego-figures was simply a part of the general characterization of them as domineering; but this is an after-thought, and may not be justified. What is far more

[5] H. G. McCurdy, "Literature and personality." *Character and Personality*, 1939, 7, 300-208.

[6] H. G. McCurdy, "Literature and personality: analysis of the novels of D. H. Lawrence." Part I, *Character and Personality*, 1940, 8, 181-203; Part II, *ibid.*, 1940, 8, 311-322.

[7] H. G. McCurdy, "A study of the novels of Charlotte and Emily Brontë as an expression of their personalities." *Journal of Personality*, 1947, 16, 109–152.

certain is that the brother-figures in the novels focus the conflict between some of the major elements of Charlotte's personality as there projected.

It is evident from what has been said that thematic analysis is carried on in terms of the *dramatis personae*. In a single work, these figures usually maintain their identity; that is, they keep the same name and the same identifying marks throughout, though exceptions do occur, as when a character assumes a disguise at some point in the narrative or as when a character is so weakly conceived that some physical feature is carelessly altered, such as the color of Caroline Helstone's eyes in Charlotte Brontë's *Shirley*. When we move from one work to another in a series, however, we are confronted by characters separated from their predecessors by various differences. Once again, what is necessary is to take a sufficiently abstract view to enable one to place the characters in manageable categories; and, once again, this is a simpler task with some authors than with others. Thus, in the case of Lawrence, it is possible to develop fairly satisfactory categories in terms simply of physique differences. In the Brontë novels, where physical delineation is relatively weak, I found it helpful to determine which *psychical* traits out of a long list published by Cattell[8] might properly be assigned to each of the principal characters; it was then possible to state on moderately objective grounds which characters were related to which in the various novels by finding the percentage of trait-overlap between them. If one is concerned only with what themes appear, such a categorization of characters is not required; but if one is also interested in how relationships within the personality structure change with time, it is. Thus, it is worth noting whether a given position in a scheme of dramatic relationships continually repeated continues to be occupied by the same type of character.

Plot-analysis and the taxonomy of characters are essential procedures. To some extent they have been used by the biographers of literary men and women always. The further analytic device now to be mentioned leads to more abstract results than those usually encountered in biographies.

In my study of the Brontës I employed a method suggested in another connection by Alfred Baldwin.[9] I counted the number of pages on which each character appeared, and thus obtained a numerical value in terms of which a character's importance relative to others could be stated in quantitative fashion. Incidentally, the order of importance arrived at by this method tallies satisfactorily with the impressionistic judgment. What the method supplies in addition is a set of definite figures which can be mathematically treated. When, for instance, these numerical values are made directly comparable by dividing each of them by the value for the leading character in the novel being considered (thus giving the leading character in each case the same value, which may be stated as 1.00 or 100%), and the resulting figures are ranked from highest to lowest, it is at once evident that there is an approximate similarity between the columns of figures (or the curves, if graphed) for the four novels of Charlotte Brontë, while the rate of descent for the one novel of Emily Brontë is rather different. En-

[8] R. B. Cattell, *Description and Measurement of Personality*, 1946.
[9] "The statistical analysis of the structure of a single personality." *Psychological Bulletin*, 1940, 37, 518–519.

couraged by these findings, I made a line-count for the characters in the seven extant plays of Sophocles. Treating the numerical values in the same way as for the Brontës, I found that the averaged figures for Sophocles fell close to those for Charlotte Brontë, though they were slightly higher at seven out of eight comparable points. I next made a line-count for the characters in thirty-six plays of Shakespeare. The sequence of ranked and averaged values was once again similar in general form to the Brontë and Sophocles sequences, though distinctly separated from them at all the compared points. With three different authors from three widely different periods, then, while individual patterning was evident, it appeared to be a kind of necessity that the average quantitative relationship between characters ranked from highest to lowest should conform to a general type of curve, expressible in a simple formula. In the case of Shakespeare, where the sample is fairly large, the second character has on the average 64% of the weight of the first, and the remainder of the series forms a geometrical progression in which, roughly speaking, the fourth term down from a given term has one-half the magnitude of the given higher term. In the case of Sophocles and Charlotte Brontë it is more nearly the third term down which is half the given term. The general hypothesis emerging from these results is that in the human personality the experience-nodes, to coin a term, or the sentiments or complexes, if these terms are preferred, in so far as they are expressed in the *dramatis personae* (which may be conceived of as sensory and emotional clusters), tend to fall into a musical order corresponding to the hierarchy of sentiments discussed by McDougall.[10]

The preceding illustration of one out of many possible applications of a table of weighted characters raises the unavoidable, though perhaps insoluble, question as to the ultimate nature of an author's *dramatis personae*. Authors often speak of them as having an independent life of their own. Critics concur in this opinion when they analyze their secret motives and pass judgment on them, as when one says of Falstaff that, except for moral sublimity, he is almost as great a poet as Shakespeare himself. Looked on in this way, fictional characters are the real forces and the course of the story is simply the necessary consequence of their interaction. On the other hand, one may reverse the valuation and think of the characters as nothing but the visible moving points which reveal by their motion the invisible currents flowing in the author's personality, as corks reveal the motion of the water in which they float. Or again, one may agree with a favorite Shakespearean apothegm and say that every character is the author himself in one of the numerous temporary roles which he can, and perhaps must, assume in his passage through this world which is, all of it, a stage. Whatever point of view we accept, however, I should say that we limit the concept of an author's personality entirely too much if we identify him with any single character exclusively, or with any particular course of events out of the many he projects into his work. Thus, no matter how completely Prospero seems to sum up Shakespeare as a magical and almost divine creator, there is also Caliban in him, and Miranda, and so on through all his protean changes. At the same time,

[10] H. G. McCurdy, "A mathematical aspect of fictional literature pertinent to McDougall's theory of a hierarchy of sentiments." *Journal of Personality*, 1948, 17, 75–82.

even Shakespeare is not absolutely unlimited; he too, like the rest of us, is cabined, cribbed, confined within his mortal separateness and peculiar selfhood. Running through his plays from first to last there is, for instance, the perpetually recurring theme of true love betrayed.

Finally, a word needs to be said about the wisdom of taking time into account when studying an author's personality. On the theory of projection, a given imaginative work displays the personality structure, at least in part, for the period when the work was written. This structure may not be permanent. A series of works written over a long span of years, arranged in chronological order, may reveal profound changes. I am confident that such is the case with D. H. Lawrence. Even in the short series of four novels by Charlotte Brontë there are quite detectable progressive changes in the thematic structure and in the fulfillment of certain tendencies. In brief, when studying an author's works chronologically, we get the impression of a living organism of great complexity which changes gradually and according to its own laws.

The proper ambition of the psychological analysis of literature, as I see it, extends beyond the understanding of the personality structure and processes of some one or another author to the more comprehensive aim of understanding human personality in general. Such an ambition cannot be realized, however, by random undisciplined observations here and there, and, like every other scientific venture, the enterprise depends for its success upon the development of sharable methods.

Writers and Madness
William Barrett

from

Partisan Review, vol. 14, no. 1, 1947.

Writers and Madness

WILLIAM BARRETT

1. *The Ancients. The Power to Convince. Authenticity. Swift.*

Is MY TITLE extreme? It is, if you will, just the same subject that has been very much discussed recently under the titles "Art and Neurosis," "Art and Anxiety," etc. But I choose the more ancient and extreme term precisely to maintain continuity with all the older instances. Is anything born *ex nihilo,* much less a phenomenon so profound and disturbing as that estranged neurotic, the modern writer? Even when the poet existed in his most unalienated condition— in ancient Greece—the similarity of madness and inspiration was the common saying; and Plato did not invent but only gave literary formulation to the belief about the poet's madness. Pause for a moment over this extraordinary paradox. They sat on sacred ground, precinct of the god, the day and drama were surrounded by all the occasions and overtones of religion, the myth known and on the whole taken as true, and yet. . . . And yet this audience too must exact a terrible price of its poet before they can take him seriously. A secret guilt perhaps? As they sat in broad daylight indulging their collective fantasy, pretending to believe that what was before their eyes was in fact something else, did an uneasy stirring at this indulgence drive them to exact from their poet in revenge the penalty of madness-inspiration? But what, in any case, we do know is this: that even when dealing with myths whose form and details were completely laid down for him, the Greek poet had to launch out into this sea (of "madness," if we believe Plato) in order to return to pour his own personal being into the preformed mold. Otherwise, his play could not have convinced an audience that already assumed their myth as a matter of fact—such is the paradox from which we start!

Everything Swift wrote, Leslie Stephen says with penetrating good sense, is interesting because it is the man himself. (If this is true of many other writers, there is on the other hand a special and compelling sense in which it holds of Swift—another reason for my finding his case so apposite.) Does it look as if I were only about to say, with Buffon, "the style is the man"? But "style" does not say enough, and it is not enough to remain happy with the judicious aphorism or with Stephen's judicious critical observation. The modern critic cannot rest easy with this eighteenth-century piece of astuteness, which long ago passed into the stock of our critical assumptions; we begin to know too much and we must dig mines beneath its truth.

But it is well to begin from such broad and obvious data of criticism (instances of which we could multiply indefinitely) for we may now pass on to the more complex and really monumental example provided us by James Joyce. In his *Portrait of the Artist* Joyce develops a theory of literary creation, anchored on the metaphysics of St. Thomas but essentially expressing the Flaubertian view of the writer as a god who remains above and beyond his creation which he manipulates as he wills. But in *Finnegans Wake* the universal human symbol of the writer has now become the infant Earwicker twin scrawling with his own excrement on the floor! (Between the two, somewhere near the midpoint of this remarkable evolution, Stephen Dedalus declares, in the famous discussion of Shakespeare in *Ulysses,* that the writer, setting forth from his door for the encounter with experience, meets only himself on the doorstep.) If Joyce is the great case of a rigorous and logical development among modern writers, each step forward carrying the immense weight of his total commitment and concentration, we are not wrong then to find in this changing portrait of the artist a measure of how far he has matured as man and writer from the once youthful and arrogant aesthete. And if we will not learn from our own experience, do we not remain formalists toward literature only at the expense of neglecting Joyce's far deeper experience?

But in fact we already know there is no escape from ourselves. Existence is a dense plenum into which we are plunged, and every thought, wish, and fear is "overdetermined," coming to be under the infinite pressures within that plenum of all other thoughts, wishes, and fears. Fingerprints and footprints are our own, and Darwin has pointed out that our inner organs differ from person to person as much as our faces. The signature of ourselves is written over all our dreams like the criminal's fingerprints across his crime. The writer, no more than any other man, can hope to escape this inescapable density of particularity. But his difference is precisely that he does not merely submit but insists upon this as his fate. It is *his own* voice which he wishes to resound in the arena of the world. He knows that the work must be his, and to the degree that it is less than his, to the degree that he has not risked the maximum of his being in it, he has missed the main chance, his only chance. The scientist too may insist on the personal prerogative of discovery: he wants the new element, planet, or equation to bear his name; but if in this claim for prestige he responds to one of the deepest urges of the ego, it is only that this prestige itself may come to attend his person through the public world of other men; and it is not in the end his own being that is exhibited or his own voice that is heard in the learned report to the Academy.

So we have come quickly to the point, and may now let the categories of *authentic* and *unauthentic* out of the bag. I am not very happy about the terms, I wish we had better in English, but it should be clear from our instances so far that they are not really new notions, and that they do come forth now at the real pinch of the subject matter. If a certain amount of faddism has recently and regrettably become attached to their use, they have on the other hand also become obsessive for the modern mind—a recommendation which we, existing historically, cannot help finding a little persuasive. The Marxist will not fail to point out that a highly developed technology, which is not directed toward human ends but capable on the other hand of over-running all areas of the social life, has plunged us into this civilization of the slick imitation, celluloid and cellophane, kitsch and chromium plating, in the morass of which we come inevitably to speak of "the real thing" and "the real right thing" with an almost religious fervor. And he will go on to explain then why the category of authenticity should play such a crucial role in modern existential thought. He would be right, of course, but he ought also to drop his bucket into the deeper waters of the well. One deeper fact is that modern man has lost the religious sanctions which had once surrounded his life at every moment with a recognizable test capable of telling him whether he was living "in the truth" or not; Hegel drew a map of the divided consciousness, and Freud explored it empirically beyond anything Hegel ever dreamed, showing us, among other things, that Venus is the goddess of lies; and so we come, as creatures of the divided and self-alienated consciousness, to wrestle with the problem of how we are to live truthfully. But if these categories have become historically inevitable, and we borrow their formulation from existentialist philosophers, we have on the other hand to insist that it is not these philosophers who can tell us, after all, how authenticity is to be achieved either in art or life. Freud, not Heidegger, holds the key. The mechanism by which any work of art becomes authentic—

flooded in every nook and cranny with the personal being of the author—can only be revealed by the searchlight of psychoanalytic exploration.

How then is authenticity—this strange and central power of a fantasy to *convince* us—achieved? A first and principal point: it seems to involve a fairly complete, if temporary, identification with the objects of fantasy. The difference between Kafka and most of his imitators becomes a *crucial* instance here. When Kafka writes about a hero who has become an insect, about a mouse or an animal in a burrow, he is, during the course of the lucid hallucination which is his story, that insect, mouse, or animal; it is he himself who lives and moves through the passages and chambers of his burrow; while his imitators, even when they are fairly successful, strike us as simply using so much clever machinery borrowed from him and often more ingeniously baroque than his, but which lacks precisely that authenticity of identification. But this identification with the objects of fantasy is also in the direction of insanity; and perhaps this is just what the ancients knew: that the poet in inspiration ventures as close to that undrawn border as he can, for the closer he goes the more vitality he brings back with him. The game would seem to be to go as close as possible without crossing over.

Now imagine, for a moment, Swift in the modern pattern. After the downfall of the Harley ministry he retires to his wretched, dirty dog-hole and prison of Ireland, has a nervous breakdown, a crack-up, is patched together by several physicians and analysts, continues in circulation thereafter by drinking hard but spacing his liquor carefully, and dies at an earlier age of cirrhosis of the liver. Shall we call this: Living on the American Plan? It is the violence of the new world, after all, that has made a system of violent drinking. Now to be drunk and to go mad are both ways of overcoming the world. If in the interests of human economy we are left no choice but to prefer the American Pattern, would we not, however, feel a little cheated had Swift's actual history been different? Before the ravening gaze of his miserable species he flings down his madness as the gage of his commitment and passion, and it has now become an inseparable part of the greatness of the human figure that rises out of history toward us.

When Simon Dedalus Delany, amiable and easygoing, remarked of a mutual acquaintance that "He was a nice old gentleman," Swift retorted, "There is no such thing as a nice old gentleman; any man who had a body or mind worth a farthing would have burned them out long ago." Does not this become his own comment on his eventual madness? The man who retorted thus, it is clear, lived with his whole being flung continuously toward the future at the end of the long corridor of which was the placid if disordered chamber of madness. To have gone mad in a certain way might almost seem one mode of living authentically: one has perhaps looked at the world without illusion and with passion. Nothing permits us to separate this life from this writing: if the extraordinary images the biography provides us—the old man exclaiming, over and over again, "I am what I am," or sitting placidly for hours before his Bible open on Job's lament, "let the day perish wherein I was born,"—if these move us as symbols of a great human ruin, they are also the background against which we must read the last book of *Gulliver*. The game is to go as close as possible without crossing over: poor Gulliver the traveler has now slipped across the border into the country of the mad, but this journey itself was only a continuation of the Voyage among the Houyhnhnms. A moment comes and the desire to escape takes on a definite and terrible clothing, and the whole being is shaken by the convulsions of what we may call the totem urge—the wish to be an animal. Rat's foot, crow's skin, anything out of this human form! The Ainu dances and growls and is a bear, the Bororo Indians chatter and become parokeets; Swift wanted to be a horse, a beautiful and gentle animal —and probably nobler on the whole than most human beings. This is the madness already present in *Gulliver*.

We do not mean to deny all the other necessary qualities that are there: the once laughter-loving Dean, lover of *la bagatelle,* King of Triflers, the great eighteenth-century wit, the accomplished classicist. Precisely these things give Swift the great advantage over a writer like Céline, whose rage is, by comparison, choking and inarticulate—like a man spitting and snarling in our face and in the end only *about* himself, so that we are not always sure whether we are being moved by literature or by a mere document of some fearful human extremity. What for the moment I am calling "madness," the perhaps simpler thing the Greeks called "madness," must somehow flow freely along the paths where all men can admire. If it erupts like a dam bursting it only inundates and swamps the neighboring fields; conducted into more indirect and elaborate paths, it irrigates and flows almost hidden to the eye. The flow from the unconscious of writer to reader would seem, then, to be more effective precisely where the circuit is longer and less direct, and capable therefore of encompassing ampler territory in its sweep. Lucidity, logic, form, objective dramatization, traditional style, taste—all these are channels into which the writer must let his anguish flow. And the denser his literary situation, the more he is surrounded by a compact and articulate tradition, the more chances he can take in casting himself adrift. But whatever Swift's advantages in literary and moral milieu, we cannot forget that he himself lived to write his own epitaph and in this final summing-up had the last word on the once laughter-loving Dean. And it is just his *saeva indignatio*—the mad wrath which, as he said to Delany, did "eat his flesh and consume his spirits"—that establishes the deeper authenticity of *Gulliver* which separates it from any other production of eighteenth-century wit. He himself as Gulliver towers over his Lilliputian enemies, and flees from the disgusting humans into the quiet stables of the horses. How far his madness had already taken him, he could scarcely have guessed, for it had unconsciously carried him, an unquestioning Christian, for the moment outside Christianity: the rational and tranquil Houyhnhnms do not need a Messiah's blood and an historically revealed religion in order to be saved, while the Yahoos could not possibly be redeemed by any savior. Swift might not have gone mad after writing *Gulliver,* but much of the power of that book comes from the fact that he was already on the road.

Once a writer imposes his greatness on us he imposes his figure totally, and we then read every scrap and scribble against the whole, and we will not find it strange that Joyce should invoke even the scrawling of the Earwicker twin as part of the image of Everymanthe-writer. The man who wrote the charming prattle of the *Journal to Stella* is the same who comes to howl at bay before the human race. In his life he made two bluestockings love him desperately (a significant choice this, that they should be bluestockings; but one, to his surprise, turned out, as sometimes happens, a very passionate blue-stocking); and one he loved all his life long. In the simple *Prayers for Stella,* sublimating, he gropes, touches, fondles her in God. What happened beyond this we do not know. But we need no very fanciful imagination to guess the frustration which produces that mingled disgust and fascination at the biology of the female body. He did more, however, than release this into a few scatological verses about milady at and on her toilet; he was able to project his frustration and rage into the helpless Irish face about him, the insouciant Saxon face, churchmen, bishops, Lord Mayors, quacks, and pedants; "the corruptions and villainies of men in power"; and through these into a total vision of the human condition.

Here at last we come close to the secret: if one characteristic of neurosis is always a displacement somewhere, then perhaps the test of a writer's achievement may be precisely the extent and richness of displacement he is able to effect. In the process of literary expression, the neurotic mass acquires energies which are directed toward reality and seek their satisfaction in reality. As the writer displaces the neurotic mass further afield he is led to incorporate larger and larger areas of experience into his vision. Everything begins to appear then *as if* the world he pictures were itself sufficient to generate this vision(which we may know, in fact, to have been rather the product of quite unconscious compulsions and conflicts); *as if* the ego, really master in its own house, were simply responding appropriately to the world as seen in the book. Thus the peculiar sense of conquest and liberation that follows literary creation cannot be analyzed solely as that fulfillment of wishes which normally occurs in daydreaming or fantasy. Why in that case would it be necessary to complete the literary work at all? And why should the liberation it gives be so much more powerful and durable? No; this conquest is also one for the ego itself, which now seems momentarily to have absorbed the unconscious into itself so that the neurotic disgust itself appears an appropriate response to reality. And if this is an illusion from the analyst's point of view, it may not always be an illusion from the moralist's point of view. The world as it appears in Swift's writings is, in the end, adequate to his madness.

2. *Power and Guilt*

Now Swift's (unlike Cowper's, to cite another literary madman) was a very strong ego, and the fact that he broke in old age only tells us how great were the visions, tensions, and repressions he had to face. We do not know enough to establish his "case," but we know enough to say that his madness probably did not have its source in the literary condition at all—however much incipient madness may have informed and made powerful his writings.

Do we build too much on his example then? Perhaps; but his figure, in its broad strong outlines (and the very simplicity of these outlines is to our advantage here), takes such a grip on the imagination that, pursuing this rather nocturnal meditation, I am loth to let him drop. He has taken us so far already that it seems worthwhile to journey a little way with him still into the darkness.

Certainly there is nothing, or very little, about Swift to make him a modern figure. He sits so solidly amid the prejudices and virtues of his age that we search in vain for any ideas in him that would seem to anticipate us. He was a man of parts rather than of ideas; and his very "rationality" is a kind of eighteenth-century prejudice, having little in common with what we struggle toward as our own, or even what the same century later in France was to discover so triumphantly as its own. He lived before modern political alternatives became very real or meaningful, and only his human hatred of the abuses of power might connect him remotely with some of our own attitudes. As a literary man, he is at the farthest distance from that neurotic specialist, the modern litterateur; he is not even a professional literary man in the sense of his contemporary, Pope, much less in the sense of the consecrated *rentier,* Flaubert. Thus we have no quarrel at all with certain professorial critics who point out that Swift was primarily interested in power and that he came by writing as an instrument of power or simply as a diversion. (What an unhappy conclusion, though, if we thought we had therefore to exclude him from something called "literature"!) And we might even go along a certain way with the generous hint of these critics that the frustration of his desires for power explains both his misanthropy and final insanity.

But does not logic teach us that an induction is strengthened more by a confirming instance further afield? and which at first glance might not seem to fall altogether under the class in question? And if Swift, who sits so solidly in his own age, leads us, when we but plunge deeply enough, into the world of the modern writer, should we not feel all the more assured that we have got at least a little below the surface? Already, beneath the solid outlines of his eighteenth-century figure, I begin to descry the shadows and depths of a *psychic type,* the writer—which has emerged, to be sure, spectacularly only in the two following centuries.

Now the trouble with the professors (and not only when they censure Swift for his craving for power) is that they have unconsciously created a figure of the writer in their own image: a well-bred person with well-tubbed and scrubbed motives, who approaches something specialized and disinterested that they call "literature" as if his function in the end were merely to provide them with books to teach. Perhaps the great writers themselves have unwittingly helped toward this deception? Has any one of them ever told us why he had to become a writer? They tell us instead: "To hold a mirror up to nature"; "To carry a mirror dawdling down a lane"; "To forge the uncreated conscience of my race"; etc., etc.—great blazons of triumph, formulae of their extraordinary achievement, before which we forget even to ask why they had to become writers. The great writer is the victorious suitor who has captured a beautiful bride in an incomparable marriage. There seems almost no point in asking him why he had to love and seek marriage: his reasons seem all too abundant, he has only to point to the incomparable attractions of his beloved. He has lost his private compulsions in the general— in the positive and admirable qualities, known to all men, of the thing achieved. (The Kierkegaardians, by the way, should remind themselves that life must be just such a conquest and appropriation of universals.) But life does not contain only such happy bridegrooms, otherwise we might never know all the enormities and paradoxes of love; and if there were only great geniuses among writers, perhaps we might never know this other truth: the compulsions and paradoxes on the dark side of their calling—which they, the great ones, could afford to forget in the daylight blaze of their triumph.

The mistake is not to have invoked the idea of power but, once invoked, not to have seen it through: we have but to pursue it far enough and we can find it present everywhere in Swift's writings, and indeed the central impulse of his prose itself (perhaps the best in English). What is that stripped and supple syntax but the design of greatest possible economy and force, by which he launches each sentence at its mark like a potent and well-aimed missile? (And each missile thuds against the bestial human face from which he would escape.) Swift's lack of interest in being a literary man as such may account, then, for some of his strongest qualities. The conception of literature as an instrument or a diversion or even a vanity may exist along with the power to produce the greatest literature: Pascal's conviction of the vanity of eloquence is one reason why he is a greater prose-writer than Valery, the aesthete, who mocks at this conviction. Here it seems almost as if from examining Swift's writings themselves we might arrive at Freud's perception: that the writer is more than commonly obsessed by a desire for power which he seeks to gratify through his public fantasies.

Because of an introverted disposition, he is unable to gratify this desire in the usual arenas of external action. Introversion is the brand of his calling: he is the divided man, his consciousness always present but a little absent, hovering over itself, ready to pounce and bring back some fragment to his notebooks. The introverted disposition suggests some excessive and compelling need to be loved; and we would suspect that here too it must result primally from some special strength or strain in the Oedipal relation. But whatever our speculation as to its source, the point of power remains clear; and if he seeks it by a detour, the writer's claims are nonetheless total: it is power of the most subtle kind that the writer wants, power over the mind and freedom of other human beings, his readers.

Such extraordinary claims of power, and particularly their indirectness of gratification, suggest immediately an ambivalent connection with that more than usually acute sense of guilt with which writers as a class seem to be endowed. (That Swift suffered from extraordinary obsessions of guilt toward the end of his life, we know by accounts of several sources; but most of his life, since he accepted Christianity without question, these guilt feelings were tapped and drained off into religion; hence it is that in his writing we usually encounter the aggressive and outgoing parts of his personality.) Georges Blin in "The Gash" (PARTISAN REVIEW, Spring 1946), has presented very eloquently some of the sadistic motives that operate in the artist. We should expect—in accordance with the usual ambivalence—a masochistic pattern to be equally operative, and perhaps even more to the fore because of the essential indirectness of the artist's drives toward power and sadism. What else explains the writer's extraordinary eagerness for the painful humility of his yoke as he crouches over his desk stubbornly weaving and reweaving his own being hundreds of times? "Thought, study, sacrifice, and mortification"—how he trembles with joy to put on these hairshirts of his solitude and calling! These punishments he inflicts upon himself over his desk will help to make clear then why writing should satisfy the claims of guilt upon him; why he should search so passionately for redemption upon the written page, and why as the paragraph takes shape beneath his pen he can feel for moments that his step has become a little less heavy on the face of the earth. But we should also know this ambivalence of power and guilt from phenomenological scrutiny. We never live in a purely private world, our consciousness is penetrated at every point by the consciousness of others, and what is it but one step from seeking redemption in one's own eyes to seeking it in the eyes of others? The movement by which we stoop to lift ourselves out of the pit of self-contempt is one and unbroken with that thrust which would carry us above the shoulders of our fellowmen.

And is not this ambivalent urge to power-guilt but the sign of that excessive need to be loved which has driven the writer into a profession where he must speak with *his own* voice, offer to the public gaze of the world so much of his own existence? Love to be conquered by force, or taken as a gift of tenderness and pity for his confession.

But both the satisfaction (of power) and relief (from guilt), though they glow brightly, glow, alas, only for moments, and we live again in the shadow of ourselves. Nothing in the world (we are told) is a substitute for anything else, and if there is a point beyond which the writer can never satisfy these urges in literature itself, then this inability can no longer be regarded as peculiar to Swift, a deficiency of his "case," but an essential and mortifying aspect of the literary condition everywhere. So we come back to our point: Swift is certainly not a modern literary man, but we only had to go deep enough, and we have arrived at a world of impulses and motives that we recognize as our own.

3. The Moderns. Aytré's Journey.

Despite the ancient recognition, the modern world of the crack-up and breakdown has really become a new and almost discontinuous phenomenon. (First the continuity; now we must do justice to the other aspect, the discontinuity of the modern.) It is time we had an exhaustive and statistical study of the problem, done with the grubbing thoroughness of a Ph.D. thesis; for the present I would only suggest some of the main statistical categories: the madmen, those who broke, Swift, Cowper, William Collins, Christopher Smart, Hoelderlin, Ruskin; figures who were not altogether normal, if not altogether mad, like Blake; who, like Coleridge and DeQuincey, had to salvage themselves through drugs (the Romantic equivalent of the American Pattern); or who produce their writing out of a maximum anxiety, their personal rack of torture, like Baudelaire and Eliot; and from these on we could ramify off into all the various subtler neuroses that have afflicted literary men. Even from this sketchy suggestion of a list it begins to appear that the incidence of aberration, neurosis, or outright madness is such that one really begins to doubt whether these misfortunes are accidental to the profession of letters as such.*

---

* The reader should compare, for a somewhat different view of the matter, Mr. Lionel Trilling's "Art and Neurosis" (Partisan Review, Winter 1945). By indicating my disagreements with Mr. Trilling's admirable essay, perhaps I may sum up, in more scientific terms, the psychoanalytic view which lies at the base (perhaps a little hidden) of my own discussion.

Mr. Trilling's main point, perhaps, is that neurosis by itself will not make anyone a great writer; a proposition with which I am in complete agreement.

I would also agree with him that there are many neurotics among business-men and scientists (though I doubt the scientists could match the incidence

And at this point perhaps we ought to face openly the question whether there is not some original flaw—original sin, if you will—about the profession such that the writer's struggle to live it out completely must inevitably involve him in some kind of hubris; and whether, after all, the game is really worth the candle. Freud at one earlier point did suggest something like this: that art is a survival in our day of primitive magic, with some of the magical still hanging about its aspirations; which did not at all prevent him, we may notice, from deriving very deep pleasure and insight from great works of literature.

The fault, the accumulating difficulty, seem to come from the very advance itself of Western culture and history. In a story by Jean Paulhan, "*Aytré qui perd l'habitude*" (Aytré Loses the Knack"), the hero keeps a journal while leading a trek across Madagascar. En route across the country the entries in the journal are very simple and direct: we arrive, leave, chickens cost seven sous, we lay in a provision of medicines, etc. But with the arrival in the city of Ambositra the journal suddenly becomes complicated: discussions of ideas, women's headdresses, strange scenes and characters in the street. The most

---

among literary men). But granting such widespread latent neuroticism (the wives of businessmen could tell us a lot, if they chose), the point would be that with the writer it is not latent but consciously exploited. My difference with Mr. Trilling is that I do not consider the question as primarily statistical: whether a certain group known as scientists contains as many neurotics as another group called writers. My main point, rather, is one about the *literary process* itself: that this process does, in a certain way, imitate the neurotic process and does exploit neurotic material.

Here it is pertinent to indicate my principal disagreement with Freud, who analyzes the effect of a literary work in terms of the pleasure obtained from fantasies and daydreams. This may do justice to our childish delight in romances —or to the level at which we read *Gulliver's Travels* in childhood. But it hardly does justice to the power which the fiction of Kafka, Joyce, or Proust has over us in our adult years. I hold instead that it is the writer's *identification* with his fantasy, rather than the aspect of fantasy itself, which has power over us, convinces us. (The phenomenon of identification, by the way, is very sparingly discussed by Freud, probably because the psychic transaction involved in it is still quite obscure.) And in this identification with fantasy the writer imitates, *up to a certain point,* one of the deepest and commonest phenomena of pathology.

Since Freud speaks of the cathexis (i.e., charge of psychic energy) which the child has toward the objects of play, he should have seen that the cathexis of the writer toward the objects of fantasy is more significant than the aspect of fantasy itself. We cited Kafka as a crucial case; equally crucial would be the case of Joyce, who rarely moves us through the elaborateness, surprise, or ingenuity of his fantasies, but by *the powerful charge he is able to lay on the most banal episode.*

The second element in my analytic view is, admittedly, more speculative, and concerns the *psychic type* which now seems to emerge with the modern writer. If we demand of the writer a deeper authenticity—identification with

ordinary incidents of daily life become complicated and almost unex-
pressible to Aytré struggling to keep his journal. Paulhan is after other
game in this tale, where we need not follow him; enough for us that
we can take this journey of Aytré for a symbol of the march of
writers in history as they progress toward subjects ever more complex,
driven by the compulsion to "make it new." From this point of view
Paulhan's title itself becomes something of a misnomer: Aytré's
trouble is not that he has lost the knack—quite the contrary, he now
has altogether too much of it. Become infinitely complicated, all-
absorbing, possessive, now the knack *has him*. Aytré, in short, has
become a modern writer. He had begun as the simple scribe of the
clan.

"Make it new," Pound cried, and Eliot further explicated:
Modern poetry must be complicated because modern life is complicated. Both have passed into famous slogans in defense of modernism;
but both abbreviate what is a much more complicated process, and
have to be expanded in the light or darkness of Aytré's painful jour-

---

fantasy—then I think we must expect that more and more only a certain
psychic type will be at once capable of this, and also driven to embrace it as
his own painful profession. We have suggested (speculatively) that the individual
who is driven to exhibit such large slices of his psyche to the world is compelled
by an excessive need for the winning of love. Whether or not this hypothesis be
verified by literary and biographical evidence, it should not surprise us, at any
rate, that the modern writer (capable of satisfying our severe demands) has
become, by and large, a neurotic type.

The third element of my view, however, attempts to separate the neurosis
of the writer from that of other men. The writer's neurosis, through displacement
and appropriation, attempts to square itself with reality—but only in the work.

Here I reach some agreement with Mr. Trilling—but not completely or fundamentally. When he speaks of the writer's ability to "shape" the neurotic
material, he seems to suggest that this latter may be some kind of clay external
to the writer, and that there is some portion of the mind which remains completely outside the neurosis. This notion of control seems also to imply that the
writer attains, through the work, health and wholeness in his life too.

This strikes me as quite unguarded from an analytic point of view. The great
counterexample that comes immediately to mind is one from painting: the case
of Van Gogh (recently discussed by Mr. Meyer Shapiro), who, a few days after
painting "Crows in the Wheatfield" and writing to his brother that the country
was "healthful and strengthening," committed suicide! The triumph of the ego,
in short, is in the work and not the life. It is, as I have said, an "as if" triumph.
Swift did not heal himself by writing *Gulliver's Travels*.

The source of the catharsis, by the way, that Van Gogh obtained from that
particular painting has to be analyzed in terms of this essay: the momentary
triumph of the ego is that it has now appropriated elements from reality corresponding to its own torments, and depicted a scene to which these torments
seem an adequate response, and so has the illusion that its own reality principle
has been restored and safeguarded.

ney. The writer objectifies his fantasies (that much of Freudian formula we have to use in any case) but he must return to view them with the analytic eyes of daylight and criticism. But this reality to which he submits is not what he meets if he gazes out into the world with the naked eyes of the first-born man; the reality principle for the writer is one qualified by the works, the recorded experience and knowledge of man, already in existence. After Proust no one can write about love with the old charming simplicity of Prevost. It would be pastiche: archaic and unauthentic. In Prevost it charms us, it is real and convincing. At his cutural moment, love—as the simple lovely disease of sensibility—was itself an extraordinary *donnée,* and the writer could find such release in it that he was capable of the necessary identification with his fantasy. (Even when a form like the novel swings back momentarily into a simpler pattern, the new simplicity is quite different from the old; the simplicity of Gide is not the old simplicity of the classical French novel, but a new one—self-conscious, difficult, refined, defining its slender line from the sum of its rejections.) Hence it appears that Pound's manifesto, and Eliot's recommendation of a complication to parallel the complication of modern life, formulate effect rather than cause; we ought instead to put it that the writer, existing in his time, in his place, and with his past must make such discoveries as to secure the completeness of release necessary to achieve authenticity. If he repeats what is already discovered, he has no chance of making it *his.* That is why his existence is relentlessly historical and he has to travel Aytré's journey. Now the reality principle functions in life chiefly (or its function is felt more forcibly there) to inhibit the gratification of desire. Its literary analogue functions in the same way: it checks the writer from releasing himself into the fantasies that are unreal, trivial, or superficial. To find his authenticity, a material into which he is completely released, the writer has now to dig ever deeper, the unconscious that is released must be at deeper and deeper levels. So he finds, like Aytré, the literary "knack" become absorbing and terrifying. Hence the burden of neurosis that weighs more and more heavily upon the modern man of letters.

4. *Increasing Burdens.*

The more gifted the writer the more likely he is to be critically conscious of his literary tradition—the more conscious, that is, of the reality principle as it operates in the literary sphere—and the harder it becomes for him to fall into one of the easy publicist styles of his day. Recently I read about a young writer who had written a bestseller in four weeks and made $400,000 out of it—$100,000 a week, almost as good pay as a movie star. If books could be written from the top of one's mind merely (even books of this kind), it is naïve to think a major writer would not do it: after four weeks of absence he returns to support himself for many years in the prosecution of his own unremunerative and serious tasks. But it seems impossible to write a best-seller in complete parody, one has to believe in one's material even there, and it is impossible to fake unless one is a fake. Joyce has written in *Ulysses* a superb parody of the sentimental romance for schoolgirls, but it is quite obvious from that chapter that Joyce could not have turned out a novel in this genre for money: his irony and self-consciousness would have got in the way, and the book would not have attracted its readers but in the end only Joyce's readers. The writer writes what he can, and if he decides to sell out it is by corrupting and cheapening his own level, or perhaps slipping down a step below it; but writing is not so uncommitted an intellectual effort that he can drop down facilely to a very much lower level and operate with enough skill there to convince that kind of reader. Joyce did not write *Finnegans Wake* out of a free decision taken in the void, but because his experience of life and Western culture was what it was, and he had to write that book if he was to write anything.

It is perhaps not a very pleasant thought, but it seems inescapable, that even the commonest best-seller is the product of the personal being of the author and demands its own kind of authenticity. Life also imprisons us in its rewards; and we may draw some satisfaction from the thought that these gay reapers of prestige and money, if they are to keep on terms with their audience, can have in the end only lives adequate to their books: *On écrit le livre qu'on merite.* Our satisfaction might be greater if we were not on the other hand also painfully acquainted with the opposite phenomenon: the gifted people who find it difficult to produce precisely because they are too intelligent and sensitive to tailor their writing to the reigning market. The very awareness of standards inhibits them from writing, and, not being geniuses, they are unable to break through and produce anything adequate to those standards. The literary future in America, and perhaps the West generally, seems to be leading to this final and lamentable split: on the one hand, an enormous body of run-of-the-mill writing (machine-made, as it were), becoming ever more slick as it becomes more technically adequate through abundant competition and appropriation of the tricks of previous serious writing, and in the end generating its own types of pseudo authenticity, like Steinbeck or Marquand; on the other hand, an occasional genius breaking through this wall here and there, at ever more costly price in personal conflict, anguish, and difficulty. Modern poetry already provides us its own and extreme version of this exacerbating split; think of the extremity of personal difficulty required to produce the authentic poetry of our time: the depth of anguish which secreted the few poems of Eliot; and Yeats, we remember, had to struggle through a long life of political unrest, personal heartbreak, see the friends and poets of his youth die off or kill themselves, before he came into his own and could produce poems capable of convincing us that this poetry was not merely a kind of "solemn game."

Some of the more internal difficulties that beset the pursuit of literature are being very much discussed in France by writers like Maurice Blanchot and Brice Parain. Blanchot finishes one essay, in which he has explored certain aspects of anxiety, silence, and expression, with the devastating remark, "It is enough that literature should continue to seem possible," though the reader by the time he has waded through Blanchot's rarefactions to that point may very well have lost the conviction that even the possibility remained. These French researches are of a quite special character, continuing the tradition of Mallarmé—or, rather, attempting to see the aesthetic problems of Mallarmé from the human anguish of Pascal. (As the burdens of civilization become heavier and we see existence itself with fewer illusions, we have come perhaps to share Pascal's attitude toward poetry: a vanity, a "solemn game"; at any rate, we seem to demand more of the modern writer before we take him very seriously.) These difficulties are extreme and we need not share them in that form: after the rigors to which Mallarmé submitted poetry in his search for a *"langage authentique"* no wonder silence should appear as the only and haunting possibility of speech. After Mallarmé, poetry had to swing back toward the language of what he calls *"universel reportage,"* and Eliot's poetry has shown us that this language, suitably charged and concentrated, can be the vehicle of very great poetry. Blanchot's difficulties persist but in another form (especially in a commercial culture). Not silence but garrulousness ("unauthentic chatter," as Heidegger would say) may be the threat confronting the writer; but always and everywhere the difficulty of securing authenticity.

The difficulties we face in America—a society which turns, as Van Wyck Brooks says, its most gifted men into crackpots—are obviously of a much more external and violent kind than in France.

External pressures abet the internal tensions, which become unendurable, and at long last comes that slide over into the more tranquil and private self-indulgence of fantasy with a consequent weakening of the reality principle. One (a critic) develops a private language; another spins out elaborate literary theories without content or relevance; a third has maintained his literary alertness and eye for relevance through a sheer aggressiveness which has cost him his ability to maintain personal relations—and which appears therefore in his work as a mutilation too. Scott Fitzgerald's confidante in "The Crack-up" (perhaps his most mature piece of writing, at that) gives him the extraordinary advice: *"Listen. Suppose this wasn't a crack in you—suppose it was in the Grand Canyon. . . . By God, if I ever cracked, I'd try to make the whole world crack with me."* And she was right and profound, but Fitzgerald was tied by too many strings to the values of American life to see her truth. His crack-up was the dawning of a truth upon him which he could not completely grasp or recognize intellectually. Swift in that position would have seen that the crack is in the Grand Canyon, in the whole world, in the total human face about him. If he is powerful enough—now against greater odds—to make the world crack in his work, the writer has at the least the gratification of revenge, and the ego that deeper conquest (described above) where its anguish now seems no more than an appropriate response to a world portrayed (and with some fidelity) as cracked. But, alas, these energies which seek reality and are capable of transforming the neurotic mass into the writer's special and unique vision of the world can also be blocked by the external difficulties in the literary situation. And when that happens we open the door, as Freud says, to the psychoses—at any rate, to the breakdown and crack-up.

5.   *Abi Viator*
               *Et Imitare Si Poteris**

And so I am brought back into the center of my theme. If I appeared to have abandoned the theme of neurosis for the difficulties, external and internal, that confront the modern writer, it was only because these difficulties as part of his alienation are the aggravating causes and public face of his madness.

But why (in the end) should it be the writer's fate—more than of any other intellectual profession—to confront this crack in the face of the world? Because his subject is the very world of experience as

---

* From Swift's epitaph: "Go, traveler, and imitate him if you can."

such, and it is this world, this total world, which he must somehow salvage. The scientist has his appointed place in the community of researchers, he confronts carefully delimited fragments of experience, the data from which he proceeds are publicly recognizable, and his whole being is to be, as it were, an incarnate outward public mind. But the writer is alone—potentially twenty-four hours a day, the luminol pill and the writing pad beside his bed for whatever welcome or unwelcome presence comes that night. On the other hand, it might seem that the philosopher, since he confronts in his own way the totality of experience might also show some fatal tendency toward aberration. But the philosopher deals with concepts and out of these he may construct some kind of "meaning" for the world: when speculative systems were still believed, he had only to be agile enough to design one of these towering arks of salvation, and what if it leaked a little, he was a professor and he had something to do the rest of his professorial life plugging its gaps; now when the pretense to speculative theories is no longer even taken seriously the philosopher can construct an equally elaborate theory showing that the question itself has no meaning, and so philosophy continues to be possible. Whatever the impasse of insoluble antinomies at which his thought finally arrives, he can continue to arrange these in neat parallel columns, chip away at their edges and perpetually recast their statement as if preparing bit by bit for a solution which in fact never arrives; and so continues in business, he has something to say, he "gets published"; and after the initial shocks and disturbance mankind has shown itself capable of settling down peacefully into positivism, and few people are more intellectually adjusted than the positivists. But it is not at the level of concepts that the appalling face of the world is seen, and it is another kind of "meaning" that the writer must construct. Out of the ravages of his experience, his desperate loneliness, he must put forth those works which look back into his gaze with conviction and authenticity and wear about them the gleams of interest—cathectic charges, in the technical term—which have fled from the vast bare blank face of the world as seen in the extreme situations of *his* truth: in sleeplessness, the nervous darkness, against death and against the inexorable and dragging vista of time which is his being.

English Literature and the Revolution
Douglas Goldring

from

Coterie, 3, 1919.

ENGLISH LITERATURE AND THE REVOLUTION

ANY one who picks up one of the weeklies, provided he knows something of literary London, can visualise the cliques and sets, the personal animosities, the log-rolling and the snobbishness which underlie their smooth-flowing columns of praise or blame. A writer who does not lunch with other writers, who has no friends among the literary "best people," who is not published by some smart publisher clever enough to exhale an aroma of "Oxford," will not as a rule receive much attention from the "leading organs of critical thought." The London papers whose reviewing ignores social or commercial influences can be counted on the fingers of one hand.

Now it is the function of criticism to act both as a tonic and as a corrective. When criticism decays and loses vigour the arts at once fall into an unhealthy state. The progressive decay of criticism in England during the past half-century has now brought English literature to such a pass that only the most violent remedies can cure it of its many diseases. During the past fifty years writers with original or "revolutionary" ideas have found it increasingly difficult to get a hearing during their lives. Publishers have declined their MSS. as being unsafe, and in cases where the publisher's vigilance has been eluded, the reviewers have either received the dangerous works in silence or have violently denounced them. Mr. Bernard Shaw, realising all this clearly enough, has managed, it is true, by sheer force of character, to make himself the exception which proves the rule. No doubt a knowledge of what Samuel Butler had to put up with showed him at an early stage in his career what precisely he was "up against." But though Mr. Shaw has triumphed over the shoddy crowd of literary parasites who guard the pass to public recognition, he has not done so without making enemies. These people are like a certain kind of toad. If you step on them they squirt a poisonous liquid at you. Readers of a certain notorious review of Mr. Shaw's *Heartbreak House* will realise what it is that he has been able to tread on and to overcome.

Mr. Shaw's success in this direction is, so far as I can discover, unique. For the most part, authors have not his cheerful combative instinct, his capacity to lay about him with freedom and good-humour. Thus it is that the devices which have been, and are, adopted by English writers, small and great, to enable them to squeeze past the barrier into the charmed circle of literary fashion are often so pathetic. The employment of these devices very often causes an agony so excruciating that, although confessions of all kinds have lately had an unprecedented vogue, no man of letters has to my knowledge dared to lay his soul bare in regard to the things he has done to ". get through."

To the commercial author the problem is, of course, merely a business problem like another. The man born for success will have begun his career by making friends with the best people at school and university. These friends, when he makes his descent on London, will stand him in good stead. If he writes verses they will soon log-roll a literary prize for him. If he begins by reviewing other men's work, the usual process, he will be sure to find some man of an older year already installed in the office of a comfortable review, who will make the way easy. And then, when his first novel is ready, his social *savoir-faire* will have smoothed the path for its reception. The wife of his future publisher will have gone down to dinner with him, and found him "such an interesting boy." Perhaps he will have floated about London a little with one of those girls whose veneer of culture—added to good looks and an inherited position—enables them preposterously enough to make or mar a reputation. Thus even his amours will push him along the road to fame and fortune!

There are, of course, many other routes open to the commercial author who is determined to arrive. They could be described in detail, but the psychological interest attaching to them is very small, because the commercial author feels no uneasy shrinking from those methods of achieving his aim which present themselves to his intelligence. The commercial poet does not feel uneasy if, for example, he combines with half-a-dozen other poets in an offensive and defensive alliance formed for mutual "boosting." The commercial novelist does not shudder at the necessity of giving evening parties with a purpose, or strategic luncheons. It is only when we consider the authors whose motive is ambition to succeed in their art and to achieve the admiration of those who can appreciate, the authors with whom that powerful vanity which has given the world half its loveliest things is the real stimulus to production, that the psychological interest begins. And among these, what miseries have been endured in the struggle for recognition, what foolish, pathetic, and even base things have been done to attain it! Very often these unfortunates ape the methods of their brass-bound commercial competitors with tragic inefficiency. They blow ear-splitting blasts on the trumpet, when the situation requires delicate and flute-like modulations ; they cringe when they should prance, toady when they should contemn. And always the unsatisfied vanity, more violent in its operations than the unsatisfied appetite of sex, forces them relentlessly forward. It has pushed them, before now, to suicide as a last resource.

This, roughly, is the position of English writers to-day : to the creative effort required to produce a work of art must be added the finesse of a social struggler and the bland assurance of a bagman, or else either the MS. will not be printed at all, or if printed and published will be smothered in unbroken silence. The root of the evil is deep-seated in our social life ; it is one more of those symptoms of national corruption and spiritual deadness which are the preludes to upheaval.

Now a revolution is a setting free of forces which have been violently constrained. The intellectual energies of England, so far as her younger writers are concerned, are to-day bottled up. The natural outlets are closed and barred. The written word must go through a watering down, trimming and softening process before it can hope to squeeze through the needle's eye of a publisher's office and reach the open. The social and commercial censorship exercised by English snobbery, and made possible by the decay of English criticism, is in its effects far more deadening than that naïf censorship which absurd and rather lovable officials exercised during the war. And so in England to-day the artist's way to freedom lies through that drastic change in our social life which it is convenient to refer to as the Revolution. That this is no idle fancy but a statement of fact must be realised by all those who have any appreciation of the change which has come over the continent of Europe during the past two years.

Those who have visited Soviet Russia, those who saw something of Hungary under the revolutionary government, even those who have visited Germany during the past few months, will know to what I am referring. The effect of revolution on the creative capacity of a people is like a renewal of youth ; like a change from winter to spring. The windows of the stuffy room are thrown open, the unhealthy stove extinguished. Sunlight pours in and fresh air, and in all the world there is an uttering of joyous leaves. Germany has not yet achieved her revolution politically, but in the domain of thought it is already accomplished. It was my good fortune to spend some weeks in Germany in the month of September, and the difference of intellectual atmosphere which I found between Berlin and London defies description. In Berlin all was energy and activity. " Sorrow brings forth," says Blake in one of his aphorisms, and it seemed that the sufferings of the German people had indeed rejuvenated their creative instinct. The interest in ideas was universal, and everywhere ideas were finding no hindrance—other than a negligible political censorship—to their expression. Every line of thought which presented itself to the human intelligence could be followed up without fear, and the results of these intellectual explorations published for the examination of other travellers. In Germany to-day, the intellect has been set free, the imagination of the artist liberated from bondage. And in London? Stagnation, intrigue, snobbery, log-rolling, deadness! Our ideas, like the air in our House of Commons, are subject to a process of warming, drying, softening and "disinfecting" before they are allowed to filter through to the public. In England the *bourgeoisie* is still established in control, and—until the New Day dawns—the man of letters must either starve or adapt himself to its standards and do obeisance before the shrines of its false gods.

The Artist in the Community
Charles Morgan

from

The Yale Review, vol. 35, no. 4, 1946.

THE ARTIST IN THE COMMUNITY

By CHARLES MORGAN

IN this essay I propose to discuss what I believe to be the next great problem which modern civilization has to face and solve: the problem of how to preserve liberty of thought from the attack of fanatical dogmatism, of how to strengthen the community of freedom against the authoritarian encroachments which now threaten it: in brief, of how to make sure that we and our children live and think and die as men and women, possessing our own minds and souls, and not as a censored and driven regiment with no virtue but obedience.

Next, I shall ask what place an artist has in a free community: what is his duty towards it and what its duty towards him? I shall suggest that the relationship between the artist and the community is, in one aspect, enduring, in that it arises from the nature of art and the nature of society itself; and, in another aspect, constantly changing, in that it arises from changes in artistic practice and in the forms which society assumes in different epochs.

Finally, regarding this relationship between the artist and the community as, in part, constant, and, in part, variable, I shall inquire what the true relationship is now and is likely to become, and shall submit a concluding proposition: that by preserving this true relationship we may help to safeguard the liberty of thought and the community of freedom itself, for an artist is neither the community's priest nor the community's slave, but a member of it who holds in his especial charge certain qualities essential to its spiritual life. He is, as it were, the breath of the people's imagination without which they perish; and the people must learn, in each new phase of history, how to adjust themselves to art, how to receive it, how to make of it an ally with religion and science in every man's quest of truth; how, in each new climate, to breathe freely and deeply; for, if they do not, the authoritarians will stifle them, and the spirit of man, though it cannot die, be cast down, for long centuries, into obscurity and submission. Mrs. Charles Kingsley, in her life of her husband, spoke a little strangely, as it may now seem to us, of her husband's "sympathy with Art, and deeper matters." We may smile at her phrase but at the same time honor her sense of art's relationship to all that she most valued in life. We, in our turn, are called upon to re-gather our strength from Athens and the Renaissance that, after the terrible retrogression which our lives have witnessed, we may prepare a way for what our children or our grandchildren, if they survive, may dare to call the Re-enlightenment.

I will, then, attempt, first of all, to state the problem as I see it. When, in the distant future, historians sit down to write, what title will they give to the chapter which describes the second half of the twentieth century? What is life going to be about?

There are many who say that what lies before us is predominantly an economic struggle, and a few others that our central problem will be of foreign policy. Both views are reasonable, but they are evidently interdependent, and there is danger in insisting on either of them to the exclusion of the other. What is possible economically depends not upon abstract theory, Marxian or other, but upon what our international relationships make possible; and we forget at our peril that foreign policy is the condition and sanction of home policy, and that security against foreign enemies is a first charge on social security and economic advance.

Among the principal subjects with which any historian of our times will have to deal is our attempt to relate foreign policy to economic policy and our ability to persuade ourselves, and to persuade others, to accept, for the sake of gradually establishing an international law, certain limitations upon national sovereignty. That this is the direction in which peace-loving and unfanatical men will try to move the world is scarcely open to doubt. But will they be prevented by impatient and bloody extremists? This, I believe, is the question underlying all the questions of our time. Our differences of economic theory and foreign policy cannot be resolved, can scarcely be profitably discussed, until we have answered within us the personal question: do I speak and think as a free man or as an authoritarian? Do I wish to live in a free community with men who differ from me in theory and faith, seeking with them— and with other nations—a reconciliation of practice, or am I determined to extirpate, in pursuit of what I believe to be right, whatever faith and theory differs from my own?

Some may feel that this presentation of the alternative is too abrupt. British men and women of my own generation and of a generation older than mine may think so, for we were brought up in an atmosphere and habit of liberty, but the alternative, I am sure, will not be considered too abrupt in France, where the tyrannies and ideologies have stalked into men's homes, or in Poland or Italy or Spain; nor, I believe, does the alternative, bitter though it is, seem unreal to Scotsmen and Englishmen of a generation younger than my own. It is to the young I dare to speak, for it is their life, not mine, that will carry the remaining burden of this century, and the Re-enlightenment, if it comes, will be their children's, and perhaps their own reward.

It was a very young man who first confronted me with this alternative. He was a fighter pilot, shot down and terribly burned in the Battle of Britain. When he had recovered from his wounds, and the plastic surgeons had rebuilt his face, and he was struggling for that permission to fly again which being granted, led to his death, he came to dine at my house in London. Through all the bombardments, I had tried to preserve one amenity there; we dined by candlelight and an open fire; and I remember that, after dinner, we went upstairs, I with the decanter and he with the candelabra. I remember it because it was in the upstairs room, just after we had entered it, that he, standing in mid-floor with a candelabrum in each hand, said: "Nowadays, wherever I go, I ask myself that question about everybody. At dinner, I was asking it about you." For the moment I had lost his drift. He was carrying on our dinner-table conversation, and I meanwhile had been thinking of other things. "What question?" I asked. He put down the candelabra and told me, and we talked of it half the night.

His point was this. He felt that everyone in the modern world—everyone, soldier, priest, scholar, tradesman, or housemaid—was potentially, whether he knew it or not, either a Communist or a Nazi. "Potentially," he insisted. "As yet, I'm neither myself. But I know which way I'd go if I had to choose. And that's the question I ask myself about other people: which way would they go if they had to choose? Which way *will* they go *when* they have to choose? Which side are they on?"

I said: "Are they necessarily on either side?"

He answered: "Yes, I think they are, inside themselves. I think they must be. The world being what it is, a man can't remain an indifferentist."

That was the word I challenged. It seemed to me false to suggest that the whole area of opinion lying between the two opposed totalitarian polities was indifferent, neutral, colorless, waiting only to drift helplessly into one or other of the warring armies.

He said: "That at any rate is the impression that both sides try to give. To a great extent, they are succeeding. They are planting the idea that not to be in one camp or the other is a form of uncourageous compromise, and that the whole idea of freedom as a positive force is dead."

This was the discussion that held us into the night. He assumed that the battle to destroy the community of freedom was over or almost over, and that soon there would be no choice open except between one form of authoritarianism and another. Many in Europe feel as he did. The choice has been thrust upon them. I still believe that, in the long view of history, he and they will be seen to have been wrong. I think that it is in the destiny of the English-speaking peoples and, ultimately, after many vicissitudes, of a recovered France, to prove them wrong. But the other alternative remains. The question may not yet be: "To which authoritarianism shall we submit?" Not yet: "To which slave-master shall we surrender ourselves?" But already and urgently the question is: "Shall we be bond or free?"

What the fighter pilot said that night was a young man's evidence that the pressure of authoritarianism was heavy upon him. It is to be felt everywhere in the modern world, in the way in which religion is discussed, in the criticism of art on a basis of politics, in the penetration of common speech by ideological jargon, in the reluctance of so many men and women to defend their own opinion against the attack of extremists. It is to be felt, too, in the tendency, from which few of us are exempt, to be swayed by passing enthusiasms and passing indignations, to reverse our judgment of great issues and even of great nations in accordance with the swaying fortunes of a battle or the flow of some popular emotion, to be carried forward by slogans and headlines rather than by the reasoned development and application of principle. There was alarming evidence of this tendency in our attitude towards the confusion which arose in Athens when the Germans had gone out. I happen to believe that our government was right to intervene, but I will not now discuss the merits of that dispute. What was remarkable about it, and relevant to our present subject, was that, when the trouble began, a great part of British opinion, instead of suspending judgment and waiting to ascertain the facts, instead of trying to discover patiently where the true interest of freedom lay, aligned itself hastily on the Left or on the Right, and began to think and talk and write for or against one or other of the authoritarian ideologies. It was as if the minds of the British people had already begun to stiffen, to congeal into two clots of opinion, as if we had begun to lose our independence of judgment, our resilience of imagination, our power to refer each new problem, not to some rigid rule, but to our own consciences, our own sense of compassionate justice. It is the radical principle and the invariable practice of all authoritarian systems to freeze imagination, to prevent men and women from thinking for themselves. It is the radical principle of art to unfreeze the imagination and to enable men and women to think for themselves.

The problem of the future, as I understand it, now lies before us. Let us next consider what part an artist may play, and what part the community may enable him to play, in the solution of it.

What I am now seeking to discover is whether there are any elements in the nature of art and in the nature of society which may be said to establish an enduring undercurrent of relationship between them. If these elements exist, if they are enduring like the tides, they will be a condition of the relationship between art and society in a particular epoch.

Now, if anything in the doubtful history of our race is certain it is that before society existed there were men, and that before schools or coteries or classifications existed there was art. Indeed the first artist was presumably subjective. He made his work of art, his song or the picture he drew on the wall of his cave, in order to express his sense of happiness or fear, or *his* sense of the form of the natural object he depicted. In other words, his art sprang from within him; it was not at first designed to produce an effect upon others. But one day, as he was drawing on the wall to please no one but himself, his wife said: "My dear, that is not at all my idea of a mammoth. A mammoth, surely, has a longer tail," and so the relationship of art to society was begun. All our aesthetic troubles, and perhaps all our matrimonial troubles, began in that moment, for the first artist, we may be sure, was both flattered and annoyed —flattered because he really had been drawing a mammoth and his wife had recognized it; annoyed because there was, after all, great variety in mammoths and wide scope for the interpretation of them in their relationship to rocks or mountains—it all depended on what *impression* they made upon you —and the first artist thought it unreasonable that his wife should concentrate on the length of the animal's tail. So he said: "It isn't a mammoth; it's what I feel about a mammoth" —half a lie, half a truth; and she said: "Well, anyhow, it isn't what I feel about a mammoth. Let us ask Belinda."

Belinda was their child, and when Belinda saw the picture she thought it was god; she fell down on her face and began to make propitiatory noises; and her father said: "Well, really, this is too much!" and the man within the artist slapped her soundly. But the artist within the man was flattered, and after a little while he began to say: ' Well, after all, whether I intended it or not, the effect was that I drew Belinda's idea of god. Perhaps that is what art *is*."

Here, I think, he was right; he had, at any rate, hit upon one aspect of the truth; he had understood the relationship of his art to Belinda. There was, of course, another aspect of the truth, which no doubt troubled him again as soon as he took up another flint and began to scratch on another wall—namely, the relationship of his art to himself. Was he trying to reproduce a mammoth or, like Cézanne, to re-present it? Was he giving information about a mammoth, about the length of its tail for example, or was he, in his re-presentation of that debatable animal, giving information about himself? Or was he perhaps not giving information at all? Did he really care what his wife or what Belinda thought? There was a part of him, an extremely important part, that cared nothing for the effect of his drawing upon others or indeed for its likeness to a mammoth or a god; a part of him that was neither zoological nor theological nor social, nor even deliberately self-expressive; a part of him, an impulsive essence, the very seed of art, its innermost mystery, which, without rhyme or reason, said to him: "Draw!" so that he drew, not for his own sake or for society's sake or for god's sake or even for art's sake, but because something inside him said: "Draw!"

To this impulse, this absolute of art, many names are given. Some have spoken of it as "art for art's sake"; some as "art to the glory of God"; some as a desire for absolute beauty which, to them, is truth and "a joy forever"; and in giving to the impulse these names they have unwittingly exposed it to the attack and ridicule of men who neither understand the names nor the thing. Let us beware how we attack or ridicule these names because perhaps to us one or other of them may seem limited or pretentious. Of course, they are limited; they are an attempt to express the illimitable. Of course, they sound pretentious; they are an attempt to express the inexpressible. Of course, foolish cults grow up around them, clinging to the approximate name without having experienced the essential thing. But whatever the name, the impulse of art is holy and absolute as the impulse of love is holy and absolute, not to be traced to its origin, not to be accounted for by its effects, such an inward-feeling and outward-shining glory, such a "silence within the heart of a cry," as you may see upon the face of Correggio's Io in the moment of her visitation by the god. I wish to establish this ecstatic impulse, neither self-regarding nor world-regarding, as the essence of the artistic act—as it is the essence of the act of love—because, without its saving presence in our minds, we cannot hope to understand rightly the relationship of an artist to the community. A hint of this relationship was given to the first artist when Belinda threw herself upon her face and began to worship not his mammoth but her own god. Towards his wife he had as an artist failed. All she had said was that the animal's tail was too long. Why had he failed? Because in her he had provoked nothing but a slavish desire to have reproduced for her what she had already seen; she wanted repetition and uniformity which, together, are hell, not imagination and variety which are a way to heaven; she was not provoked to a fresh imagining of anything—not even of a mammoth, much less of a god. But with Belinda he had succeeded because by his work of art she had been carried beyond his work of art; it had, so to speak, broken up the coagulation of her mind as a poker thrust into a sleepy fire breaks up the coagulation of the embers; and a flame had jumped out and burned and dazzled her, and the flame was god. It might not have been god. It might have been anything—if she had been younger a divine doll, if a little older an almost divine lover. At all events, it was hers, not her father's: that is the point. It had grown in her soil, like a flower from a seed. What her mother had wanted was what society so often demands of artists—something ready-made, useful and familiar, something that fulfilled her preconceptions and required of her neither adjustment nor growth nor imaginative effort of any kind, a clearly recognizable mammoth down to the last inch of its tail. But that was because the mind of Belinda's mother had became fixed, frozen, authoritarian, and the art of Belinda's father had failed to break it up. But with Belinda herself he had succeeded, and, when he had recovered from the shock of having his mammoth taken for a god, he said to himself: "I made the girl imagine for herself." And then he added: "That is what art is for. What art *is* is a different matter. I know and feel that inside myself, and Correggio will know and feel it when the time comes for him to paint Io in the moment of her visitation by the god. Meanwhile I know what art is for. It is to enable men to imagine for themselves." And he thought, in saying this, that he had solved the problem of the relationship of the artist to society, and I think he had taken a necessary step towards the solution of it; but he had not solved it because two vital questions remained unanswered and the answers to these differ, or appear to differ, from age to age.

These questions are: "By what means shall an artist enable men to imagine for themselves?" and, secondly: "What shall he enable them to imagine?" To the second question the authoritarian answer is simple: "The people shall not be enabled to imagine freely. They shall be compelled or persuaded or tempted to imagine what is good for them, and what is good for all is good for one and what is good for one is good for all." Sometimes the authoritarians dress up this answer in a more dignified and ancient dress, and say: "The people shall be made to imagine the Truth," and, when authority says that, we are on the way to the fire and the torture chamber, to the death of Socrates, to the scourge and the crown of thorns. Why will men torment one another for the kingdom of this world, which is worthless when they have attained it? Why will they torment one another for the kingdom of God, which is within them? If art has anything to teach it is that these torments are vain, and that to mistake one supposed aspect of truth for Truth itself and so to imprison men's curiosity and aspiration in the dungeon of an ideology, is the unforgivable sin against the spirit of man.

An artist is bound by his vocation to recognize as sin the authoritarian's claim to be a monopolist of truth. For that very reason the word "truth" cannot be excluded from his answers to the two vital questions. When he is asked what he will enable men to imagine, he will answer, in summary: "Aspects of Truth." When he is asked by what means he will do this, he will answer, again in summary: "By communicating my own visions of Truth." You will observe that the word "visions" is in the plural: "visions," not "vision"; you will remember that Thomas Hardy called a volume of his poems "Moments of Vision" and that he was careful to renounce all claim to a monopoly of truth. "I have no philosophy," he wrote, "merely what I have often explained to be a confused heap of impressions, like those of a bewildered child at a conjuring show." And you will not have failed to notice that when that giant among artists, Tolstoy, reached that stage of his life which is called his "conversion"—when, that is to say, he exchanged his many visions of truth for one vision of it and established an ethical system—he became so much the less a practising artist and indeed repudiated art altogether as he had formerly understood it. But Hardy's saying that he had no philosophy is not to be understood to mean that he had no point of view. He stood on a hilltop and from it surveyed experience, and it was his own hilltop; he was not inconsistent in the sense of being without distinct individuality; he was not forever blown hither and thither by the opinions of others, joining leagues and clubs and fashionable groups and peering out at life through their blinkers. He preserved his integrity, guarded his individuality, looked out from his own hilltop. But he did not look only north, or only south, or only east or west. He did not fix upon a favorite view and say: "This is Truth. There is no other." He surveyed the whole landscape of experience with what eyes he had, and said to us: "Look: what do you see with your different eyes?" And we looked, and, though we did not see what he had seen, we saw what we had not seen before and might never have seen but for his visionary flash.

What is it, then, that an artist enables men to see? I think that ideally he enables them, looking out from the point of view of their own individualities, to see their own experience in a light of Truth—in *a* light, not *the* light, for there are many. But the phrase "in a light of Truth" is a vague one except to the man who uses it. I have used it, and cling to it, because it indicates to me something that is essential to my idea of the function of art in a community, but I will try to express in more concrete terms my answer to the question: "What is it that an artist enables men to imagine?"

An understanding of art's effect upon us, of its real value to mature men and women, may be reached by trying to remember what its effect was in childhood. Do you remember, can you still feel, what it was then to fall under the spell of a book? I remember well how, as I read, a circle seemed to be woven round me forbidding my thoughts to wander, so that attention became concentration, and concentration became at first effortless, then involuntary, then necessitous, and at last something more—absorption, self-surrender, a passing into another world. So the spell would fall. But the world into which I entered was never altogether the author's world, though I saw it by his light. My own identity was no more lost than a dreamer's identity is lost during his dream; but it was, as it were, distilled; what moved in the imagined world was not I, with the inhibitions of my self-consciousness, but the essence of I, freed from the knowledge that I was eight years old, or that I had a brother and two sisters, or that my preparation was not done, or that, if I walked round the little wood that bordered the tennis lawn, I should come to the kitchen garden: freed, that is to say, from the relationships of age, of person, of duty, of place, which tied me in my ordinary life: liberated from my social and temporal bonds, and yet liberated in such a way that I did not become, in the transition, anti-social, for I was liberated from my egotistical bonds as well. This was the first part of the spell—liberation, intensification, purification—a penetration of that film of personality to which name and circumstances are attached—a walking clean through the looking-glass.

On the other side of the looking-glass was not, as some pretend, an escape from life, but a new impulse and vitality. On this side of the looking-glass we are bound by an unreal sense of order, of partition, of what is congruous and what incongruous; we think of time as if it were a calendar on the wall, each day to be stripped off in turn, the past, the present, and the future impenetrable by one another; and this is spiritually untrue; all time is simultaneous; my end is in my beginning. On this side of the looking-glass, we are bound always by a sense that each individuality is locked within itself, so that, even between two people who love each other, though there is communication like the tapping on prison walls, there is no fusion, and we struggle continually towards this fusion unattainable in this world, giving many names to our struggle: sometimes the name of personal love, sometimes of friendship, sometimes of congregation in the worship of a god, sometimes of society or community. Under the spell of art this separateness may be transcended. On the other side of the looking-glass the prison walls are down. There is interpenetration of individuality, of time, of place. I well remember that, in childhood, under the spell of a story, I used to feel, without any sense of incongruity, that I myself was present at the siege of Troy though I remained fully aware that the narrative belonged to the past; on my way home with Odysseus, I found Nausicaa playing ball with her maidens on a stretch of seashore where I had bathed yesterday; she had her own face, *and* the face of a beautiful girl whom I knew, *and* a face that was featureless, indescribable, like the face which Michelangelo left unpainted in his unfinished picture, "The Entombment"; she had many beauties, and, as well, an absolute beauty. And I knew, when I read of the Agony in the Garden, that where Jesus kneeled to pray was in a corner of the lawn in front of my own house, just as Giovanni Bellini knew, when he painted the scene, that Jesus kneeled on a little mound in the midst of an Italian landscape; and it seemed not unfitting or untrue that, within two hundred yards of this tennis lawn, was a steep dell or pit into which Joseph was cast by his brethren; nor was it unfitting or untrue.

And this breaking down by art of the compartments of the

mind belongs not only to childhood. I first read Keats's "Eve
of St. Agnes" when I was a young naval officer in the China
Seas. My mind accepted the poet's description of his scene—
the ancient castle, the bloodhound at the gate, the painted glass
of the upper room.

> Full on this casement shone the wintry moon,
> And threw warm gules on Madeline's fair breast,
> As down she knelt for heaven's grace and boon;
> Rose-bloom fell on her hands, together prest,
> And on her silver cross soft amethyst,
> And on her hair a glory, like a saint:
> She seem'd a splendid angel, newly drest
> Save wings, for heaven—

For me then, for me now, full on this casement shines the win-
try moon, and yet, at the same time and with an enhance-
ment, not a dissipation, of the illusion, it shines also into a cabin
of H.M.S. *Monmouth* at sea, in which cabin forever Made-
line sleeps.

That is the spell—not in this room, not in this large company, but in the cabin of the *Monmouth* at sea, that was the
spell which broke down the divisions of time, place, and circumstance, and set the spirit free to go on its voyages. The
greatest tribute that a writer earns from us is not that we keep
our eyes fast upon his page, forgetting all else; but that sometimes without knowing that we have ceased to read, we allow
his book to rest, and look out over and beyond it with newly
opened eyes, discovering all else. Then lies open to earthbound
man the firmament of the spirit; he takes wing and travels in
it, liberated from the chains of partial judgment and from the
blindness of close appearances. Like a bird released from a
cage, he soars, and sees truth in new aspects. And though the
spell of art breaks at last and he returns to earth, it is not to the
cage of his former prejudice that he returns. The spell of art
breaks, the "Eve of St. Agnes" is ended; the young officer finds
himself in the cabin again, feels the throb of engines, listens to
the whirr of an electric fan. It is five minutes to eight bells, and
he goes onto the bridge to keep his middle-watch. But he has

been a liberated spirit, and thereafter, in all life's embittered divisions, in all his faults and follies and self-imprisonments and hardnesses of heart, he never altogether ceases to be aware of the unity of the living with the dead, and in all his temptations to hatred or fear he cannot be without compassion. Art has planted in him a seed from which his own imagination shall spring; has fertilized his earth that of it he may be reborn. An artist does not renew society; he enables men to renew them-selves and so, in the long run, the society in which they live.

In saying this, in suggesting what an artist may enable men to imagine, I have, perhaps, already implied an answer to the other vital question: how does an artist produce this effect? I shall not here elaborate that answer, for I do not wish to plunge into a discussion of technical processes or into a matching of one school with another. I seek a common factor, and this much, I think, is clear; that if the true effect of art is to enable men to re-value their own experience in terms of the absolute values—that is to say, in terms of Compassion, Beauty and Truth—the artist himself must value life in those terms and must be able to communicate his valuation in a way that is not merely a statement of his opinion or even an account of his vision but is fertilizing.

This view of the function of art receives endorsement as soon as we ask ourselves what the difference is between a good book, important in its own age, and an immortal book which has continuing life in generation after generation. When you and I read the "Decameron" of Boccaccio or the sonnets of Shakespeare or Emily Brontë's "Wuthering Heights," our pleasure and excitement are not the same as the pleasure and excitement in which these masterpieces were written. We are different creatures, nurtured in a different age, and what we imagine is not what those dead writers imagined. In brief, their books are alive because their life is renewed in us, because we re-imagine them; and their genius consists in their power to enable us to do so, in their fertilizing power. They are not beautiful flowers pressed in an album; they seed, and, though they die in one generation of men, they bring forth in another. So Keats, who was far removed from Boccaccio and did not see what he saw, was nevertheless inspired by a story of Boccaccio's to write "Isabella, or, the Pot of Basil" and we, reading "Isabella," though we do not see what Keats saw, are impregnated by his vision to bring forth our own.

Now, if we agree that, from the point of view of the community, what is important in an artist is his impregnating power, and that, from the point of view of an artist, what is important in the community is its power to be impregnated and to re-present his vision in an eternal vitality and freshness, does it not follow in the first place that the subject of a work of art, though important, has not, and cannot have, the primary importance that a part of modern criticism, and particularly authoritarian criticism, is inclined to attach to it?

The subject of a story or poem—and I continue to speak in terms of literature, though the same principle may be applied to the other arts—the subject of a story or poem is evidently important because neither story nor poem can exist without a subject; but the subject is not the essence or the immortal, fertilizing quality of the work of art, but a limitation upon it. No one, unless he is a historian in quest of material, now reads Dickens because he wrote about prison reform or Turgenev because he wrote about liberalism in Russia or Victor Hugo because he attacked Napoleon the Third; and no one in the future will read Mr. Wells because he once chose as his subject certain doctrines of the Fabian Society. Or, rather, people may *read* these authors because they are interested now or in the future in subjects related to these subjects, but their own imaginations will not be fertilized by the subject—for then any pamphlet would serve as well—but by the excitement with which the author wrote about the subject. The fertilizing power is not the subject, but the aesthetic passion which the author pours into it; and this aesthetic passion is expressed not in subject alone or in treatment alone but in a harmony between them. Therefore we are not to say except at the peril of an ultimate sterility: "This subject is admissible, that subject is barred," or: "This treatment is admirable, that treatment is ruled out," and this is precisely what the authoritarians of all ages do say. It is madness and folly for us to cry: "But we are modern. Our particular brand of authoritarianism really is right. Our preference for free verse—or what you will— really is the last word in prosody. Our particular swerve towards ecclesiasticism or proletarianism or romanticism or realism—or what you will—really is the law and the prophets." In saying this, we are ourselves committing all the sins which we condemn in others as we read the history of literature. We say of Victorian criticism that it insisted too much on the religious or ethical content of the work it criticised. And so it did. But it knew what it was doing; according to its lights it could sometimes be wonderfully fair, and we find that when Mrs. Humphry Ward published "Robert Elsmere," a novel which struck to the very heart of Victorian religious controversy, "The Spectator" could say: "Profoundly as we differ from Mrs. Humphry Ward's criticism of Christianity we recognize in her book one of the most striking pictures of a sincere religious ideal that has ever yet been presented to our generation under the disguise of a modern novel." How many modern reviews are there which, being wedded to one or other of the authoritarian ideologies or even to one of our slightly less ferocious economic "isms," would thus praise on its merits the work of a writer from whom they "profoundly" differed? It is within the recollection of us all how, in the period between this war and the last, a powerful section of criticism looked upon certain subjects and certain treatments with such horror that they were excluded from discussion and from the anthologies. With the exception of one unrepresentative poem about clouds, Rupert Brooke was completely shut out from Yeats's "Oxford Book of Modern Verse"; his war poems and his love poems were treated as if they were obscene. In the same volume another poet of the same generation, Robert Nichols, is given a place, but his war poems also are unrepresented.

Yeats would not give room to this, which will live when two-thirds of the poems he included are forgotten:

> Was there love once? I have forgotten her.
>> Was there grief once? Grief yet is mine.
> O loved, living, dying, heroic soldier,
>> All, all my joy, my grief, my love are thine!

And if Yeats, a great poet, compiling not a personal anthology but an Oxford book, could be thus cabined by a partisan distaste for certain subjects and treatments, how much fiercer and narrower was the partisanship of the camp-followers whose very livelihood depended upon their closely following the camp! They took the view that art should, in its subject, reflect what Yeats calls their "social passion" and what I should call their political fanaticism. They insisted further that certain treatments, certain ways of writing, should be regarded as the brand of Cain. They howled against romanticism as Victorian spinsters howled against sex.

> Great Heaven! When these with clamour shrill
>> Drift out to Lethe's harbour bar
> A verse of Lovelace shall be still
>> As vivid as a pulsing star.

The verse is William Watson's, and Yeats himself quoted it in his preface to the "Oxford Book." How strange that he should quote it and himself fall into the very error that it condemned!

No: we are not to dictate to an artist either subject or treatment, nor are we to deny to him any subject or any treatment. We are not schoolmistresses. We are not censors. All that matters is that the subject be one that awakes the artist's aesthetic passion, and that the harmony between subject and treatment be such that it casts a spell upon him, enabling him to be visited by his god, and so casts a spell upon us, enabling us to be visited by ours. "The excellence of every art," said Keats, "is its intensity." And what did he mean by that? Fortunately he tells us. "Capable," he continues, "of making all disagreeables evaporate from their being in close relationship with Beauty and Truth." Do not misunderstand him. By "disagreeables" he does not mean things that are unpleasant to us; he means those things which do not agree together, which clash in our immediate experience, but which harmonize when seen in the aspect of eternity. Keats's "disagreeables" are what I have called our incongruities, of time, of place, of individuality, of right, seemingly opposed to right, of loyalty conflicting with loyalty. It is the function of art by its intensity to penetrate these incongruities, to perceive some aspect of order in the chaos of living, some aspect of beauty in that order, some aspect of truth in that beauty, and so to distil experience that we are made partakers of its essence and are enabled to re-imagine it and to renew ourselves.

It would seem, then, that though, as I suggested at the outset, art continually changes its practice and society its forms so that to us, who float upon the surface of experience, there appears to be a variable relationship between them, and though, in a sense, the relationship *is* variable and we have continually to adjust ourselves to it, the adjustments we make should always be so designed as to preserve the true and essential relationship. This willingness to see the artist as an impregnator of the spirit of man and not as a propagator of his own, or our own, opinions, is of the more importance in a period of swift and radical social change. The tendency of our time is for human thought, alarmed by the rapidity of change, by the seeming dissolution of society into a condition of flux, to congeal into stiff, uniform chunks of fierce and frightened orthodoxy—the orthodoxy which condemned Keats because he did not write like Pope, the orthodoxy which condemned Swinburne because he was unchristian, the orthodoxy which in our own day invented the ignorant word "escapist" and pretends that social consciousness is the criterion of art. And so we are in danger of demanding, as authoritarians do, that an artist fall in with our platoon, or of insisting that he must be in our sense a good citizen before we will regard him as a good artist. In fact, it is probably desirable that an artist should be, as a man, a good citizen; that he should obey the laws and fight his country's enemies and care for the happiness of the people. But though good citizenship may be desirable in him, it is evidently not always so; certainly we are not qualified to define good citizenship for him and to reject him, as an artist, because as a man he does not conform to our definition. Do we condemn Thomas Mann because by Nazi standards he has not been a good citizen of his own German state? Do we exclude Shelley because, as a citizen, his behavior was extremely odd? No: we may enforce our laws upon the man but not our opinions upon the artist. And he, in his turn, must understand that, though he is entitled to express his opinions, he is no more entitled to drill the community than the community is entitled to drill the artist in him. He is entitled to express his opinions if the subject of those opinions is what at the moment stirs his aesthetic passion; in this way, great religious poetry has been produced; but woe to him if his art does not transcend his didacticism and carry him away from it and beyond it! Woe even to Shelley if he had not so often and so gloriously forgotten to be a propagandist! Immortality is not to be voted at a political meeting. Posterity will not stay in any man's school. We are wilful and enchanted children, by the grace of God. Our school classes and our school books and our school rewards and punishments matter very little to us in the end. For an hour or two we may earnestly concern ourselves with them, and turn our solemn, communal eyes on the teacher who presides over these things; but what in our heart of hearts we want to know about is the world beyond this classroom of his. He whom we love and remember is not he who thrusts upon us his own dusty chart of the Supreme Reality, scored over with his arguments, prejudices and opinions; nor he who will draw a map of heaven on the blackboard and chastise us with scorpions if we will not fall down and worship it; but he who will pull the curtain away from the classroom window and let us see our own heaven with our own eyes. And this enablement of mankind, I take to be the function of true education, for the very word means a leading-out, and to lead out the spirit of man, through the wise, liberating self-discipline of learning and wonder, has been the glory of great teachers and of great universities since civilization began to flower.

We are citizens, but we are men and women; we are men

and women, but we are spirits. We live in the spirit, though we are instructed in the mind—

> The mind, that ocean where each kind
> Does straight its own resemblance find;
> Yet it creates, transcending these,
> Far other worlds and other seas.

And to these, and to the truth that dwells in them, we come not by instruction but by vision, the vision that penetrates to the spirit through the senses. Shelley knew; he stopped preaching and drew attention to something that was not a bird and far transcended the skylark. Keats knew: he did not preach at all, and in his vision forgot even the nightingale. And Hardy knew:

> Love is, yea, a great thing,
>   A great thing to me,
> When, having drawn across the lawn
>   In darkness silently,
> A figure flits like one a-wing
>   Out from the nearest tree:
> O love is, yes, a great thing
>   A great thing to me!
> Will these be always great things,
>   Great things to me? . . .
> Let it befall that One will call,
>   "Soul I have need of thee":
> What then? Joy-jaunts, impassioned flings,
>   Love, and its ecstasy,
> Will always have been great things,
>   Great things to me!

So let us not think too communally on the relationship of the artist and the community, for along that path of thought lie the gauleiters on the one hand and the commissars on the other. What then? As you like it or what you will.

> . . . Joy-jaunts, impassioned flings,
> Love, and its ecstasy . . .

skylarks, nightingales! Take them, but take them into yourselves. Give the artist freedom that he may discover; preserve yourselves in freedom that you may receive and re-create.

The Decadence of the Novel
Anon.

from

The Author, vol. 19, no. 5, 1909.

THE DECADENCE OF THE NOVEL.

IS it permitted to have doubts regarding the decadence of the novel ?

"Where are your Dickens, your Thackerays, and your Scotts?" immediately retorts the impugner of contemporary fiction.

To which the best reply is,

"And Fieldings ? "

Because, sad to say, it is ten to one that the detractor has not read Fielding. In consequence of which he will at once proceed to entangle himself in efforts either to conceal his ignorance, which will be impossible, or to justify his neglect, which will put him out of court.

If "Tom Jones" is to be the standard, the English novel has been certainly on the down grade since February 28, 1749. But this is not a reasonable way of regarding any phenomenon of literary production. For some reason, not yet explained, the superlatively best in every literary form makes its appearance very soon. Greece never produced anything to rival the Iliad ; nor, indeed, has it been approached by any work in any one of the Western literatures, all of which are essentially offshoots of the supreme Homeric torrent spreading itself in the divergent winding streams and backwaters of a delta. No Greek dramatist rose to the height of the Orestea. No Roman lyric successor of Horace,

> " Princeps Aeoleum carmen ad Italos.
> Deduxisse modos,"

ever equalled him. Quintilian opined "Lyricorum Horatius fere solus legi dignus." Had time, and the Byzantine monks, spared us the works of Terpander and of the other early Greek lyric poets, should we have found in them things not surpassed by Pindar ? It is certain that the poetess who can rival Sappho has still to make her appearance ; and seems very unlikely to appear. No Englishman has written such blank verse as Milton. And so on. Indeed, that the best is soon reached appears to be a phenomenon dominant in all provinces connected with letters. No document is so indestructible as a Babylonian tablet. The script of the oldest inscriptions and manuscripts is the handsomest. The Mazarine Bible still remains an unrivalled example of letterpress ; and no printer has ever produced pages and type of more beautiful proportions than those presented by the "Hypnerotomachia Pamphili."

Possibly a partial explanation of this dominant phenomenon is to be found in the fact that for those who came first

> " The world was all before them where to choose :

and they chose the best. Afterwards their less fortunate successors had either to tell the same story, to use the same form, or to take what the first comers had prudently eschewed. But seeing how far-reaching is this phenomenon of the best being very soon reached, it is evidently always an easy thing for anyone who wishes to insist upon literary decadence to prove his point.

At the same time it is open to question whether the works of authors whose writings are adduced to shame the labours of their successors are in all cases so perfect as they are represented to be. This does not apply to the very greatest, to such novelists as Fielding and Cervantes. But Sir Walter Scott has certain *longueurs*. It would be difficult entirely to exonerate Dickens of exaggeration and " playing to the gallery." And will any one defend "her eyes were full of almost tears," " different to," " many opprobrious epithets in the English and French language," all which flowers of speech are to be found in " Pendennis " ? Is it possible to find the parallels of these in the pages of any novelist of 1908 who is careful about his style ?

" But many are disgracefully careless. You must judge by an average."

Oh, but there were novelists who were not Scotts nor Thackerays even when Scott and Thackeray were living! And it is instructive to peruse on the fly-leaves of fiction of fifty years ago the press notices of the novels of the day. They are generous, those press notices ; exactly as are many press notices now. And if what they said was to be taken "au pied de la lettre " those stories ought still to be favourites. They are not. Their titles are forgotten ; and it is often difficult to find any one who can say who the authors were. But these writers were the contemporaries of Dickens and Thackeray and ought to count. In effect, the comparison of all that is being written to-day with the exceptional work of fifty and more years ago which has been found worthy to survive is essentially unjust.

A smaller number of novels than might be supposed survives a decade : only a fraction survives a century. It is not entirely the fault of the work. Sir Walter Scott remarked very justly that after fifty years a novel to be rightly understood requires notes. Or if it does not require notes, it demands of the reader some such knowledge of a state of society that has passed away as only well-informed people possess. In consequence to obtain anything resembling a lucid view of the actual situation it is not only requisite first of all to distinguish novels of very various merit published at the same date, but also no less necessary to distinguish the various classes to which these novels appeal.

Are the " serials " at present running in half-penny prints, and (whatsoever may be their merits or demerits) devoured with avidity by a certain class of readers, inferior to the tales in the "Penny Readers" of fifty years ago? Those "Penny Readers" had a public. Had they not had one they would not have been published. It seems not at all improbable that their publishers reaped a larger profit than is at present reaped by the publishers of the penny fiction at the present day offered to a public of about the same intellectual level. There were then by far fewer publications of this kind; and it is now many years since a newsvendor observed to the present writer "If there were only one or two of these weekly penny fiction periodicals they would be a gold mine. But there are so many that they are of no value to any one." And since then the competition for the penny of the reader of cheap weekly fiction has certainly not diminished.

Here we probably touch the secret of the "decadence," if there is a decadence. Undeniably the conditions favour decadence. And the conditions are not to be justly charged against either authors or publishers. They are in no small degree results of human nature.

Now, it is useless to quarrel with human nature. Human nature is a phenomenon of the same kind as gravitation and magnetism, and, whether it is what any one would wish it to be or not, it has to be accepted as it is. Neither does it help to say,

" It is, but hadn't ought to be."

In "Don Quixote" Marcela justly excuses herself for having turned the head of Grisostomo by remarking, "As the viper deserves no blame for its sting, although it be mortal, because it is the gift of nature, neither ought I to be reviled for being beautiful." And it is one of the gifts of nature to humanity to scramble for halfpence; or, if the coin be of any larger worth, to scramble with proportionately keener ardour. That has to be accepted as the viper's " sting " has to be accepted, howsoever much it " hadn't ought to be."

A publisher is a man who hopes to make an income by bringing out books. To do that he has first to get the copy, and afterwards to purchase paper, to pay the printer and binder, and—this last is the rub—to sell the books. It is said that there are people who will give away copy; and it is certain that mechanical inventions have reduced the cost of paper, printing, and binding, to prices that would once have been considered impossible, though these prices may still not be so small as a publisher could wish. In fact, none of the preliminary expenses are very serious. But to sell the book demands genius. Books do not sell themselves; publishers wish they would. Nor will the public part with their money for any book that is offered them. If the public would do that, the

situation would become too sunny. Every author would bring out his own works, and there would be no publishers. But the public will purchase, by no means generously, if their expectations have been properly tickled, if they can be persuaded (no matter how) that they are going to have a little more than their money's worth for their money, and, this is the chief thing, if the humour takes them. What they ought to purchase is a problem for the critic, not for the publisher. What they will purchase the publisher desires to supply in the largest quantity saleable at a profit. If the public wanted the "Rig-Veda" in the original, the publishers would be delighted to sell them the "Rig-Veda" up to any number of hundreds of thousands; and some publisher would no doubt offer the complete Sanscrit text, edited by a first-class scholar, for fourpence-halfpenny—to "cut out" the other publishers.

Well, the public do not want the "Rig-Veda." And they do want a certain number of novels. How many they want no one knows. But they would like them at cheaper rates. This also is of a piece with the viper's "sting" and Marcela's beauty, a gift of nature. But no matter how ingeniously the cost of production may be manipulated, as the selling-price is ruthlessly diminished at the bidding of a furious competition, the actual profits tend towards a vanishing point. Many small profits now become the remedy for shrinking returns; and the publisher plays for a profit of $\frac{x}{3}$ on three novels instead of a profit of x upon one. That multiplies the output of novels; not necessarily of volumes, 500 of A, and 500 of B, and 500 of C, taking the place of 1,500 of A.

Next the author does the same; and, be it noted, with by far less excuse. Publishing three books instead of one, as above, means only spending rather more on composition. It is true that the modification is one that leads to sinister effects upon percentages of gain, more capital being invested to earn the same return. But if a man has the capital, and particularly when he can invest the same capital thrice successively in three small ventures, the result may be merely a considerably increased production of books with no very great corresponding extra expenditure. But the author who, because he finds the value of copy reduced from y to $\frac{y}{2}$, coolly sets to work to write two novels in place of one is committing literary suicide. The time necessary to write a novel, and still more the all-important period of incubation that must precede the invention of any story, will be very different in the case of different individuals; just as the final result will differ in consequence of their different abilities. But no writer can " put on steam " and run out two novels in the time that he would normally spend upon one, without incurring an enormous risk of drifting into mere journeyman work. No man can in such circumstances do his best. And the novelist who is not writing his best would be by far better advised in not writing at all. It is, however, no secret that some men have been trying to remedy a reduction in prices by an increased output.

Such tactics would certainly make for decadence.

But the mischief does not end with the probable deterioration of the work of the individual. When publisher and author deliberately combine to play a double game of forced production at low profits, the output must be inevitably exaggerated. Probably it is already grossly exaggerated ; and the books exceeding the demand stand in one another's way. So much is this avowedly the case that it will not be indiscreet to hazard a conjecture that a certain proportion of the much wider popularity of some of the novels of the past was due to the fact that the tales got a wider reading in consequence of there not being others that could be taken up instead. At present of ten novels that are published, seven never have a fair chance. The numerous others that succeed them week by week rob them immediately of their claim to be *new* novels. And the *new* novel is the biggest of all the fetiches of the novel-reading public. Swept headlong by the combined forces of feverish production and demand for nothing but what is " new," " newest," and " only just out," fiction is threatening to become purely ephemeral. If that should arrive, if the novelist is to know that as the journalist's work has a life of a day only, his is to exist but for a month, is it possible, is it in human nature, that he should put into his book the qualities that a man might labour to compass in a work that might hope to be a favourite with a generation, that had a chance of being remembered when its writer had passed away ? If there is a decadence, if less and less of the work at present done has permanent value, to what extent is that due to the novelist's labouring for the moment only because he has lost hope of a future ?

It is possible enough that when time shall have sifted the work, and shall have brought a date from which the literature of to-day can be viewed in due perspective, the fiction of the present generation may be found quite worthy to reckon with that of the generations that have preceded it. If in all but the very best a distinct decadence is visible that will have been in no small degree the result of idiotic competition.

Modern Writers in the World of Necessity
Stephen Spender

from

Partisan Review, vol. 12, no. 3, 1945.

Modern Writers in
the World of Necessity

STEPHEN SPENDER

T HE FASCISTS in their downfall have left us a sinister inheritance,
a world which they have lost but on which they have been able to
set their curse. The curse is the spell which they invoked in order to
achieve their triumphs. It is the curse of a necessity which hangs over
everyone and everything, justifying conscription, economies, censorship, discipline, because there is a continual crisis in the world which
can only be solved by the most ruthless use of governmental power.
When the fascists expired in flames of self-destruction, they were like
that old peasant who, on his deathbed, told his children that there
was a treasure of gold buried at the bottom of the field. He knew
that they would have to dig for the rest of their lives. And the fascists
know that we must build and control everything and almost everyone
after they have gone. They may think that after their deaths the curse
which they laid on their own countries in their lives will be laid on
the whole world.

The difference, of course, between fascism and this heritage
from it is that with fascism the conditions for the conscription of
every branch of life into the totalitarian effort were largely forced;
with us, ruin, shortages, the disasters left by fascism. have made the
total organization of society really necessary. The difference is between necessity as an excuse, and necessity as a reality. If the fascist
governments had been superseded by other forms of government,
before 1939, then these other governments could have ruled without
introducing measures of control and conscription. Any government
now, whatever its party, if it is to govern, must control and ration and
organize at home, while approving of equally strong measures in its
foreign policy abroad, to bring world order out of the chaos left by
fascism.

The problem of our time has always been power. The evils of
power are fully proved to us, and our age is a classic demonstration
of Lord Acton's famous saying that all power corrupts and that absolute power corrupts absolutely. Yet it is impossible for us to renounce

power, because none of the problems of the modern world can be solved without exercising it. We must learn to use it justly and wisely. This means that governments must be able to exercise the controls necessary to the postwar world without giving way to the temptation to set themselves up in a position in which they are irreplaceable. It means that what is considered necessary must include culture and criticism, and not just that which is immediately desirable. It means that the democratic governments must reject the evil inheritance which fascism has maliciously left them—to become overruling, imperialist and totalitarian. It also means that the people in the democracies must deliberately avoid slipping into the mood of acquiescence which was typical of the peoples living under fascism. They must accept the sacrifices which are necessary, but they should not do so merely because the government has mentioned the magic word "necessity." They should insist that strong government does not mean no possible alternative to the existing party or coalition in power.

Freedom has been defined as the recognition and acceptance of necessity. This means that in a situation where men are compelled by a sense of common social necessity, they recognize freely the reasons for their actions and they accept them. It does not mean that necessity can be used by the government as an excuse for every kind of censorship and infringement of liberty. In fact, what determines freedom is the spirit of criticism and vigilance, so that the controls which seem to be imposed by the government are willingly imposed on themselves by free individuals for reasons which they understand.

But what is necessary for society in a state of emergency hardly ever coincides with the wishes of the individual, precisely because the margin which distinguishes an individual personality from a mere economic and social unit almost disappears in a society undergoing continual crisis. Today people notice the gap between the massive, generalized, levelling, ruthless, mechanical public activities which are directed in the interests of all, and yet which coincide exactly with no one's wishes for himself, and the eccentric, yet creative needs of individual self-expression. Government becomes more and more concerned with imperative necessity, an either/or meaning that unless individuals act as is required of them, consciously suppressing their desire to express themselves extravagantly, they will be romantic rebels against the measures necessary to feed and clothe the victims of the war, and to prevent further wars.

The idea of necessity tends to swallow up every cause that cannot be integrated within the problem of distributing available goods and satisfying minimal needs. Flamboyant and rhetorical tastes, which produced the most beautiful architecture of the past, appear anti-social in a time when governments are conscious of the limited uses to which they can put their limited stocks of building labor and materials. The dynamic need for self-expression which made the nineteenth century flourish despite all the flaws of its judgment, is dwarfed by the enormously exposed public wounds of whole nations in our time which must be healed before anything else is attended to. Thus personalities and causes are made insignificant by the perception of necessity. Overnight the struggle between the propertied and the poor classes in several countries of Europe disappeared when it became evident that everyone in those countries was almost equally dependent on aid coming from America. Ironically, the triumph of Russian communism has occurred just at the moment when communist revolutions are less than ever in a position to solve the problems of countries, and thus communists themselves have abandoned the idea of the proletarian revolution for that of a struggle of power between powerful, realistic interests, some of them formerly conservative, some of them formerly revolutionary.

In this world of necessity, there is danger of the individual who clings to personal values becoming as cynical and apathetic as many individuals under fascism. The definition of scruples, free choice, opinion, differentiation, is tending to disappear from the picture of the postwar world. Whether for or against the interests of the future of humanity, arrangements are being made and will continue to be made which will inflict injustice and misery on whole populations and involve a painful sacrifice of principles in the minds of every fair-minded spectator. Recent events in Poland, and also in Greece, are examples of a situation which is likely to repeat itself many times after the war, in which fair-minded people will have to say, with the emphasis of a new kind of patience:

> *Be still, be still, my soul; it is but for a season:*
> *Let us endure an hour and see injustice done.*

All these terrible injustices will have to be measured against the necessary changes in Europe. Moreover, physically, the new world we build cannot be a beautiful one. Prefabricated or temporary or steel houses on emergency sites, standardization, the most rigid economies in materials—there is no functionalist who would dare suggest that cities rebuilt under these conditions will look beautiful. All that can be said is that it is necessary to provide houses for as many people as possible, with limited materials and quickly, just as it is necessary to compromise with Russia over Poland, perhaps reluctantly to abandon the cause of the Central European Social Democrats, or of the Yugoslav monarchy. Necessity is no respector of persons or of parties. The only demand one can make of it is that it should really be necessary.

In the postwar world dominated by the god of necessity, it seems likely that many people will turn away from politics and seek to construct small worlds out of their private relationships, based on personal values. In doing this, these people will be imitating art: for this has been exactly the tendency of various literary movements during the past hundred years.

The significance of the attitudes of the various literary movements toward politics lies in their not having been directly political or allied to any political party: or if they had political alliances, these were for some other reason than a purely political one. The poet considered himself to be sensitively in communication with the most significant realities of life, which might be summed up under some such idea as the experience of beauty, and if he happened, like William Morris, to be a socialist, it was for the sake of beauty rather than for the sake of socialism. The politics of the artist are the politics of the unpolitical, decided on for the sake of life and not of politics. Therefore even the non-political and anti-political attitude of artists is a criticism of politics by life, though it may also imply a criticism of the artists themselves if they have an incomplete or a false attitude toward life. Thus, if one realizes that the attitude of artists who are critical of all politics is ultimately a political attitude, since politics are and must be concerned with the same kind of life as forms the subject matter of art, then it will be seen that, as so often happens, the artistic attitude foreshadows one which later may become widespread.

The attitude of the esthetes of the end of the last century toward political organization is epitomized in Whistler's famous apothegm to his fellow students whom he saw exercising with dumbbells: "Can't you get the concierge to do that sort of thing for you?" Politics, like gymnastics, were the business of the public servants while the esthetes got on with their art for art's sake, which might also be called life for life's sake. The attitude that politics exist in order that one may forget about them is, in fact, a political attitude, based on the truth that art and life are separate from and more important than the machinery of living. Unfortunately, though, in the highly organized, rationalized modern age, this idea is only a half truth. The other truth which is complementary to it, is that in the immense world organization of modern wealth, everyone has an obvious dependence on his position in the economic system, everyone is to some extent conditioned by his environment, and one of the most obvious characteristics of modern thought is that we cannot dissociate the individual completely from his environment. A modern St. Francis who stripped himself of all his possessions and lived a life of saintly poverty might be respected today, but could not be regarded as likely to influence the conditions of life because we have too clear a picture of the interconnectedness of the modern system to believe that anyone can help humanity by separating himself completely from it within some attitude of personal saintliness. The artist who proclaims himself isolated within the values of his art is in much the same position as the modern St. Francis would be. "Art for art's sake" may be treated with respect, but the connection of the esthetes with a political and economic situation is felt by everyone except themselves. Therefore the attempt today to be a pure artist, having renounced all political connections with society, although it has been made and will be made again and again, is simply a failure to be conscious of the artist's position in the modern world. Ruskin and William Morris were right to draw the conclusion that if the artist does not accept the social system in which he lives, he cannot wash his hands of it; unless he is for it, he must be against it.

The esthetes foreshadowed the attitude of many wealthy people in fascist countries towards fascism. Disdaining the social system in which they lived, they sought to cultivate a world of their own values, isolated from it, while accepting the position which the system gave them. Ultimately they supported fascism, because it supported them. It is interesting to note that the survivors of the esthetic movement, D'Annunzio, the futurist Marinetti, the imagist Ezra Pound, and W. B. Yeats, all showed a certain enthusiasm for fascism, because they saw in it a violent assertion of the aristocratic principle, which although decaying, kept them in their position of detachment from society. While I am writing this, a bitter controversy is raging among Italian writers. The school of "hermetic" poets claims that the mysterious obscurity of their poems written between 1923 and 1942 proves that they would never compromise with fascism. An embittered group of anti-fascists points out, however, that it is exactly this "pure" style of literature which fascism could afford to support, and whose exponents, in fact, supported fascism.

Here, though, I am not concerned with recriminations which are only of local importance, in so far as certain unfortunates (Ezra

Pound, for example) gave political support to fascism. What is important for art is that almost every view of life today has social implications. The various schools and movements of the last few years have attempted to develop an artistic aim, a psychological truth or a view of personal relationships split off from the modern social problem. Yet, as with the esthetes of the '90's, social implications are involved even in the most personal or private world, and thus we find a writer like D. H. Lawrence, who concentrated on developing a very one-sided view of relations between men and women and the inner depths of sexuality, sympathizing with the atavism of the Nazis. The fact is that D. H. Lawrence, like Yeats and Pound, was too big a man to exclude from his mind the social problem, and the attempt to avoid it in his work put him in sympathy with the repressive lords of blood and soil. The development of the complete view of life which was potentially within him would have made him sympathetic more with his own people—the miners of Nottingham—but this would have meant a broadening of his vision and a denial of his intuitive personality altogether too painful and difficult for him. As with Lawrence, so with the Imagists, the Symbolists, the Surrealists, the Apocalyptics, the Personalists: there is an attempt to embrace any reality, however narrow, remote, violent, neurotic, visionary, private or mad, so long as it can be appealed to as part of an inner world of individuality more important and durable than the external world which seems outside the control of the individual. Yet there are elements of false prophecy and desperate remedy about all these efforts to get away from an overwhelming present history:

Newman, Ciddy, Plato, Fronny, Pascal, Bowdler, Baudelaire,
Doctor Frommer, Mrs. Allom, Freud, the Baron and Flaubert,
Lured with their compelling logic, charmed with beauty of their verse,
With their loaded sideboards whispered, "Better join us, life is worse."

Yet the outside life has a way of overtaking and overthrowing the most elaborate positions of the "art for art's sake" which is "life for life's sake." The elaborate self-disguises of the esthetes become too expensive to be kept up, the madness of the surrealists is excelled by the behavior of a world at war, personal relationships are torn aside, the journeyings of a D.H. or a T.E. Lawrence become impracticable. The innner world of personality is certainly the most important reality we know, but unless it can be related to the outer world, all attempts to develop it only reveal its isolation and weakness. This inner world is the world of civilization, but civilization is a reality in society, it is not just personal relationships, jokes between friends, surrealist extravaganzas, sex nightmares and mysteries. Whoever cares for it must fight to achieve it not only in his life but also in society.

Doubtless it was partly considerations of this kind which persuaded writers as detached from political passions as E. M. Forster, Maritain, Gide, Benda, Bergamin and Thomas Mann, to play a political role in the 1930's. They realized that the inner life of civilization which they maintained in their art, was in process of being destroyed in the external world of political action. Accordingly, they intervened, and although recently in England there has been a cooling off of relations between writers and leftist politicians, that does not affect the ultimate repercussions which their intervention will have. The 1930's were a turning point because they marked the realization of many artists that they had a responsibility toward civilization in the world outside themselves and their friends. The doubts that have arisen since are not as to this responsibility, but as to the part that the writer should play: whether he should lend himself to party propaganda, whether he should give up time for writing to appear on political platforms, whether he should, as T. S. Eliot suggests, define for himself very exactly the part which the man of letters may take in supporting cultural activities and limit himself to that.

The political activities of writers in the 1930's led to misunderstanding for a clear reason. The writers, for the most part, supported leftist causes, such as that of the Republicans in Spain, because they believed that, on the whole, the Republicans and the socialists were the defenders of civilization. In addition to this, in supporting the Republicans they were supporting the great cause of social justice which many intellectuals have supported in Europe ever since the time of Voltaire. But although they were indeed supporting a movement which was fighting for the cause of intellectual freedom, this movement itself had very little use for poetry and for art, except perhaps in Spain itself among Spaniards. When supported by some of the most brilliant young writers of the decade, the English Communist leaders had no idea of putting them to a better use than the crude one of getting them killed as quickly as possible on the battlefields of Spain, and of then using their names as propaganda. In this the Communists were not malicious, they simply revealed their complete ignorance of the very highest values of the freedom of the spirit for which they were supposed to be fighting, and their pathetic faith in the idea that the only use of any talent outside that of party politics is the value to which it can be turned as political propaganda.

The writers who were not killed physically were at any rate killed as creative writers, because there was no way in which they could fit their talents into the movement, the line, the party program. This has been the experience of the writers who have sympathized with proletarian revolution all over the world, in England, in Russia, in China, and in America. It is possible that socialism has defeated its own ends, because, in attaching enormous importance to the attainment of economic liberty of the workers it has lacked respect for the highest freedom of all—the freedom to explore the truth of the philosopher and the artist without any predetermined conclusions. The insistence on philosophic materialism, the myth of the superiority of the proletariat, the obsession with the idea that every other cause must subserve the revolution, create a mental prison of socialist ideas, precisely because the revolution does not point to the release of any ideas greater than materialism, the revolution and the proletariat. Socialism is afraid of ideas, of a conception of humanity which includes the rich as well as the poor, of the unfettered imagination. One has only to think of past causes, such as the French Revolution, Nineteenth Century Liberalism, even, for that matter, the Spanish Republic, to remember that they have inspired men because they have stood for things greater than themselves, greater than politics and politicians: liberty, beauty, genius and ideals.

In the partly managerial, partly socialistic society, dominated by necessity, of the immediate future, the intelligentsia will be in a position in which, whether they like it or not, their work will have an unprecedented influence, because it will be almost the only outlet of free self-expression in a world where most commodities and employment are rigidly controlled. There are two directions in which their thought may develop, and I suggest that this is one of the turning points in history in which the ideas of the intelligentsia may really alter the lives of future generations.

One direction, which would be consistent with the tendencies of the literary movements of the past two generations, is already adumbrated in the vague movement called "personalism." The theme of this and similar tendencies is that society has nothing to offer which can satisfy any individual: the scale of power politics, planning, controls, etc., is quite unrelated to the human scale of separate individuals: the only reality to which we can cling is that of personal values. Views such as this, which are to be found in English literary magazines, could probably only flourish today in England and in America, where a good many people have learned nothing from the war except to hate control and conscription.

The other tendency in European literature comes from the continent, especially from France and the countries occupied by the Nazis. This springs from the literature written during the Occupation. It is a literature of resistance, of hope, of faith, active and full of energy, which is yet not imprisoned within the limited and material aims of any political party. It is a poetry of writers such as Eluard, Aragon, Jouve, Emmanuel, Seghers, and others who have integrated their personal vision with an understanding of the absolutely essential tasks confronting the poet as the most fully conscious member of society. In these writers the gulf which separated the private, personal, antisocial aspect of the poet and the political aspect seems to have been bridged. The tendency is toward integration of the idea of the separate personality with that of the social being. As a result of this integration, these writers are not the intellectual by-products of politics. In other words, they aim at the expression of personality and the freedom of the imagination, while they also recognize their responsibility toward society. They create an ideal above politics, which political movements should seek to interpret in action.

An acute observer who has recently returned from France, pointed out to me: "The French writers are still faithful to the principles of the Spanish Republic." It is interesting that their close contact with the Nazis should have had this result. In the postwar society obsessed and overwhelmed with material problems, it may well be that only thinkers and creative writers can keep steadily before the world the idea that, besides the organization and distribution of material resources, it is necessary to remember that we are human, with all the limitations and all the grandeur, the full social responsibility and the necessity of freedom, which this implies.

Economic Correlates of Artistic Creativity
Vytautas Kavolis

from

American Journal of Sociology, 70, 1964.

Reprinted by permission of Chicago University Press.

Economic Correlates of Artistic Creativity

Vytautas Kavolis

ABSTRACT

A survey of economic correlates of historical fluctuations in artistic creativity suggests two generalizations. First, the motivation for artistic creativity is maximized by a balanced tension between the needs for achievement and for expression in the personality system. This type of motivation is most likely to be produced in relatively early stages of increasing prosperity. Second, social demand for art tends to be stimulated, in a minor mode, by disturbances of socioeconomic latency and, in a major mode, by the necessity for social-emotional reintegration of a social system subsequent to intensive adaptive activity. From these observations a general sociological theory of artistic creativity is derived.

Studies of the relationship between economic conditions and artistic creativity[1] have generally been based on somewhat imprecise historical data from the urban cultures of classical and modern Europe. They suggest the presence of a direct relationship between economic achievement and artistic creativity.[2] It may be argued, however, that the virtual exclusion of the data from preliterate cultures, together with inadequate attention to intervening variables, have frequently resulted in generalizations about the economic backgrounds of artistic creativity which lack both universality and theoretical significance.

In the present survey, a tentative attempt will be made to deal with this relationship in a somewhat wider perspective, and to formulate a conception of the mechanisms responsible for the observed associations between economic and artistic conditions. The processes to be related to artistic creativity will be conceptualized within an interpretive framework derived from the sociological theory of the phase cycles.[3]

THE PHASE-CYCLES THEORY

A general statement of the phase-cycles theory may be formulated in the following manner:

1. All social systems have a number of basic functional problems to solve. Among these, instrumental *adaptation* to the external environment, organization of the legal-institutional machinery for *goal attainment*, internal social-emotional *integration*, and *tension reduction* (and latent pattern maintenance) are of paramount importance.

2. Social systems produce only limited amounts of social resources (such as wealth, administrative power, disposable time, and popular interest) and, in addition, may be able to mobilize only a part of the resources for problem-solving action. Furthermore, specialization with regard to any particular system problem tends to some extent to circumscribe, even if resources are available, the possibility of action oriented toward the solution of any

---

[1] "Artistic creativity" is defined as referring to (*a*) an increase in the quality of art production in a definable socio-historical unit and/or (*b*) the culmination(s) of artistic attainment of such a unit, as judged by a reasonably general consensus of artists and art critics which, in most cases, eventually tends to emerge as "historical judgment."

[2] Shepard B. Clough, *The Rise and Fall of Civilization: An Inquiry into the Relationship between Economic Development and Civilization* (New York, 1961), p. 261.

[3] Robert F. Bales, "The Equilibrium Problem in Small Groups," in Talcott Parsons, Robert F. Bales, and Edward A. Shils, *Working Papers in the Theory of Action* (Glencoe, Ill., 1953), pp. 111–61; Talcott Parsons and Neil J. Smelser, *Economy and Society: A Study in the Integration of Economic and Social Theory* (Glencoe, Ill., 1956), pp. 242–43.

other problem. For example, when the emphasis is on tension reduction, some of the potential resources for creative action are likely to be unproductively dissipated, by virtue of the negative effects of a prevalent "latent tension-management and pattern-maintenance" orientation on the readiness to commit resources to purposive action.

3. For these reasons, basic system problems tend to be dealt with in a cyclical manner. Major emphasis is placed on one type of problem, to the relative neglect of others, at any particular time. As a functional problem is being successfully resolved, resources are increasingly recommitted to previously neglected tasks which the solution of this problem has made salient. The process can be conceptualized in terms of several typical phase sequences which can be directly observed in small-group studies and also abstracted from complex historical events. In problem-solving processes, the normal phase sequence is as indicated under statement 1.

In terms of this theory, it is hypothesized that artistic creativity will tend to be stimulated in the phase of social-emotional integration,[4] and relatively inhibited in the other phases of any type of large-scale social process. The main body of the present paper consists of an application of this theory to two types of economy-related processes. First, however, to demonstrate the need for such a theory, it must be shown that artistic creativity cannot be explained, even in part, as a natural product or a symbolic expression of concentrated wealth (or of comfortable general prosperity), as some of the existing theories implicitly suggest.

THE DEGREE OF ECONOMIC ACHIEVEMENT

To indicate the dependence of artistic creativity on economic capacity, evidence can be cited to show that an advance in prosperity[5] or the attainment of economic dominance in a culture area[6] is frequently associated with increases in artistic creativity. Contrariwise, a long-range decline in economic activity or prosperity does appear to be associated with a lowering of artistic creativity.[7]

However, these kinds of data may merely mean that changes in economic prosperity are correlated with variations in artistic creativity. No absolute level of prosperity can be identified as necessary for artistic excellence. The cave art of the European

[4] "Because the phenomenon of expressive communication" is related "to the problem of order," the discharge of motivational energy "without reference to adaptive exigencies ... is a process peculiarly bound up with integrative exigencies" (Talcott Parsons, Robert F. Bales, and Edward A. Shils, "Phase Movement in Relation to Motivation, Symbol Formation, and Role Structure," in Parsons et al., Working Papers . . . , p. 190).

[5] In Athens, Pitirim A. Sorokin, Social and Cultural Dynamics, III (New York, 1937), 231; in China, Peter C. Swann, Chinese Painting (New York, 1958), p. 33; in Egypt, A. L. Kroeber, Configurations of Culture Growth (Berkeley, Calif., 1949), p. 240; in Mesopotamia, Encyclopedia of World Art (hereinafter cited as "EWA"), I, 856; in Rome, France, and Germany, Pitirim A. Sorokin, Society, Culture, and Personality: Their Structure and Dynamics (New York, 1947), pp. 549–50; in the Romanesque age and in Renaissance Italy, Arnold Hauser, The Social History of Art, I (New York, 1957), 183, and II, 12–13.

[6] In the Hellenistic age, Clough, op. cit., p. 114; in the Italian Renaissance, Hauser, op. cit., II, 29; in the fifteenth-century Low Countries, Kroeber, op. cit., p. 363; in seventeenth-century Holland, George Edmundson, History of Holland (Cambridge, 1922), pp. 120–21, 186, 298. The British efflorescence of the eighteenth century (when Dutch art was stagnant) was preceded by the ascendancy of London over Amsterdam as the center of "international financial business" (G. N. Clark, The Seventeenth Century [2d ed.; Oxford, 1957], p. 45).

[7] Jean Gimpel, The Cathedral Builders (New York, 1961), pp. 40, 176, 178; Richard Ettinghausen, Arab Painting (Lausanne, 1962), p. 183. The economic welfare of Benin state, based in part on slave trade, declined in the seventeenth and eighteenth centuries, and Benin art "flourished from the 16th to the 17th century" (Roland Oliver and J. D. Fage, A Short History of Africa [Baltimore, 1962], pp. 122–23); EWA, III, 380. "In fact, historical evidence supports the proposition that . . . declines in civilization have accompanied falls in abundance per capita" (Shepard B. Clough, Basic Values of Western Civilization [New York, 1960], p. 55).

Paleolithic hunters, the rock art of South Africa, and the powerful image-making of the Australian natives are all associated with quite limited material resources.[8] "In Oceania . . . life is often very precarious indeed," especially "in the swampy areas of New Guinea or in the very inhospitable coral islands," yet it is "these areas in particular" which "have yielded some of the finest works in the whole of primitive art."[9]

As Redfield has observed, "such a contrast as that between the Haida and the Paiute Indians reminds us that generally speaking a people desperately concerned with getting a living cannot develop a rich moral or aesthetic life."[10] This generalization, however, points to the artistically adverse effects *not* of a low-attainment economy, but of a near-total preoccupation with economically instrumental action. Such a preoccupation may be a consequence of a low-attainment economy in areas with difficult access to natural resources, as in the American Plains before the introduction of the horse. But where a low-attainment economy is combined with more easily accessible natural resources, as in many parts of Oceania (and on the Northwest Coast of America), economic backwardness may coexist with high-level artistic creativity.[11] On comparable levels of economic development, a cultural emphasis on the accumulation of wealth appears likely to preclude an adequate commitment of social resources to artistic pursuits, as a comparison of the Tchambuli, the artistic headhunters, with the Kapauku, the capi-

talistic businessmen, of New Guinea suggests.[12]

Our illustrative comparisons imply that it is not the level of economic achievement, but the proportion of social resources which is allocated to non-instrumental pursuits that is causally related to artistic creativity. Artistic achievement is not proportional to the amount of wealth accumulated; nor is it impossible in the absence of a considerable economic surplus. Art *creation* is hence not primarily a symbolic projection of material prosperity (though self-conscious art *collecting* may serve this purpose).[13]

THE EFFECTS OF ECONOMIC ADVANCEMENT

While, in a static cross-cultural comparison, prosperity is not a prerequisite of artistic creativity, the latter seems to be stimulated by *recently attained* prosperity. The accumulation of urban wealth in Europe, beginning in the eleventh century, is followed in the twelfth and thirteenth centuries—an age of "magnificent prosperity" —by the period of Gothic cathedral-building.[14] The creation of the great fortunes in America during the nineteenth century is succeeded in the twentieth by the first original American contributions to visual art.[15]

[8] Hans-Georg Bandi, Henri Breuil, Lilo Berger-Kirchner, Henri Lhote, Erik Holm, and Andreas Lommel, *The Art of the Stone Age* (New York, 1961).

[9] Alfred Buehler, Terry Barrow, and Charles P. Mountford, *The Art of the South Sea Islands* (New York, 1962), p. 48.

[10] Robert Redfield, *The Primitive World and Its Transformations* (Ithaca, N.Y., 1958), p. 18.

[11] There is, however, a tendency in nomadic cultures which lack both permanent settlements and stable centers of religious activity to develop extensive ceremonial as a functional equivalent of more objectified kinds of art.

[12] Margaret Mead, *Sex and Temperament in Three Primitive Societies* (New York, 1950), pp. 168–70; Leopold Pospisil, *The Kapauku Papuans of West New Guinea* (New York, 1963), pp. 15, 18–31.

[13] Cf. Thorstein Veblen, *The Theory of the Leisure Class* (New York, 1931), pp. 36–37, 45, 74–75. But "the idea of collecting and displaying works of an earlier period was hardly known in those cultures where the need for art was strong and widely diffused" (Kenneth Clark, "Art and Society," *Harper's Magazine*, August, 1961, pp. 77–78).

[14] Gimpel, *op. cit.*, pp. 38–42, 178.

[15] In 1831, de Tocqueville still held "the general mediocrity of fortunes, the absence of superfluous wealth . . . and the constant effort by which everyone attempts to procure [comfort]" responsible for the low level of the arts in the "democratic nations," exemplified by the United States of his

In general, "the flourishing periods of fine art do not come in the periods when a rising upper class is building up its wealth and power, but afterward."[16] One linkage between the recent achievement of prosperity and artistic creativity is the leisure which the former makes possible, as in "Athens in the classic period and Florence during the Renaissance."[17] In this context, artistic creativity could be regarded either as the product of recommitment of resources from instrumental to expressive activity, or what may be only a special case of the former more general tendency, as a means of symbolic legitimation of recently acquired socioeconomic dominance. It does not, however, seem possible to account for this linkage by assuming that, in urban as contrasted with preliterate cultures, artistic creativity is generally a consequence of the accumulation of wealth and might be regarded as a response to the demand for luxury goods, which great wealth presumably generates (at least in non-puritanic cultures).

In some cases, "refined luxury" coincides indeed with "creative spontaneity" in the arts, as in the Warring States and in the late Shang periods of Chinese history.[18] At other times, by stimulating a demand for luxury goods great wealth merely increases the capacity to afford, but not the ability to create, works of artistic value. "The four centuries of the Han *Pax Sinica,* like the four centuries of the Mediterranean *Pax Romana* . . . encouraged the development of a rich material civilization. In both cases the period of creative spontaneity— in the Mediterranean world the apogee of Athens and Alexandria, in China the 'Warring States'—had ended. Civilization

passed through a stagnant and apparently happy period in which the luxury arts, on both sides, played a considerable role."[19] "Luxury art," observes an art historian, "has a deadening effect. The most obvious example is the art of eighteenth-century France."[20]

The comparison of the effects of recently attained prosperity and of stabilized great wealth on artistic creativity implies that artistic efflorescences are indeed, to a significant degree, the result of spontaneous recommitment of social resources from instrumental to expressive pursuits, which the achievement of what is felt as *relative* prosperity makes psychologically possible (and perhaps even necessary). Social resources may be committed to expressive action, as in Melanesia, where economic achievement is low, provided that, within the context of the prevalent cultural aspirations, it is felt to be relatively satisfying.[21] However, within more dynamic economies the successful accomplishment of a significant economic advance apparently makes the diversion of social resources to artistic creativity more probable. But it seems to be only in the earlier (and less "luxurious") stages of such diversion that artistic creativity is maximally stimulated. To explain the frequently evident reduction of artistic creativity in the later stages of economic advancement (marked by greater "luxury"),[22] the dynamics of the achievement drive must be considered.

[19] *Ibid.,* p. 103.

[20] Clark, *op. cit.,* p. 77.

[21] In the long run, satisfaction with low economic attainment is likely to be reduced when direct comparisons with more economically productive cultures are possible. This may be implicit in V. Elwin's observation that "the explanation for this relative poverty of artistic inspiration" in the tribal cultures of central India "lies partly in the general depressed state of the populations that for centuries have been subjected to political and economic pressures from economically more advanced peoples . . ." (*EWA,* I, 840).

[22] Sorokin, *Society, Culture, and Personality,* p. 544.

day (Alexis de Tocqueville, *Democracy in America,* II [New York, 1957], p. 50).

[16] Adolph Siegfried Tomars, *Introduction to the Sociology of Art* (Mexico City, 1940), p. 171.

[17] Irwin Edman, "Art," *Encyclopaedia of the Social Sciences,* II, 226.

[18] René Grousset, *Chinese Art and Culture* (New York, 1959), p. 43.

THE DYNAMICS OF ACHIEVEMENT
MOTIVATION: SOME PSYCHO-
LOGICAL EVIDENCE

Evidence of a change in the patterning of individual motivation with increasing prosperity is implicit in a series of psychological analyses of fantasy-production samples from four historical societies. On the basis of literary and graphic evidence, Berlew and Aronson have demonstrated the need for achievement to have been strongest during the "growth" stage of classical Greek culture (900–475 B.C.), to have declined during the "climax" (475–362 B.C.), and to have been still further reduced in the "decline" phase (362–100 B.C.).[23] In Spain, the climax in painting can perhaps be placed (if El Greco is to be included) in the period from 1580 to 1660; and four different types of literary indexes of the need for achievement show it to have been declining from 1200 to 1730.[24] However, the first significant growth of modern English painting, in the eighteenth century, coincided with a period of increasing need for achievement—which McClelland attributes to the Wesleyan revival.[25] In their analysis of American children's literature, de Charms and Moeller have demonstrated an increase in the frequency of achievement imagery up to 1890 and a continuing decline in every decade since 1900.[26] In three cases out of four, the attainment of economic prosperity has

been associated with a lowering of achievement motivation (and it might have been in England as well, if not for the unpredictably intrusive factor of the Methodist movement). Presumably, in those cases, the level of prosperity attained has been felt to be sufficiently gratifying to legitimate the diversion of some motivational energy toward other kinds of activities, including those of the expressive kind. The decline in achievement motivation is roughly linked with increasing artistic creativity.

However, the Greek and Spanish data suggest that it is in the transitional period of *declining* achievement motivation that artistic creativity may be most stimulated. An extremely low level of achievement motivation, after a period of continuous decline, appears to be associated with a demand for material luxury, but also with a reduction in artistic creativity. This suggests that artistic creativity may in general be linked with changing patterns of motivation,[27] and that, consequently, high-quality art may have socially integrative and psychologically stabilizing functions to perform (which luxury in itself, presumably, does not).

These inferences are borne out by the observations of an economic historian on Renaissance Italy. "After the first decades of the thirteenth century and in the first half of the fourteenth . . . the urban economy of medieval Italy may be said to have entered its prime." But "by the fifteenth century," toward the culmination of the Renaissance, "Italy no longer occupied the same place in the economy of Europe as in the two preceding centuries . . . the old power of expansion was enfeebled," partly because of what seems to be a reduced achievement drive: "the new aristocracy of money" tended by now "to withdraw their capital from industry and trade and invest it, from motives of security and social prestige, in town and country proper-

---

[23] David C. McClelland, *The Achieving Society* (Princeton, N.J., 1961), pp. 119, 125. The need for achievement is measured by the relative frequency of achievement-related imagery in fantasy productions.

[24] *Ibid.*, p. 131.

[25] However, he believes that this increase in achievement motivation occurred primarily in the "middle and lower classes" to which Methodism had its chief appeal (*ibid.*, pp. 139, 145–49). Achievement motivation may in fact have been declining in the ruling class, which provided the greater part of the audience for such painters as Reynolds and Gainsborough—and lost the American war, though not because of its artistic taste.

[26] *Ibid.*, p. 150.

[27] Cf. the association of role change with artistic interest (Vytautas Kavolis, "A Role Theory of Artistic Interest," *Journal of Social Psychology*, LX [1963], 31–37).

ties." This was, however, a period of continued prosperity, and "during the fifteenth century court life in Italy attained its highest point of splendour."[28] The forfeiture of artistic leadership by the Italians after the High Renaissance may be associated with a hypothetical further decline in achievement motivation.

The evidence presented in this section suggests the general interpretation that increasing prosperity tends to reduce the motivation for achievement and to strengthen that for expressive action; and that it is in the extended moment when the two types of motivation are, in some at present not precisely definable manner, balanced in strength that highest-level artistic achievements are most probable. The theoretical justification of this expectation lies in the natural dependency of creative attainment in art upon the presence, in a strongly developed form, of *both* types of motivation.

With further increase in economic prosperity, however, achievement motivation tends further to decline and expressive motivation to become still stronger. This may be sufficient, on the one hand, to terminate economic advancement[29] (and even to reduce abundance per capita) and, on the other hand, to cause the further growth of a self-conscious interest in art works, as objects of luxury to which no profound emotional significance need be attached. But, in this stage, achievement motivation would seem to become inadequate to sustain creative achievements of the highest order, even in the sphere of artistic expression. Indeed, once this stage is reached, an *increase* in achievement motivation may stimulate the capacity to create great art.

ECONOMIC ACTIVITY AND
ARTISTIC CREATIVITY

It is possible to conceive the data surveyed in the previous section in terms of an

extremely long-range *psychoeconomic* phase cycle. Within this framework, the historical observations of the achievement-motive school suggest that artistic creativity tends to be inhibited in both the adaptive (pre-prosperity, high-achievement motivation) phase and in that of socioeconomic latency (stabilized wealth, low-achievement motivation). Conversely, it is stimulated in what may be regarded as the integrative phase, following immediately upon the attainment of relative prosperity (when achievement motivation is comparatively balanced against the drive for self-expression).

As contrasted with this psychoeconomic cycle, defined by the motivational accompaniments of economic achievement, a *socioeconomic* phase cycle may be conceptualized on the basis of changes over time in the commitment of social resources to economic action. While the nature of the relationship between the two types of cycles may be viewed as problematic, the phase-cycles model seems applicable, with appropriate modifications, to both types. As will be seen, however, it provides more useful information when applied to the socioeconomic data to be reviewed in this section.

Our theory predicts that the adaptive phase, indicated by sharply increased activity oriented to adaption to the external environment, should be inversely associated with artistic creativity. Two strategic cases will be considered. The decline of the earliest great artistic tradition, that of the European Stone Age, appears to be due, at least in part, to the new need for re-adaptation to the post-glacial environment, which must have absorbed the social resources of the population.[30] In principle, this case is comparable to the sharply increased need for re-adaptation effected by the Industrial Revolution, both in the West and in the developing non-Western societies; and its (possibly transitional) anti-artistic effects[31] are explicable as the prod-

---

[28] Gino Luzzatto, *An Economic History of Italy from the Fall of the Roman Empire to the Beginning of the Sixteenth Century* (New York, 1961), pp. 85, 142, 146, 143.

[29] McClelland, *op. cit.*, p. 120.

[30] Bandi *et al.*, *op. cit.*, p. 69.

[31] On such effects in Oceania and New Zealand, see Buehler *et al.*, *op. cit.*, pp. 51, 191. "Each of

uct of a radical movement, in the socioeconomic process, into the adaptive phase.

If this is valid reasoning, the period of the industrial transformation in which economic growth proceeds at the most rapid rate should be marked by reduced artistic creativity. Such periods were 1819–48 in Great Britain, 1868–93 in the United States, and 1928–40 in Russia.[32] When the dates of artistic debuts of the most prominent painters of the period are considered, the expectation is borne out for the two European societies,[33] and, possibly though not certainly, for the American as well.[34]

While the most intensive concentration on economic action appears to inhibit artistic creativity, there are indications that the gradual *beginning* of an economic transformation, before it gets into full gear, may have an artistically stimulating effect. Rostow has placed the dates of the "take-offs" to industrialization at 1783–1802 in

Great Britain, 1830–60 in France, 1843–60 in the United States, 1850–73 in Germany, and 1890–1914 in Russia.[35] In each case (with the possible exception of Germany), the beginning of a modern artistic efflorescence follows closely upon the take-off.[36] However, the artistically stimulating effect of the disturbance of relative socioeconomic latency by the beginning of a phase of intensive adaptive action tends later to be weakened by a more extreme commitment of social resources to adaptive action.

A second, and major, revival of artistic creativity should follow the transition from the adaptive (and goal-attainment) into the integrative phase of the total social process. Two sets of data will be used for identifying such transitions: (1) the beginning of contraction in the area, value, or amount of foreign trade,[37] and (2) the beginning of a long-range decline in the number of discoveries (in the case of Greece and Rome) or (in all other cases) in the percentage of the sum total of important inventions and discoveries made in a particular nation.[38] The latter index is

the epoch-making inventions which has caused an 'industrial revolution,' has caused an immediate decline in the artistic level of the pre-existing crafts" (Sir Hubert Llewellyn Smith, *The Economic Laws of Art Production: An Essay towards the Construction of a Missing Chapter of Economics* [London, 1924], pp. 146–47).

[32] W. W. Rostow, *The Stages of Economic Growth: A Non-Communist Manifesto* (Cambridge, England, 1962), p. 40.

[33] In Britain, the "generation of 1775" (approximate average birth date of Turner, Girtin, Constable, Cotman, and Crome) appeared just before the maximum growth period (Aurelien Digeon, *The English School of Painting* [New York, 1955], p. 10). And the next artistic development, the founding of the Pre-Raphaelite Brotherhood, in 1848, coincided with its termination. The only contributions of Russia to modern visual art were all made in the first two decades of the twentieth century, although some of them were subsequently further developed, by expatriated artists, in the West (Camilla Gray, *The Great Experiment: Russian Art 1863–1922* [New York, 1962]).

[34] Winslow Homer, the most significant American painter of this period, began to acquire fame just before the maximum growth stage. There was, however, little to decline from in American art during this stage.

[35] Rostow, *op. cit.*, p. 38.

[36] In France, the "great decade" of Impressionism, which originated in the 1860's, "was 1870–80" (Peter and Linda Murray, *A Dictionary of Art and Artists* [Baltimore, 1959], p. 162). In American art, the beginning of the activity of Homer, Ryder, and Eakins follows immediately upon the take-off, though the content of their work suggests a negative reaction to industrialization. In Germany, the really significant artistic developments (expressionism) were delayed until after the turn of the century. This "delayed effect" may be due to the intense preoccupation with political organization during this period. Artistic efflorescences tend to *follow* such periods. On Great Britain and Russia, see n. 33.

[37] McClelland, *op. cit.*, pp. 120, 132, 139.

[38] Sorokin, *Social and Cultural Dynamics*, II, 148, 150. Data for Greece and Spain suggest that the movement of inventions is associated with the level of foreign trade rather than with the need for achievement. The latter declines in both countries throughout the period at hand, whereas the rate of inventions and the level of foreign trade first rise and then fall in a similar, though not identical, pattern in both countries. In England,

only a tangential indicator of the degree of commitment of social resources to economically relevant adaptive activity, and consequently, so far as the present theory is concerned, it should be a less precise predictor of periods of artistic creativity.

On the assumption that artistic creativity is maximally stimulated in the phase of integration after intensive action, *before* this phase passes over into that of social latency, it is hypothesized, for the purpose of facilitating measurement, that the maxima of artistic creativity will occur within one hundred (plus or minus fifty) years after the beginning of a long-range decline in the commitment of social resources to economic action, as defined by the two previously cited indexes. The first set of data, then gives the following *predicted* maxima of artistic creativity: Greece, 550–450 B.C.; Spain, 1560–1660; England, 1634–1734. The second set gives the following maxima: Greece, 300–200 B.C.; Rome, A.D. 100–200; Spain, 1450–1550; Germany, 1100–1200, 1525–1625, and 1875–1975; France, 1200–1300 and 1825–1925; Italy, 1350–1450; Holland, 1551–1651 (or 1675–1775);[39] England, 1100–1200 (or 1250–1350), and 1800–1900.

To provide a rough test of this hypothesis, the "artistic climaxes," as judged by Sorokin, of the respective nations will be listed, first for sculpture and then for painting: Greece, 559–350 B.C. and 450–300 B.C.; Rome, 30 B.C.–A.D. 100 and A.D. 50–110; Germany, 1120–1260, 1400–1550, and 1450–1560, 1800–1900 (?);[40] France,

1140–1325, 1450–1550, 1850–1910, and 1620–70, 1760–1880 (?);[41] Italy, 1420–1600 and 1420–1600; England, 1220–50, 1758–87, and 1715–1850.[42] The periods of greatest artistic creativity in Holland and Spain may be set at approximately 1580–1660. While there are artistic peaks which do not seem, at least in this rough comparison, to be associated with the economic variables used here, there is apparently a very consistent tendency for periods of incipient decline in the commitment of social resources to economic action to coincide or overlap with significant artistic efflorescences. This correspondence is the more remarkable in view of the imprecision of the data, which have not been collected for the purpose at hand. As has been expected, the first index seems to be a somewhat better predictor of artistic peaks, except in the case of England where the Puritan Revolution may have "postponed" an otherwise expectable artistic efflorescence (although even in this case it overlaps with the predicted period).

The hypothesis that artistic creativity is associated with the passage from the adaptive into the integrative phase can apparently also be supported, though with less certainty, by prehistoric data. The important artistic tradition of the European Paleolithic hunters was created by an "advanced hunter culture" which had reached a "dead end along a particular path of development," while "two other types of economic activity, hoeing of the soil and pasturing cattle . . . in combination led to settled agriculture," without producing, during this period, art of comparable value.[43] It was this materially adequate,[44]

---

changes in the need for achievement are very closely associated with the level of foreign trade; hence, both are associated with the invention rate (McClelland, *op. cit.*; Sorokin, *Social and Cultural Dynamics*). The two indexes of economic action appear to be more closely interrelated than is either of them with the measure of achievement motivation. This (*a*) provides some validation for the former, and (*b*) suggests that the "psychoeconomic" and the "socioeconomic" cycles may not necessarily be closely co-ordinated.

[39] The data for Holland fail to reveal a clear pattern for the period from 1551 to 1675.

[40] This is a somewhat questionable estimate of a peak, which should probably be placed at 1900–1930.

[41] I would place the peak of modern French painting at 1820–1920.

[42] Sorokin, *Society, Culture, and Personality,* pp. 549–51.

[43] Bandi *et al., op. cit.*, p. 12.

[44] Georges Bataille, *Lascaux; or, the Birth of Art: Prehistoric Painting* (Lausanne, 1955), pp. 20, 23.

yet no longer progressing, culture that was responsible for "the birth of art."[45] A parallel association of relative economic backwardness with artistic creativity presents itself in the case of rock engravings so profusely carved, in several areas, in the period of transition from the Stone to the Metal Age.[46]

Other variables being at all comparable, the lack of economic progress in one society, while other societies under similar circumstances are advancing, implies relative satisfaction with the level attained. This suggests an orientation to the integrative rather than the adaptive exigencies in the social system of the Stone Age hunters who created the greatest art of their age.

Summarizing the materials presented in this section, it can be said that artistic creativity tends to be stimulated (a) in the period of initial response to the beginning of economic transformations and (b) in the phase of social-emotional reintegration following successful adaptive action in the economic sphere. It is adversely affected (a) in the phase of most intensive adaptive action in the economy and (b) in the phase of economic latency—which has been here identified as the condition of relative equilibrium preceding the beginning of a basic transformation of the socioeconomic system.

Clearly, artistic creativity does not arise from a state of relatively stable social integration, but from a felt need to achieve reintegration. Objectively viewed, the need exists during all stages of an economic transition, but the requisite resources are made available only in its very early stages (when they are not yet primarily committed to economic action) and in its *relatively* late stages (when the results of economic action are felt to be sufficiently satisfying to justify an increasing release of resources for symbolically expressive activities, and

[45] Bandi et al., op. cit., p. 26.

[46] Emmanuel Anati, *Camonica Valley* (New York, 1961), pp. 76–77, on northern Italian; Bandi et al., op. cit., p. 90, on eastern Spanish; and p. 127, on Saharan rock carvings.

before the need for reintegration is felt to have been adequately resolved).[47]

CONCLUSION

In the course of this survey, an extremely general sociological theory of artistic creativity has emerged. That economic data have been used as indexes of measurement is, in the most basic sense, incidental to the theory. The interpretations presented should have made clear that what is regarded as causally related to artistic creativity is not economic processes or achievements as such, but certain psychological and sociological conditions which can be empirically correlated with economic as well as, presumably, with other kinds of social processes.

The *psychological* factor favoring artistic creativity has been identified as a relatively balanced tension, in the personality system, between the drives toward achievement and toward expression. There is a very real problem, which our data do not help much in resolving, whether, in a highly differentiated society, this type of motivation must be present only in the personality systems of creative minorities, or whether it must be more generally prevalent to make possible an artistic efflorescence. It is assumed that this personality characteristic constitutes the patterning of individual motivation which is most conducive to artistic attainment.

The *sociological* factor which the data suggest to be an important causal agent in

[47] Artistic creativity which is caused by the beginning of an adaptive disturbance of social latency should be less likely to provide potent symbolic foci of sociocultural integration than the creativity stimulated in the "social-emotional" phase following that of intensive adaptive action, when social resources are *increasingly* released for non-instrumental pursuits. As cases in point, Romanticism may be compared with the Renaissance (and with Greek classicism). This distinction suggests an important element in the analysis of the "alienation of the artist." Because he has a smaller (and perhaps declining) claim on the socially distributed resources and for this reason can accomplish less, the artist should feel more alienated in the initial disturbance than in the reintegration phase.

artistic efflorescences is a widely felt need for reintegration of the social system. While this need has been treated here as a theoretical construct to account for the pattern of data, its existence has been experimentally demonstrated in small-group research, from which the conceptual model of this investigation has been derived. The collective perception of this need is viewed as the cause of an increased demand for art and consequently of a tendency to commit social resources to the action of artistic creation. It is not assumed, however, that the social demand for art is caused only by the integrative need.

The relationship between the two basic variables—the patterning of individual motivation and the commitment of social resources—must be regarded as intrinsically problematic. If the kind of motivation which is most conducive to artistic attainment has not been developed in the personality system, a widespread social demand for art will probably be insufficient to cause an artistic efflorescence. It is only by exploring the historically variable relationship between the two variables that a systematic sociological theory of artistic creativity can be developed.

Regarded by itself, no economic or any other social process can be expected always to have the theoretically predicted effect on artistic creativity. First, a tradition of high art must be present for any social factor to have a significant artistically stimulating effect, and such traditions cannot be taken for granted. Second, the artistically propitious phases of one type of cycle may overlap with, and in their effects be offset by, unpropitious phases of other partly differentiated cycles (political, religious, communal), or vice versa. Third, any historically real cycle movement may be interrupted by the beginning of a new cycle before the former has reached the integrative phase, in which its artistic effects should be most strongly felt.

In spite of the blurring effect which the complexities of historical data have on any theoretically conceived pattern, the evidence presented tends to indicate that the theory of phase cycles constitutes a useful approach to the study of artistic creativity, certainly one of the areas to which the authors of the theory have least intended to apply it.

DEPARTMENT OF SOCIOLOGY
DICKINSON COLLEGE

Questionnaire on the Cost of Letters, with Responses
by Twenty-one Writers.

from

Horizon, 14, 1946.

QUESTIONNAIRE:
THE COST OF LETTERS

1. How much do you think a writer needs to live on?

2. Do you think a serious writer can earn this sum by his writing; and if so, how?

3. If not, what do you think is the most suitable second occupation for him?

4. Do you think literature suffers from the diversion of a writer's energy into other employments or is enriched by it?

5. Do you think the State or any other institution should do more for writers?

6. Are you satisfied with your own solution of the problem and have you any specific advice to give to young people who wish to earn their living by writing?

*   *   *

J. BETJEMAN

1. As much as anyone else.

2. No person requiring intoxicating drinks, cigarettes, visits to cinemas and theatres and food above British Restaurant standard can afford to live by writing prose if he is not 'established'. Not even a *popular* poet, if there is one, can live by his poetry.

3. I can speak only for myself. I would like to be a station-master on a small country branch line (single track).

4. I do not know.

5. The State cannot possibly help a creative writer since, properly viewed, a writer is as much part of the State as a Civil Servant. You are therefore asking should a writer do more for *himself*? A Government Office certainly cannot help since it is concerned, or should be concerned, with making living conditions tolerable, with giving us enough to eat, proper roads and drains and heat and light and arranging wars for us when our existence is threatened from outside. A few writers find their inspiration in writing about politics—most of them write vilely— but I would have thought the subject-matter of a writer is irrelevant to this question. I do not see why writers, as much as

school-teachers or manual workers, should not be entitled to a State pension when their powers are over. As it is, they are subject to the publicity and niggardliness of the Civil List. A decent pension should be the limit of help from a Government Office.

The Society of Authors might arrange that when the State approaches a writer to write something, the State should offer a fee commensurate with a generous periodical instead of apologizing for the lowness of the fee and excusing it on the grounds that it is Government work.

6. No. Who is? But if someone is born to be a writer nothing will prevent his writing. Perhaps the bitter tests of today are a good thing. But you need great strength of character. At all costs avoid an advertising agency where you will either have to write lies or embellish facts in which you are not interested; such work is of the devil. Journalism is a better way out for weak characters, such as I am, who are slaves to nicotine and drink. It teaches you to write shortly and clearly. It allows you to say what you think—at least reputable journalism does. It forbids you to be a bore.

But because I believe that there is such a thing as a balance between mental work and manual work and because I believe that in Britain today people are subjected to too much of one or too much of the other, I would advise a young writer to equip himself for manual work which he thinks he will enjoy. It is pretty certain to be better paid than is writing in its initial stages. If I had my life over again, I think I would take up some handicraft—making stained glass or weaving or french polishing or woodcarving—and with this to fall back on and to content the manual side of me without destroying my soul, I would be refreshed and confident when I wrote. But I would have taken on such work with writing as my chief aim. I would have taken it on in self-defence because I knew I must write and that God had called me to be a writer, but demanded that I do my quota of work with my hands.

ELIZABETH BOWEN

1. I should say that, as in the case of any other kind of person, this depends on his liabilities and his temperament. In my own case, I should like to have £3,500 a year net.

B

2. I should say that, with *all* past books in print and steady production still going on, a writer, if his or her name is still of value, should be able to command two-thirds of the sum I have named by the time he or she is 60 or 65.

3. I should say in a man's case a suitable second occupation would be either medicine, architecture or law. Very few women would have time to carry on two professions simultaneously as their personal life and domestic responsibilities take up a good deal of time in themselves.

4. I should think that a writer's writing would be improved by any activity that brought him into company with other than that of his fellow writers. Literary sequestration, which seems to be increasing, is most unfortunate. On the other hand, the diversion of energy is a danger. If a writer is doing two things at the same time he is likely to have more to write *about*, but runs the risk of writing with less high concentration and singleness of mind.

5. I find this difficult to answer, as I am not clear how much the State does already. Writers who have worked hard and shown distinction (in any field, or of any kind) should certainly be entitled to some help, or even a degree of support, in the case of illness or old age. And, equally, some sense of responsibility should be felt by the public towards the dependants (young children, etc.) of such writers. As far as I know, an extension of the Literary Fund, and possibly a contribution to this from the State, should meet the purpose.

6. I doubt if one ever does arrive at a specific solution of the problem—it is a matter of getting along from year to year. My advice to young people who wish to earn their living by writing would be to go at it slowly, with infinite trouble, not burn any boats in the way of other support behind them, and not either expect or play for quick returns.

ALEX COMFORT

1. I cannot lay down an income scale for 'writers', as if they were a race apart from anyone else. I live on a combined income of about £500 per annum, with a wife, and one child expected.

2. In other words, can a writer who conscientiously produces work he considers artistically worth while live on the proceeds

of it? Yes, obviously he can, if he happens to write in one of the genres or styles which are commercially subsidized, but in the present world it seems to me highly inadvisable for him to do so. It means that one has to impose some sort of quota in order to live comfortably; it renders one dependent on the phases of an opinion which one ought to be forming, not obeying, and it continually dangles the temptation of subsidy-conditional-on-conforming under one's nose. I would not try to live entirely upon literary work myself, even though at the moment I probably could get paid for everything I write without being obliged to alter it. The writers who are working experimentally, or in forms such as lyrical poetry, would be quite unable to live out of their work, if only because of the relatively small volume which can be produced by one man. I have no sympathy with the Chatterton-Rimbaud fairy stories which lead writers to starve in garrets, or, the more modern equivalent, sponge on non-literary friends, because they are poets and find work too mundane. Artists are not privileged people—art is probably the human activity most deeply dependent on a responsible attitude to other people.

3. This depends upon the attitude which you adopt towards life. I believe that the most consistent and factually justifiable attitude towards life and art is Romanticism, by which I mean a philosophy based upon two postulates—that Man individually and collectively is engaged in continual conflict to assert the standards, beauty, justice, and so on, which are the product of his own consciousness, against an inert universe and a hostile environment, on the one hand, and power on the other: and that by reason of this conflict we have a definite, inescapable duty and responsibility towards all other human beings. We are afloat on a raft in a sea of mindlessness—our cargo includes all the things which consciousness regards as valuable, and there are one or two people on board who have lost their heads and are busier trying to assert their own authority than working to keep the raft afloat. We have to fight them with one hand and the elements with the other. The two fights are part of one single conflict, and for me art is the name we give to the struggle for spiritual survival and science (the genuine article, not the kitsch variety) the fight against death and our environment. One can add revolution, the fight against the human allies of the dead

environment. That is why I regard scientific activity as fully continuous with artistic activity—I don't know where one stops and the next starts. I do not suggest that all artists should try to become research workers, but I think that their second occupation should be one which bears some relation to the general effort of Man, which I call mutual aid.

4, 5, 6. My answers follow from what I have said. Non-literary activity always enriches creation subject to my provisos. As to the State, since one of the major battles of the sane man in the present period is against obedience, an enemy second only to death, I don't think the artist should touch the State or its money with a barge-pole. The same applies to commercial patronage, increasingly, from day to day. In a period of barbarism one has to be able to cut oneself off from all patronage—put yourself in the place of the European underground writers, and remember that the responsible human being is a member of a permanent underground movement who must be ready to carry on his work in the devastated landscape of the next hundred years.

6. Yes, entirely satisfied. What I have written here and elsewhere about this question is the only advice I have to offer. It boils down to this—be human, fight death and obedience, work like anyone else, since that is part of humanness, despise kiss-breeches and collaborators, and produce the work which you feel compatible with these ideas.

For your information, my own non-literary posts at the moment are M.O. in a Borough Children's Clinic and research assistant at a hospital. I am paid for the first, but not the second.

CYRIL CONNOLLY

1. If he is to enjoy leisure and privacy, marry, buy books, travel and entertain his friends, a writer needs upwards of five pounds a day net. If he is prepared to die young of syphilis for the sake of an adjective he can make do on under.

2. He can only earn the larger sum if he writes a novel, play, or short story, which is bought by Hollywood and/or chosen by one of the American book societies, but he can add considerably to his income if he tries to publish everything he writes simultaneously in American periodicals, who all pay most handsomely. This is the only dignified way of making more money without giving up more time.

3. A rich wife.

4. If you substitute 'painting' for 'literature', it becomes obvious that no art can be enriched by the diversion of an artist's energy. A good book is the end-product of an obsession; everything which impedes the growth and final exorcism of this obsession is harmful. All writers like to have hobbies and side interests to fill up the interval between obsessions, but this is not the same as having other employment. Compare Pope with Gray, Tennyson with Arnold, Baudelaire with Merimée, Yeats with Housman. Pope and Yeats *grew*, the two dons, despite their long holidays, remained stationary.

5. The State, in so far as it supplants private enterprise, *must* supplant private patronage. But private patronage was not based on results, and the State should not count on them either. Free gifts of money should be made to those setting out on an artistic career, and at intervals of seven years, to those who persist in one. Most of our good writers need at the moment a year's holiday with pay. Furthermore, pensions to artists and their widows should be trebled, both in value and quantity, and considered an honour, not a disgrace. All State-conferred honours to artists should be accompanied by a cash award. Furthermore, all writers and painters should be allowed a fairly large entertainment allowance, free of tax, and one annual tax-free trip abroad. Books and framed paintings (as opposed to articles, sketches, posters, etc.) should be regarded as capital and the income from them not taxed. This would encourage the production of books rather than the better-paid journalism by which most writers now make their living. Money spent on buying books and works of art by living artists should also be tax-free. Big Business, too, could do much more for writers and painters. Shell and London Transport before the war were setting the example. Even the general public can send fruit and eggs. The State's attitude towards the artist should be to provide *luxe, calme et volupté*, and when it receives *ordre et beauté* in return, to be sure to recognize it.

6. No, certainly not. What a question! As for the young, don't become writers unless you feel you must, and unless you can contemplate the happiness, security and cosiness of respectable State-employed people without loneliness or envy. Otherwise, like most of us, you will resemble the American 'who wanted to be a poet and ended up as a man with seven jobs'.

C. DAY LEWIS

I could not generalize about any of these questions. Ideal thing, for most writers: a private income—small enough not to encourage laziness or dilettantism, large enough to relieve the worries, obsessions and grosser expedients of poverty, say £150 to £300 a year. Failing this, should a young writer make his basic income from (*a*) literary hack-work or (*b*) a second occupation? Depends so much upon the individual. Advantage of (*a*) is that it has (or can have) some relation to his serious work, something to do with words and ideas and even with the imagination; and one only learns how to write by writing—and 'hack' writing has its discipline, its opportunities to shirk, to twist, or to be honest and careful, just as does 'serious' writing: serious writing, in one sense, is any writing you take seriously. Advantage of (*b*), for the beginner at any rate, is that it is the best way for him to find out whether he is really meant to be a writer: if he is not, the interest of the second occupation will soon overshadow the interest of writing; and he will have made a start with this other profession, instead of having to start again from scratch. The most suitable second occupation for a serious writer? A routine job, with regular hours, spare time, and (particularly if he is a novelist) one which brings him much into contact with people: for the novelist, who needs a wide range and diversity of personal contacts, medicine, the law, or commercial travelling might be recommended: for the poet, in so far as he needs a deeper, narrower experience, the instinctive kind of human relationship which comes from working with other people is perhaps best— the relationship of a Civil Servant, a schoolmaster, or for that matter a soldier or a miner, with his colleagues. The poet is a special case, anyway: other serious writers can, with luck, and without loss of integrity, make a living from their writing when established; the poet cannot, by his poetry alone. Ideally, he should arrange his life more regularly than the novelist; there is a systole and diastole in his creative workings, and his life should be adapted to these—a period of taking in followed by a period of giving out. He, if any writer, should receive support from the State; for, on the whole, his writing will be apt to suffer more than others' from diversion of his energy either into hack writing or a second employment: but State support should involve him in no obligations except to his poetry; therefore it would best come from some non-political organization such as the Arts Council. On the other hand, since friction stimulates, no writer should have things made too easy for him, materially, morally, psychologically: a smooth, cosy life in the bosom of the State, or the intelligentsia, will not do: it is in his struggle with the ordinary business of living, even more than in his struggle with problems of technique, that the writer finds his own level of seriousness.

ROBERT GRAVES

1, 2, 3. 'Serious writer' was, I think, a term invented by the young experimental writers of the 'twenties to distinguish themselves from the commercial, academic, and elder writers whom they lumped together as their common enemies. But if HORIZON is using the word in a less provocative sense, it includes such different types as the modern novelist who writes for entertainment but not according to a commercially dictated formula, the literary historian, and the poet.

Novel writing is not an all-time job, and there is nothing against a novelist having a secondary profession if he does not happen to have inherited, or married, money. Fielding was a police magistrate, Trollope a post office official, and for contemporary instances consult *Who's Who*.

The literary historian requires whatever it needs to live in a University society with ready access to specialist libraries and specialist colleagues. The snag is the difficulty of getting a salaried post that does not involve so much routine teaching that he cannot get on with his real work.

To be a poet is a condition rather than a profession. He requires whatever it needs to be completely his own master. This need not involve great expense—W. H. Davies solved the problem by being a professional tramp.

4. This is too broad a question for me to attempt an answer here.

5. Those who pay the piper call the tune. The State (or any State-sponsored institution) is a dangerous patron of literature.

6. Everyone has to solve the problem in his own way. First by deciding to what category of writers he belongs. Many begin as poets or experimental writers, and end as journalistic hacks. On

leaving the Army after the last war but one, I took a vow of poetic independence which I have kept ever since. The only job I took and held for a few months was that of Professor of English literature at Cairo University, but I was my own master, had only one hour a week lecturing, and resigned as soon as difficulties arose with my French and Belgian colleagues. That was twenty years ago, and I have lived ever since by writing biography and historical novels: a profession which I find more easily reconcilable than most with being a poet. Shakespeare himself admitted the difficulty of a secondary profession in his sonnet about the dyer's hand; and to say that I am satisfied with my solution would be indecent—it would imply a greater satisfaction with my work than Shakespeare seems to have felt with his.

As for advice, if the young writer really wants it: never write anything that you do not really want to write for its own sake, whatever the fee is. And if you have made no critical discovery about life or literature that you feel so important that you must write it down, putting everything else aside, in the most direct and careful language of which you are capable, then you are not a serious writer. Apply for a job with a newspaper, an advertising agency or the B.B.C. But if you are a serious writer and have no money, then live on your friends, relations or wits, until you can collect a public large enough to support you. (That took me twelve years.) If you must take a job, find one wholly unconnected with writing, leave it as soon as you are proficient in it, and either live on your friends again or take another quite different one.

I cannot answer the question in terms of pounds, shillings and pence, because I live abroad and, anyhow, never keep accounts, and have a large family to support.

ROBIN IRONSIDE

As an aspiring critic, mainly of painting, I require, for the satisfaction of my aspirations and having due regard to the present cost of living, a net income of £15 a week, an amount I have never possessed and am never likely to possess. Because I am too poor, I have never been to Greece or to America; with £15 a week, I believe I could contrive to do so without great discomfort. The propriety, for a critic of fine art, of a visit to Greece, is obvious;

nor is it possible to speak with any real authority on important aspects of French painting without some acquaintance with collections in the U.S. Such visits, even with the income I have proposed, would be exceptions to be paid for out of savings. But I should be able, without practising extreme thrift at home, to make brief annual excursions to France and Italy, and to visit any exhibitions, houses or museums, in the United Kingdom. Without these facilities, an aptitude for art criticism cannot adequately develop.

I regard £15 a week as a reasonable minimum, not as a bare minimum, and emphatically not as an optimum amount. Such qualities as my writings may already possess would improve as my income grew larger. I should be more diligent if I could work in a beautifully furnished room, if I could buy the books I wanted, if I could offer good food and wine to my friends, if I could be conveyed from place to place in a car, etc., etc. I am prepared to listen to people who tell me that there is a point at which money becomes a burden. But I do not really believe them. I could most profitably spend £10,000 in five minutes at Christies; if I were excessively rich I would hand out the excess to others; if wealth is burden, it is a burden that is very easily removed.

Serious writers without private resources must necessarily make a living by some means or other. State patronage would be incompetent to deal with this difficulty. It is hard to imagine any scheme of Government support that would not, at some stage of its career, be exposed to the danger of passing a megaphone to the bad writers with one hand, while it silenced the good ones with the other. I believe that everyone interested in the prosperity of the arts should look to a general reduction of working hours. Humanity is only too conscious of its right to work; in fact, this 'right' is not a right at all, but a necessity; what we need is a recognition of our right to leisure. If the normal working day could be reduced say to four hours, the State could exercise its discretion in the matter of patronage with the certain knowledge that, however misjudged the distribution of its benefits, anyone wishing to write would at least have some time in which to prove his abilities; and time, of course, is even more necessary to a writer than a satisfactory income. I am aware that a general reduction of working hours is not immediately realizable. But it is an ideal that requires, like other ideals, to be acclaimed and pursued now, if it is ever to be achieved in the future; and I am led to suppose (perhaps mistakenly) by the pronouncements of scientists and economists that its achievement, in a world at peace, need not be regarded as a remote or Utopian eventuality.

I am not satisfied with my own solution of the problem. I have, for a writer on art, the apparent good fortune to be employed at the Tate Gallery. But the administrative needs of this very important but unhappy institution are such that, within its doors, I must largely renounce the pursuit of knowledge and that official occasions for enlarging my appreciations elsewhere hardly, if ever, occur. It is a situation that must frustrate more than it can assist any ambition to qualify fully as an art critic.[1] If I possessed a private income of even £5 a week or a capital sum of £1,000, I would resign in the brave but slender hope that additional sums earned by writing and painting would provide a tolerable life for a substantial period of time.

Since I do not believe it is possible to make a living by writing criticism, I have no advice to offer to young people who wish to do so. I should be ashamed to dissuade and afraid to encourage them.

ROBERT KEE[2]

There is something inside all artists which remains themselves whatever happens, and this has nothing to do with income unless income is so low that they have neither time nor energy to be themselves.

The trouble is that few writers can be certain of obtaining regularly from their writings even the £400 a year which I regard as necessary to supply the time and energy with which to write. They have to turn to bureaucracy or journalism or some other activity which demands allegiance to society and thereby castrates them as writers. However, if there is no other way for a writer to get his £400 a year, a part-time extra job is at least preferable to a full-time one. And as a writer's business is to do with words it is obviously more sensible for him to turn to some form of word-using rather than to glass-blowing or road-making. But let him

[1] Adoption of the improvements recommended by the Massey Committee on the National and Tate Galleries would in great measure invalidate these observations.

[2] Winner of one of the recent Atlantic Awards.

be quite clear about what he is doing. There should be no attempt to compromise between money-earning and writing. There are already too many writers who, in the higher forms of intellectual and literary journalism, have lost sight of their real work. The principle should be: the easier the money, the more suitable the second occupation. If a writer cannot find enough to write about in what goes on all round him, without being 'enriched' by other employments, he might as well give up being a writer altogether.

But the idea of a writer having to descend to tricks to be able to follow his trade is unpleasant, and the society which tolerates it is being short sighted merely because it means that so much less serious writing will be done. How then is a writer to get his £400 a year? I suppose publishers could be made to surrender a great deal more of it than they do at the moment. The present relationship between writer and publisher seems as absurd as if a man were to be paid pocket-money by his butler. But this is really irrelevant because even if publishers did pay fairly it would not help the writer who produces little or who is not in sympathy with his time.

Therefore the State, as the instrument of society, should make £400 a year available to anyone who wants to be a writer. This would be renewable every year at the option of the writer. The only condition would be that no other employment could be taken during that year. There would be few abuses of this system. £400 a year is not enough to tempt the crook. Moreover, any charlatan who had no intention of writing would get so bored with nothing to do on so little money that he would be eager to escape at the end of the year. Admittedly some appalling writers would be given a chance but, regarded as experimental waste, this would be a minor drawback. We are prepared to tolerate several million pounds-worth of experimental waste to produce a new atom bomb. Surely we could afford a few thousands to produce a new writer?

This £400 a year would in no way be an attempt to reward the writer for what he does. It would merely make it possible for him to write. The writer should be paid for what he is, not what he does. However, the State should also see that those writers who do produce something are more suitably rewarded than at present. No income tax should be payable on income derived from writing, though it would be payable on the basic £400. A considerable sum—say, the cost of about one afternoon at war—should be set aside every year to be distributed as prizes for poems, novels, criticism, editorship, etc. And if anyone thinks that this State interest in literature would lead to the same results as in the totalitarian countries, I would say that our literatures would resemble each other just about as much as our State legal systems do at present.

In answer to your last question I can only say that I now enjoy £250 tax-free for one year on similar conditions to those which I have suggested. In so far as this is not £6 a week and will not continue after the end of the year, I am dissatisfied. In so far as it does give me a chance to write, I realise that I am more lucky than many writers who have already produced distinguished work.

LAURIE LEE

The commodity most necessary to the writer is not money at all, but time. The writer needs guaranteed time, long avenues of it stretching far away before him, free from congestion, side-tracks or concealed entrances. For ignoring the occasional lyric cart-wheel, which covers no more than a moment of paper, serious writing is one of the most pedestrian occupations that exists.

I think few serious writers can earn this necessary time, legitimately, by the sort of writing they most wish to do. There are always the speed-kings, of course, but they pay heavily with blurred and half-seen images and phrases mutilated by the wind. A writer needs time to pause, to explore, to cultivate in detail the prospect before him. He needs to take time, and having taken it, to consume it in his own time.

But who among us is free to do this? Look at the panting cross-country novelists. Look at the six-day-bicycle-riding script writers, struggling at poems while changing tyres. Their doom is in the pace and the payout; they are paid off by the number of milestones they cover, and not by their discoveries of the country in between. These are the things which break their hearts and wind.

Old-day patronage was in many ways evil, but at least it gave the artist time without tears. Its modern counterpart—State or commercial sponsorship in their present forms—is a great deal worse, for this, geared to the speed-neurosis of industry, induces in the writer all the jumping-jack hysteria of the factory-worker faced with the dictatorship of the moving belt.

What are the present alternatives? A he-man's job as wood-cutter or crane-driver, with a couple of hours writing in the evenings? Romantic fallacy! The body's exhaustion is also the mind's. A State job, then—Ministry propagandist or B.B.C. hack? No; they fritter and stale like nobody's business.

What then? A State pension for all writers, with no questions asked? Not altogether; but that is more like it. Hardship and near-starvation are not bad for the young: they force the broader view, they stimulate, they atomize the coral-coasted island; they give birth to thoroughbreds of sublimation out of frustration. Let younger writers first serve this apprenticeship, and show something for it. Then, when they have passed the test, let the State provide them with sufficient pasture to live on, a free hand, and a bonus for special achievements. But do not let this be free altogether from the demands of commission. A fat pension, with no provisos, only encourages fatness; but extra sugar for spec-tacular leaps will keep the beasts in condition.

As to a present personal solution of the problem: my own serves me well enough, but I cannot say it would serve others. My rules are these: To avoid as far as possible the dissipation of regular work for others. Never to despise a commission unless I dislike it. Shelve any commission whenever the compulsion to do private work arises. But generally I welcome the rewards of scattered commissions; the discipline involved often provides channels for genuine personal expression. Anyway, I like writing for a waiting audience; and ever since my schooldays I have enjoyed making poems to a set subject. I only wish publishers and editors would issue that kind of challenge more often. Records are never broken except on a set course.

ROSE MACAULAY

There can't be any general rule as to how much a writer needs to live on. But whatever it is, it is very unlikely that he will earn it at all early in his career, unless he happens to make a lucky hit, get chosen by book societies in this and other countries, perhaps even get filmed. The ordinary young writer, whether serious or not, must depend on something else for some years. If he (or she) has good-natured and moderately well-off parents, they may consent to keep him (or, more likely, her) till he finds his feet, or, alternatively, finds that he had better adopt another career. If the parents refuse this burden, as well they may, and if there are no other means of support, the young writer should enter some profession, the less exacting the better. If possible, he should choose a job that does not run counter to and stultify his creative instincts; either purely mechanical or physical work, whose hang-over would not impinge on his leisure, but which he could forget entirely when he laid down his tools each day and turned to his writing; or work that ministered to his imagination. It might be useful to get a job abroad for a time. Southey had a notion that he would be happy and fruitful if only he could get the consulship at Lisbon —''Tis a good thousand a year'—though as a matter of fact the Lisbon consuls have always been busier than he supposed, and have had little time for literary pursuits. On the other hand, diplomats, whether ambassadors or holding some lesser post in a legation, have often written a great deal. Councillors and First Secretaries have been eloquent, and chancelleries have been nests of singing-birds or of experimenters in prose. But diplomacy, of course, is out of the reach of most young writers; it is a profession approached over stiff hurdles. Easier to be a tourist agent abroad (if you know any languages), or get a job in a café or a foreign bank or firm. That way, the writer will see life a little, which should be good for him. Much better not enter an intellectual profession, such as the law, medicine, or teaching, which will absorb his mind. In former times, the country parson's was often a life which gave scope for literature and scholarship; the fact that this is seldom now the case may indicate the decline of intellectual quality among clergymen. The number of our clerical authors in the past—and down almost to the present generation—is greater than in any other one profession; the quality of their work perhaps higher. However, if the writer succeeds in finding the job to suit him—preferably a series of jobs—his professional work should enrich his talent.

The State might well consider helping young writers with temporary maintenance. 'Let there be patrons,' as Herrick (himself patroned by Emmanuel Porter) urged in moving verse. Patrons have gone out; the State might do something to fill the gap. There might be a committee for the purpose of selecting worthy candidates. As no one can tell at first whether a serious writer is a bad serious writer or a good one, a few risks would have to be taken, and a few bad writers helped, as they were often helped by patrons of old. This does no great harm; better that than good young men and women should be forced to earn their daily bread by work that uses up all their energies and stultifies their talent. All the same, writers should be ready to live a little hard; to travel cheaply if at all, to eat and drink simply. They had better not be in a hurry to get married; this leads to expense, and, if they are young women, to devastating distraction of energy. (Unless, of course, they manage to marry money, which solves the problem at once.)

J. MACLAREN-ROSS

Your questionnaire arrived at an opportune moment, when I was at my wits end to know which way to turn for money. This situation is always arising with me. Hence, my answer to your first question is: A writer needs all he can lay his hands on in order to keep alive.

How much he actually should have depends on the writer himself: his tastes and habits. In other words, he should be able to live comfortably, in a style that suits his temperament. If he is a drinker he shouldn't have to worry whether he drinks beer or spirits or wine, though he shouldn't necessarily have enough to get sozzled every night. If he is a smoker he shouldn't have to buy Woodbines if he prefers Perfectos. If he wants to buy a book he should be able to buy it, not wait until it is sent to him for review or lent to him by a friend. If he doesn't drink, smoke, read books or go to the cinema, then he almost certainly has other vices, or else a wife or mistress to spend money on; well, he should have enough to spend. A writer's standard of living should be at the least as high as that of a solicitor, or any other professional man.

I am a metropolitan man and I need a minimum of £20 a week to live on, given the present cost of living; and that's *not* including rent. Whether I get it or not is another matter.

Which brings me to your second question: How can a serious writer earn this sum by writing? It's very difficult. Suppose, like myself at the moment, you have written short stories but now want to write novels. How do you raise the sum of money needed to sit down and concentrate on writing a novel in moderate peace of mind? You can't do it except by more short stories, radio plays, or what have you, the writing of which takes up most of your time and vitiates your energy. So the novel doesn't get written, that's all.

Suppose, however, you are fortunate enough to obtain an advance of £300, you certainly spend more than that while writing the book, so you're no better off; in these days of small editions and reprints at long intervals, your advance almost covers the total royalties on your sales. Then there is the interval between delivery of MS. and the appearance of the book: nine months to a year if you are lucky, three years if you are not, as in one case I know. After that there is a further period until statements of sales go through and royalties are paid up; any attempt to obtain money in between is regarded by the publisher as an imposition, or, if he doles out some small sum, as an act of charity.

Besides, advances are rarely anything like £300. They are more likely to be, at the most, £75 or £100. The *Artists' and Writers' Year Book* is still talking about £25 as a suitable advance, 'but only in rare cases can publishers be made to see this'.

Therefore a novelist is supposed to spend six months writing his book and then live for a further eighteen months or so on his advance—about £100. Plainly impossible, with the present cost of living, even for a man of the most spartan tastes.

Publishers should be made to acknowledge the higher cost of living and to pay advances in proportion; a minimum of £300 should be forced upon them, and even that will not keep anyone for eighteen months. The rates paid by editors for poems, articles, stories, are far higher now than they were before the war. Why haven't publishers raised their rates accordingly?

Until they do, the writer is compelled to exist by means, in my opinion, detrimental to his serious work. In many occupations, like film-script writing, the B.B.C., etc., he has neither the leisure nor the energy, when the day's dull work is done, to settle to what he really wants to do. I don't think there can possibly be any occupations suitable to the writer other than that of writing what he wants when he wants and of being well paid for doing so.

I don't think, either, that the State or any other institution should support writers. Such a state of affairs would inevitably lead to limitation or control of subject-matter and theme. It is the publishers and editors, who make money and reputation out of printing writers, who should do more for the people on whose work they in turn depend for their living.

But this solution to the problem does not satisfy me, since I see no hope of the present vicious system being altered; and if I have advice to give to anyone who wants to write for a living, it is this:

(*a*) Don't attempt it.

(*b*) If you are crazy enough to try, be tough; get all you can.. Price your work high and make them pay. Don't listen to your publisher's sob-stories about how little he can afford. He'll have a country house and polo ponies when you are still borrowing the price of a drink in Fitzrovia. Remember, *he* makes the money; make him give you as much as you can extort, short of using a gun or pincers. Art for art's sake is all cock, anyway.

And by the same token, please pay promptly for this contribution, because I am broke.

GEORGE ORWELL

1. At the present purchasing value of money, I think £10 a week after payment of income tax is a minimum for a married man, and perhaps £6 a week for an unmarried man. The *best* income for a writer, I should say—again at the present value of money—is about £1,000 a year. With that he can live in reasonable comfort, free from duns and the necessity to do hackwork, without having the feeling that he has definitely moved into the privileged class. I do not think one can with justice expect a writer to do his best on a working-class income. His first necessity, just as indispensable to him as are tools to a carpenter, is a comfortable, well-warmed room where he can be sure of not being interrupted; and, although this does not sound much, if one works out what it means in terms of domestic arrangements, it implies fairly large earnings. A writer's work is done at home, and if he lets it happen he will be subjected to almost constant interruption. To be protected against interruption always costs money, directly or indirectly. Then again, writers need books and periodicals in great numbers, they need space and furniture for filing papers, they spend a great deal on

C

correspondence, they need at any rate part-time secretarial help, and most of them probably benefit by travelling, by living in what they consider sympathetic surroundings, and by eating and drinking the things they like best and by being able to take their friends out to meals or have them to stay. It all costs money. Ideally I would like to see every human being have the same income, provided that it were a fairly high income: but so long as there is to be differentiation, I think the writer's place is in the middle bracket, which means, at present standards, round about £1,000 a year.

2. No. I am told that at most a few hundred people in Great Britain earn their living solely by writing books, and most of those are probably writers of detective stories, etc. In a way it is easier for people like Ethel M. Dell to avoid prostitution than it is for a serious writer.

3. If it can be so arranged as not to take up the whole of his time, I think a writer's second occupation should be something non-literary. I suppose it would be better if it were also something congenial. But I can just imagine, for instance, a bank clerk or an insurance agent going home and doing serious work in his evenings; whereas the effort is too much to make if one has already squandered one's energies on semi-creative work such as teaching, broadcasting or composing propaganda for bodies such as the British Council.

4. Provided one's whole time and energies are not used up, I think it benefits. After all, one must make some sort of contact with the ordinary world. Otherwise, what is one to write about?

5. The only thing the State could usefully do is to divert more of the public money into buying books for the public libraries. If we are to have full Socialism, then clearly the writer must be State-supported, and ought to be placed among the better-paid groups. But so long as we have an economy like the present one, in which there is a great deal of State enterprise but also large areas of private capitalism, then the less truck a writer has with the State, or any other organized body, the better for him and his work. There are invariably strings tied to any kind of organized patronage. On the other hand, the old kind of private patronage, in which the writer is in effect the dependant of some individual rich man, is obviously undesirable. By far the best and least exacting patron is the big public. Unfortunately the British public

won't at present spend money on books, although it reads more and more and its average of taste, I should say, has risen greatly in the last twenty years. At present, I believe, the average British citizen spends round about £1 a year on books, whereas he spends getting on for £25 on tobacco and alcohol combined. Via the rates and taxes he could easily be made to spend more without even knowing it—as, during the war years, he spent far more than usual on radio, owing to the subsidizing of the B.B.C. by the Treasury. If the Government could be induced simply to earmark larger sums for the purchase of books, without in the process taking over the whole book trade and turning it into a propaganda machine, I think the writer's position would be eased and literature might also benefit.

6. Personally I am satisfied, i.e. in a financial sense, because I have been lucky, at any rate during the last few years. I had to struggle desperately at the beginning, and if I had listened to what people said to me I would never have been a writer. Even until quite recently, whenever I have written anything which I took seriously, there have been strenuous efforts, sometimes by quite influential people, to keep it out of print. To a young writer who is conscious of having something in him, the only advice I can give is not to take advice. Financially, of course, there are tips I could give, but even those are of no use unless one has some kind of talent. If one simply wants to make a living by putting words on paper, then the B.B.C., the film companies, and the like are reasonably helpful. But if one wants to be primarily a *writer*, then, in our society, one is an animal that is tolerated but not encouraged—something rather like a house sparrow—and one gets on better if one realizes one's position from the start.

V. S. PRITCHETT

1. Before the war I remember J. Middleton Murry held that a writer could honestly earn about £400 a year. Aldous Huxley estimated the need at about £700. The post-war equivalent would be about £1,200 to £1,400 gross.

2. A vastly successful novelist, playwright, etc., can, of course, earn much more. But the promising, the rising, the merely successful, cannot earn anything like the above sums, by writing books or serious criticism or good short stories or poems, alone. The good creative writer will have to supplement his income

from journalism, broadcasting, publishers' reading, editorial work, some other job—or a private income.

3. Any secondary work.

4. But it is essential that it should take up very little time and energy. This hardly ever happens, and the result is an evident decline in the quality of creative literature. The writers are worn out, overworked; they are not worn out by creation but by the various grindstones by which they earn the major part of their living. I would say that up to the age of thirty it does not matter what a writer does with his time. An outside job may be valuable. After thirty, the outside job is inevitable in our high-costing, highly taxed society, where the private income is vanishing—inevitable, and in the long run fatal.

5. The question really amounts to this: should the State replace the support given by sinecures and the private income? No. State writers are bought and censored writers. I am against writers' co-operatives. I am in favour of the people who now have the large private fortunes being obliged, by the State, to support literature. These private fortunes are not in private hands. They are in the hands of the Boards, the shareholders of the great industrial firms. Shell-Mex, Unilever, London Transport, etc., should be obliged to give patronage—but not in return for publicity.

6. Advice to a young writer: discipline yourself to the *habit* of writing. Write every day. Keep office hours. Inspiration comes from the grindstone, not from heaven. Do not hope to move up from popular writing to more distinguished levels. Popular journalism corrupts very quickly. Write for yourself alone as long as you can; the conditions of the profession will gradually vitiate the highest standards. The failures of overwork are fewer than the failures of idleness. Move heaven and earth to get time, and put time before money whenever you can. Be born with a small private income; or get yourself supported by a husband or wife.

HERBERT READ

1. How much a writer needs to live on will depend on his personal appetites, but if he is married, has two or three children, likes decent food and a comfortable house, he will need with present costs at least £1,000 a year.

2. A serious writer cannot possibly earn this sum by writing.

A serious book takes two or three years to write. To earn the necessary sum by book royalties, he would have to sell between thirty and fifty thousand copies of each book: in all probability he will sell only three to five thousand copies.

3. The most suitable second occupation for him is one which is no drain on either his intellectual or physical energy. 'A nice job in a museum', jobs in publishers' offices and cultural organizations like the British Council and the B.B.C., are the worst possible kinds of occupation. They are too interesting: they overlap into his literary work. They create mental confusion and lead to all kinds of trivial activities which are intellectually exhausting and completely unremunerative.

Farming and small-holding, which have superficial attractions (especially for romantic writers) are physically far too exhausting. They drug the mental faculties with a poisonous fatigue.

The best kind of occupation is represented by Spinoza's lens-polishing. If I were beginning my life again, I should seek a job in the light engineering industry, especially one in which, by piece-work, the necessary amount of work could be varied according to the needs of the moment.

4. The more a writer has experience of the normal activities of human beings, the better it is for his writing. I can think of no great writer in the past who has not benefited from non-intellectual activities. I can think of many whose work has suffered from academic or hedonistic seclusion.

5. No. The State can only demoralize and debase literature.

6. I am far from satisfied with my own solution of the problem. I have tried several solutions—Civil Servant, museum assistant, university professor, editor of a magazine, and now a publisher. They have all been unsatisfactory, for the reasons given in my answer to Question 3 above. They bristle with the 'grappling-irons' which Cézanne so rightly feared, and although a strong-minded individual might be able to avoid the public responsibilities which will eventually attach to eminence in such a position, nevertheless all such jobs are by their nature 'contact jobs', and whichever way one turns one meets the devouring pack—until in the end one is reduced to a condition of dazed indifference, the paralysis of the cornered animal.

My advice to young people who wish to earn their living by writing is at all costs to avoid following my example.

HENRY REED

I find it easier not to answer Question 1 first. Question 2: I believe that after three or four years of practice a writer who is willing to do subsidiary literary work should be able to keep himself by writing. The position of the poet and the novelist is much the same: both have to earn their leisure to write; I think it is best, for most writers, to earn it by subsidary writing of a civilized type; this is often extremely helpful in loosening a writer's tongue. The avenues open are obvious: free-lance journalism (especially for the 'good' provincial daily papers); commissioned reviewing (which should not be difficult to get, since reviewers are always drifting *out* of it); broadcasting, and writing for broadcasting. After a time it is wiser for a writer to confine this honourable hack-work to commissioned work. There is less risk and more money in it. I think it bad for any writer to write down; I deplore the writer who, *without enjoying it*, writes low fiction (e.g. detective stories) or dance-lyrics in order to earn money. To do so is to give play to a cheap part of the mind (present in all writers, I suspect—cf. some of James's plays) of which a writer must, in fact, strive to rid himself. There is a danger—though clearly a decreasing one—in writing for films.

3. The trouble with most secondary jobs available to writers is that you often have to write as well in order to bring your income within bearable limits. The best job is teaching, because of its incomparable holidays. It is, however, a job very exhausting to the brain, the emotions, the throat and the legs; I have found that office-work is less tiring mentally and physically, but its hours often make work in the evening impossible. A university life is ostensibly ideal for writers; but here there is the grave disadvantage of your company; with angel-exceptions (some of whom I have met) the don is by nature prejudiced against the creative artist; in no profession is the belief more strongly held that all art *ceased* just before Mummy got married; there is a Freudian explanation of this, but it remains one of those obstinate psychological cloggings which get round the bend where the brush cannot reach. Its atmosphere savages the soul. A disadvantage of *all* secondary jobs is that they are apt to become primary. This induces in a writer self-pity and lethargy, both fatal.

4. You have but to look round to see how badly 'literature' suffers from the diversion of a writer's energy elsewhere. Very serious writers do not let their knowledge of outside *milieux* intrude unduly in their work; but minor writers are not very strong-minded about this. On the other hand, think what we should miss if Melville had never gone whaling, or Joyce Cary never been in the African Service; note, however, that they both digested these experiences before writing of them, and that they are great enough writers to order their recondite experiences into art.

5. I believe emphatically in the value of State help, and help from other institutions who will be willing to risk no returns. But the funds should *not* be administered by the donating institution, least of all by the State. Artists—cf. the Soviet novelists and our own official War Artists—are only too ready to play the whore and the toady to any institution which will pay them to do so. The universities, and particularly the provincial ones, should, I think, administer such funds; and as soon as practicable those who have benefited should help to choose future recipients. This brings me to Question 1. I think the three hundred pounds offered for one year by the Atlantic Awards is an admirable basic sum (it is, I believe, free of income tax). It is enough for various forms of existence, including, I venture to think, married life and possibly a fairly small child. £300 a year, however, still entails worry in the background; I think a youngish writer (i.e. younger than 35) can live fairly happily on £800 to £1,000 a year.

6. I am quite content with my own 'solution'. I have a good deal of advice to offer. For writers without a private income, it is advisable to face the process of a possibly slow *conversion* to a position where they have to make fewer and fewer concessions for the sake of money: i.e. it is advisable for them to put up with the more reputable forms of hack-work till they need no longer do so. When they can, they should drop hack-work like hot bricks, however easy it has become. In any case, they should be very chary of the implications of each *kind* of hack-work: specifically, and without frivolity, I would advise all young writers not to take on regular novel-reviewing. It is one of the most exacting and lowering jobs in the world.

And poets: the poet must (but above all secretly) think of

himself as a potential Shakespeare, *and not less than this;* he will rarely find difficulty in excusing to himself his occasional failures. He must manage his relations with his novelist-colleagues very carefully. The novelist is always kind to the poet, but the income-difference is always there. How true it is that every novelist would prefer to have been a poet I am not sure; I rather doubt it. At any rate the poet feels among novelists like a poor tolerated relative who has the good looks of the family but nothing else. Try to avoid a stab of anger and jealousy at the thought that even a good novelist earns about fifty times as much from his novels as you do from your poetry. Finally, no writer should live too far below his income; avoid cheap or irregular meals; and if he stays on after a party, he should try to insist on a proper bed, not the floor or the sofa.

JOHN RUSSELL

All true writers exist in the hope of creating a masterpiece. This fact must be the central chimney and warming flue of their lives, and all other activities are, in the last resort, merely ways of buying the time which they need for their best work. All such writers write ultimately for themselves, and in obedience to inner canons of perfection; vanity, want and lust are potent local stimulants, but to the central impulse we must acribe, if hesitantly, a certain absolute, moral grandeur. This quality is held by modern society in organized disrespect; and nobody needs telling that, although good work occasionally meets with a copious financial reward, it does so only by luck or accident. Writers need, therefore, some auxiliary limb or iron lung, if they are to make a living. This can be acquired within their own field; for although few people live by literature, a great many live off it; and a life, for instance, of desultory writing for periodicals must now exert a great charm. Most other employments for young men offer a crushing load of work and a nugatory initial reward. Herbert's rectory, Stendhal's consulate and Pater's fellowship at Brasenose seem gone for ever, and leisure, even purposeful leisure, is difficult to secure. As against this, good writing will always be rare, and will always be sought after; for the first five or ten years an aspirant with unusual or acceptable talent will earn, with relative ease, as much in this way as would be paid to him during his first years in diplomacy, at the bar, or in any learned profession.

He will see himself at a bound among those whom he had hitherto regarded as Delphic arbiters of taste and judgement. His way of life is itself delightful; he can stroll up from the country on Tuesday afternoon; he need never be early for breakfast or late for the theatre; he can pass a normal life in society—or, if he wishes, a fruitfully abnormal one. Spring migrations are his for the asking; and on wet November mornings he can spare a glance, from his study window, for the dutiful bowlers of his friends as they splash along towards Whitehall.

In twenty years, however, his memory and ear will have been debauched by the habit of rapid composition to order; he will have lost the power of disinterested reading; his income will not have increased, though his commitments may well have trebled. He will never have dared to take a sabbatical year of travel and rearmament, for fear of that Tartar horde so vividly evoked by Sir Max Beerbohm—'younger men, with months of work before them'. His habits of mind will be known to the last twitch, and editors will dread his fixed grin or unvarying scowl. Most galling of all, he will see his beastly, dull contemporaries soar high above him; collocations of letters will hang to the tails of these comets; K.C.B., P.C., K.C.M.G., K.C., he will read. And as the junior Ministers move from N.W.3 to S.W.1, they will quietly drop him, and forbid their children to play with his. Illness will beggar him, and in perhaps another twenty years they will get him put on the Civil List, at forty pounds a year.

Writers are born, of course, with all their preservative instincts in a state of exceptional strength and tenacity. Most horny and tusky is this vital part of their being, and enclosed in a protective belt of Asian guile. Sublimest of spongers, the Duinese elegist has shown how the highest ambitions of the spirit need not exclude a deft and rapacious instinct for comfortable living; and I have heard it said, perhaps in envy or malice, that among our ranks long-sighted legacy-hunters and successful stalkers of rich wives occur in unusually high proportion. Be that as it may, I believe that the only serious enemies of a writer's best work are within himself; all outward obstacles can be overcome, and many may even do useful service as goads and challengers; and the advice or suggestions of others count ultimately for little. Most writers work, in Aubrey's phrase, 'as boars piss—scilicet, in jerks', and it is for the weeks and months of creative idleness that they and their patrons have to plan; but it would be difficult to convince any legislature of the realism of this view. Our task should rather be to improve the quality of the audience, and in this to begin with ourselves; it is arguable that, though the number of readers (or rather, of persons able to read) must be many times greater than at any other period in literary history, the informed audience has never, in proportion, been smaller. The State also has its duty here; for now that writers cannot hope to find the indulgent patrons or the commodious sinecures by which at one time they might have hoped to tide over their years of fasting and preparation, there is surely a case for the temporary endowment of at least a few young writers, and a stronger one for the protection of those who, in middle or later life, deserve better than indigence. If a small tax were levied upon all lending libraries, and the proceeds given to the Civil List, this might at last become a roll of honour, and its benefits be enlarged to the level of a decent subsistence.

EDWARD SACKVILLE-WEST

Another interrogatory! As if writers hadn't enough to do to keep their heads above water! But I see I have already begun to answer your questions, so I may as well go on.

The amount of income a writer needs to live on must, I should have thought, differ according to the kind of work he does. If he is a journalist with a family living in a town, he will need a lot more money than a novelist living alone in the country. But even then, what does 'need' mean? Some writers can be happy living very simply; others actually need what some would call superfluities—pictures, gramophone records, travel, lovers— to enable them to do their work properly. What appears to me certain is that a basic ration of *unearned* increment is essential to a 'serious' writer—so that he can afford to turn down hackwork that will fritter away his time, and not to be obliged to hurry his work, and even to lie fallow for a year or so if he feels the necessity of it. The only way a writer can earn a sufficient income today is by driving his quill as hard as it will go and harder, regardless of the results to his style, his taste and his sensibility.

There is no such thing as a 'suitable second occupation' for a writer—except in the sense that writing books on philosophy was a suitable second occupation for the late Lord Balfour.

Serious writing is a whole-time job, and a very hard one, too. When a writer takes to regular pot-boiling, his work is bound to suffer sooner or later. (Those who think this doesn't matter are unfit to live in a civilized country.)

Your fourth question is less easy to answer. Of course nearly all writers must accumulate a certain capital of emotional and practical experience. In some cases this has to be replenished from time to time, in others not. But—at any rate when first youth is over—any employment that continues to absorb most of the would-be writer's energy can hardly fail to sap his creative vitality and will quite soon destroy it altogether. On the other hand there are, of course, all kinds of daily chores and interests which, far from diverting a writer's energy, nourish and promote it.

I certainly do not think the State a good substitute for the private patron of past times. In theory the State may have all the right intentions towards artists, but in practice its patronage is bound to be far too rigid, since the 'benevolence' is entrusted to little men in ivory offices, who either fear to carry out their instructions in a liberal and imaginative way, or else interpret them according to ignorant personal prejudice. Look at the way Shostakovitch has been ruined by the dogmatism of the Soviet regime. Subsidiary institutions (university colleges, publishing houses) are an improvement in this respect, but even they tend to upset the situation by insisting on too quick a return for their money. In this connection it is worth recalling the case of Robert Bridges who, during his tenure of the laureateship, wrote practically no occasional verse at all; devoting all his energies to the completion of *The Testament of Beauty*. Which, in the circumstances, was exactly as it should be.

Am I 'satisfied with my own solution of the problem'? Of course I am not! If I were, I shouldn't be wasting my time answering your questionnaire: I should have chucked it into the waste-paper basket and gone on working at the novel which I ought to have started long ago, had the demon of journalism not got me by the throat. Rightly or wrongly, I consider myself as first and last an imaginative writer who is forced, by the pressure of present-day English life, to fritter away the years in purely ephemeral activities.

My advice to the young writer? First: cajole, bully or black-mail your parents, guardians or whatever, into giving you an independent income just large enough to keep the wolf from the door. Time—quite a short time—will show whether or not you have the root of the matter in you. If it becomes clear to yourself, as well as to others, that you have not, then will be time enough to take to some sort of hackwork.

One final word: don't begin by reviewing other people's books. Many—even most—young writers think this the easiest way of starting on the career of letters. In fact, it is among the most difficult of all literary undertakings. While your lyrical faculty lasts (and it is unlikely to last as long as you imagine), write novels and poetry; there will always be time for criticism later' on, when middle age has cooled your imagination, and deepened and sharpened your judgement. You can write several good novels, and even more good poetry, with next to no experience of life; but criticism is essentially the business of maturity.

WILLIAM SANSOM

1. At the present cost of living, I should say a minimum of £400 to £500 a year—this to obtain privacy and a certain mobility, but not to support a family or remove pressure-forming anxieties as to the future. But averages are difficult to suppose: a writer, I expect, is usually in some way not normal—and according to his character might prepare his best work in restrictive or normally unsavoury conditions. Prisons, gardens, slums, society, have all produced literature. Perhaps the most reasonable average desideratum would be some comfortably private ivorite tower with the habit (and even the necessity) of frequent sorties therefrom.

2. At the moment, with luck, yes. Provided his output is regular, and he is to some extent established. But he must necessarily risk the complete failure of experiments.

3. No commercial writing. However limited this sphere may be, there is the temptation to excel within the rules of the game and the creative cells are sapped. Manual work is probably the best alternative, though this only rarely could bring in sufficient extra income. Perhaps the usual—one of the quieter Civil Services, if they exist any more? Teaching? Librarian? Somewhere are to be found individually suitable libraries and lighthouses. But again these are severely personal choices: it is always possible, for instance, that a metropolitan mind isolated with a gross of

mixed stuffed stoats in a small museum, not a hundred miles from
Hadrian's Wall, might at some time begin rather to pity itself.

4. Any fresh experience can provide its stimulation. But if the
writer feels imprisoned, he is likely to spend all his effort in dream-
ing himself free. A state of free leisure is the really important
condition. In degree, the enrichment of experience must be
accompanied by enough privacy and leisure to absorb and
record it.

5. There is the chance always of a decline into directed State
inspiration—but this should be risked. Patronage from any source
is invaluable. It is wrong to assume that strings are attached to
every generosity, right to marvel that fairly disinterested good
does exist at all in the human arena.

6. Yes. Over a period of years I decided to save, and did. These
savings gave me the chance to live and write freely for a couple
of years. (Since, I have been so fortunate as to receive a bursary;
this naturally has further eased matters, removed further the
temptation of a salaried job.) So I suppose any advice I could give
would be save, save, save. If you can. Modest living, if you can
bear it, discovers a greater interest in simple things, and reduces
the headache of desire. And any accumulating money develops a
fair feeling of security, and thus a freer mind.

D. S. SAVAGE

So many social, cultural and religious issues are raised by the
question of the writer's economic position that it is impossible
to deal with them in a small compass. The position of the 'clerisy'
is determined by the distribution of wealth/power/privilege and
by the cultural standards obtaining in society. Wealth in our
racketeering society is distributed, to put it mildly, unjustly; and
our cultural standards are debased. I am dead against the theory
which, raising the banner of 'the artist', would make of writers
a privileged élite existing in æsthetic detachment from, and yet
actual dependence upon, an enslaved and militarized people.

How much does a writer need to live on? What sort of a
writer; what are his responsibilities, liabilities? But it's quite
useless to discuss this matter in general terms. For myself, I am
not interested in earning a living by writing. I am interested in
writing. Also, I have to earn a living for myself and my family
—if only to be able to continue writing. In fact, I've never yet

been able to earn the barest living for the five of us out of the rewards of authorship. I have been compelled to improvise, taking up one ill-paying job or occupation after another in the vain hope of eventually getting into a position in which I should have the more leisure and mental ease to read, think, write, in accordance with my irrepressible urge to those activities. My employments and my writing have each hindered success in the other.

There is no precise answer to Question 3. Question 4 raises the point of the relationship of writing to living. In the daily struggle which is my life I am brought up against the brute facts of human existence; through experience I get to know them, to comprehend something of the very structure of existence. This knowledge is inevitably reflected in my writing at the same time as the necessity for coming to terms with the material conditions of living puts a practical obstacle in my way as a writer. Naturally I'd like the obstacle removed—in which event the struggle would be transposed elsewhere.

I am cynical about State support for writers. I don't give a damn for the State either way. No, I'm not satisfied; in fact I haven't a solution. And I'm not a bit interested in the fate of people, young or old, who merely 'wish to earn their living by writing'. I am interested only in those who wish 'to write', and not even, very much, in all of those.

But I admit it's a problem, and the question still remains, what, under existing bad conditions, can be done to take some of the obstacles out of the way of serious writers (always remembering that there are degrees of 'seriousness') so that they can get on with the job? I have often wondered why, under the conditions of a capitalist society, no collective action has been taken to improve the writer's position—why it is that there is apparently no intermediate stage for the writer between that of outcast and celebrity, and how it is the celebrity shows so complete an unconcern with the tribulations of the outcast. If anything practical is to be done (and whatever is done is bound to be unsatisfactory), rather than State interference I should recommend the setting up of a commission by, say, the Society of Authors, to investigate the economic position of writers—particularly young writers—and to institute a fund for the purpose of making grants for needy writers to proceed with specific works of literary value. This fund, within the unwholesome conditions of a competitive economy, might well be swollen by some diversion of the proceeds from out-of-copyright works of dead authors, period of copyright being extended by law for this specific purpose, while celebrated writers, as well as publishers and other middlemen who profit from literature in one way and another, might be bullied and shamed into making substantial regular contributions to the fund. This would be used not merely for making direct cash grants but for financing one or more journals of a solid character which would provide a market for serious work, in much the same way as some American Universities support and finance independent quarterlies. An authors' publishing corporation, even, might be developed, co-operatively run and setting an example to the commercial publishing houses in its concern for the welfare of writers and for literary standards.

STEPHEN SPENDER

1. Of course, what a writer needs depends on many things, such as his age, whether he is married, etc. The one impregnable position is readiness to make every economic sacrifice to his vocation and, if necessary, to involve everyone round him in such sacrifice. But very few writers can do this. Allowing for travel and occasional treats, I should say an unmarried writer needs £500 or £600 a year (free of tax), if he lives in London. A married writer, if he makes his wife his cook, needs £700. However, if he has children, if he does not wish his wife to be a domestic slave and if he has any social life, he needs £1,000 a year or more.

Directly he needs as much as this, difficulties of income tax arise, for he needs actually to earn £1,500 a year. Writing is a social occupation and in London he will find that entertaining is one of his chief expenses. If he were a business man, the government would pay for his lunches with his colleagues, but as he is an artist, entertainment of other writers will not be recognized as a legitimate expense of his profession.

2. Try to earn £1,000 a year or more from writing today and see what happens. If you write books your publisher will not have paper to print more than 5,000 copies, which will bring you in £250 to £350. This means you must either write four to six books a year, or you must turn to journalism. Assuming you are paid, on the average, £3 3s. for 1,000 words, you will have to write

333,000 words a year to gain £1,000. Myself, I find that if I write three or four articles a week (*a*) I become irritable, (*b*) I get into a condition in which I find it very difficult to read seriously, (*c*) least of all can I read what I write myself. I can write an article far more easily than I can bear to read it, for the purpose of proof correcting, (*d*) there follows a general disgust with my own ideas, my way of thinking and talking, and (*e*) a tendency to write more and more journalism and less poetry, because I feel unworthy to write serious work.

3. I can only state the problems in general terms. These are (*a*) to avoid expressing merely in words on a level which lowers one's standards, (*b*) to avoid exhausting oneself physically and/or mentally, (*c*) to avoid becoming absorbed in some task which eventually becomes more important to one than one's writing, (*d*) to avoid being forced to play some role in life—such as an official or a pedagogue or an important person—which usurps one's creative personality.

The safest part for a writer to play in a job is a return to childhood. Do some job which enables one to learn something which will be useful in writing. Accept the fact that one is once again the stupidest boy in the class, the backward son in the family. One's best relationship with one's colleagues is for them to think of one as slightly mad but full of good will. Be a cog and allow oneself to be gently ground between the heads of departments. Reassure people by allowing them to think that one is distinguished without one's ever menacing their own position. For God's sake never be in a position of responsibility and have no ambitions. Do not seek honours and do not refuse them. One should aim at being a rather superior and privileged office clown who excites no one's envy, and on whom one's colleagues project a few fantasies. One encourages all this by arriving always a little late (but not too late). Prepare for the worst, when the boss shows you his (or his wife's or his son's) poems. Pretend to like them, ask for a testimonial and resign immediately when this happens.

4. This depends entirely on the quantity of the writer's energy. If he has the energy to do another job and to write, I cannot help thinking that his writing gains by a contact with the machinery of ordinary life. A scientist, a managerial leader or a statesman who realizes an idea which has to pass through the whole machinery of a modern organization, is creative in a

way parallel to an artist who overcomes technical problems in order to state an idea in his particular medium. If one can retain the sense of a creative attitude in one's environment and not be crushed by a routine, one will learn much from ordinary work. Myself, I think that the best and most serious modern literature suffers from unworldliness. Literature should be made of the same worldly muck as are the historic plays of Shakespeare, the courtly drama of Racine and of Lopez de Vega, the materialistic novels of Balzac and the Duchy of Parma in *La Chartreuse de Parme*. Byron was the last worldly poet. What we want is a fusion of Byron and Blake.

5. Only in the way of recognizing and protecting the writer's professional position, by providing paper for modern books, giving creative writers the travel facilities of journalists, allowing the social contacts of writers with their colleagues to count as tax-free business expenses, etc.

6. At the moment I am happy because I work with an intelligent and sympathetic international group of people who, not being English, expect of me what I can give, do not make me feel guilty and have an unobtrusive recognition of my value in their work and also in my own which has a certain value for them. I am not unpatriotic, but I fear that the mainspring of English industriousness is a sense of guilt and for this reason the position of writers who have to work for their living in this country is particularly difficult. They are forced into the dilemma of feeling they have to choose between two kinds of work. In France, this is not so, with the result that many French writers combine official positions with writing.

I advise the young writer to be perfectly honest with himself about the all-important problem of how he is expending his energy. The only rule in this work is to know what you want to do and do it, at all costs. If you can do other things as well, you will probably gain by it. But if you can't, you're *foûtu*.

DYLAN THOMAS

1. He needs as much money as he wants to spend. It is after his housing, his feeding, his warming, his clothing, the nursing of and looking after his children, etc., have been seen to—and these should be seen to by the State—that he really needs money to spend on all the luxurious necessities. Or, it is then that he doesn't

D

need money because he can do without those necessary luxuries. How much money depends, quite obviously, on how much he wants to buy. I *want* a lot, but whether I *need* what I want is another question.

2. A serious writer (I suppose by this you mean a good writer, who might be comic) can earn enough money by writing seriously, or comically, if his appetites, social and sensual, are very small. If those appetites are big or biggish, he cannot earn, by writing what he wishes to write, enough to satisfy them. So he has to earn money in another way: by writing what he doesn't want to write, or by having quite another job.

3. It's no good, I suppose, saying that I know a couple of good writers who are happy writing, for a living, what they don't particularly want to write, and also a few good writers who are happy (always qualified by words I'm not going to use now) being bank clerks, Civil Servants, etc. I can't say how a writer can make money most suitably. It depends on how much money he wants and on how much he wants it and on what he is willing to do to get it. I myself get about a quarter of the money I want by writing what I don't want to write and at the same time trying to, and often succeeding in, enjoying it. Shadily living by one's literary wits is as good a way of making too little money as any other, so long as, all the time you are writing B.B.C. and film scripts, reviews, etc., you aren't thinking, sincerely, that this work is depriving the world of a great poem or a great story. Great, or at any rate very good, poems and stories do get written in spite of the fact that the writers of them spend much of their waking time doing entirely different things. And even a poet like Yeats, who was made by patronage financially safe so that he need write and think nothing but poetry, *had*, voluntarily, to give himself a secondary job: that of philosopher, mystic, crank, quack.

4. No, to both questions. It neither suffers nor is it enriched. Poems, for instance, are pieces of hard craftsmanship made interesting to craftsmen in the same job, by the work put into them, and made interesting to everybody, which includes those craftsmen, by divine accidents: however taut, inevitably in order, a good poem may appear, it must be so constructed that it is wide open, at any second, to receive the accidental miracle which makes a work of craftsmanship a work of art.

5. The State should do no more for writers than it should do for any other person who lives in it. The State should give shelter, food, warmth, etc., whether the person works for the State or not. Choice of work, and the money that comes from it should then be free for that man; what work, what money, is his own bother.

6. Yes and No, or *vice versa*. My advice to young people who wish to earn their living by writing is: DO.

What are Writers Worth?
Richard Findlater

A Survey of Authorship prepared for the Society of
Authors, London, 1963.

Reprinted by permission of the author.

TEN years ago "Critical Times for Authors"—"a survey of present conditions prepared for the Society of Authors," and issued as a supplement to *The Author*—predicted "the end of professional authorship as we have known it in the past," if the complex situation in which the British writer was caught were "allowed to continue for long". Since then, the complexity of the writer's situation has been intensified, in a way that could scarcely have been foreseen in 1952. During the past decade the British author has been closely affected by radical and continuing changes in the production and distribution of the printed word and also by the reverberating side-effects of social change at home and abroad, not only as a victim (as "Critical Times" suggested) but perhaps as a beneficiary, too. "The end of professional authorship as we have known it in the past" is now certainly not far off; yet this does *not* mean the end of the professional author.

In the 1950's literary life in Britain, generally speaking, had been organized on the same design for about a century. Books were published in hard covers for a middle-class minority, with a partially guaranteed sale to the lending libraries ("commercial" and public). To many people this system seemed immaculate and immutable. Neither the "commercial" library nor the clothbound novel, however, is indispensable to the continuation of professional authorship, any more than were the circulating library and the three-volume novel of the 1840's. Not even letterpress printing is immortal, as the writer's sole means of visible support. New forms, new patrons, new channels of expression and communication are emerging. As yet, their development may seem to be haphazard and chaotic, and obvious dangers and difficulties lie ahead. Yet there are great opportunities for the English writer and the English language. At home and abroad, the public potentially within his reach is far larger than it has ever been before. Let us bear that roseate prospect in mind as we look at the condition of authorship in Britain today.

How many professional authors are at work in Britain and how do they all make a living? Right from the start of this brief survey, I must emphasize that there is no full and accurate answer to these questions—and to many others raised here, including the one on the cover. Although the Society of Authors and others have done their best to map the central mysteries, it remains discouragingly true that, in the words of *The Economist*, "for an industry whose product is the printed word, the book trade has strangely little information on record about its own fortunes"; and what Sir Charles Snow has called "the occupational camouflage of publishers and writers" still ensures that large areas of the literary landscape are charted only by guesswork. Even the term "author" is apt to be misleading if left undefined: for our purposes, he is a man whose books are published. No value-judgment is attached here to the *kind* of books. We are concerned not only with the makers of literature but also with the entertainers, propagandists and pedagogues, with the smallest fry as well as with the big fish, working on the premise that authors are *needed* by a society, and that the culture of a society may be partly assessed by the way that its authors are treated. In the belief that the reading public might like (and probably ought) to know a little more about the writing, publishing, selling and borrowing of books in Britain today; and that the author himself should have a better knowledge of his trade, which comprises all these processes; the Society of Authors has asked me to outline some of the facts of life, as far as we know them, and as far as a short pamphlet can comprehend them.

Who are they? ✳ ✳ ✳ ✳ ✳ ✳ ✳ ✳ ✳

WHITAKER'S *Reference Catalogue of Current Literature* lists between 55,000 and 60,000 authors, of whom perhaps 45,000 to 50,000 are both alive and British. Yet most of them do not rank as *professional* authors —certainly not in their own eyes, on the evidence of the census, which goes by what people *say* they are. In the 1951 census self-declared authors were included, in Group 811, with caption writers, crossword compilers, turf correspondents and other "editors, journalists and publicists": in all, 23,822. My own guess is that less than a third of Group 811 in 1951 were professional authors, in the sense that they had written full-length books and would be eligible for full membership of the Society of Authors; and that in 1962 the number was about the same—between 6,500 and 7,000, writing not only books but also film scripts and plays (for television as well as the theatre) with some degree of continuity and productivity. "Technical" and "educational" authors—estimated unofficially in 1951 at some 4,000—may be pigeon-holed in a separate and expanding category, which by 1962 numbered perhaps 5,000 people. Most of these do not regard author-ship as their prime occupation, and many may be found among the 300,000 teachers registered in the 1951 census.

It may be that during the past decade the number of authors has slightly increased; but certainly their social status has been sharply deflated—officially, at least. In 1951 they were ranked near the summit, with lawyers and doctors, in Class I of the census. Teachers were rated no higher than Class II, while actors and musicians were relegated to Class III. "Allocation of occupations to the five groups," the census explains, "has varied from census to census in accordance with economic conditions and with the intention of preserving the gradient rather than literary continuity." Now, in the 1961 census, writers have been pushed down to Class II, on a par with actors and musicians, who have been promoted. Has the gradient, in fact, altered so noticeably since 1951? Have economic conditions deteriorated? Somerset House's devaluation suggests that this is true.

Since the publication of "Critical Times" some useful facts about the earning-power of writers have been unearthed. In 1957 the Society of Authors published the results of a questionnaire sent to its members for completion anonymously. Over 600, about a fifth of the total membership, supplied details of their incomes from writing of all kinds —enough to give a fairly representative picture. Three quarters of these authors had published three or more books, and half of them had published over six: they were, in fact, seasoned professionals. Yet only 82 of them earned more than £1,500 a year from writing; only one in ten earned between £20 and £30 a week; 18 per cent. earned between £5 and £10 a week; and as many as four of every ten authors who filled in the questionnaires said that they earned no more than £5 a week, if that, from their work. These figures should not, of course, be taken as a comprehensive guide for 1957, let alone for 1963, but they are to some extent reinforced by information supplied in 1961 by two leading agents, one of whom estimated that 60 per cent. of his clients earned £500 a year and under, while the other's estimate was as high as 77 per cent.—compared with the 58 per cent. in the Society of Authors' analysis.

In other words, the majority of professional authors earn from their writing of all kinds well below the national average wage (around £15 weekly in 1962) and far below the income-levels taken for granted by most lawyers, doctors, dentists, etc. What is more to the point is that many authors have suffered from a relatively sharp drop in their standards of living, at a time when many of the people they write about, in all classes, are doing better than ever before; and at the same time there has been no improvement in their national status. In Britain the professional writer has never in recent times been rated as highly as he is in France, Germany or the U.S.A. Even the great fame of Shaw, Bennett and Wells rested not so much upon their books and plays as on their journalism, their crusading and, above all, their performances as "characters." To win attention, if not respect, the writer should be very young or very old or very rich; he should have a stormy private life or public cause. It is not enough to write. He has to act as well, for press reporters or for the television screen. Increasingly the writer is becoming a part of show business; yet this does not appear to be gaining him a wider acceptance by society. Mr. Priestley has expressed this lack of prestige with characteristic vigour:

> Any English writer has only to go abroad to feel immediately that his status has changed for the better . . . When the board of governors, the directorate, the executive committee, the trustees are being chosen, the worst politician, lawyer, moneylender or busybody will be preferred to an author. It is the same with honours. Players turn up in every list, but not playwrights. It is the same with honorary degrees. I am willing to bet that English universities, new and old, give fewer honorary degrees to authors than any other universities in the world.

Lingering still in the darker corners of the national mind, it seems, is a blimpish belief that writing is something done either by a servant for money or by a gentleman for fun: it is not to be taken seriously as a full-time profession or to be granted special social privileges. This perhaps helps to account for the unfair treatment of authors by the state—particularly by its taxmen.

Some progress has been made since "Critical Times" was published. After a long campaign by the Society of Authors, particularly through its members in Parliament, the Government finally conceded in 1953 that for tax purposes a writer could spread back his earnings from a sudden success over three years instead of having to pay a penally high rate on what is often the result of many years' work. Moreover, the author has, with other taxpayers, benefited by cuts in the standard rate and increases in the earned income relief and personal allowance. For example, on an income of £600 in 1962 an unmarried author would pay £20 less tax than on the same income in 1952; on an income of £1,000 he would pay over £40 less tax; and on an income of £2,000 over £110 less tax. Such changes have helped to camouflage the effects on authorship of an inequitable system.

An author is still not allowed, as other men are, to treat as a capital gain the sale of his property—his copyright, which unlike other forms of property becomes valueless to his heirs 50 years after his death. If he sells outright the film rights, publication rights or any other part of his copyright, the receipts are taxed as ordinary income—as Sir Compton Mackenzie discovered to his cost and to the disgrace of the state. In his 70's, this distinguished author sold the copyrights of 21 books, part of a lifetime's labour, for £10,000—only to be mulcted of £6,000 of it by the Inland Revenue, after he had fought them himself in the Court of Appeal.

It is ironical that an author's publisher and an author's agent can both sell their property for lump sums without paying anything at all in tax, while the man on whose work such businesses are built is penalized when he sells *his* property. It is perhaps equally ironical that on an author's death his income is "capitalized" for the purpose of assessing estate duty. In life as in death, then, the author is—in this respect, at least—victimized by the state. "In France a writer is taxed less highly because he is a writer," wrote Tennyson Jesse bitterly to the *Daily Telegraph* some years ago, "If it were possible in England he would be charged more for the same reason."

The author's share ＊ ＊ ＊ ＊ ＊ ＊ ＊ ＊

ACCORDING to the Financial Secretary to the Treasury, reported in *Hansard* in May 1962, wages and salaries would have had to rise 30 per cent. between 1951 and 1961 to make up for the rise in the cost of living and the depreciation in the purchasing power of the pound; and in fact, he said, the average increase during that period was 77 per cent. How has the author fared? The superficial evidence looks hopeful. Between 1952 and 1962 the average retail price went up by 46 per cent., and this corresponds roughly with the price-increase in most categories of fiction. Taking samples in various size-ranges, it was found that during the same period there were increases of 70 per cent. and 80 per cent. for longer and "heavier" kinds of non-fiction. "Overall reading per head", as Mr. Graham Hutton has put it, also increased during the 1950's: national expenditure on "books, newspapers and magazines" went up, according to his calculations, from £176 million in 1954 to over £190 million in 1961. The total turnover of publishers soared from £41,500,000 in 1951 to nearly £79 million in 1961.

None of these apparently encouraging figures, however, proves that the majority of authors—those 90 per cent. who in 1957 earned £20 a week and under (on the evidence of the Society of Authors)—are now enjoying better times; or, indeed, have even managed to maintain their standard of living. Although the price of books is higher, it has not risen far enough to match the rise in the cost of their production. (Paper prices have fluctuated since 1952, but printing, binding and other costs have increased—see pages 28 and 29.) This gap is still, as it was ten years ago, one main factor in the economic crisis of publishing and therefore in the economic crisis of authorship. Publishers are selling on average more books in a year, but they are making a smaller profit out of each individual book sold. In order to cut the costs, some publishers, especially in the field of light reading once supported by the "commercial" libraries, are cutting the wordage; a few are economizing on standards; and some are saving money at the author's expense. These economies are made in various ways. Authors who commonly publish two books a year are restricted to one; royalty rates have been reduced; and advances have been frozen or even, in some categories, cut.

The jump in the total sales turnover should mean that authors are earning more from their books. The fact is, however, that home sales are inching downwards: it is in the overseas trade that publishers have found their expanding market, especially for technical and educational books; and the group of specialists who write such books with a main eye on the market abroad are thriving. But for the "general" author every copy of a book sold abroad brings the author a far smaller return than if it were sold in the U.K., his royalty usually being charged not on the published price but on the publisher's receipts —after deductions of abnormally high discounts. To earn 30 per cent. more in the last ten years, from overseas markets alone, he would have had to sell—in many cases—nearly three times as many more copies as he would have to sell at home. The boom in the export trade, therefore, is small advantage for many professional writers and the increase in the annual number of new titles helps to depress the individual author's economic status; for, taken in conjunction with the fall in the total of British bookshops, it means that too many books are chasing too little selling-space. Paperbacks, moreover, as yet do not benefit the majority of writers directly. To some their disadvantages seem more conspicuous than their assets. Older authors, not quite in fashion, have lost their traditional opportunities of prolonging the life of a book through a cheap hard-bound edition, without the certainty of getting it into paper covers. They watch the swelling flood of softcovers washing the hardbacks away and they know that you may well have to sell ten times as many books in paper as in cloth to get the same return. They see in the growth of paperback publishing the dissolution of the relative continuity and security which they enjoyed before the 1950's, and the contraction of minority reading.

Both in hardbacks and softcovers, furthermore, the author may be damaged by concentration upon the latest, up-to-the-minute model, which is discarded and ignored after an increasingly short interval. In the words of *The Times Literary Supplement*:

> . . . a principle seems to have filtered into the book business that is not unlike the doctrine of "built-in obsolescence" preached in other consumer industries . . . Applied to the publishing business this means that the booksellers are pressed to stock up with a list of new books rather than go on selling the old ones; that [commercial] libraries clear out their fiction shelves so that there is a continual process of turnover; that literary journalism concentrates almost entirely on the current output . . . Slowly but in some cases disastrously the life of the unsuccessful seller has shortened, till a novel (say) that fails to make an initial impact is counted dead after three months.

If this trend continues, not only the survival of the "unsuccessful seller" is endangered, but also the staying-power of the *moderate* seller, and indeed of all books but the immediate mass-hit. Yet there are hopeful signs that such a doom will be averted.

Books for hire * * * * * * * * * *

THE novelist is among the most uncomfortable victims of economic change. Although far more titles of all kinds are published annually than before the war, the number of novels has fallen, and the proportion of fiction in the yearly total has shrunk since the 1930's from nearly a third to just over a sixth. There is one very material reason for this: that because of the rise in production costs a publisher must print at least 3,000 copies of a novel instead of the 1,500, say, which were an economic minimum in 1939 (of which only half might be bound); and he must sell at least 2,500 of them; but the public for first or unknown novels has not doubled in the last quarter-century—if, indeed, it has grown at all. The publisher cannot, accordingly, take the same risks on new and minority fiction, and the novelist finds it increasingly difficult both to get into print and to stay in print.

One cause of his difficulties is the gradual disappearance of what has been for many years one of the novelist's most reliable customers: the commercial library. It was its predecessor, the circulating library, which helped to ensure the novel's prosperity in the nineteenth century, when "three-decker" fiction relied upon Mudie's and its kin as a main link with the Victorian middle-class reading public. After 1890, when the three-volume novel at 31s. 6d. was replaced by the single volume at 7s. 6d. or less, the book-borrowing system—charging readers an annual, graded subscription—was extended; and the chain of chemists' shops owned by Boots and the newsagents' empire of W. H. Smith, with Harrods and The Times Book Club at the summit of the social pyramid, became dependable buyers of new fiction (of the right, respectable kind). It was not until the 1930's that working-class readers began, on a wide scale, to rent their fiction—from the "twopenny libraries" which spread rapidly throughout the country before the war, and have vanished nearly as quickly in the past decade. The books which they stocked were those which the subscription libraries had bought two or more years earlier, on their first publication; now these novels were re-issued in cheap, hardback editions, with colourful wrappers. Although they were on sale at railway bookstalls for as little as half-a-crown, the new "libraries" rented them out at twopence a week a volume to people who could not afford to pay the annual subscriptions of the middle-class establishments, who did not want to buy books, and who could not find the brand of light reading they favoured on the shelves of the public libraries. In the 1950's, however, a number of social factors combined to push many of the "rental libraries" out of existence, at both ends of the scale. The increase in book prices and the disappearance of the cloth-bound cheap edition since the war meant that the rental had to be put up, and it was—or seemed—too high for many people. These potential borrowers—both weekly and annual payers—now spend their money and their leisure in different ways, notably in watching television and buying paperbacks; and, what is more important, they can usually get their recreational reading *for nothing* from the public libraries, which are investing an ever-growing amount of money in light fiction. The liquidation in 1961 of the W. H. Smith chain—with 286 branches, around 60,000 subscribers and a stock of 750,000 volumes—marked the end of an era, in a disquieting way for the professional novelist. The Boots chain remains, but one by one the branches are closing down—30 in 1962; and even though there are still about 4,000 shops in Britain which lend books at a weekly charge, they work on a very limited scale within a very narrow range. As a result of the evaporation of these commercial libraries, many authors' sales have dropped in the last three or four years by between 1,500 and 2,500 copies on each title; and it seems unlikely that this market will ever be recovered by "entertainment" books in the lower reaches. Compensations for some writers, however, are derived from TV and paperback rights and from translations. The growing volume of English books, of all kinds, translated into other languages every year is one of the rosier minor auguries for the future, even though a translation into any one foreign language may bring in only a small return.

If established authors feel the pinch in the opportunity state, it is scarcely surprising that novices find the going much harder. In 1938 a young aspiring writer without dependants, without influence and with only his talent for capital, could get by on £4 a week. This was enough for a furnished bed-sitter in central London, for keeping in touch with films and plays, and for a weekly meal out in Soho; and it could be earned with relative ease on the fringe of the literary world so that he had time for his own writing. By 1952, however, a young man living in that way would have needed at least £9 a week; while by 1962 the minimum was £12 a week, for a Spartan existence without much to spare for playgoing (or smoking). In tax alone, he would have to pay twice as big a share of his earnings in 1962 as in 1938; his room—17s. 6d. in 1938—would cost him at least three times more in 1962; and it would be much harder to earn his £12 *and* keep some time for work at home. Many of the sources of income in 1938, especially in journalism, had dried up by then, while the new sources which have opened up are not, on the whole, to be tapped as casually for occasional subsidies to private writing. Instead of living on essays, reviews and reading for publishers, the new-model freelance is more likely to write revue and cabaret sketches, advertising jingles or plays for television; while the pressure to *join* is much stronger than it was in the 1930's. As in the U.S.A., there is a growing tendency for writers to join the salariat, on the payroll of film, advertising, publishing and television companies, apart from those who have to take school and university jobs. Yet this should not necessarily be taken—for authorship in general—as a symptom of decay and defeat: except by those romantics who still believe that writers must be rebels, and that it is better to starve than to submit. There is less living-space for the pin-money dilettante today, yet there are more sponsors for the free-wheeling talent above a certain level. Below it, in Grub Street, it is much harder to keep the dream alive.

Publishers and their problems ✳ ✳ ✳ ✳ ✳ ✳

As many as 1,750 names are listed in Whitaker's *Publishers and Their Addresses*; since the war as many as 105 publishers have closed down, and over a score have been taken over by competitors, but no more than 400 firms are to be taken seriously as publishers, of which some 360 belong to the Publishers' Association. Most of the leading companies were established in the last century, and some of them are still controlled by the same families. In general publishing the dynastic principle still shows. It is worth noting, in considering the social rating of writers and their relationships with publishers, that an investigation by the Society of Young Publishers in 1962 among some 80 per cent. of its members revealed that nearly a quarter had come into the business through friends and relations; 70 per cent. had been educated at a public school; and 40 per cent. had private incomes.

In publishing, as in other industries, there is a narrowing concentration of power in a few expanding groups: it is becoming more difficult for small firms, working on their own, to survive or, at any rate, to keep their independence. Some of the groups are now controlled by outside commercial and industrial interests: big business is entering publishing—not yet on the American scale, but with growing impact. Exactly what effect this will have upon the condition of authorship, in the long run, it is impossible to say; yet the injection of capital into an industry which has long been chronically short of it can only be regarded as a sign of progress. The Heinemann network, which includes Secker & Warburg, Peter Davies and World's Work, is part of a big holding and investment group, Thomas Tilling Ltd.; Max Reinhardt, who also controls Bodley Head, Werner Laurie, Putnam and Hollis & Carter, is supported by the City banking firm of Henry Ansbacher & Co.; Michael Joseph and Nelsons have been acquired by the Thomson organization; the Financial News (besides several magazines) has acquired Oliver & Boyd, E. & S. Livingstone and J. & A. Churchill; Sidney Bernstein of Granada has bought MacGibbon & Kee, which also controls Arco and Staples, and he has a large holding in Jonathan Cape; Charterhouse holding group has a small stake in Associated Book Publishers, which includes Methuen, E. & F. Spon, Eyre & Spottiswoode, Chapman & Hall and also the Sweet & Maxwell group.

Every year the number of titles increases, from 18,741 in 1952 up to 25,079 in 1962—double the number published thirty years ago. And every year the share of a few firms grows bigger. In the first six months of 1961 8,576 titles were published, but as many as 12 per cent. of the titles were issued by only six firms (Collins, Heinemann, McGraw-Hill, Macmillan, Hutchinson and the Oxford University Press). Yet there is still a wide freedom of choice for the author in search of a publisher.

About 300 million volumes, it is estimated, are now published every year—roughly four times as many as in the 1930's. Around 175 million of them are educational books, the backbone of the industry: this side of publishing is likely to be even more important in the next decade, with the expansion of British schools and universities and the further development of the overseas market. It is primarily because of the possible Commonwealth market, for educational books in particular, that U.S. firms have begun in the last three years to buy up, or buy their way into, British publishing houses, which control the Commonwealth rights. Some attempts have failed, but other successful ones will intensify the competition for educational markets abroad—perhaps with a beneficial effect on British authors' overseas royalties. (Doubledays now control W. H. Allen; the New American Library has combined Ace and Four Square into the New English Library; and Harcourt Brace has bought Rupert Hart-Davis. Other American deals may be expected during the 1960's.)

As we have already mentioned, British publishers now sell a much bigger proportion of their products abroad than they did before the war: exports now account for half the volume and over 40 per cent. of the total turnover (compared with 30 per cent. in the 1930's). In the home market around 75 per cent. of the titles are "net"—that is, they are sold by publisher to retailer on the agreement that they will not be sold to the public below the list price. "Non-net" books are mainly educational ones, sold in bulk for use in schools by contractors rather than through the bookshops. If spending on these books is deducted from the total of home sales, it will be seen—as the President of the Publishers' Association, John Boon, pointed out in 1961—that during the last five years there has been a declining rate of increase. Some firms export from 60 to 70 per cent. of their total turnover, and they tend to neglect home in favour of overseas buyers—with unfortunate results for many authors.

Publishing profits vary widely from year to year and between firm and firm: publishing losses are not unknown. In giving evidence before the Restrictive Practices Court about the Net Book Agreement in 1962, Mr. Arthur Bagnall, Q.C.—who appeared for the Publishers' Association—said that a publisher "aimed at a gross profit of 40 per cent. on his turnover, with the hope that he would be left with a net profit of 10 per cent.". Mr. Bagnall quoted the following figures to illustrate publishers' "disparity of experience" (without relating them, of course, to disparity of skill and judgment and luck):

One published in the first year under review 98 books which were all profitable; in the second year he published 104 (of which 100 were profitable, 4 broke even); and in the third year 115, of which 113 were profitable, one broke even and one made a loss. By contrast, another publisher in the same financial group (annual turnover under £350,000) published 73 books in the first year, of which 10 broke even and profits and losses were about half and half. In the next year, out of 51 books published, 22 were profitable, 10 broke even and 19 were losses; and in the third year, out of 62 books, 18 were profitable, 6 broke even and there were over twice as many losses as profits.

It is in such a run of bad luck that the advantages of being buttressed by a group become most evident. The safest and richest buttress of all, however, is still a good educational backlist, and in the last ten years several firms have bought up educational publishers to get it. It is here that one may look for the explanation of the gross trading profit of a million pounds made in 1960 by Collins (plus Bibles, diaries and a printing works), and the near-million made by Longmans in 1961. Yet many publishers—like most authors—have to pedal twice as hard to stay in the same place: there are no easy pickings of the size available in other, less prestigious occupations. Before the war, says Mr. Ian Parsons of Chatto & Windus, you would need a turnover of £100,000 to make a net profit of £20,000; now, to make the same nominal profit, you would need at least double that turnover.

Paperbacks and authors ✳ ✳ ✳ ✳ ✳ ✳ ✳

DURING the past decade the most significant change in the world of British writers—even though not all may feel, as yet, affected by its repercussions—was the wildfire spread of paperback publishing. In the words of Mr. Anthony Godwin of Penguin Books, "Paperbacks were still no more than a minor sideline in 1948, a promising trend in 1954. By 1960 they had come to be recognized as the most dynamic factor in the publishing world." Since 1960 that recognition has been forced upon the most sheltered brethren of the book trade (both gentlemen and pros) by the sheer pace and volume in the expansion of publishing *and* reading, and by the effects of the new paperbackery on the conventional relationships between writers, publishers, librarians and booksellers. Yet so inconspicuous was the paperback only ten years ago that it was not even mentioned, as a factor of potential importance, in "Critical Times for Authors".

At that time there were well under a thousand titles in print in soft covers. Yet when *Paperbacks in Print* was first published in May 1960, as a "reference catalogue" of paperbacks on sale in Britain, it listed as many as 5,866 titles; and by June 1962 this total had risen to 9,578—an increase of 65 per cent. in two years. This available stockpile included, moreover, a range of books whose variety would have astonished not only the pre-war reader accustomed—in the century-old Tauchnitz tradition—to regard "paperback" as synonymous with "novel", but also the post-war bookman brought up to believe that readers would pay no more than half-a-crown for a book in soft covers. In the mid-1962 *Paperbacks in Print*, many novels were priced at 5s. and even 7s. 6d.; hundreds of non-fiction titles—in history, religion, psychology, the arts and sciences—were listed at prices up to 15s.; and 2s. 6d., instead of being the *maximum* price, was now the *minimum* price. In a random sample of 250 titles, not much more than a third were priced at 2s. 6d. (88); nearly as many (81) were in the 3s. 6d. to 5s. group; 40 were in the next price-range, up to 10s. 6d.; and 44 were over 10s. 6d.

Some of these titles represent a stock of only a few hundred volumes, remainders imported from the U.S.A.; some have a first printing of 10,000, others of 100,000; some are published by long-established British hardback firms, others come from the lists of paperback specialists under American control; in all, they present a muddled but major fact of life which the British book trade is assimilating only with acute difficulty. Nobody knows, as yet, the exact *volume* of this major fact: among the few round figures ventured in the press are those of the *Financial Times*, which said (in 1961) that about 75 million paperbacks were published in Britain in 1960, and which mentioned (in 1962) that about 50 million paperbacks were *sold* in 1961. Mr. Edmund Penning-Rowsell estimated (in the *Observer*) that paperbacks made up 7½ per cent. of the titles published in 1962 (which would mean a softcover total of 1,880), and up to 25 per cent. of the volumes printed; and the *Economist* made a "guess" in 1962 that they made up a third of the number of books sold in a year (another total which nobody knows), and 15 per cent. of the total retail value. Many are sold abroad: the percentage of their annual product claimed by export trade amounts to 25 per cent. for Corgi and Digit, 50 per cent. for Pan, 42 per cent. for Penguin (over 50 per cent. with their U.S. and Australian subsidiaries).

Whatever the true number may be of millions sold and unsold in a year, there is abundant circumstantial evidence of "the paperback revolution": the cliché can be verified in nearly every street in Britain— in supermarkets, tobacconists' and department stores, on the shelves of newsagents and public libraries, and in thousands of homes where— less than ten years ago—a book was another name for a magazine or was, at best, something which was borrowed but never, never *bought*. Compare this picture with the scene in 1935 when—against the strong opposition of the book trade, well primed by "realists" who *know* (then as now) what the public wants—Allen Lane inaugurated the Penguin experiment. Paperback series had been on sale at railway stations, on and off, for nearly a century, and some of the early books were considerably cheaper in relation to the hardback novel than the first (or indeed the latest) Penguins. (George Routledge's Railway Library books sold at a shilling each, when a hardback novel still cost 31s. 6d., in three volumes.) Yet it is right to date the modern Paperback Era from those first ten volumes, sold at sixpence each, with the penguin on their jackets. Then, it is said, the advances paid on those forerunners came to less than £500: today a paperback publisher would probably have to pay £5,000 for ten books of this kind, and if he were starting from scratch (as Allen Lane was) he would probably need at least £150,000 for rights alone to begin with no more than an adequate list. Back in 1935 Allen Lane printed 20,000 copies of each book, bound 10,000 and estimated that he could break even on a sale of 17,500; yet within three years the minimum print-run was 50,000. Between 1936 and 1961 Penguins published over 3,250 titles and sold over 250 million copies; and it is a sign of the sudden acceleration of paperbacks' popularity that between 1951 and 1960 the annual Penguin sale jumped from around 9·8 million to over 17 million copies. Even if one allows, in that last figure, for the somewhat specialized success of *Lady Chatterley's Lover* (which accounted for over two million of the total), such statistics indicate how much *the balance of power* has altered since the publication of "Critical Times for Authors".

By 1962 Penguins—the first in the field—still took the biggest share of the market, about a quarter of the annual sales; and it may still claim not only the largest pre-tax profit, but also the widest range of publishing, the highest standards of production, the biggest number of titles (around 400 a year, and about 1,400 kept in print), and the highest proportion of new, commissioned work to reprints. Although the proportion of originals is gradually increasing, nearly all the industry outside Penguins is concerned only with reprints. Most firms produce about a dozen titles every month, divided roughly into the following categories: one war book, one or two romances, Westerns, horror stories, and film tie-ins; two to five general novels, and crime or thriller stories; one non-fiction book; and at the summit the "leader"—the smash-hit novel on which the selling machine is focused, and for which there is keen bidding among the rival houses.

According to the June 1962 edition of *Paperbacks in Print*, 133 publishers are concerned. Of these I estimate that around 40 per cent. are either American-based or American-controlled: these firms probably claim no more than 30 per cent. of the British market. Over 60 of the 133 are British hardback publishers, but only a dozen of these produce softcover books on a sizeable scale. Many use paperbacks as convenient cheap editions of "egghead" books on their lists, and some have been amazed to discover that these paperbacks, at prices not much below the original level, have sold so much better than the hardback edition. Neither wholesalers (as in France) nor new paper and magazine publishers (as in the U.S.A.) are as yet interested in the business. The power, the glory and the main profit are shared—most unequally— by only a handful of publishers: nine firms (including Penguins) control about 88 per cent. of the British market. Next to Penguins, in the 1962 running order, comes Pan with 14 per cent. of the trade: around 10 million Pans, it is estimated, are sold every year, and there are over 300 titles in stock. Macmillans and Collins are in joint control: both also have their own paperback imprints (St. Martins and Papermac, and Fontana). After Pan comes Corgi, with 11 per cent., concentrating mainly upon American fiction: it is under U.S. control, linked with one of the biggest magazine-publishers in America (the Curtis Publishing Company) and a number of book-publishers. Fourth in importance is the New English Library, with 9 per cent. of the business, comprising the former Ace and Four Square imprints: it is now controlled by the New American Library, publishers in the U.S.A. of Signet and Mentor Books, and under the wing of the Times-Mirror Company of Los Angeles. The New American Library's chairman, Mr. Victor Weybright, was—in his own words—"urgently and repeatedly implored by the majority shareholders to make proposals to purchase" all or part of Pan Books in 1961, before Macmillan and Collins assumed dual control; and in the same year his firm was reported to have bid for the fifth biggest paperback publisher in the U.K., Panther, which also claims around 9 per cent. of the market. It remains under the ownership of Hamilton & Co. (Stafford) Ltd. Thereafter follow three paperback satellites of hardcover firms: Fontana (Collins: 4 per cent.); Hodder (Hodder & Stoughton: 4 per cent.); and Arrow (Hutchinson: 4 per cent.).

U.S. investment—here as in hardbacks—is growing; but immediate American influence is felt not so much in the take-over of British firms as in the flood of imported paperbacks, which are unsaleable across the Atlantic because of chronic overproduction. Although in 1961 Americans were said to be buying a million paperbacks a day, they could not —and cannot—cope with the torrent of print gushing from the U.S. presses. Pushed into about 100,000 "outlets" on a sale-or-return basis, about a quarter of them—around the 100 million mark—are pushed back again to their publishers, who then ship a big slice of them to Britain. About five to six million books a year arrive here from the U.S.A. Their distributors frequently allow a much larger discount to the retailer than he could get from a British-made book, and this influx of U.S. remainders—competing for the dwindling amount of display-space—was among the factors leading in 1962 to a small but noticeable fall in the sales of British paperbacks. It also helps to account for the increase in available titles.

Publishers will maintain that "practically all the good authors are already with one of the firms"; but to most paperback publishers the only good author is a selling one. In fact, the selection of British writers who can be read in softcovers is patchy and unrepresentative, both of the quick and the dead. Taking a rough count of the authors of General Fiction listed in that indispensable "catalogue", *Paperbacks in Print*, we find that over a third are American and that living British writers amount to less than half the total (about 450). In the "Bibliography and Literary History" section the proportion is much smaller: out of about 220 authors, only a quarter are both British and alive. If some technological catastrophe dissolved all hardcover books, and we had to rely on paperbacks now in print for our acquaintance with English literature, we should find five books by Dickens, for 35 by Peter Cheyney; none by Henry Green, but 16 by Zane Grey; none by Peacock, Burns, Galsworthy and Richardson—to take a few eminences at random. Publishers have understandably concentrated upon marketing the most immediately and sensationally successful of current hardback novels, for which most of the advance publicity has already been floated by the original hardback publisher. As things are, three main kinds of author are still ignored by most paperback publishers: the *young* writer with talent who has not yet scored a hit; the *middle-aged* writer whose hits were scored the day before yesterday, when yesterday—at the latest—is the only admissible past in what Americans call "the literature business"; and the *older* writer undeservedly forgotten, not only by the critics and the public but by his publisher, who has allowed the writer's books to go out of print and has made no effort to cut a new channel for them to a different generation of readers. Even the writers who do get into softcovers are often only allowed a short life in print. At least one paperback publisher remainders books if they have not made a good showing within six months. While the superstition spreads among the newly literate that "if it isn't in paperbacks, it can't be any good", this narrowness of choice may appear dangerous. Yet we are still, after all, only at the beginning of the Paperback Era—an era in which, I believe, all but a handful of authors will take paperback publication for granted. Considering the anarchic conservatism of the industry as a whole, and the economic processes at work, it is surprising how far the paperback revolution has already gone.

For some readers it is necessary to restate one basic fact here— that paperbacks are cheaper than hardbacks not because their covers are softer but because their runs are longer. While other economies count—the standardization of format, for instance, reduces costs in production, storage and transport, and the lower rate of royalty paid to the author is not unhelpful—the main reason for the gap between the softcover and hardcover prices of any book lies in the size of the print-order. To substitute soft for hard covers would make very little difference to the budget of a conventional octavo novel, if only 3,000 copies were printed. The minimum run for, say, a Corgi or Pan novel is ten times as much. Yet the spread of "egghead" paperbacks has demonstrated that the minimum can be far lower than was once thought to be feasible: between 8,000 and 10,000. This is economic because the egghead paperback can be sold for three or four times as much as the paperback novel: the trade had underestimated the size of the "egghead" reading public and its willingness to pay. In all categories of the business, indeed, price-increases have been accepted which are, proportionately, far greater than those belatedly made by hardback publishers. Whereas the price of an average hardcover novel has doubled since 1939, paperback fiction now costs at least five times, and even seven times, as much. Paperback publishing has proved already to be far more flexible—socially and economically—than was generally supposed after the war; and with a greater flexibility of distribution it is reasonable to hope that by 1973 *Paperbacks in Print* will catalogue a far broader and less random list of titles.

But will British authors, by 1973, be getting a fairer deal and a better reward? At present the general royalty rate normally paid by paperback publishers is $7\frac{1}{2}$ per cent., which the author may or may not have to share with his hardback publisher: this compares with the usual 10 per cent. minimum in hardbacks and with 5 per cent. in U.S. paperbacks (on which the authors get a bigger advance). Only a few big names, in the "leader" class, get $12\frac{1}{2}$ per cent. Authors should, in time, take 10 per cent. as a virtual minimum rate. They should also win a juster division of the proceeds of sub-leased paperback rights, a matter over which the Publishers' Association, in 1961, tried to maintain a retrogressively rigid attitude, invoking "the firm principle of the traditional 50/50 division" as the guiding rule for sharing paperback royalties, although such a division was neither traditional nor by any means unanimously observed. By the end of 1962 the publishers' official hard front had been badly dented, thanks largely to the solidarity of members of the Society of Authors. And as paperback royalties began to rise, even the most hidebound hardback publishers began to adjust their 50/50 claim accordingly.

Who sells the books? ❋ ❋ ❋ ❋ ❋ ❋ ❋ ❋

Many of the new readers reached by paperback publishing have never entered an orthodox bookshop in their lives: to them it seems out of bounds, the precinct of another class (much as the theatre still seems to a generation of working-class Englishmen), and the management of many bookshops does little to dispel it, unwelcoming and unimaginative as it is. The paperback format is so popular that increasingly in public libraries, where they are stocked for hire, a hardback book will be ignored if the title is available in a softcover edition.

As in the U.S.A., paperback firms are finding difficulty in efficient marketing, partly because of the weakness of the British wholesaling structure. Most firms employ wholesalers for all their export (Penguins are the exception) and a large part of their home sales; Penguins and a few other firms are using an increasing number of their own salesmen in this country—an example which is likely to be generally followed in the years ahead. Wholesalers get a discount of 40 per cent. on the selling price from Penguins, up to 50 per cent. from Corgi, and up to 65 per cent. from Digit; but although they provide a channel which, at the moment, most publishers would find it uneconomic to make for themselves, they are not rated highly in the trade.

Roughly half the paperbacks produced go through the bookshops. About 12,000 shops in Britain include books among the commodities they sell; some 3,000 of them are members of the Booksellers' Association; but the bulk of the home trade is shared by no more than 500. (Between 450 and 500 take 80 per cent. of the books marketed through the Book Centre, which handles 10 per cent. of the industry's home sales.) While the number of titles and the volume of books increases every year, the number of shops to sell them steadily declines: in 1956 324 went out of business, in 1957 there were 479 casualties, and in 1958 there were 621, while replacements averaged only about 200 annually. Among the dwindling survivors, moreover, the space available for books is shrinking, because of the competition from more profitable commodities such as fancy goods, greeting cards and garden ware.

The bookseller gets far more money, on every individual book he sells, than the man who wrote it. On specialized books his discount is usually $16\frac{2}{3}$ per cent.; on technical and educational books, 20 to 25 per cent.; and on general books, including fiction—which make up the greater part of his stock in hand—he gets a third or more of the selling price. (There is wide and complex variety in terms offered by publishers; the Restrictive Practices Court was told in 1962 that there were at least 300 standard terms of sale and 2,300 variations upon them.) To the author this often seems an extortionate percentage, especially when he feels—as most authors *do* feel—that the average bookseller does nothing to earn it.

It is certainly true that, in this respect alone, the book trade is absurdly lop-sided and anarchic. The vast expense of talent, time and money on the writing and production of books is not matched by any comparable investment in their distribution. In an "occupation for gentlemen" the selling side has too long been undervalued and hence undercapitalized; and it is not *entirely* due to the ignorance and apathy of the non-buying public that the shops for those who *do* buy are often so inefficient and unwelcoming.

Yet, however unjustly large his discounts may seem to an author, the bookseller cannot do without them under the present system: they compensate him for the risk he takes in venturing to sell books to the British without a preliminary order (and even preliminary orders, accepted by the shop in good faith, are sometimes unconfirmed, so that the bookseller is left with expensive books on his hands.) His rate of profit is still tiny—as the drop in the number of bookshops suggests. In 1935 the net profit of 25 booksellers, under special investigation, averaged only 1·55 per cent. (£155 profit for every £10,000 worth of books they sold); and an investigation on similar lines in 1952 into 17 booksellers showed an even worse result—of 1·22 per cent. On new books the average was only ·45 per cent., that is to say, £45 for every £10,000 worth of new books sold: in other words, to earn a profit of £450 a year—the starting wage of a bookseller's assistant—you would have (taking the average price as 15s.) to sell about 420 new books a day! Neither the rate of profitability nor the conditions of trading have improved much, if at all, in the past ten years. Prices have risen, discounts have been increased, and carriage costs are now met by most publishers. Yet the boom in high-street land values has pushed many shops into side-streets (with damaging effects on their trade), and the swelling volume of increasingly perishable new titles (with the drop in reprints) has added to the bookseller's difficulties.

Many of the delays and inadequacies of bookshop service seem inseparable from the current system of distribution. The basis of the system is the single order: that is to say, the bookseller orders nearly all the commodities he sells one at a time from hundreds of different firms, under hundreds of varying terms, in dozens of different categories. The Book Centre distributes 1,200 tons of books a year (a fifth of its annual turnover) among 11,500 retailers, and 38 per cent. of its orders have a net invoice value of under a pound. The Book Centre, moreover, only handles 10 per cent. of the trade: the bookseller generally orders directly from the publisher, often to find that the book is out of print, usually to wait for weeks, sometimes to get the wrong book (for publishers' warehouses are frequently manned by staff as relatively untrained and inefficient as those of the booksellers who deal with them). Giving evidence before the Restrictive Practices Court, Richard Blackwell quoted one day's business in the celebrated Oxford shop with which he is connected, one of the best and biggest in the country. On the spot, and by post, it received orders for 2,786 titles published by British publishers, of which 1,188 were available in stock: the remaining 1,598 were ordered from 246 publishers, and of these only about two-thirds were available—192 were not yet published, 141 were binding, printing or out of stock, and 180 were out of print. Although this is not, of course, a representative shop or a typical bookseller's day, it suggests the intricacy of the business in a graphic way.

The continuation of the Net Book Agreement has protected the booksellers—and therefore the publishers and the authors, too—from the evils of competitive price-cutting seen in the U.S.A. For the time being, this means that they are also protected from the application of the kind of "realistic" logic illustrated by Mr. H. A. P. Fisher, Q.C., counsel for the Registrar of Trading Agreements, in the 24-days' hearing before the Restrictive Practices Court. "Anything which stands in the way of adaptation of the retailing system to the changing requirements of the times is detrimental", said Mr. Fisher; but he made some erroneous assumptions about what these "changing requirements" entailed, the worst of which was "there was no significant difference between the considerations affecting the production and distribution of books and those affecting all other merchandise". This assumption was quashed by the Restrictive Practices Court, which solemnly confirmed that "books are different". Yet the Net Book Agreement's continuation does not, of course, solve any of the basic problems: it only allows the trade a reprieve for reform.

It is not the job of this pamphlet to outline how such reforms can be achieved. Yet there is one obvious fly in the ointment: the public library. To support and encourage good bookshops—as an indispensable part of the amenities of a civilized community—should surely be a civic responsibility, discharged through the local library authority. What happens today in Britain is very different, as the evidence given to the Restrictive Practices Court revealed. Most libraries buy a large proportion of their books from specialized "suppliers", not from bookshops. There are 20 of these companies, which have mushroomed with the expansion of public library spending, and about eight of them are big-scale enterprises with staffs of nearly 100 and stocks of over 100,000 books. They do not sell to the public but only to the libraries, providing them with services at a cheaper rate and—so librarians say—with greater speed and efficiency than the average bookshop can guarantee to show. Both suppliers and bookshops give the standard discount of 10 per cent. on the published price, but the supplier may charge a penny or two less per copy than the bookseller does for preparing it for use in the library. For librarians, this is one decisive argument in favour of the supplier. Yet by snubbing their local bookshops they help to keep bookselling in a permanently depressed condition. The trade which libraries could divert to the shops, given a more generous allocation for buying, could help to regenerate British bookselling, with happy results for British authors.

Publishers could also do much more to help booksellers. As a matter of urgent self-interest, they might press ahead with plans for an adequately capitalized, efficiently staffed central clearing-house, or with a system of interlinked, decentralized co-operatives; might consider the investment of capital in particular shops already of proven quality and in need, or in particular areas where bookshops are required; and might collaborate in promoting the book-buying habit among potential customers.

Free libraries? ∗ ∗ ∗ ∗ ∗ ∗ ∗ ∗ ∗

BOOK-BUYING in Britain lags a long way behind book-borrowing, which has spread rapidly since the war. Many public libraries have transformed their image, under the pressure of a vast new readership—much of it from a social group for which a free library seemed as much alien ground before 1939 as a bookshop appeared to the class below them (libraries were too *common*; bookshops too *posh*). The number of books issued in a year has risen from 76 million in 1924 to over 441 million in 1960/1: roughly 70 per cent. of this is fiction. Even in the past five years there has been a notable expansion in borrowing: in 1960/1 libraries had 75 million books in stock (nearly 66¼ million in 1956/7), and spent over £5½ million on books (£3,863,000 in 1956/7). There are now 548 public library authorities, who provide about 40,000 "service points". Nearly 30 per cent. of the population are registered readers (on average each borrower takes out a book every fortnight). Libraries buy about 10 per cent. of the book trade's output, at a discount of 10 per cent.

This expansion is a significant aspect of the social revolution of our time, in which the library itself has been an instrument. At their best, the libraries have been power-stations of ideas, supplementing the inadequacies of the educational system and making up for the lack of purchasing-power in the lower of the Two Nations. They have also supplied a steady market for many authors and many kinds of book, taking some of the risk out of publishing by buying a third to half the initial printing of a first novel.

Librarians, however, have often claimed too much, in fighting—with oddly disquieting bitterness—the proposals widely supported in Parliament and elsewhere, for some form of charge against the borrower. Sir Alan Herbert, who has led the campaign for Public Lending Right with his usual verve, discovered that two books by him in a public library had been borrowed around 5,600 times in twenty years, and that—including replacement copies—this reading on loan had earned him £3 in the whole period. If each of those readers had bought a book, the return would have been about £180. It is probably true that most of those borrowers would never have read the books if they had not been in the library, and that many of them could not afford to buy a book for pleasure: but should this mean that Sir Alan—and all other authors—must be content with a pittance from the local authorities? Why should not readers, directly or indirectly, pay something towards the remuneration of the men who make the books they borrow? Why should librarians, who have an especial responsibility for the health of professional authorship, so violently rebut writers' claims to some material return for their increasing popularity on loan? Why should some of their supporters in the press and elsewhere, while admitting that authors are inadequately paid, uphold the shibboleth of Free Reading on moral and social grounds, as if its abandonment represented a betrayal of democratic liberties and the British way of life? Clearly the libraries and their local authorities must act as patrons of authorship in a more positive way than was expected of them before the welfare state changed people's reading habits.

One essential improvement is to give the librarians more money to buy books. Although they have had more cash during the past decade, they still—even under the most enlightened local authorities—don't have nearly enough; and budgets still vary wildly. Some authorities spend on books as much as 17s. per head per year, others spend well below the 2s. minimum a head considered by an investigating committee in 1959 as the chief test of a library's efficiency. Only about a quarter of total library spending in Britain is invested in books: other factors—salaries, fabric charges and service charges—have also cost more in recent years, sometimes at the expense of book-buying.

Writing for the press ✳ ✳ ✳ ✳ ✳ ✳ ✳ ✳

IN Britain, as elsewhere, the professional author has usually depended upon the press—both newspapers and magazines—to supplement his income; but here, too, there have been marked changes. Between 1949 and 1962 as many as 17 daily and Sunday newspapers closed down, and only four new ones were launched. Among the survivors, the concentration of ownership has ominously increased. In 1948 the three major groups—Associated Newspapers, the *Daily Mirror* group and Beaverbrook Newspapers—controlled between them 45 per cent. of the total circulation of all daily papers. By 1961 they controlled 67 per cent. If this trend continues it is likely to have a bad effect not only upon the relative freedom of journalism but also on the status of authorship. Most authors, moreover, have a smaller chance both of writing and of being reviewed in the national (and the periodical) press. Although newspapers have increased their size (and their circulations) in the past decade, most of them devote a bigger proportion of their space to magazine features, especially those addressed to women, and scarcely any space at all to the stories, essays, reviews and light, literate journalism from which the talented pre-war freelance might pick up a fairly easy living. The steady pressure for bigger readership, upwards to the million, has already modified the older patterns of press entertainment for the "educated classes", and with them have disappeared many of the traditional ways of freelancing.

Outside London the press has evaporated: in the past 40 years nearly 250 weekly papers have closed down. In magazine publishing there has also been a massive concentration of power in several mammoth groups, so that around 300 periodicals are now controlled by one company. There are *more* magazines, in spite of the rationalization of production that has resulted from various mergers—3,997 were listed in the 1962 edition of the *Newspaper Press Directory*—but the decisive changes have not been in the general author's favour. Twelve years ago, when Rowntree and Lavers made a survey of *English Life and Leisure*, they reported that the most popular periodicals were *Picture Post, Illustrated, John Bull* and *Lilliput*. Three of these have disappeared, and the fourth (*John Bull*) is unrecognizable in its current shape (as *Today*). Gone are *Public Opinion, Chambers' Journal, Truth, Literary Guide, Adelphi, World Review*, and others. If one looks at the casualty list of the 1930's as well, the pattern of disease becomes clearer: *Life and Letters, Nation, Saturday Review, Week-end Review, G.K.'s Weekly*, and all those magazines which were among the war's first victims—*Bystander, Family Journal, Grand, Happy, Man and Woman, Pearson's, Red, Violet* and *Windsor*. It is the weekly review, the family "general" magazine and the fiction magazine which have faded away, as the old-style middle-class's spare-time occupations have changed. Here, as in other ways, it is the novelist—especially the young aspirant—who feels the pinch most painfully. Back in 1922 as many as 13 new magazines were launched, all publishing "a substantial proportion of fiction": only one survived in 1962. There were 27 "fiction magazines", both fortnightly and monthly: only two of them were left in 1962. The demand for stories today is narrower and more specialized, for the main market is in the women's magazines which dominate the field with sales of up to three million copies a week. Throughout the world of periodicals, in every category, there is a greater reliance on formula writing by staff insiders and on big names for outside authors. It is increasingly hard for the small name to get bigger, by telling stories in print.

The rewards of writing for British magazines, below the summit, are all too often miserably inadequate, measured against the changing cost of living and the rising revenue of the publishing networks. Forty years ago Mr. Michael Joseph notified readers of *Short Story Writing for Money* that "twenty pounds is a good price for an English magazine to pay for a story of ordinary length—about 4,000 words", while he declared that "a magazine of any standing ought to pay at least two guineas per thousand". No complete or consistent information is available, yet from the Society of Authors' records it seems clear that many magazines of "standing" have not so much as *doubled* their price for a story since 1923, although the cost of living has increased by well over 300 per cent., and that some magazines pay below the 1923 level. A guide to current earning-power may be taken from the fact that the most profitable markets, the women's magazines, pay— to all but top names—25 to 45 guineas; one of the very few surviving short-story magazines pays from 35 to 45 guineas; and the short-story's biggest customer, the B.B.C., has raised its fees from £15 to £21 in the past ten years. Quick-selling authors at the top of the publishing ladder may earn big money from serialization of their books in British periodicals (in addition to American ones). But in general storytelling is underpaid and crowded out. British writers look increasingly to the selective U.S. market, which pays three to ten times as much.

The biggest expansion in the magazine field has been in technical and do-it-yourself publications, which have increased in number by 50 per cent. since 1952. Information is in demand: the newly affluent readers—with cars to run, homes to decorate, children to educate— want to *know*. Practical, factual journalism leads the field. (In the 1962 total there were 1,933 trade and technical publications.) As in book-publishing, the "technical" author has come forward, while the "literary" and the "entertainment" authors have dropped behind.

In other channels ✳ ✳ ✳ ✳ ✳ ✳ ✳ ✳ ✳

OUTSIDE the world of the printed word, a somewhat different prospect has opened for an increasing number of writers during the past ten years, in a way that demands another pamphlet to do it justice. Let us take the theatre first. On the debit side, there are still not enough stages for the drama, especially in London; for it is on the West End, nearly as much as in 1953, that the dramatist must depend, for cash if not entirely for kudos. The tendency of long runs to get even longer, and so to freeze theatres for years at a stretch, has meant a smaller play-turnover inside the commercial system; and rising costs have cut still further the run of a play that does not score an instant success. This hit-or-flop disease, chronic on Broadway, has grown more acute since 1953. Like some publishers, some managements are trying—here and there—to reduce their risk by squeezing the author, asking him to accept a lower royalty rate until production costs are paid off, demanding a bigger slice of his subsidiary rights. The dramatist can no longer count on income between plays from work on tour: during the last decade this business has evaporated, and by 1962 there were seldom more than a dozen productions on the road at a time (most of them pre-London tours) compared with around 70 or 80 in 1953, and with about 180 in the 1930's. Television has drawn away audiences, technicians and actors: casting difficulties may now cause even longer delays between a play's acceptance and its production.

On the credit side, the West End system is in some ways more flexible and diversified: there are a few more independent managements, more adventurously concerned with new playwrights, and the power of the "bricks and mortar" interest has declined a little. Authors staged in London with success can pick up a reasonable income from repertory, amateur, film and foreign rights. (A play in the *Sailor, Beware!* class can earn about £1,000 a year for ten years in provincial reps: film payments vary from £10,000 for *Seagulls over Sorrento* to £125,000 for *Separate Tables*.) "Weekly rep" had almost disappeared by 1962; with state aid, through the Arts Council, a growing number of companies have introduced fortnightly rehearsals and even fortnightly changes of bill—an improvement of standards which benefits the dramatist. New patrons for the theatre have appeared since 1952 among local authorities, universities, trusts, and industrialists. The Arts Council's aid to the drama—from a budget which rose from £76,193 in 1952/3 to £252,144 in 1961/2—has been of great value, directly and indirectly, through personal grants to authors, guarantees to companies against loss on new plays, and the maintenance of new enterprises.

The first of these was the English Stage Company, which set out in 1956 with the declared ambition of creating a "writer's theatre", and sponsored a new group of dramatists in a break-through which has had repercussions not only in the theatre but in the other arts as well. At the Royal Court, at Theatre Workshop (for a decade) and at the Aldwych under the Royal Shakespeare banner, writers found something new— relative permanence and continuity of organization, with a kind of freedom and vision (however erratic) which it is impossible to achieve in the casino conditions of the long-run system, to which there had for too long been no working alternative. Although these theatres live precariously, they have already had a striking effect on the status and prestige of the dramatist.

From the Royal Court, the new playwrights—led by John Osborne —have begun to influence the cinema, and the writer's place in it, with the help of new theatre directors and novelists. Against all the prophecies of trade "realists" in Wardour Street, the new-wave films— identified, so far, with a sharper social realism—have proved not only to be popular but to be much bigger box office than the standard industrial product. Elsewhere, the success of such writer-producers as Bryan Forbes is another pointer to a change in status for the author in films, as in the theatre. Yet the area of change is still very small. While the number of Britain's cinemas drops (from 4,568 in 1952 to 2,711 in 1961), the machinery of exhibition and distribution remains the same—weighted against nonconformist, minority work, against "shorts", against a higher valuation of the diminishing cinema public's I.Q., against a higher proportion of British film scripts, against more power for the artist. Production stays at roughly the same level—125 feature films in 1950/1, 122 in 1960/1—while the state subsidy, on which production partly depends, keeps at about the same level of a million pounds, and the audience slumps steadily down (from 1,635 million in 1946 to 460 million in 1961). Many authors have occasional windfalls, of varying size, from the film rights of books, plays and stories—the industry traditionally buys far more than it can ever use—but the cinema still does not offer much scope, directly, to more than a couple of dozen specialists.

In television, on the other hand, there have been great changes in the past ten years; and the situation is still so fluid that it would be premature to attempt to crystallize any definition of the writer's relationship to the new medium. By 1962, however, it had plainly developed into a guaranteed market for a relatively small group of dramatists and scriptwriters, many of them discovered by television and working for television only. (There are 500 full-time members— those with two or more "major credits"—of the TV and Screen Writers' Guild.) Up to 1955 the only channel was the BBC, which televised about a score of new plays every year and paid £100 each for them. By 1962 it paid an average £300, while ITV averaged £450 (a few at the top get £1,000 and over). From 1955 to 1960 there was a boom in output —between them, the BBC and ITV screened around 500 hours of "drama" a year. In the early 1960's, play-output was cut: films were cheaper to televise. Even so, the TV and Screen Writers' Guild reported at the end of 1962 that 40 per cent. of their full members earned over £20 a week, and 11 per cent. earned over £80 a week, from writing of all kinds; and although the Guild is understandably dissatisfied with the writer's share of television and film budgets, these figures of earning-power stand in revealing contrast with those previously quoted for members of the Society of Authors, even if the five-year-interval is taken into account. There are great possibilities in television's future growth, both for "entertainment" and for "educational" authors: not as a full-time occupation, but as an expanding source of auxiliary income (not least in the appetite it whets among a mass public for books and plays) and as a means of communication to the millions.

In sound radio the writer has found a valuable outlet for the past forty years: for short stories, talks, poems, adaptations, scripts for comedy shows or serials, and plays. Television offers richer pickings, but it has not—as pessimists predicted—eclipsed sound radio so far as to threaten its employment of authors. On the contrary, the drop in the listening public which followed the spread of TV appears to have been a temporary recession; and although in the field of light entertainment the proportion of words to music has slumped since 1952, elsewhere the BBC still offers many authors a useful way of making a little money, at rates adjustable to the rising cost of writing. Between 1952 and 1961 the minimum rates for serials and plays rose by around 50 per cent. (from about a pound to thirty shillings a minute). A questionnaire completed by a hundred members of the Radiowriters' Association showed that, of authors writing radio plays regularly for the BBC, in 1950 a quarter were earning less than £1 a minute; a third were earning less than 25s.; by 1959 no one was earning less than 25s. In 1950 no one was earning as much as 30s., but by 1960/61 55 per cent. were earning between 30s. and 40s., and 20 per cent. were earning 40s. and over a minute.

Signposts to the 'Seventies ✳ ✳ ✳ ✳ ✳ ✳ ✳

LOOKING ahead, some general predictions may be made about the British author; only a few are offered here. For better or worse, economics are squeezing the amateur out of "entertainment" writing, and that field is being narrowed down. The decline in the volume of fiction published annually is likely to continue; the "commercial" libraries will wither away; there will be a cut not only in the number of titles produced every year but also in the number of firms over-producing them. Gradually, the price of books (and newspapers and magazines) will be increased; and the rewards of the author should rise as well. More and more writers will earn a bigger proportion of their living from overseas sales, subsidiary rights, and such media as TV, radio and films.

Writing for hardback publication in the home market is becoming less profitable for the generality of "general" authors. Yet they can contemplate the prospect of a much vaster reading public, at home and abroad, transcending the "educated classes" on which professional authorship depended before the war. There were 50,000 undergraduates in British universities in 1938: in 1970 there will be around 200,000. Thousands of new readers are trained every year in the Commonwealth. Millions are learning not only to read books but also to borrow them and even to buy them, as the paperback extends its empire over the English-speaking world. The softcover book, once treated as a kind of fringe benefit, will be recognized as the main commodity of British publishing (already in the U.S.A. one third of the titles published are in soft covers). The enormous further increases in the sales of educational books and textbooks will bring new wealth to the publishers, who ought to be able to reward their authors more justly (especially for their sales abroad) and help to promote the reforms in bookselling which are so urgently required. Publishers may also be expected to collaborate in tackling the problems of the industry, in cutting production costs by improving and standardizing techniques, and in urging on the notoriously bookless people of this country the need to pay for their reading. With help from the public libraries, the universities, the big foundations and trusts, and the state itself, as all these acknowledge more fully their responsibility for the health of professional authorship, the British writer will have better opportunities to ensure that he is paid what he is worth and treated as he deserves.

Appendix: Publisher's Estimates
1950

English textbook   **200 pages**   **Size: Large crown $7\frac{3}{4}$ in. $\times$ 5 in.**

	10,000 printing			15,000 printing		
	£	s.	d.	£	s.	d.
Composition	151	15	6	151	15	6
Machining	146	9	6	186	9	6
Paper	200	12	11	300	19	6
Sheet cost	£498	17	11	£639	4	6

	s.	d.	s.	d.
Sheet unit cost		1 0		10·25
Binding unit cost		11		11
Unit cost		1 11	1	9·25

On selling price of 5s. 6d.

	s.	d.
Price received	4	4·25
Less royalty @ 10 per cent. ..		6·6
Overheads: 25 per cent. of price received	1	1·06
Profits: 15 per cent. of price received		7·84
	2	0·75

1962

History textbook   **208 pages**   **Size: Large crown 7¾ in. × 5 in.**

	10,000 printing £ s. d.	15,000 printing £ s. d.
Composition	260 10 10	260 10 10
Machining	185 7 10	244 17 10
Paper	280 0 0	420 0 8
Sheet cost	£725 18 8	£925 9 4
	s. d.	s. d.
Sheet unit cost	1 5·375	1 2·875
Binding unit cost	1 1·25	1 1·25
Unit cost	2 6·625	2 4·125

On selling price of 6s. 6d.

	s. d.
Price received	5 1·75
Less royalty @ 10 per cent. ..	7·8
Overheads: 25 per cent. of price received	1 3·44
Profits: 15 per cent. of price received	9·26
	2 5·25

These figures—for textbooks only—are given as an indication of some factors in the relative costs of producing books during the past decade. It will be seen that while in 1950 a publisher could afford to print 10,000 copies of a textbook and to price it at 5s. 6d., in 1962—for a book of the same size and function—he had to raise the print order to 15,000 and the price to 6s. 6d. if he was to meet his costs. Both costings take into account an author's royalty of only 10 per cent., although in fact the royalty rises, in both cases, to 12½ per cent. over 5,000 and to 15 per cent. over 10,000.

The Industrialization of the Writer
Elmer Rice

from

Saturday Review of Literature, 12, April, 1952.

Reprinted by permission of the *Saturday Review of Literature*.

The Industrialization of the Writer

ELMER RICE

Elmer Rice

THE Authors' League of America was organized in 1912 for the purpose of protecting the rights of creators of copyrightable material. When I joined it in 1914, the membership consisted almost entirely of fiction writers, dramatists, composers, and free-lance illustrators, that is to say, of "self-employed" individuals who created something and then sought a market for it. In 1920 I helped organize the Screen Writers' Guild in Hollywood, and when I came back East, the following year, I represented the Guild on the Council of the Authors' League. Since then I have served almost continuously on the Council in one capacity or another. Hence, I have been in a good spot to observe the changing status of the American writer in the past three decades.

In its first years the League dealt almost entirely with problems pertaining to the literary rights of authors (the illustrators dropped out to form their own organization), in particular with copyright, royalties, dis-

Elmer Rice, distinguished American playwright and novelist, has been actively associated with the Authors' League of America, the Dramatists' Guild, American Civil Liberties Union, and the National Council on Freedom from Censorship.

position of motion-picture and other subsidiary rights, enforcement of contracts. But the expansion of the motion-picture industry, the emergence and·mushroom growth of radio, and now the even more rapid growth of television have brought about radical changes in organization and emphasis. The Screen Writers' Guild and the Radio Writers' Guild have become the recognized bargaining agents for writers working in those industries; and television writers, though not yet fully organized, are presently engaged in collective bargaining with networks and advertising agencies. The meetings of the Authors' League Council, clearing-house for all the Guilds, deal more and more with straight trade-union problems: minimum wages, conditions of employment, shop elections, loyalty oaths, strikes, boycotts, blacklists.

The meaning is unmistakable: the status of the writer is shifting, at an accelerating pace, from that of an independent creator to that of a wage-earner. I do not have the figures at hand, but it is safe to say that one third to one half the 8,000 or so members of the Authors',League are in the salaried category. Nor is this the whole story; for while the League membership includes most of the "name" writers in all major fields, it does not include the uncounted tens of thousands of professional writers who are salaried employees of newspapers and newspaper syndicates, of periodicals, of trade, Governmental, and professional publications, of publicity services and advertising agencies.

It is only in the theatre and in the book-publishing field (and to some extent in the magazine field) that the author still functions freely as an independent creator; and there are few dramatists or novelists, even among the most famous, who do not occasionally do a motion-picture or television job for hire. I seem to remember reading somewhere that only about a hundred American writers subsist entirely upon their royalties. Whether the number is fifty or two hundred is unimportant. The fact is that today almost every American writer derives all or part of his income from salaried employment.

BEFORE we examine the significance of this new and startling development in the world of letters it would be well to ask how it came about. The answer is not hard to find. The change in the status of the writer is merely a phase of the revolutionary process which has mechanized and standardized nearly every kind of productive work. A century ago manufacturing was still carried on largely by craftsmen. But because of its inability to compete with machine production, handicraft is rapidly becoming obsolete—not only in the United States, but throughout the world; the individual (and often highly creative) artisan has become an almost unidentifiable robot on an assembly line. Farming, too, becomes more and more industrialized; the erstwhile tiller of the soil is today an operator of complicated mechanical contrivances. This we call progress—and perhaps it is, insofar as it lightens labor and multiplies the supply of consumable goods. Anyhow, it is a process that is not

"Well—you see, I compose on an electric typewriter!"

likely to be arrested. Its increasing application to the world of letters must therefore be a matter of deep interest to all who value the independence of the human mind and the free flow of ideas.

Until the beginning of the present century, writing was almost entirely a self-instituted and highly personal enterprise. Even newspapers were largely organs of opinion, flavored by the prejudices and enthusiasms of their editors. But the independent newspaper is vanishing; the salty, homespun editor has almost entirely disappeared. As production methods become more efficient and circulation grows, the number of newspapers actually diminishes; the empire of the syndicates expands and the content of the individual newspaper becomes more and more standardized; news reports, columns, recipes, editorials, comic strips, book reviews, jokes are all produced for the mass market by assembly line techniques. Many newspaper writers have by-lines and a few, perhaps, write pretty much as they please; but in the main the writer for the daily, weekly, or monthly publication is an anonymous employee who is paid to write to order.

When we look at the new channels of communication — motion pictures, radio, television—it is not surprising to find that the industrialization of the writer is almost complete. For these media did not originate as spontaneous forms of human expression. Unknown until the twentieth century, they were born out of business enterprise by technology. From their incep-

tion, they were organized along industrial lines, and the role of the writer has been that of a skilled technician, essential to a manufacturing process. (I am not referring, of course, to the writer of books or plays who supplies the raw materials from which motion pictures and radio-television presentations are constructed, but to the salaried employee who fashions the material according to the requirements of the industry.)

Even the relative independence of the book writer and the playwright is precarious—may, perhaps, be doomed. For—to stick to the economic line— the manufacture of books and plays remains in the handicraft stage of industrial development, and may be obsolescent. Since assembly-line production methods are not easily applied, manufacturing costs are so high that the finished product cannot possibly be sold in competition with the mechanized output of the motion-picture or broadcasting studio (particularly of the latter, which appears to cost the consumer nothing!). The theatre is a shrinking business. In 1926, there were seventy theatres in New York and something like 200 plays produced. Last year, there were thirty theatres and about seventy productions. The road is dwindling; professional stock companies have largely disappeared. Production costs are so excessive that the financing of plays becomes increasingly difficult; very few productions pay off, and even successes show only a small margin of profit. The publisher, too, sees his costs mounting and mounting. Formerly, he could

come out on a sale of 1,500 copies; now it is more like 7,500—obviously a figure that very few books attain.

The effect of this shrinkage of the market is to make it harder and harder for the young writer or the unorthodox writer to find an outlet. (I am not even talking about making a living!) Even the idealistic publisher and producer—and there are such!—must face the practical alternatives of making ends meet or going out of business. So the writer or would-be writer either gives up entirely or else hires himself out to a newspaper, motion-picture, or broadcasting factory. (I am not theorizing; I have known many able writers who have had to trade freedom for security.) It is no answer to say that there is always plenty of room at the top, that the brilliant writer will always find someone to produce or publish him, and an audience to appreciate him. No doubt. But literature, as a social and cultural institution, does not consist only of works of superlative genius. In a historic or ethnological sense it is the whole *body* of writing that expresses the mores and the thought of a given era and links it to the past and to the future. Furthermore, no writer works or can work in a state of splendid isolation; without the right climate and the right milieu, he cannot function freely or happily. Everybody wants to watch Ted Williams or Bob Feller in action, or see Helen Hayes and the Lunts perform, but neither baseball nor the theatre can exist without relief pitchers and pinch-hitters, or bit players and understudies. Even Shakespeare was no lonely peak, towering over a plain of mediocrity. He wrote in an atmosphere of fervid and unrestrained literary productivity. Today, though he outshines his contemporaries, he by no means eclipses them.

NOTHING that I have said is intended as a slur upon the author who writes for money, though I do not go all the way with Samuel Johnson's dictum that no man but a blockhead ever wrote except for money. Certainly Grub Street is one of the oldest thoroughfares in the world and the first hack was probably an Assyrian scribe who hacked out a cuneiform eulogy of his royal master. Though Voltaire may not have seen the necessity, writers continue to feel that they must eat. Even to the well-fed author, money is proof of the existence of an audience; and to most writers that means as much as bread.

But an author may have an eye on the box-office or the best-seller lists and still write what he wants to write —or, at least, persuade himself that

(Continued on page 62)

THE INDUSTRIALIZATION OF THE WRITER

he is doing so. Psychologically, and perhaps artistically, the author who is hired to do an assigned job, under arbitrary rules in the making of which he has had no part, is in a very different situation. Not only the quality of his work but his self-esteem must suffer (and does suffer). Most of the fine and potentially fine writers who have become industrialized are not happy and are not doing the best work of which they are capable. Whether or not the sacrifice of independence and spontaneity is too high a price to pay for economic security is something the individual writer must decide for himself. But of the loss to literature and to society there is not even a question.

Indeed, seen from the point of view of freedom of expression, the situation is truly alarming. Two conditions are essential to the healthy and democratic functioning of free speech: multiplicity and diversity of outlets, and the absence of arbitrary restraints and prohibitions. Do these conditions prevail in our present-day industrial society? I think not.

The tendency in all economic areas today is toward concentration of ownership and control. The field of communications is no exception. Ownership in the newspaper and periodical industries becomes increasingly centralized. And behind the owners is the very real economic power of the advertisers upon whose patronage the publications depend. The radio-television industry is almost completely dominated by four or five national networks; and here the influence of the advertiser is almost supreme, for advertising is the sole source of operational income. The production of motion pictures is largely in the hands of seven or eight big corporations, which are linked, directly or indirectly, to a few chains of exhibitors. (There are independent producers, but they are controlled by the bankers to whom they must look for their financing.) It is no exaggeration to say that a few hundred men have effective control over 95 per cent of what is read, seen, and heard in newspapers and magazines, and on the motion-picture and television screens.

I am not suggesting that these men are evil or even ill-intentioned. I am merely saying that such monopolization of control operates against diversity of outlet and variety of expression and constitutes a dangerous threat to free speech. This is particu-

larly true in view of the fact that the ownership group is fairly homogeneous and that its political and economic opinions tend toward orthodoxy and uniformity. The rebel, the iconoclast, the innovator among writers is looked upon as unsound—or, at any rate, as a bad business risk. Hence, conformity becomes the price of continued employment.

This is vividly demonstrated by the codes regulating the motion-picture and television industries. The opening paragraph of the recently adopted Television Code states: "Television is seen and heard in every type of American home. These homes include children of all ages, embrace all races and all varieties of religious faith, and reach those of every educational background. It is the responsibility of television to bear constantly in mind that the audience is primarily a home audience, and consequently that television's relationship to the viewers is that between guest and host." This is developed, at some length, with the customary obeisances to "education," "culture," and "good taste."

The Code then gets down to cases. In twenty-four sections and several sub-sections, it specifies unacceptable program material. Here are some samples: "From time to time, words which have been acceptable acquire undesirable meanings. . . . The Television Code Review Board shall . . . issue . . . a continuing list of specific words and phrases which should not be used. This list, however, shall not be considered as all-inclusive." "Attacks on religion and religious faiths are not allowed." "Divorce is not treated casually nor justified as a solution for marital problems." "The consumption of alcohol, in American life, when not required by the plot or for proper characterization, shall not be shown." "The use of horror for its own sake shall be eliminated." "Suicide as an acceptable solution for human problems is prohibited."

THERE is, of course, nothing new or surprising in all this. The Television Code embodies most of the shibboleths and proscriptions of the so-called Hays Code, under which the motion-picture industry has been operating for a generation. Its adoption is another

capitulation to the mandates of the leaders of organized religion and of other self-appointed censors. For the concentration of ownership and control of the major outlets of expression makes them easy targets for the pressure groups whose incessant and increasing demands are rapidly choking off free speech. These special-interest organizations, formed for the legitimate purpose of protecting the rights of a particular racial, religious, or economic minority, and often serving a useful social end, have in recent years taken the position that minority interests must be fostered even at the expense of the rights of the majority. Thus each group (as may be seen by studying the TV and motion-picture codes) endeavors not merely to *combat*, but to *suppress* whatever it considers inimical to its own objectives, regardless of the effect upon freedom of expression or the rights of those who hold opposing views.

Thus the Catholics insist that there be no attack upon religion and no approval of divorce, abortion, or birth control. Other sectarian bodies demand acceptance of their peculiar views on drinking, gambling, and lovemaking. Veterans' organizations will tolerate nothing that violates their own conception of patriotism. The Jews protest any unflattering depiction of a Jew; the Negroes take the same position with respect to their own race. Indeed, there is hardly a national or professional group that does not claim exemption for itself. Here is how it is stated in the TV Codes: "Racial or national types shall not be shown on television in such a manner as to ridicule the race or nationality." Why not? As an ardent advocate of the rights of minorities, I should like to point out that the right to equality of opportunity and of equality before the law does not carry with it the right to immunity from criticism or even from ridicule. A victim of injustice is not necessarily flawless. Ridicule has always been an effective weapon in the writer's armory and its use has often led to individual and social betterment; just as heretical, anti-moral, and revolutionary ideas have brought about the revivification of old ways of living or the creation of vigorous new ones. (Incidentally, the most pointed anti-Semitic stories are usually of Jewish origin.)

One would think that it would be obvious to the leaders of the pressure groups (who frequently represent only a small fraction of their putative constituents) that the claims of any one minority must be contingent upon the rights of all other minorities and, of course, of the majority. But they do not see it that way. Their demands grow more insistent, and the industrialists, fearful of shrinkages at the newsstand, the box-office, the drug counter, obey. The hired writer obeys too—and without even freedom of choice. He can give up his job, of course, but there is always a worried father waiting in the outer office, eager to step in.

We know what happens to civil liberties and to the arts in totalitarian countries. Freedom of speech and of opinion become extinct; the writer becomes a pitiable figure, without dignity, without courage, without zest, concerned only with saving his skin by tasteless conformity, cutting his cloth according to the dictates of a Hitler, a Mussolini, a Stalin. We decry censorship, we decry the regimentation of writers, we recognize that there is a melting-pot of ideas as well as of peoples, we demand the right to speak and to hear, to compare, to weigh, to choose. We take a rightful pride in our democracy, in the provisions of our Bill of Rights that protect free speech.

But all censorship is not official, all regimentation is not governmental. The concentration of economic power

can work as effectively as the concentration of political power. We are a long, long way from Hitlerism or Stalinism. Our dissident writers are not yet headed for the gas-chambers or the slave-camps. But, for the majority, conformity has become the price of bread. Conformity not only to the codes, the Nielsen ratings, the orders from San Simeon, Culver City, and the RCA Building, but conformity in their personal lives and private opinions. For there are loyalty oaths, morals clauses, blacklists, too. You not only have to write right, you have to think right, perhaps even prove that you don't think wrong.

This is a complex subject on which I have barely touched. To make it understood in all its ramifications and implications requires a job of research and analysis by the economist, the social historian, the literary critic. It is a job that should be done, for there is no subject more relevant to our political and cultural development. The writer is always the first victim of dictatorship. He is like the canary in the front-line trenches of World War I. When he stops singing, when he droops and dies, look out for poison gas.

The Criminal Record

The Saturday Review's Guide to Detective Fiction

Title and Author	Crime, Place, and Sleuth	Summing Up	Verdict
THE SEASON FOR MURDER *Hugh Lawrence Nelson* (Rinehart: $2.50)	Plane on hush-hush mission crashes in Rockies and Zebulion Buck & Jim Dunn look for bodies and cash, while villagers, fishing season, forest fires impede.	Amiable but confusing mish-mash of local color. Too many plot strands, too little motivation for too many murders. Characters meant to be lively but never make it.	Half-and-half
THE LONG GREEN *Bart Spicer* (Dodd, Mead: $2.50)	Phone call from Tucson summons Carney Wilde from Philadelphia to aid of vacationing millionaire client, whose granddaughter has been kidnaped amid luxury and cactus. Murders and chases ensue.	Good short-story idea dragged out by hard-bitten speeches, portentousness, ridiculous misunderstandings— and another 'tec hero who can go without sleep boringly long.	Readable enough
WAKE THE SLEEPING WOLF *Rae Foley* (Dodd, Mead: $2.50)	Laura Field thinks she has twice tried to kill her novelist husband with an erratic golf drive. Then husband's double is murdered and Laura is in for it, till Clarke Turner, explorer, goes fathoming.	Ingredients sometimes strangely mixed — but writing nicely straightforward and characters drawn in-the-round. Mystery not deep, but story persuasive.	Very good
FROM THIS DEATH FORWARD *Robert Bloomfield* (Crime Club: $2.50)	Damsel-in-distress Connie Daniels digs into deeper trouble by marrying sodden millionaire in Southern California. Murders and truckers and racketeers increase the woe.	Story quite improbable and disjointed — no logic at all. But author keeps you reading with held breath; some characters are weirdly memorable — even hateable and lovable.	The man can write

—KATHLEEN SPROUL.

The Minority Writer in England
by Geoffrey Wagner

from

The Author, vol. 64, no. 1, 1953.

THE MINORITY WRITER IN ENGLAND

By GEOFFREY WAGNER

1952, we now know, was a record book year for Great Britain. Almost twice as many novels were published here as in the U.S.A. But apart from the large group of small sale fiction which this publishing effort represents, the main selling groups in the literary market place in England are " Chemistry and Physics," " Engineering, Electricity and Mechanics," " Medical and Surgical," " Technical Handbooks," and so on. It is clear, from the latest breakdowns of book sales in this country, that the new classes given money by the socialist revolution, or experiment, have not yet become interested in creative literature. What our new middle class really wants is to take home a book on electronics, or how to tune up the bike on Sundays. The former middle class, comprising doctors, lawyers, and the like, who have been deprived of money recently, consisted of men largely educated by the Arts degree. The new middle class have not yet had their chance to develop these interests perhaps. I am not here arguing as to whether this is right or wrong, but in analysing the plight of the English minority writer one has to realize that the changes in our society since the last war have hit him hard.

If we are to believe Michael Joseph, our novelists could during the war years " count on " a sale of 10,000. To-day I wonder how many young novelists are, excepting the various book society recommendations, exceeding the 2,000 mark. I think it would be fair to say that the average British novelist to-day makes about £200 on an early novel. This has, to my mind, a devastating effect on the novel as form in our country ; for if you are only likely to earn sixty or seventy pounds on a novel this form of literature inevitably must become equated in the minds of its practitioners with the short story or factual article, for three of which, strategically placed in England, I earned more than for my last novel.

It is said that the story era in England was the nineteen-twenties and that now the market that supported writers of the order of Maugham or Conan Doyle has closed down. In 1918 there were more than twenty magazines, like *Strand* and *Argosy*, all taking stories on this level. To-day *Argosy* and *Blackwood's* are the only survivors of this period. It is safe to say that the modern British miscellany, like *The Cornhill*, publishes a better story than the average *Strand* of the twenties, but the job it is meant to be doing is giving an outlet to the serious minority writer, and printing a British equivalent of the story to be found in, say, the *Kenyon Review*. This I am afraid it is all too obvious it does not do.

The decline in British fiction, especially in

story fiction, seems to me to be due largely to the fact that the reading public is given no chance to sort itself out in England. In America you find fairly strictly stratified tastes.

In England the fiction-reading audience is far more monogenic, and of this general level I would say that there is a closer approximation to the tastes of the *Saturday Evening Post* than to *The Partisan Review*. Even *Atlantic* and *Harper's* print a totally different sort of story from the so-called " slicks " and are far bolder in what they give their readers in this way than *The Adelphi* or *The Cornhill*. But in England the woman's story shades off into the *Lilliput* story, which in turn shades off into *The Cornhill* story. I can see nothing to exclude most of the stories published in *World Review* or *The Cornhill* over the past few years from being printed in *Housewife*. That there is nothing left in British fiction to disturb the heartbeat of a flea is well seen by comparing *John O' London's Weekly* with its American " middlebrow " counterpart, *The Saturday Review of Literature*. It is the latter that seems, by comparison, " long-haired," I fear.

Now I am by no means one to despise the mass media. Indeed they would seem an exciting challenge to the minority writer, a round robin delivered in the name of demos which we should all sign with a chuckle of delight, instead of a *De Profundis*. But it must be realized that they are apart from literature. What happens in England, however, is a wide merging and flattening of the periodical audience until you get that state of affairs so admirably reported by Geoffrey Rans in *The Hudson Review* recently, an overall dilapidation of taste and the death of the story. Was a single one of Frank O'Connor's recent Knopf collection of stories first published in a British magazine ? It was not, although in America not only *The New Yorker*, but also *To-day's Woman*, could find space for samples. And since the novel is now paid at the same rate, approximately, as the short story, I predict the general demise of this form also in England.

There is already, in fact, no patronage for our minority writer left, so that any attempt to try to rise above the general level of com- petent mediocrity simply cannot collect an audience. First *Life and Letters*, then *Polemic* and *Horizon*, and now *World Review*, a mild enough miscellany in all conscience and backed by a rich publishing group, have gone. All this is especially disastrous when it is realized how little-magazine publication has made for continuity in English literature of this century, from Ford Madox Ford's *The English Review* to *The Egoist*, *Blue Review*, *The Criterion*, *The London Mercury* to *Horizon*.

In America there is a considerable little-magazine audience. The last issue of the Mentor *New World Writing* (which finds some half million readers from somewhere or other) lists twenty little magazines, all of which publish, and most of which pay for, serious fiction. Where does one of the few short story writers of any consequence left in England, Angus Wilson, publish but in America, usually in *The Partisan Review* ?

What would happen, I ask myself sometimes as my eye slides over the urbane periods of *The Times Literary Supplement*, were a Joyce to publish a novel in London to-morrow ? The answer is that it would receive inept attention in the daily press (in about a fifth of the space allotted to literature by, say, *The New York Times* daily). It would be intelligently reviewed with a batch of other novels (with which it would thus be equated) in the opinion-forming political weeklies and in *The Times Literary Supplement* (whose factual accuracy, incidentally, appears to be growing unusually low, judging from the errors noted in the American scholarly journals). And there the matter would end.

The mass media in America keep employed writers who are far happier on the threshold of literature than they would be in Joyce's Circe episode, and who help to define for all of us aspects of popular culture in their broadest boundaries. But the literary world of the British Harrods or Boots Library is the same vague and characterless one of the British miscellany, that is, a tolerably educated, tolerably cultivated, flaccid mass of generalized fiction readers. It is enough to listen in to the B.B.C. Third Programme. The Third Programme don is the perfect representative of that spirit of compromise that is killing all vitality in our literature. It will be objected that in America there are virtually no dons on the air at all. This is true, by and large, but it permits the dons to get on with their serious work.

In America the minority writer has a real chance. In poetry things will always be difficult, I imagine, as they always have been. And an awful lot of poetry still gets respectably published in the U.S.A., while last year a leading London publisher sold just twenty copies of a highly praised collection by a reasonably established native poet. In the U.S.A. not only are the little magazines engaged in erecting standards of discrimination (which eventually decide what fiction will be even commercially valuable, after all), but the whole fiction market is being changed to-day. As with the movies, the " quality " novel is tending to make money—comparatively speaking. Paul Bowles, Angus Wilson, Jean Stafford, Thomas Mann, have all made recent appearances on the best-seller list. This is partly due to the fact that no fiction, beyond a few exceptional titles, is " selling " at all, in the old sense.

Since no author, barring the prodigious exception, is selling at all, then, the minority writer is in the running for attention. For if you are certain to lose money on a novel anyway (break-even points now being as high as 15,000 in some firms, and my own publishers, Simon and Schuster, publishing no more than two or three novels a year), why not lose on a novel of reasonable quality that may have longevity ?

Tom Hopkinson has charted in a recent article the " possible fall " of the fictional best-seller but he does not go so far as me, for I personally believe that publishers will be led to publish good fiction in America simply out of commercial interest. Huge sums have been made recently by the Dreiser and Conrad estates. Lawrence's sales are said to be enormous, while the Modern Library *Ulysses* is a perennial that must sell a steady ten thousand or so a year to the increasing student audience.

The point is that the crass audience (with which America is so glibly credited) does not impinge as adversely on the minority writer as does the same group in England. In America, after all, the " glossies " keep to themselves and leave the serious writers to get on with their business.

Now I am not pretending that serious English writers peruse *Reveille* or *Tit-Bits*. But I do maintain that in our country a general vitiation of taste, via comic-books and the like, affects the whole literary audience with repercussions on the minority writer, to which he is immune in America. The American minority writer has never been befriended by the crass audience anyway and he owes them nothing. I, for one, would far prefer the average American publisher's list to-day, numbering at least one collection of poetry alongside the obviously commercial matter, to the average English publisher's list in which a general level of innocuous gentility is preserved. The fate of our minority writer is a serious one. It may be that, as Professor Levin writes of Cyril Connolly, " His work serves more or less authoritative notice that England, long declining into a second-class power, has begun her decline into a second-class culture." Or it may be that, as an English colleague put it the other day, the situation will have to change for the better since it cannot do so for the worse.

[Mr. Wagner's article was with the printers before announcements had appeared of two new monthly periodicals, *Encounter* and *The London Magazine*, to be edited respectively by Mr. Stephen Spender and Mr. John Lehmann. Editor, *The Author*.]

Will the Commercialization of Publishing Destroy Good Writing?
James T. Farrell

from

New Directions, 9, 1946.

Reprinted by permission of the author.

WILL THE COMMERCIALIZATION
OF PUBLISHING DESTROY GOOD WRITING?
SOME OBSERVATIONS ON THE FUTURE OF BOOKS

James T. Farrell

THE magazine *Tide* (August 15, 1945) printed an article on "Book Publishing" which stated: "With the prospect of more paper for book publishers in the not far distant future, the big publishers are girding themselves for the biggest expansion and probably the greatest competition in their history." This article gives an account of the connections of the four big reprint companies which are now becoming the dominating organizations in the book business and also mentions something about their post-war plans which are not as yet fully crystallized. The major publishers, the article remarks, "agree that the industry is changing and will possibly evolve into a quite different animal." Many have said the same thing, both in public and in private discussion. Publishers, writers, editors, economic journalists and others are all asking questions about what will happen in the book business. Contradictory predictions are being made, some gloomy, some optimistic. In general, there is a great deal of interest, curiosity, alarm and uncertainty in literary and publishing circles about these recent developments.

During the war, a number of people discussed the future of books. Philistine literary critics dealt with this question in terms of mere tendency and predicted that in the post-war world writing would grow up, which meant that it would become as smug as they are. The way that writing would grow up, according to Mr. J. Donald Adams and others, was that it would become "spiritual." One of the ironies of these discussions and predictions lay in the fact that while the book critics were so concerned with the souls of authors and of the American public, and with the status of the Deity in American literature, the major developments in the book world were economic in character. Current interest in the book world is now mainly centered in the economic features of publishing.

A number of serious critics have repeatedly discussed the differences between literature and commerce in American culture. A question posed for a number of writers has been formulated in terms of the opposition between success and integrity. Now, with changes in the book business, gloomy prophets and disturbed writers are predicting that in the future it will be impossible for writers to retain any integrity and that American writing will become merely a success chronicle of commercialized writing. It will be, they say, Hollywoodized. Heretofore, questions of this kind have usually been dealt with in terms of a juxtaposition of "high culture" and "low culture." "High culture" has been treated as serious art and viewed as the concern of gifted, sensitive and educated people; "low culture" has been dismissed as cheap popular art, spiritual fare for the uneducated masses. This view can be very misleading, for what has long been happening in this country is that a commercial culture has been developing and expanding. It has confused cultural values, and has almost totally absorbed the theatre. Books have not been unaffected; in fact, the fear of commercialized culture is the source of current alarm about the future of books. At present it is easy to make rash predictions. Publishing is now in a very problematic state. It is not my purpose to try to offer any definitive answers to the questions involved or to make over-all predictions. I wish, instead, to present some observations relating to these questions which will, I hope, serve as a basis for further discussions. Authors and interested readers should attempt to orient themselves concerning the book business. It is of real meaning to them that they watch what is now happening in the publishing world.

II

Book publishers on the whole, as is well known, enjoyed phenomenal prosperity during the War. Hampered by paper restrictions and shortages in manpower and materials, they were unable to supply the full demands of the swollen market. Describing this situation, one publisher remarked that any book would sell as long as it contained either words or pictures; if it contained neither, there would be difficulties in selling it. However, he also added, if the book were too good, it might be a little difficult to sell. During this boom the reprint houses rose to a position where they now are becoming the dominant factors in the book world. Perhaps the degree of their expansion is suggested by the statement of *Tide* that Pocket Books sold 30,000,000 paper-covered reprints at 25¢ in 1944. And it is to be noted that the four big companies discussed by *Tide* are all reprint houses.

Publishing, which has always been a highly competitive business, is now moving into a period of feverish rivalries on all sides. The reprint houses are competing for distribution outlets, for authors and reprint rights, for motion picture tie-ups and for access to production facilities. This rivalry is the central fact in the economics of the book business today.

Tide lists the four major rivals and specifies their connections and the advantages each holds against the others. They are: Simon & Schuster; Doubleday, Doran & Co.; World Publishing Company; and the combination of Harper & Bros., Random House, Little Brown & Co., Charles Scribner & Sons and the Book of the Month Club. *Tide* further states: "Each of the four combines has been dabbling with one or more of the four elements that make for publishing concentration: a regular [trade] house, a reprint house, a book club and a pocket-sized book house."

Simon & Schuster, already a rich company, was bought by Marshall Field, and new capital has been invested in it. In connection with Sears Roebuck it has a People's Book Club; it owns Pocket Books; it has organized a new Venture Press, which plans to print the work of hitherto unpublished novelists. This last has been interpreted by some as a means by which Simon & Schuster would line up new authors and thereby try to squeeze out the independent publishers.

Doubleday Doran & Co. is undoubtedly the biggest of these four companies. *Tide* states that it owns its own plant and that it does a large part of its own printing and binding. This is not definitely confirmable and, in fact, has been denied; but it is reported that the company is planning to build a new plant of its own. Whether or not Doubleday Doran & Co. owns or doesn't own its plant, builds or doesn't build a new one, it is still the biggest company in publishing. Through subsidiaries it controls a large share of the reprint business by publication of Triangle Books (49¢), the New Home Library (69¢) and Star Dollar Books, Blue Ribbon Books and the Sun Dial Press (from 70¢ to $1.49). In addition to its regular trade house it controls book clubs: The Literary Guild with a reported membership of 900,000, making it larger than the Book of the Month Club; the Doubleday Doran Book Club with 400,000 members; the Book League of America with 200,000 members; the Junior Literary Guild with 20,000 members. It also has its own chain of retail book stores, established on a national basis.

The combination of four publishers recently purchased the reprint firm of Grosset & Dunlap, a large, well-established business, and it also recently announced that it would enter the 25¢ field with a new series, Bantam Books.* The Book of the Month Club, affiliated with this combine, has a reported membership of 600,000.

The World Publishing Company began by printing Bibles and dictionaries. It owns a huge plant in Cleveland, and entered the reprint field in 1934. Today it is a major and very rich reprint house, but it has no subsidiaries. One of its advantages against rivals is its network of distribution outlets in chain stores and on news stands. Through this important kind of outlet, it is now beginning to challenge the 25¢ paper-backed editions.

Besides these four big rivals there are also in this field the Avon Company, which prints pocket-sized books of short stories and mystery stories, and Penguin Books.

* Despite this combination, of course, Scribners, Little Brown & Co., Random House and Harpers will remain separate trade firms and, as such, they will remain competitors.

"Despite this impending growth," the *Tide* article concludes, "there is not much indication that Wall Street is interested in the industry but it's an even bet it will be if the reprint field develops into the big business that is anticipated."

This being the situation, let us now look at some of its implications.

III

War economy did not create this new situation; it only accelerated the momentum toward bigness in publishing, which in turn has attracted fresh capital. The war boom demonstrated positively that mass production and distribution in books are both feasible and highly profitable. These developments are irreversible. Their structural consequences are revealed in the tendency toward combinations and centralization. Inevitably every phase of book business will become more concentrated than in the past. This concentration will increase the difficulties of operation for small and independent publishers, and it will probably have the effect of requiring a higher initial investment from any newcomers into the field. In other words, the scale of publishing will be enlarged, and money will talk more than ever. It is already common knowledge that books which have the largest advertising budgets most frequently receive prompt and long reviews, and that those selected by a large book club are generally treated as important books by the majority of reviewers. The immediate, if not the permanent reputations of many writers are related to such factors.

The American publishing business has long existed in a very fluid state. Consider the number of new houses and new figures who have risen to importance during the last two decades. Here the basis of rise is not rooted in new and revolutionary technological developments. The best conditions for advancement in publishing are to be found in having a lot of money to invest, in having new ideas for promotion and advertising, in having the charms of a contact man and the inclination to live in the limelight of glamor. Book publishing, if it is to play any progressive cultural role at all, constantly demands new figures. From this standpoint, the types it needs are men with disinterestedness, sympathy for new currents in writing, liberality of view, cultivation and love of books. But such types now usually become employees, rather than publishers, and they are likely to exert a decreasing editorial influence in the future. Present conditions suggest that this tendency will continue as the concentration of publishing progresses. Centuries ago, Aquinas, writing on glory, declared: "It is better to know than to be known." In publishing, this statement is gradually being dialectically reversed.

Not the least of the effects of the rise of the reprint houses will be the strengthening of the influence and pressure of commercial considerations. The enlarged scale of publishing will require increased efforts to minimize risks. Now more than ever publishers will be forced to be receptive to bestseller books. The practice of thinking up and concocting likely best-sellers in publishing offices and the minds of literary agents will grow more widespread than it is now. Ghost writing will become a better paying occupation.

The effort to minimize risks will be reflected in the type of publicity released from many publishing offices. Authors, especially of the female sex, will be continuously glamorized. A larger number of them than is now the case will probably become, along with movie stars, the witty heroes and heroines of Café Society and the gossip columns. More important, there will be increased budgets for book advertising as long as business prospers.* On the whole, book advertising has never been much different from general commercial advertising, but the thin line of demarcation is now disappearing. Publishers are beginning to use radio, billboards and similar sources of advertising.† One of the principal emphases which will be made in these ads will be that of appeal to conformity. They will at-tempt to interest the public in books by stating that inasmuch as one hun-dred thousand or one million or more of your fellow citizens have read a certain book, you also should read it. And popular reviewing will prob-ably become more debased than it now is.

With the increase of book advertising budgets and the greater glamori-zation of authors, both books and authors will become newsworthy, thereby enhancing the strategic importance of a few regular book reviewers. Grad-ually, and in inverse proportion to the tepidness and vapidity of what is said, the slavery of column book reviewing is growing into a better paid profession, and book reviewing is becoming more centralized. The decline of book reviewing in New York and the growth of the widely syndicated book column is paralleled by the emptiness of most unsyndicated provin-

---

* At a public symposium of book publishers on the future of books held last winter one publisher characterized the money he spent on advertising as money used for "educational" purposes. In a sense, of course, this is true; advertising is education, not for mental growth, but for the market.

† The radio program "Author Meets Critic" is now a national one. With few exceptions the books discussed on this program are the ones which sell best and receive most attention from reviewers. Mr. Bennett Cerf, publisher of Random House books and the Modern Library, has for several years conducted a radio book program, "Books are Bullets." Books which re-ceived popular attention and, in addition, which usually conformed to the accepted interpreta-tions of the War were the principal ones discussed on this program. It is needless to stress the point that immediately popular books are very often only of transient significance. Programs of this kind magnify that transient significance, however, and help toward effecting greater centralization of passing tendencies and literary and ideational fashions.

cial reviews: a number of them are now scarcely even literate.* This situation is rapidly reaching the point where it is almost impossible in these days to write a bad novel. If the comments of some of our widely read reviewers be taken as honest criticism, it is clear that these United States have become groggy with genius. In fact, "greatness" is so common in current reviews that the only way left anyone to become a distinguished writer is to be a bad one.

The foregoing should make it clear that all tendencies which lead to a bestseller culture will probably be strengthened as publishing centralizes. The importance of money, of the sum invested in a book and more broadly in a publishing house should, in consequence, be more nakedly revealed. As weaker publishers are forced out of business, the stronger will grow all the more powerful. Business accelerates itself in a complicated rather than in a single, straight-line manner.

Reprint houses and regular trade houses are now linked together through the fact that the same persons control both. This is the case in three of the four major companies mentioned above. The owners and executives involved claim that this linkage will not affect the editorial policies of their associated trade houses. We can accept such declarations at face value. Undoubtedly these men have no intention of making their trade policies merely subservient to the needs of reprint houses. Nevertheless, the book business has developed to the point where factors more important than subjective intentions are beginning to play the decisive role. The market is emerging as almost all-important. This tends, especially in the reprint business, toward the creation of a kind of substitute market taste for the individual tastes of editors. It is as if the market were giving birth to its own consciousness which then reduces the significance of the individual consciousness of editors and publishers.

Competition among publishers has always been keen. In the past it often provided an economic basis for the search for freshness, vigor, variety and originality in books. In the reprint field competition will probably tend to standardize. An instance of this is the increasing rivalry for motion picture tie-ups. One reprint house has already published at least forty-two titles which have also been sold to studios and filmed. Another house has entered the same field. No matter how inconsequential a book may be, it is certain to be reprinted in large editions if it is purchased for filming. The nadir of this trend is the current practice of publishing, in large low-priced editions, novelizations of successful films which were not originally based on novels. These books are usually ghost-written for a flat fee. The obvious

* In many instances all that small town newspaper reviewers do is either to paraphrase the book blurb or repeat what has already been written by popular New York reviewers.

conditions of sale of such novelizations demand that they be done with the greatest haste: otherwise the advantage of the movie tie-up would be lost. And it is to be remembered that the film plays were written to conform to the standards of the Hays Office Production Code. Need we guess what the quality of these novelizations is like?

The need to minimize risks will be greatest in the reprint field, where more money is invested. On the average the necessary minimum investment of the reprint publisher is likely to be a thousand or more per cent higher than that of the trade publisher. Under these circumstances it is obvious that any safe book with sales possibilities is going to be reprinted. From the standpoint of the original publishers reprint rights offer added and easy profits since they entail no risk or investment and will help reduce production costs. It follows that any book which stands a good chance of being reprinted is a better investment than one which doesn't. The reprint market offers an added and important economic reason for printing safe books.*

The necessarily feverish fight for shares in the reprint market, the size of the capital investment of reprint publishers, the relatively low profit per book all demand that they constantly acquire new titles to add to their lists. They need a steady flow of new books; they need the names of new authors; and the new books and new authors must be absolutely guaranteed for them. If such cannot be found, they will have to be made. The big printing presses cannot stop running except at the peril of bankruptcy, for overhead costs mount day after day and must be paid. In time, such factors can well push the reprint houses toward taking steps to guarantee new books and authors. Already the fact that three of the four big companies are linked with trade houses further suggests this probability. Mr. B. D. Zevin, vice-president of World Publishing Company, has predicted, according to *Tide,* that he may have difficulties in buying reprint rights from the trade houses which are linked with his competitors. Here is further testimony suggesting the same probability. Strong economic motivations exist to give weight to the practice of nursing authors along for the reprint market.

The conditions of sale of the reprint market differ from those of the trade book market. In the former, books are generally sold as pure mer-

---

* There is a certain qualifying factor here which must be remembered. Data and experience in publishing history prove that serious books and even great ones are usually excellent long run investments, and that they may even have value on the reprint market. This market has made short stories of all levels of competence and significance a better investment for publishers. Not only is the market for books of stories by one author thriving, but there is a large demand for short story anthologies. The reprint rights of short stories are now far from insignificant when looked at from the standpoint of profits.

chandise.* Quality and variation do not play the same role as they do in the trade market. Reprint books are, in consequence, relatively interchangeable. If one book doesn't sell in a certain area, a certain chain, then another will be put in its place. And in addition to this the demand for sentimental and cheap novels is large and fairly steady. Our social conditions, which alienate so many people, daily recreate the need for these books, just as they do the need for escape movies. It should be clear then, that there are many reasons to predicate greater standardization in books: this in turn suggests that the reprint houses will exert, directly or otherwise, a growing editorial influence on the policies of the trade houses.

Never in the history of American publishing has there been a need for authors such as that which now exists. Publishers no longer sit in offices and wait for the mailman and the literary agents to deliver manuscripts to them. They search for authors across the length and breadth of America. Hollywood has become a regular stopping-off place for publishers' representatives on the hunt for writers. A new occupation, that of the literary scout, has been created. These scouts tour the literary sandlots of America, and with contract, check and fountain pen in hand, seek to sign up promising talent just as if they were scouts for a major league baseball team.

The need for writers explains the growth of the institution known as Writers Conferences, which are conducted by an increasing number of universities all over the country. (In most instances the teachers at these conferences try to give the amateur writers the rudiments of commercial writing.) It explains the reason for the existence of so many literary prizes and fellowships offered by publishers. The general intensification of competition has induced this almost frantic search for new writers. Under these circumstances the richer publishers have the advantage merely because they can offer larger advances and bigger prizes and fellowships. One result of all this activity is to create an over-supply of literary aspirants— disillusioned housewives, grandmothers, small town *petits bourgeois,* psycopaths, old maids, business men turned into New Dealers, and sundry other types and classifications, all seeking with might and main for some way whereby they can learn to write a novel and thereby make a million dollars.

The literary agent is gaining a more important position in the mechanics of American publishing. One of the roles he performs is that of thinking up ideas for a book which he can have one of his clients write, and so get his own commission. This is but another of the ways in which the chance

---

* This, of course, does not apply to such reprint libraries as Oxford's World Classics and Everyman's, which are based on quality. In the past the same could be said for The Modern Library, but a study of the list of titles dropped and added in recent years indicates that its editors are gradually watering down their stock.

for various people to make a lot of money becomes the premise on which a number of books are written.

The rise of the reprint houses is having the effect, as we have seen, of strengthening the ties between Hollywood and the book business. For more than a decade films have influenced writing. Thanks to the prices it can pay, Hollywood has given a strong financial impulse to the publication of books which approximate the sentimental patterns of its films. Many writers have found it most convenient to adjust their conscience, their style and their themes to the dramaturgical conceptions of Hollywood. New ties are being formed between studio offices and reprint houses. When a reprint house publishes a book in connection with a film there can be joint publicity. This will in turn lead to book advertising and publicity which will seek to fix Hollywood conceptions about books in the public mind. It is a proven fact that if a book is filmed its sale almost automatically increases. The new reprint profits will thus help to give Hollywood a greater, if indirect, editorial influence in the book world. Already the juciest literary prize now available is the Metro-Goldwyn-Mayer prize for "The Novel of the Year," so deemed by a committee of film people and critics. This prize pays the winning author a minimum of $100,000 and just about assures financial independence for life: and the publisher of the prize-winning novel is given a fat bonus for printing the book, presumably to make him happy. A critic who had served as one of the judges selecting a "Novel of the Year" reviewed the selection in his column. This critic, an honest man who never uses his column to exploit private grievances, is not known for either his acute intelligence or his literary sensibilities. However, he was well aware that the "Novel of the Year" was a standardized performance. His review was on the side of explanation and apology, showing that while it was not like really good novels, it was a Hollywood story.

IV

I have already mentioned that the direction now being taken by the big publishers has been described as the Hollywoodization of literature. One editor and poet is of the opinion that the film and the printed word are fighting a life and death struggle, and that the film is likely to destroy the printed word. Just as some years ago there were many poets and literary men prepared to bury humane letters as a corpse slaughtered by science, so now there are writers, poets and even editors who are ready to deliver the funeral orations over the novel, that great and beautiful lady who has been killed by a camera. While this rush for the mourner's bench goes on, it is necessary to look into the question a little further. The recent expansion of the reprint market offers us some interesting data.

To date the reprint publishers have not practiced an economic censorship such as that which exists in pictures and radio. The taste shown in reprint titles reflects the general level of taste in the trade publishing world. The reprint houses have bought as many titles as they could which promised to be successful on the mass market. There is one instance of an almost forgotten but seriously written realistic novel which had had a very small original sale, was reprinted, and then sold in a very large edition. There are instances of protests from chain store buyers concerning the alleged immorality of serious novels in which the publishers did not heed these protests. One publisher took the position that he had no right to censor any book which had received critical recognition and for which there existed a popular demand. There are instances in which serious novels were kept in stock by reprint houses even though paper was scarce and this meant the temporary sacrifice of sentimental books. (However, these serious novels *were* selling well.) Reprint titles in recent years show considerable variety, especially in fiction; the variety is less wide in non-fiction titles.

A mass audience, large for the book business if not for films, has shown that it is receptive to serious titles. For instance, Richard Wright's book *Uncle Tom's Children* sold heavily in a 49¢ edition, even in the South. Inasmuch as the reprint audience includes a considerable number of those who also compose the motion picture audience we have here an excellent basis for drawing comparisons. It is now easier to examine contrasts between the quality of the novel as it is written today and as it was in the past, and the film as it is made today. The opportunity now exists for large sections of the public to see a picture and then to procure the novel on which it was based in a low-priced edition. The differences in treatment between films and novels, the greater freedom of the novelist over the scenarist often offers so glaring a contrast that it is difficult not to perceive it. These differences and contrasts offer an excellent basis for analysis, for exposing the emptiness, the shabbiness of so many Hollywood films.*

Theoretically the film and the novel should complement one another. Insofar as they are placed in competition it is artificially imposed because of the social organization of culture in American society. However even in this artificially imposed competition the novelist is less at a disadvantage

---

* The case of the film *To Have and Have Not,* based on Ernest Hemingway's novel of the same title, is illuminating here, even though the novel itself is a very bad one, far inferior to *The Sun Also Rises.* The hero, in the novel, smuggled arms for Cuban revolutionists who were fighting the terroristic Batista regime; in the film, the hero helps to win the World War by putting himself in the service of anti-Vichyites. Cuba becomes Martinique. Changes of this kind were made not for any artistic reasons at all, but for purely immediate political ones. At the same time, the relationship between the hero and the heroine becomes utterly senseless. The reason for this is the Hays Code. Immediate practical needs, plus the Code, also demanded other changes and disfigurations of the novel. However, it can be added that in the case of another book, *The Informer,* the film is far superior to the novel.

than many people assume. He is more free than the screen writer. He may dare to say in public what even the most powerful motion picture magnate dares not whisper. In artificially imposed competition in the arts, money is not the only decisive factor. Freedom of expression is also decisive. In the long run he who is most free is sure to have the most important influence.

There are many forms of literature which have little or no connection with films—essays, most of the good poetry that is written, and such works as *Finnegans Wake*. There are many novels, however, which do stand in relationship with the film, the sentimental popular novel and the realistic novel being leading instances. In the case of the former the influence of the films is the strongest. But not so in the case of the latter. Novels form part of the raw material for films. The serious realistic novelist is able to explore social conditions more all-sidedly than the film writer: he has greater freedom in the use of dialogue; he can seek to grasp and use more penetrating psychological insights. Thus he is able to develop his talents more fully than the screen writer. His work is closer to the problems, the feelings, the needs of people. The film writer and the film apologist have to pretend that films are as free and as close to real needs and problems as is the serious novel. But this pretense is empty. The studios can buy talent and knowledge; but with a purchase price they cannot produce a serious work of art which will manifest its influence long after it is presented to the public. When we see many of even the best films of the past we consider them dated: we even laugh at their naiveté. But the best novels of the past retain their interest, and often they seem contemporary with the present. The healthier influence at work in the mutual relationships between films and novels is that which serious novels exert on films. It is likely to have a more lasting influence than that manifested by the Hollywood film on the novel. The serious novel is potentially a standing example which exposes the emptiness of most of the apologies made in the name of Hollywood films.

Not because of artistic needs but because of business interests and self-imposed "discipline," the film again and again must reduce, disfigure and alter the contents of novels. The situation in Hollywood is such that the past is recreated according to naive fantasies of the present. An instance of this is the film *The Adventures of Mark Twain,* a banal picture showing us an actor made up to look like Twain. There are a few events in the picture which are like those in the life of Mark Twain. The similarity ends just about there. Certainly so long as Hollywood continues to produce the films it does the serious writer need not have the slightest fear concerning the artificially imposed competition between the picture and the novel. The real advantages are all on his side. And insofar as he is placed in competition with Hollywood he doesn't compete with the screen writer. His work can even help the screen writer in the latter's struggles with his producers. The center of this induced competition is between the serious writer and the studio owners and executives. When his work exposes the shallowness of films it hits at the companies' interests, not at that of the scenarists. The best of the screen writers will try to write more freely on any and every occasion when they are given the least opportunity to do so.

In general, concerning this mutual relationship between films and novels, there is much irrelevant rationalization. This question must be explored further because Hollywood plays a peculiar role in American life.

V

The role of Hollywood—and also of the radio—in American life reveals a contradiction which has only the most irregular application in the book business. If we look at the arts of the film, the radio and the novel in terms of the problems of capitalism and culture, we will see that important differences must be noted. These differences should warn us against making arbitrary analogies. In the case of radio and the film, a major contradiction produced by capitalist economy arises between commodity sales pressure and the needs of art. In a society based on commodity production works of art become commodities. But this does not, of itself, produce the contradiction of which I am speaking.

Most radio art is sponsored by commodity producers. A major example is the soap opera, whose reason for being is advertising. Used as a mere sales come-on, this form of art is terribly censored. The hired writer of soap operas must invent, devise, contrive in any way that permits him to interest and flatter the largest possible number of people. His dramaturgical problems are artificially created by this necessity. He must make no character unpleasant if any section of his audience is likely to associate itself with that character, for these people may possibly be offended. Then they will not buy the brand of soap manufactured by the company which is sponsoring this work. The need to sell a commodity directly intervenes in the process of producing a work of popular art and it has a number of deforming consequences. It practically demands that art be turned into wholesale flattery. Here then is a direct instance of what I mean by the commodity-versus-art contradiction.

In a more indirect way it interferes with motion picture writing. The Production Code of the Motion Picture Industry states: "The history, institutions, prominent people and citizenry of other nations shall be represented fairly." The real reason for this provision is that foreign trade is important to the film industry. If a film disturbs a foreign government it can be banned. And lest we forget, in the days when Hollywood was not as anti-fascist as it recently was, it feared to produce anti-fascist films.* The late Benjamin Boles Hampton indicated years ago in *A History of Movies* that a few Hollywood persons were not blind to the connection between films and the sale of commodities. He pointed out the role of American films abroad in increasing the demand for American products. Some Hollywood people have at times denied this, but the fact is indisputable. Professor Raymond Moley, in his recent book *The Hays Office,* explicitly admitted this fact by stating that a major cause for resentment of American films abroad and for a demand that their import be restricted was because these films disturb foreign manufacturers. They create a demand for American goods rather than the home-produced brands which are often inferior. Hampton's explanation of the success of the De Mille spectacle movie is relevant. After the First World War America had a rich upper and middle class with an increased budget to be spent on social life, on parties, entertainments, decorations and consumer goods in general. Spectacle movies appealed to the consumption and leisure needs and desires of this group, especially the women in it; and according to Hampton these same pictures also helped to teach them how to buy, how to entertain and to give parties. For years the American motion picture has exerted a tremendous influence on tastes in personal appearance, in hair dressing, female clothes and such matters. Its strongest emphasis in the overwhelming majority of pictures is on leisure, on personal life. Indirectly it helps to create wants, giving new or changed tastes to people which cause them to want to buy things.† Then too, America is ringed with cartels, trade

---

* A large motion picture studio purchased the film rights of Sinclair Lewis' novel *It Can't Happen Here* and then did not dare to produce a film based on the book.

† Miss Barbara Deming, a film analyst and critic, has observed a change in the pattern of the movie dream. (Cf. her articles, "Exposition of a Method," in the magazine *Chimera* for Winter and Spring, 1944.) She writes: ". . . film after film is obedient to a compulsion to clear of any serious censure the big money man, the big breadwinner. The rich household is fumed against, but the kingpin of the household is not. Censure of the idle rich, but not of the rich who work for their money, is of course in the Puritan tradition. And it is in this tradition for the millionaire to be identified, as so frequently he is in these films, with the common man. For is he not just that—the common man who has fulfilled himself, who has scaled the ladder of success, who has made good. The successful breadwinner cannot be censured if there is to be a Horatio Alger myth." However, she observes, citing many examples, that the Horatio Alger myth is being unrolled backward. The successful Horatio Alger seeks to retain the common touch, to express a nostalgia for the days when he was just a common man. This implies—and often explicitly presents—a mood in which America as the paradise of commodities is not enough to satisfy the individual. This new emphasis in pictures is related to the New Deal climate in culture, with its verbal flattery of the common man, the "forgotten man."¹ (Here it should not be overlooked that the phrase was taken from Sumner and that Sumner's "forgotten man" was the man of the middle class.) Also it is related to the War. War needs, war sacrifices, war shortages rendered untenable the film in which America is a paradise of Horatio Algers with leisure and all of the commodities which go with the life of leisure and success. A "People's War" tended to dictate a film in which the common man, his taste, his essential humanity triumphed over that of the rich, the snobbish.

associations, occupational associations, which are jealous guardians of the value of the products and the dignity of the occupations of their members. If anything in a film disturbs these associations or its members there is usually a protest. The pressure applied by these organizations causes Hollywood to exert the utmost care about how objects are used as film properties, and similarly the types of villains which it may employ are severely restricted.* Let us take a hypothetical case: suppose that the demands of a film story were such that the villain had to be an undertaker. It is fairly certain that the undertakers of America would be on the neck of the studio which produced such a film.†

The pressure of commodity producers, sellers, and of those who sell special kinds of services, is almost as strong as that of those religious groups which guard the soul of humanity. Hollywood films reflect and relate to

During the War some film executives spoke of the new growth of social consciousness in films and promised—almost vowed—to produce films that would educate for peace and democracy. This line has shifted, and some of them speak of the film as a means of healing conflicts. A fairly recent film, *Practically Yours,* laughs at the modern home full of the newest commodities. The man who wants this is a clerk; the hero is a war hero. The girl wants the vigorous war hero, not the clerk who is going to give her a home with the latest in refrigerators and such commodities. But now with the War over and with the economic need of America that of a booming and prosperous consumer market, we can expect further changes in the movie dream. Finally, the observations of Parker Tyler on love in his suggestive book *The Hollywood Hallucination* (New York, 1944) are, in the main, consistent with those of Miss Deming. The book is to be recommended along with her articles.

* Gangsters make excellent villains, but gangster pictures sometimes bring down the social workers and pastors on the studios because of the juvenile delinquency problem. Germans and Japanese served during the War as excellent villains, but now War films—like War stories in slick magazines—are passé. Lunatics offer excellent possibilities, however, because there is no existent Professional Association of the Lunatics of America which could protest over a film casting indignity on their special occupation. Under these conditions the endless repetition of the old story of the boy who meets the girl is an easy solution of the problem. All the world loves a lover, and lovers are too busy with love to form a Cartel of Lovers of the World which would jealously protect the way in which the lover is represented on the screen.

† Professor Raymond Moley in *The Hays Office* (New York, 1945) gives real examples of this pressure. "The depiction of James Cagney as an honest, capable and competent employee in the Department of Weights and Measures . . . (in *The Great Guy*) was the signal for vehement outcries from retail grocers and gas station owners who insisted that the picture 'cast a reflection on their honesty' . . . A comedy showing the troubles of a householder with his coal furnace and ending with his decision to buy an oil burner infuriated anthracite coal producers . . . not to mention furnace makers and distributors. . . . The casual line of a popular star— 'They say white bread is not good for you'—brought literally thousands of angry letters from millers, bakers, grain-elevator men and farm organizations. . . . Heroes and heroines used to set sail for foreign parts on inferentially identified foreign ships [which] brought legitimate protests from all American shipping lines." Moley also cites an instance in which Atlantic City hotel men and businessmen protested about pictures in which characters brought their secretaries instead of their wives to that resort, and asked that once in a while in a picture a wife instead of a secretary be taken to Atlantic City. Moley comments: "Such are the fruits of inadvertent references to services, commodities, and products." He also says that the communications of the Production Code Administration to studios are filled with references concerning these matters.

every important vested economic, political and moral interest in American life. Given our economic and social structure, Hollywood is understandably fearful of these interests. However no decent conception of art asks that art and the artist be the servant of commodity production in this sense. The artist is an artist, not a salesman. To continue, the scale of picture investments demands that films have the widest possible audience, the largest possible measure of good will. As a result, the film studios will rarely oppose strong pressure; they bend to it. Hollywood censors itself and boasts of this "self-discipline." The consequences to the film as an art are drastic. Like his fellow writer in radio, the screen writer has to meet artificially imposed problems which relate to commodity production as such, and not to art as such.

VI

The contradiction between commodity sales pressure and the needs of art has not yet intervened seriously in the book world, although there are instances of it in the magazine and newspaper business. In magazines we can see many connections between the commodity and the story. In more than one slick magazine there is often a certain synchronization between the stories, the illustrations showing characters in the stories, and a number of the advertisements in the same magazine. *The New Yorker,* an ultrasophisticated magazine, prints many stories about the sophisticated New Yorker while its advertisements often show us sophisticated types in sophisticated homes who buy consumer goods which are the last word in sophistication.* In book publishing this does not yet apply except in rare instances.

The absence of this kind of pressure is one of the reasons why the freest means of communication in America has been found in the book. It is possible, in book form, to pose questions sharply and seriously; it is possible to try to think things through even to the end. In works of literary art the writer may feel very free in his choice of subject matter and his method of treatment.† And the record of publishers in defense of free

---

* For some interesting and suggestive remarks on *The New Yorker* see "The New York Wits" by Herbert Marshall McLuhan in *The Kenyon Review* for Winter, 1945.

† There are, of course, frequent instances of editors' and publishers' trying to tamper with manuscripts, and authors have had many difficulties in this respect. There are counter-instances where authors have never had to face this problem. I personally have never had this kind of trouble except occasionally with magazines. In one such instance the editor of a "left" magazine tried to persuade me to delete some mildly teasing remarks directed against a capitalist publisher. Even when publishers or editors do try to get an author to change his writing for sales reasons, or because of fear of pressures, the author is not bound to do so. If a publisher changes a manuscript without an author's permission the writer can publicly denounce the publisher and sue him. If a publisher refuses to print a book unless changes are made the writer does have a chance to try to interest some other publisher. In many cases writers willingly

speech in the courts is, on the whole, far, far better than is that of other cultural entrepreneurs. The business of the publisher is to sell a book. His commodity is one which contains ideas and artistic representations. His investment is significantly lower than that of many merchants, and up to the present, his market has been relatively limited. In terms of the total investment structure of our American economy the money invested in publishing houses is very small. Even now that publishing is becoming big business its investment is still much less than that of one of the big American industries. Factors such as these have created economic conditions which made liberalism economically feasible in book publishing. Publishers have been more or less willing to print any kind of book which will sell enough copies to give them some chance of making a profit. And the relative smallness of financial risk has often permitted publishers to print books which stood only a slight chance of returning their original investments. The prestige gained from publishing good books is of real value to a publisher. In non-fictional books there is an almost complete freedom of expression concerning all ideas and trends which exist within a bourgeois perspective. Even revolutionary books are published. Trade publishers have printed works of Marx and Trotsky, books which threaten the entire class of which the publisher is a member.* Publishers have nursed along serious literary

---

agree to changes which will enhance sales values, and in others they have not taken action publicly on changes made over their heads but have complained and griped privately. The situation is often confused in the public mind because of undue griping. Besides the question of changes prompted by the desire to make money or through fear of pressure, there is the problem of editing. Many writers, even good ones, need editorial help. Often there are conflicts and differences which are merely editorial in character. Then there is the problem of legal censorship. It is shameful for a serious author to accept economic censorship so that he can make a lot of money, and then to represent himself as a serious writer to the public. Legal censorship is another matter, and it is a practical question to be decided on the circumstances of each case. Artistic and intellectual honor do not demand that one say everything in all instances; it only demands that in each case one say all that is necessary and that one do not lie. If what one has to say is of great importance and there is a clear-cut probability that the police power of society will be applied to prevent one from saying it, then there is nothing unprincipled in making a partial statement. There are cases where authors have been abused by publishers and editors, but the common myths that all publishers always do this to authors is not true, and the facts compel one to say so. Much more common than conflicts over content are those between publishers and writers concerning money and business. These sometimes involve equity and more often they relate to the sums of money spent in advertising and exploiting a book. This is not our concern here.

* Leon Trotsky's unfinished book *Stalin* was printed and sent out to reviewers by a well known publishing house. Then changes in the world situation resulted in pressure which caused the publishers to ask that all review copies be returned; the book was locked up. The jacket blurb of this book described it as a scientific contribution to historiography. A couple of weeks after this blurb was prepared the book became not science but something which would hurt the feelings of America's Soviet ally, and that would endanger international relationships. The irony of this situation is further suggested in the fact that Trotsky's widow protested against the publication of the book as it had been prepared because she believed that the editing of it had misrepresented Trotsky's political views. She either sued or threatened

artists for considerable periods until a demand for their books was created that finally made their publication profitable. In general, the publishers have sold books to a market which includes the most serious, the most disinterested, the most educated, the most cultivated people in America. Quality is one of the demands in the market of the trade publishers. Most book buyers do not become disturbed if a book happens to cast real or alleged aspersions on a particular cake of soap. Some of them are not disturbed if a novel happens to portray unpleasantly a member of their own profession or occupation. To date, the book business has occupied a less important role in American economy than do the radio and the film. This above all else explains the absence of the contradiction between the commodity and art in book publishing, or its purely secondary role when it does appear.

The problems involved in a study of art under capitalism are highly complicated. We will only misconstrue these problems if we approach them merely from the standpoint of the general class interest of a particular cultural entrepreneur. The general class interests of capitalists as a whole do not always coincide with the particular interests of particular capitalists. This is often peculiarly the case with publishers. During the War many publishers were constantly seeking books which would have a direct bearing on war aims and which would help to build morale. One publisher proposed that no books in any way critical of the Soviet Union be printed. Doubleday Doran printed Jean Malaquais' *War Diary,* a book which most certainly could have had no value in advancing war aims. During the early Thirties many publishers competed with each other in seeking leftist books, both novels and political writings. It is necessary to emphasize that each individual capitalist is vitally concerned with his own market.

As I have already noted, the market of the trade publishers is highly selective and includes many discriminating people. If a publisher can stay in business and supply this market with what it wants or will take, he is generally free of the fear of pressure groups and of trade associations. The character of his business, the nature of his commodity, his market—these and similar factors all work so that up to now this contradiction between the commodity and art has not intervened in the book business as it has in radio and motion pictures. A number of years ago one of the phenomenal best sellers in America, both in trade and reprint editions, was *100,000,000 Guinea Pigs.* Many of the important commodity producers in America were up in arms about this book. Nevertheless it was sold widely, although

---

to sue to prevent publication, but according to the press the publishers insisted that they would be within their contract rights in publishing it with the editing to which Madame Trotsky objected. However, this instance of suppression is due to particular political causes at a particular time, and not to economic reasons.

I have heard that there were instances of individual chains which refused to handle reprints of it. A little later another best-seller was Ferdinand Lundberg's *America's Sixty Families*. Reprint bidding for this book was not as high as it has been for many others, but it *was* reprinted and sold, although it attacked the major financial vested interests of America. To date I know of no serious pressures applied in the reprint business to threaten this freedom.

However, there are certain implications in contemporary publishing which need here to be mentioned in this connection. It is possible that there may be changes in the future. Heretofore the majority of publishers have been independent merchants. We have seen how they are free of pressures of certain kinds. But now publishing is becoming bigger, and there are some houses capitalized at over a million dollars which do a huge volume of business. If with the growth of publishing the financial interests of important publishers become diffused so that publishing is but one of their interests, then the publishing business will tend to be more like other large industries. In the long run it seems likely that publishers with diverse interests of consequence in the structure of American economy *will* sooner or later begin to apply a form of economic censorship in their publishing houses. This danger is the important point to remember too, if Wall Street becomes seriously interested in the book business. If such a thing happens Wall Street control will mean that Money, Pure Money, becomes the boss. In other words, there will be absentee ownership. Such a development will be serious for the freedom of American culture and, as *Tide* indicated, it is not to be excluded as a possibility. This step would have a tremendous effect in further centralizing the book business. Another possibility is that in the next depression one of the reprint houses may go bankrupt because of over-expansion. Should this happen it is likely that the organization would be retained and the creditor banks would become the owners.*

Another centralizing tendency should also be considered. Mail order houses and chain stores are now among the largest reprint wholesale book buyers in America. It would indeed be a coincidence if chain buyers should also be men of culture with some experience in books.† Besides the role that this situation will play in effecting a greater standardization of books,

---

* Last summer the Atlas Corporation, a large investment trust, was reported to have bought *Liberty Magazine* (and other magazines in the same chain) for the sum of $2,000,000. This, to my knowledge, is the first instance of a magazine being owned by a holding company.

† Mr. Walgreen of the Walgreen Drug Stores is decidedly a man who is aware of culture. Some years ago his protests about the alleged teaching of Communism at the University of Chicago resulted in a legislative investigation of the faculty and particularly of Professors Robert Morss Lovett and Frederick L. Schuman. After this Mr. Walgreen's interest in culture deepened and he made a bequest to the University. Out of the money he gave books are even now being published.

it makes it possible for chain store buyers and executives to become secondary economic censors. Whenever customers or others protest certain books sold by chain stores and mail order houses, it is likely that the objectionable books will be dropped from sale. Inasmuch as these concerns buy so many books it is quite possible that their refusal to stock certain titles can drive these books out of reprint editions. As I have already stated, this has not happened often yet. And a factor militating against this possibility is that the reprint houses have a variety of outlets. But the enlarged role of chain stores is another instance of how centralization and expansion of the book business gradually achieves the effect of linking it more closely into the structure of the whole American economy.

The principal dangers of centralization in the book business lie in this direction. And if the contradiction between the commodity and art does seriously intervene in writing, it is most likely that it will come as a result of this kind of centralization. For when the book business becomes more intimately involved in the general structure of American capitalist economy, the general interests of the capitalists as a class will supersede the specific interests of the individual publishers. Then these interests will dictate to the big companies. The pressure of these big holding companies on the large publishers will be all the greater as a result.

VII

The publishing business enters the era of bigness at a higher level of culture than was the case with radio or motion pictures. This contrast is suggestive. As we know, among the original film entrepreneurs there were many fly-by-night characters and types. Others who have risen in the industry were salesmen, haberdashers, theatre owners and so on. Some of them have more than proven themselves to be men of force in business. But they were not men of culture. It is no secret that many of them treated this potentially powerful artistic medium no differently than they did the ties and other articles which some of them sold in little stores. The motion picture was a novelty. Its development surprised many of its leading figures. Its effects on audiences are immediate, vivid, magical. The very magic of the motion picture often tends to lull one's mind, to keep one fascinated and interested, even though there is no substance to what one sees. Developing from the ground up, there were no available bases of contrast of accomplishment by which films could be tested. Even today we do not have easily available standards for judging films. It is not too easy to see old films and to compare them with newer ones. Conversely, the great culture of the ages is preserved in book form. In ideas, in social thought, in creative writing, some of the peaks of human achievement are easily accessible to all who wish to read. Our culture, our habits of reading and feeling, the values by which men live have been crystallized in books. The film industry has not only pulled itself up by its own bootstraps (a fact which is still quite obvious in the rawness of most of its products), but it has managed to become a virtual monopoly as well. It has almost complete control of the sources of production in America. It is not difficult to limit what can and cannot be said in a film. The Production Code, for instance, is easily administered. Under these circumstances the human need for variety in art is not and cannot be satisfied in films. Films have conditioned a mass audience without providing the variety to satisfy it. On the other hand, book readers have been habituated to variety. And as the number of book readers increases this possibility of variety is at least accessible to new book readers. These facts are important. Any copy writer can claim that a cheap book is a work of genius; any book reviewer can write a critical piece which reads like an advertisement. But to make such claims stick is another matter. An interested reader can always test a book by many comparisons.

The high levels of literary culture developed in periods of the past constitute a kind of good will for publishers. They can draw on it, and they can reprint and sell books which have attained a major significance in the history of human culture. There is a need for, an interest in, a demand for such books. We can see this in the reprint market. At various times reprints of Plato and Spinoza have been popular. The greatest reprint library in existence is probably Everyman's, and its titles include a large proportion of the major literary and scientific works of the ages. The Modern Library, less broad than Everyman's, is also an important reprint library. It, however, is sometimes watered down by such books as the works of Dashiell Hammett which are, at most, a little bit less than classics of the ages. At the same time that the reprint publishers compete for a new, wide and uneducated mass market, they are also reaching a smaller but important market which is made up of people who want to buy good books at cheap prices. Even though the reprint business should become completely centralized, book taste could never become as standardized as it is in films. And whereas in films a picture based on Shakespeare will be something other than the work of Shakespeare, such will not be the case in reprints. Before absolute standardization could ever be attained in the reprint market it would be necessary that several full generations of Americans be absolutely moronized. Actually, taste has progressed in America. More honest books sell in larger numbers than was the case a few decades ago. Many readers demand a greater seriousness from novelists today than they did several decades ago. Far more people of the lower middle class and even workers are reading seriously than, say, in 1890. I doubt that anyone will conscientiously dispute this. The progress in taste has been along democratic lines, a trend suggested by the fact that with ever greater frequency the more vigorous American writers are of plebeian origin, and that writers of the upper classes try to imitate them. The serious readers are not as homogeneous as they used to be when New England culture dominated America. Also, to take another instance of a rise in taste, the publication of *Finnegans Wake* by a trade publisher would have been unthinkable in 1925. But this absolute progress in taste does not justify commercialized culture in America. For a commercialized culture is impeding a *more rapid* growth in taste. My remarks on Hollywood in this essay reveal how this is happening.* In consequence of this we are arriving at a situation in which there is likely to be a growing eagerness on the part of a large number of better books while there is an increased tendency toward standardization of taste on the part of the larger publishers.

No merchant or manufacturer can ignore his market. In a footnote above I have cited Miss Barbara Deming's article, "Exposition of a Method." Miss Deming points out how increasingly necessary it has become for films to pay heed to the "common man," that is to their audience, and how in recent years films have gravitated "toward the subject of the sins against others that result from commercialism." Movies constantly try to create a celluloid dream which wishes away this sense of guilt. The guilt of commercialism, the inner doubts that seethe beneath the surface in American capitalist society, cannot be neglected in any consideration of the problems that interest us here. Commercialization, standardization, "bigness" in the book business are running head on into a changing America. Those who sell books to a mass market will meet with this counter-force. One of the complexities of merchandizing cultural works for a mass market lies in the fact that the masses cannot really be ignored. Even though they continue to present stupid reveries the movies have had to change the patterns of their formula. This feature of a mass market for culture emphasizes the need for a large cultural entrepreneur to preserve to a certain degree a neutrality on many subjects and issues. At the present moment no reprint publisher—even in the unlikely assumption that they could wish to do so—would dare to publish a viciously anti-strike and anti-trade union book at twenty-five cents. Hollywood would not dare to produce a film of such character. Too many of those who concede in advance that taste will be utterly stupefied always seem to think of the power of big business; they never see the limits of its consumer market in culture. And there are such limits. Hollywood is at least formally neutral on many issues, and it often

---

* In my book *The League of Frightened Philistines,* New York, 1945, and in the article "Some Observations on the Communications Revolution," *Bulletin of the National Theatre Conference,* I have attempted to deal with various aspects of these problems.

reveals its neutrality by not dealing with these issues. Publishers also, as a whole, show a relative neutrality on various issues and types of books, a neutrality which varies in accordance with what is happening in society. This relative and varying neutrality is of considerable importance for all who are concerned with freedom of expression. It is directly connected with the fact that we can still write most freely in America in book form. And we note that, to date, the reprint houses have also shown a relative neutrality. There is a tendency in motion that leads toward standardization. But it is evolving more slowly than many alarmed persons assume. And I think we cannot arbitrarily predict that future developments in the book business will be nothing more than a mere carbon copy repeating what has happened in the case of motion pictures. Above all else we can say that so far the basic policy of the book business, both in the regular and the reprint houses, has been based on this relative neutrality. And because publishing rests on a relatively higher cultural level, the areas of publishing neutrality are much wider than those of film studio neutrality. This relative neutrality does not conflict with the business interests of many publishers because of the many variations in tastes, interests, and inclinations in their market.

True, in the last analysis the *market* dictates, and this applies to the book market as well as to others. But the book market is not a homogeneous lump. It is composed of live human beings, and they have many needs, desires, interests and inclinations. The variation in tastes in books is bound to be greater than that for hair oils or hand lotions. When the book market dictates, people want something. Their book wants are more variegated than their demands in the way of shoes. The market can be influenced by pressures, sales campaigns, publicity; but it cannot be totally controlled by these methods.* The book market is itself fluctuating. Its fluctuations are psychological as well as economic. There is nothing in the present situation which permits the assumption that it can be *absolutely* hardened. Nothing less than total police tyranny is likely to effect total hardening of the book market. And that is a political question outside of the boundaries of my article; suffice it to say that it is far too soon to write of the possibilities of freedom in the world.

Up to the present there has been no serious competition between the reprint and the trade publishers. In the main the former are opening up a

---

* There are, for instance, a number of book buyers in America who could by no methods whatsoever be advertised into making detective stories their major literary fare. There are others who could not despite all publicity be inviegled into joining Book Clubs. Frequently those who concede that commercialized culture has already won the day are mere snobs, and they assume that many others will never have as high a seriousness about culture as they themselves have attained. Among such people are a few of the most abysmally insensitive intellectuals now on the loose in America.

new book market. As we have seen, they are printing any kind of book which they can sell. Competition is becoming more feverish, and we are seeing a new growth of centralizing tendencies. But this is not wholly new in publishing. Doubleday Doran & Co. existed precisely as it now does before the War. Then too the reprint houses were also centralized. The irreversibility of these facts, however, does not as yet assure us as to what their final consequences will be. In other words, the degree of extension of centralizing tendencies is still problematical. The limits of the book market are unknown. It can be saturated. It expanded during the War at a period when many consumer goods were scarce, when studios were restricted in the number of new films they could produce, when gas rationing limited pleasure driving, and when other factors helped to put books in wide demand. If the expectations of the more optimistic reprint firms are realized, the mass market for books will approximate that of films. Books will even be sold in slot machines in motion picture theatre lobbies. Others enthusiastically predict that the day will come when authors are hired by reprint houses as they are now by Hollywood. They even hail this idea, assuming that a mass market for books will effect a stupendous rise in levels of taste, and that in consequence the writer will, even when hired, be able to write "his own stuff." If the publishers win a market as large as that of the films, then, under capitalism, these centralizing tendencies will become more pronounced. The area of literary freedom will become narrowed, bottle-necked. The serious writer will be pressed into his bohemia, that cultural ghetto of bourgeois society. The capital investment in books would rise; the banks would undoubtedly become partial owners of the book business. And then if, in addition, America could turn its entire educational system into a means of progressive moronization, all this and more might happen. This we grant.

But it is too soon to accept these predictions, or to find their roots in actuality. While American industry has produced the greatest mass production system in history, and while many commodities have been correspondingly standardized, the standardization and centralization of industry and commodity production as a whole has been uneven and irregular. Standardization and centralization proceed unevenly in those fields where there is the most profit. To date it has not destroyed the quality markets. In consumer industry after consumer industry we find the existence of both quality and quantity markets. The book market has in the main been a quality market. That a quality market in books will remain is certain. It remains to be proven that a book trust can produce books for a quality market by standardizing the methods it uses in the production of books for a quantity market. In the case of Doubleday Doran & Co., we can see that their trade policies have not been essentially different from those of the small independent publishers. At the moment, and in the immediate future, the independent publishers are not threatened. We have indicated that the initial cost of investment in starting a publishing house has risen. But this is a fluctuating factor. And even with this rise the sum of money needed for the establishment of a new publishing house is small in the total picture of American economy. At the same time that the reprint houses have prospered in the war boom, quality publications have likewise flourished. The New Directions Press is one instance of this; another is Pantheon Books, which has gained a foothold after starting into business only recently. The conditions for the publication and exploitation of new and serious authors have not changed. A mass production publishing house cannot give the time and the attention, and it cannot wait long enough for a return of investment, to exploit a new and serious author by mass production methods.

The emphasis on quantity in the reprint field will limit quality there. But quality will remain, and in culture officialization and standardization inevitably produce their own anaesthesia. If culture grows too far from the needs, the feelings, and the problems of people, it will rot. There is a profound historical truth in Lincoln's statement that you cannot fool all of the people all of the time. Culture is highly sensitive to the tensions and class struggles which exist in society. With the next depression there will be changes in the subject matter of books. Then many books will be serious, deadly serious. For a culture based on commodity production to be eternal, that system must itself become eternal. Capitalists themselves are now less than absolutely convinced that their system is eternal. There is no vista of endless prosperity ahead of us, with markets that never contract. And I have already remarked that in a mass market you meet the masses, as it were, face to face. The War has given the masses of the world an education which is almost unparalleled in history. The conclusions concerning this education are far from drawn. But the increased awareness of serious problems existent in the world is more clear than it ever was. With this the need for greater knowledge, and hence for greater culture, has been touched. If you once touch this sleeping need in masses of people the consequences are far from predictable. In creating the conditions of communication which make the creation of a mass democratic culture practical, capitalist society has created a problem which it cannot ultimately solve.

The real starting point of an analysis such as this one must be human needs. The actual and potential cultural and intellectual needs of masses of people cannot and will not be permanently satisfied by standardized ideas and works of art. This can be stated as a positive fact. Even Hollywood realizes this. It is searching for a new idea almost as frantically as the treasure hunters of Washington D.C.—the planners, New Dealers, and politicians—are looking for sixty million jobs.

Briefly then, the conditions for the monopolization of the printed word are not easily created. The big publishing companies may gain access to and control over important printing and distributing facilities, and to that degree they may achieve centralization. But this will not eliminate the possibility of printing books. To paraphrase Emerson, once an idea is let loose in the world no one knows what will happen. The book business develops toward centralization at a time when many ideas have long been loose in the world. And some of these ideas on the loose even get into reprinted books. Mass production standards are not and never can be substituted for ideas and for genuine art. For these latter flow out of the needs of the people, out of the problems and pressures of life. In turn they produce the need for variety, the need for differentiations. The most likely possibility is that for some time to come there may be a growing centralization in the book business and with this the greater separation of quantity and quality. But quality slowly and subtly will continue to eat away the strength of quantity. We can forecast this on the basis of analyses such as that given earlier on the relationships between the novel and the Hollywood film.

A cultural renaissance is unpredictible. Such a renaissance does not or need not flow out of great freedom and great prosperity. In many periods there is cultural depth and growth because crucial problems are felt widely and all-sidedly. When there are severe contradictions in society, when these are registered in the minds and hearts of ever-growing numbers, you have one of the kinds of situation which help to create a cultural renaissance. Witness Tsarist Russia. The depth of the problems of today, the growing consciousness of their meaning—these facts and conditions may yet help to condition a cultural renaissance in America. In these United States all of the conditions for cultural growth exist. The technical means for the creation of the most widespread culture in history have been perfected. On the one hand cultural growth is impeded by the social organization of culture; on the other hand, the sleeping needs of millions for knowledge, for ideas, for culture have not been stirred. These needs will never be stirred merely by selling millions of books. These needs will be stirred by problems, by the very fact that the contradictions in our society are consciously felt. If and as these sleeping needs are slowly stirred—as I remain convinced that they will be—the social basis will be laid for a quickening of cultural energy.

These possibilities suggest that the writer has a role to play. It is well for us to remember this fact.

VIII

A number of those who now predict the doom of good writing confuse business success in literature and book sales with *influence*. They approach the problem of influence merely from the standpoint of the trade publishing business; without realizing what their premise is, they see influence purely in terms of arithmetic. Let us examine this problem.

Face to face with the publishing business, many new and gifted writers will meet with difficulties, even the most trying ones. Rarely is there an immediate market for new works of literary art. However it usually happens that most literary artists who have something to say do get published. Very frequently they are still published by the trade publishers. I doubt that many artists of weight go unpublished, even though they may earn little money, even though the circumstances of their personal life be most trying. At the present time the intense competition for new writers is so keen that trade publishers are likely to be very receptive to new writers, even to some advance-guard ones. The greatest likelihood of the immediate future is that, at the most, increased centralization in parts of the publishing business will limit the volume of sales of new writers rather than prevent their being published. But this will not be a new development. It is likely that there will be fewer publishers who will nurse a new author along for an extended period. But this tendency may be partially countered by the fact that the more intelligent independent publishers will quickly realize that the best basis on which they can maintain themselves in the face of powerfully organized and richer rivals will be by the publication of works of quality. And then too we must consider fashions and fluctuations in taste. We cannot correlate in a one-one equation the taste of the War years with the condition of the book market in these years. At home during the War there was prosperity. With prosperity there was great anxiety, and millions were overworked. These are particularly good conditions for the spread of so-called escapist literature. Periods of prosperity are not always the best periods for an advance in the levels of taste. As I have already emphasized, reading habits change because of problems. We can see this in the changes in literary and ideational tendencies in America before and immediately after the depression of 1929. With the depression there was a leftward swing of the intellectuals. Reading became more serious and so did many books and writers.

Often monetary values will influence taste more pronouncedly in periods of prosperity when economic problems sink into the background than they will in periods of crisis. It is a mistake to assume that in the immediate future the efforts of book publishers to expand necessarily will mean that they will merely print more of the same kind of books that have been printed in the past. The pressures of war, the fear of expression felt by so many during the War, are now of the past. There is now a new generation ready to begin writing. And many in the older generation are almost throbbing with the desire, if not the capacity, to try now to say much that was left unsaid during the War. There is possibly a real symptomatic significance in the recent autobiography, *Raw Material,* by Oliver La Farge.* There La Farge confesses that for years he had been an escapist writer, writing the same love story with variations. He stated that he had developed a formula which usually permitted him to sell stories at a thousand dollars a crack. He wrote: "Analysis of my writings showed that I had one theme and one fundamental love story. I had rewritten the theme from every angle; the only new treatment I could see for the love story would be to set it up between homosexuals." We can be sure that Oliver La Farge, not a writer without gifts, is not alone among escapist writers who are worn out with what they have been writing. The world of literary success is full of self-doubt; it is groggy with its own emptiness. Let me repeat: it is far from impossible that in the immediate years ahead, and especially after the next economic crisis, we will see sharp changes in writing, in literary and ideational currents. And these currents flow with some independence of the bestseller lists.

At this point it is pertinent to remind readers that the most important novel in world literature of the Twentieth Century was not first printed by the regular book publishers and that it was even confiscated by the Customs authorities. I refer to Joyce's *Ulysses.* For years this novel influenced the best of the younger generations in all of the civilized countries of the world, but it was completely outside the channels of commercial and bestseller culture. In the field of politics many of the most influential books—for instance some of the writings of Marx, Lenin, Trotsky, and Rosa Luxembourg—were published and distributed outside of the regular channels. The course of influence is not always that of business success. Literary tendencies and influences do not work precisely as do political ones. They do not need mass appeal. Their influence bears most importantly on writers, and of these, on the newer generations. A new literary tendency, a new writer of great promise, may not be recognized in the popular literary organs: he may even be unknown to the literary pundits of the day: his work may not be published by the trade publishers. And yet it may slowly and surely manifest its influence. Further, there is a difference between the aesthetic rebel and the political revolutionist. Aesthetic rebellion is

---

*I have discussed this book in detail in an article "The Artist in Our Time" in *Tomorrow* for October, 1945.

always more easily assimilable by bourgeois society than is revolutionary political thought. Bourgeois society, not only in America but also abroad, has successively assimilated its generations of aesthetic rebels. We can see this by merely looking at the present status of the anti-bourgeois literary artists who were the contemporaries of Karl Marx. Flaubert, Baudelaire, and Rimbaud have all been more or less assimilated: but not Marxism. The picture of the Impressionists and of Cézanne which caused such furors of Philistine indignation are now investments worth thousands of dollars. Too many of those who make dire predictions concerning the future of art because of the official and bourgeois Philistine standards of the moment have themselves a bourgeois perspective. It would be better if serious and good writers always outsold hacks. But even if they don't, it does not follow that the hacks will exert the permanent influence. By and large the literary works of the past which we read and respect, and in which we can find something that makes us feel that these works are contemporary for us, are works written by literary artists, not hacks. It is well to remember this. New writers often face terrible difficulties. But we gain little by complaining and griping over difficulties. The point is not to complain about conditions but to fight them. And in the field of writing itself, one of the means of fighting is by writers' pursuing their own bent, and by criticism, pitiless criticism. If we approach these problems in this spirit, our outlook for the future becomes different, if not always too hopeful in the economic sense. The future of art does not and never can belong to the hired artist.

"Neither a nation nor a woman can be forgiven for the unguarded hour in which a chance comer has seized the opportunity for an act of rape," wrote Karl Marx in *The 18th Brumaire of Louis Bonaparte*. No more can the gifted writer be forgiven for the unguarded hour when he has allowed a chance literary agent, a chance Hollywood producer, a chance publisher to rape his artistic honor with a fat contract, and thereby turn him into a wretched hack. The writer need be no passive instrument. Without writers there can be no writing. No one has ever put Huxley's monkeys before a typewriter and gotten any results; no genius has invented a machine that will substitute for writers. Most predictions about the gloomy future of humane letters do not even take the writer into account. These assume that the writers will all become hacks, or else that they will be crushed. It is for the writers to answer these assumptions: this task lies on the shoulders of the young generation. Do they and will they answer that they are passive instruments? Are they prepared to let themselves be pressed and driven into literary ghettoes? Instead of asking: will literature *be* standardized? let us ask: will writers *allow* themselves to be standardized? and especially in the immediate days ahead when publishing competition gives so many temporary advantages to the writer. Regardless of what the popular reviewers say, they have worn themselves out praising fake genius; they swoon from the junk they read and like, or pretend to like. Under attack, they usually dodge, hedge, apologize. They too have their inner doubts. This is another important symptom to remember. Art, to be of weight in this world, must be of sterner stuff than what we get; and so must the artist.

In his preface to *Thérèse Raquin* Zola wrote: "The public as a whole resents having its habits changed, and the judgments which it passes have all the brutality of a death-sentence. But there comes a time when the public itself becomes an accomplice of the innovators; this is when, imbued with the new spirit, weary of the same stories repeated to it countless times, it feels an imperious desire for youth and originality." Speaking of the historical drama of his time, Zola said: "The historical drama is in its death-throes, unless something new comes to its assistance: that corpse needs new blood. It is said that the operetta and the dramatic fantasy have killed the historical drama. This is not so: the historical drama is dying a natural death, of its own extravagances, lies, and platitudes. . . . And melodrama, that bourgeois offspring of the romantic drama, is in the hearts of the people more dead than its predecessors; its false sentiment, its complications of stolen children and discovered documents, its impudent gasconades, have finally rendered it despicable, so that any attempt to revive it proves abortive. . . . But now that everything is torn down, and swords and capes rendered useless, it is time to base out works on truth. . . . There should no longer be any . . . formulas, no standards of any sort; there is only life itself, an immense field where each may study and create as he likes. . . . We must look to the future, and the future will have to do with the human problem studied in the frame-work of reality. . . . The well-known receipts for the tying and the untying of an intrigue have served their time; now we must seek a simple and broad picture of men. . . . Outside of a few scenic conventions, all that is now known as 'the science of the theatre' is merely a heap of clever tricks, a narrow tradition that serves to cramp the drama, a ready-made code of language and hackneyed situations, all known and planned beforehand, which every original worker will scorn to use."

We can repeat these words of Zola with the greatest pertinence today and apply them to the entire fields of creative literature and motion pictures. And repeating them now, we have learned much since Zola's time, much about art, about politics, about society, about history. We have seen how the Philistines of other years have raved for their little hour, and vanished. We have seen how the works they damned, and this includes both naturalistic writings and advance guard literature, have been precisely the works which have entered into the living currents of literary influence. Increasing tendencies toward centralization in publishing and the enormous influence of Hollywood cannot, singly or combined, kill living creative literature. But writers will kill it themselves if they surrender, if they passively acquiesce. It is true that we have in America a swollen commercial culture. But at the core it is empty. And we can see that it is hollow by noticing how, when serious books do have an opportunity to sell, they often maintain themselves in competition with the base products. For instance, there is the phenomenon of Richard Wright. But his example does not suggest the full situation. For the advance-guard writer and the poet do not have the same chances as does the realistic novelist. Still all serious and honestly written literature has the influence of helping the literary artist. Literary taste must be created, and this can only be done by examples, by examples of seriousness and truthfulness. In the final analysis the problems of literature and commerce will remain as long as we have a capitalist form of society. But the literary and cultural situation is a fluid one. The Hollywood film may be produced more or less on the basis of a monolithic industry. There may and most likely will be pronounced monolithic tendencies in book publishing. But the character of the industry itself, the unevenness of monolithic economic development, the great variety in tastes, cultural levels, and cultural needs produce a very fluid and complicated book market. The publishers intend to make money. They will, within this compass, have a more or less neutral attitude on what they publish. They are now competing on all sides. Their very competition gives the author a certain independence of position, vis-a-vis commercial publishing. The production and distribution of books in America may be organized in terms of the needs of the commercial book trade. But literary influences can, if with difficulty, grow even outside of this organization. Thus the writer himself has a role to play, and he has some voice.

Even though the gloomiest of predictions be fulfilled these tendencies must work out in time. And here time is of the essence. They have not worked out to their end of total standardization. The channels of serious communication in America have been narrowed in recent years, but this narrowing has occurred more in the field of ideas and political thought than it has in that of literary work. As long as channels remain open the object of the writer should be to use these channels. Viewing these problems from the standpoint of the writer who opposes the commercialization of art, we see that counter-efforts must be made to provide different examples, different types of work. The conditions of the social organization of literature are given for the writer. He does not control them. But Napoleon was fond of remarking: "Engage in battle, and see what happens." The writer must do likewise. He must engage in battle and see what happens. His battle, as a writer, is made through his effort, through his op-position to shoddy standards of writing, and thereby, through the creation of counter-examples that are not shoddy.

As these centralizing tendencies do evolve to the degree that they may, it should become increasingly clear to the writer with a conscience that his long-run interests as a human being and as an artist fail to coincide with the interests of capitalism. But this conclusion, leading the writer toward socialism, does not, in itself, give him a literary perspective. By reaching this conclusion the artist will not thereby necessarily assimilate socialism as a perspective which motivates his work. Some of these problems are problems involving the economic position of the writer, and the degree to which he desires to struggle in order that he be able to write out of his own needs, his own feelings, his own tensions and emotions, his own ex-periences, rather than on the basis of the fluctuations in the book market. An analysis such as this one is not directly concerned with a discussion of the problems of orientation and perspective out of which a writer develops and works according to his own bent. This problem is a separate one, and to introduce it here would be as likely to confuse as to clarify. It is best treated separately. Further, we can now see that from the standpoint of the writer the direct and immediate problem he faces is precisely the same as that which his predecessors have faced—the problem of success versus in-tegrity. The circumstances of that problem have changed somewhat, and the attractiveness of success is greater than ever. The rewards of writing for the market are higher. In consequence, the serious writer will meet with more competition from those who see in writing merely and solely an opportunity for the big money. But greater competition does not change the problem in its essentials. For some time to come at least, this problem will remain posed for the writer as it is at the present moment. In meeting it his own decisions constitute a factor of great importance. This point cannot be over-emphasized. *The writer is an active not a passive agent in this situation.*

Long ago, when discussing the question of freedom of the writer, Karl Marx remarked: "Is a press which degrades itself to a trade free? A writer must certainly earn money in order to exist and write, but he should not exist and write in order to earn money. . . . The first freedom of the press must consist in its emancipation from commerce. The writer who degrades the press to a mere means of material livelihood deserves as a punishment for this inner slavery that outer slavery called censorship, unless his very existence is already his punishment." After quoting this, Marx's biographer Mehring stated: "All his life Marx lived up to these principles and to the same standard which he demanded from others: a man's writing must always be an end in itself. Far from being a mere means for himself and others, he must, if necessary, sacrifice his own existence to his writing."

Marx was a great revolutionary. But creative artists have written and clung to this same principle. Tolstoy did. Joyce did. And we love the memory of these men, not only for their literary greatness but also for their artistic conscience and honor. Decidedly the time has come for writers to speak up, to assert themselves, to take a stand on the future of books. The time has come for them to say, and with scorn in their voices, that they will not be hacks. The field of the future is theirs. Year in and year out bestsellers have come and gone. Real books will not go like that. They will stay. For we know that the future of books is involved in the future of culture. And the future of culture is a not insignificant part of the future of mankind. We have not lived through the *last* mass revulsion in taste in history. We have not lived through the *last* change in history. We have not lived through the *last* revolution. Now less than ever should the literary artist surrender to the Philistines and to commerce. The future is more important for writers, for the new generation, than the bombast and glamor which so many now call culture. A half-monopolized culture can only reproduce worn-out and wretched formulas, patch them up with cellophane, and let the press agent do his job. You can saturate humanity with everything, including this sentimentality. Clear and honest work *will* stand out against such saturated sentimentality. Years ago, Zola boldly proclaimed: "The truth is on the march." That is the role of the writer—to try to make that truth march.

What Happens to First Novelists?
Alice Hackett

from

Saturday Review of Literature, 26, February, 1944.

Reprinted by permission of *Saturday Review of Literature*.

What Happens to First Novelists?

A Box-Score Covering the Last Ten Years

ALICE HACKETT

APPROXIMATELY one hundred "first novelists" of the past decade, 1934-1943, inclusive, are tabulated in the chart below. The yardstick used here is that of new writers whose first published book achieved some measure of critical or commerical success, or both. A few whose highly successful first novels appeared during this period have been omitted because their prominence in other literary lines or similar activities was so great that their first novels should be considered as portions of already-established careers. Among such writers are George Santayana, Walter Duranty, Lin Yutang, Carl Carmer, Ilka Chase, Granville Hicks, William Saroyan, Nancy Hale.

In the first column are the names of the authors and the titles of their first novels, arranged chronologically, with a very casual word of comment upon their literary careers to date. The second column scores the outward success—in sales, prize awards, book club selections, critical attention, or what have you. This second column shows that, out of the entire group, thirteen are winners of literary prizes. Nineteen were tapped by the book clubs. Notice that the same publishers appear time after time. Some of them, like Houghton Mifflin and Alfred A. Knopf, have established Literary Fellowships to attract new talent. Harper promotes its "finds" and, like Little, Brown-Atlantic, has well-known and substantial prizes offered periodically. Farrar & Rinehart has its Discoverers

Club; Simon & Schuster and Macmillan, who account for quite a number on the chart, are outstanding as seekers for new writers. During the more recent years, the influence of book clubs, magazines, and movies in building up new writers is increasingly apparent.

The third column records the novels which have followed the new writers' first books. These range from a regular every-other-year output to the Gibraltar of "Gone with the Wind," upon which Margaret Mitchell has taken her stand. Watch the fourth column for repeats. It reveals, briefly, the success of these subsequent books, leaving judgment as to their value as literature or entertainment to the statistician and the critic.

First Novel and Comment	What It Did	Subsequent Work	First Novel and Comment	What It Did	Subsequent Work
1934			JOSEPHINE JOHNSON *Now in November* (Simon & Schuster) Brilliant start. What has happened to her?	First novel by an unknown author, which won the Pulitzer Prize.	1937 — *Jordanstown* (Simon & Schuster).
MILDRED WALKER *Fireweed* (Harcourt, Brace) Consistent, if a bit uneven output, five novels in ten years and two book club selections since her first prize winner.	Hopwood Award winner, sold about 5000 in its first season.	1935 — *Light from Arcturus* (Harcourt, Brace). 1938 — *Dr. Norton's Wife* (Harcourt, Brace). 1940 — *The Brewers' Big Horses* (Harcourt, Brace). 1941—*Unless the Wind Turns* (Harcourt, Brace). 1944—*Winter Wheat* (Harcourt, Brace).	VICTORIA LINCOLN *February Hill* (Farrar & Rinehart) Long-lived book that has had a career as a reprint, and in dramatized form, too. We'd like a successor!	One of the best liked, most remembered books of the period.	1938—*The Daughter* (Simon & Schuster).
JAMES M. CAIN *The Postman Always Rings Twice* (Knopf) The title of his first book has become a part of our language, but subsequent novels have not equalled his first two in popularity.	Startling success for one of the first of the tough, hard school.	1937 — *Serenade* (Knopf). 1941 — *Mildred Pierce* (Knopf). 1942 — *Love's Lovely Counterfeit* (Knopf).	**1935**		
			BESSIE BREUER *Memory of Love* (Simon & Schuster) Good beginning.	Sold about 2000 a week at its height.	
TESS SLESINGER *The Unpossessed* (Simon & Schuster) Later volumes are books of short stories.	Attention by reviewers.		RACHEL FIELD *Time Out of Mind* (Macmillan) After achieving top-ranking success both as a writer of adult fiction and juveniles, Rachel Field died in 1942 before the publication of *And Now Tomorrow.*	Chosen by American booksellers as most distinguished novel published in 1935.	1937—*To See Ourselves* (with Arthur Pederson) (Macmillan). 1938—*All This and Heaven Too* (Macmillan). 1942—*And Now Tomorrow.*
JOHN O'HARA *Appointment in Samarra* (Harcourt, Brace) His first two great bestsellers, mainly followed by short stories.	Famous. Shocked and entertained a big audience.	1935 — *Butterfield 8* (Harcourt, Brace). 1938—*Hope of Heaven* (Harcourt, Brace). 1940—*Pal Joey* (Duell, Sloan & Pearce).	LOUIS PAUL *The Pumpkin Coach* (Doubleday, Doran.) Prolific writer who won the O. Henry Memorial Award with his first short story.	Literary Guild selection. Well reviewed.	1937 — *Emma* (Doubleday, Doran). 1938 —*The Wrong World* (Doubleday, Doran). 1940—*A Passion for Privacy* (Knopf). 1941 — *Reverend Ben Pool* (Duell, Sloan & Pearce). 1943 — *Ordeal of Sergeant Smoot* (Crown). 1943 —*This Is My Brother* (Crown).
MARY ELLEN CHASE *Mary Peters* (Macmillan) Consistent output, popularity increasing with each new novel.	Two printings of 10,000 each almost sold out on publication.	1935—*Silas Crockett* (Macmillan). 1935—*Uplands,* (Little, Brown). 1938—*Dawn in Lyonesse* (Macmillan). 1941—*Windswept* (Macmillan).			

First Novel and Comment	What It Did	Subsequent Work
H. L. DAVIS *Honey in the Horn* (Harper) Has only published a book of poems since his first achievement.	Harper Prize Novel which also won the 1936 Pulitzer Prize.	
LOUIS ZARA *Blessed Is the Man* (Bobbs-Merrill) Chicago writer who is most popular through the Midwest.	Moderate success.	1936 — *Give Us This Day* (Bobbs-Merrill). 1937 — *Some for the Glory* (Bobbs-Merrill). 1940—*This Land Is Ours* (Houghton Mifflin). 1943—*Against This Rock* (Creative Age Press).
HORTENSE LION *The Grass Grows Green* (Houghton Mifflin) Substantial historical novelist.	10,000 printed a month before publication.	1941—*Mill Stream* (Houghton Mifflin).
DOROTHY McCLEARY *Not for Heaven* (Doubleday, Doran) Original writer, worth watching.	Co-winner of *Story* Magazine-Doubleday, Doran prize novel contest.	1937 — *Naked to Laughter* (Doubleday, Doran). 1938—*Paved with Good Intentions* (Doubleday, Doran).
HUMPHREY COBB *Paths of Glory* (Viking Press) Critic, booksellers, and public liked this first book.	Paeans of praise for this one. Book-of-the-Month Club selection.	
ROBERT RYLEE *Deep Dark River* (Farrar & Rinehart) Promising first novelist whose second is not remembered.	Most successful. Also a Book-of-the-Month Club selection.	1937—*St. George of Weldon* (Farrar & Rinehart.)
GALE WILHELM *We Too Are Drifting* (Random House) Off the beaten track. A book every two years for a not very large but appreciative audience.	A first writer published first in an edition limited to 1200 copies. In the regular edition sold over 12,000.	1936—*No Letters for the Dead* (Macmillan). 1938 — *Torchlight to Valhalla* (Random House). 1940 — *Bring Home the Bride* (Morrow). 1942—*The Time Between* (Morrow.)
CHARLES G. FINNEY *The Circus of Dr. Lao* (Viking Press) Original writer who has not yet hit the mark with the public.	The booksellers of America voted it the most original book of 1935.	1937 — *The Unholy City* (Vanguard Press.) *Past the End of the Pavement* (Holt).
FREDERIC PROKOSCH *The Asiatics* (Harper) His reputation grows with each new novel.	Critical success.	1937—*The Seven Who Fled* (Harper). 1939 —*Night of the Poor* Harper). 1941 — *The Skies of Europe* (Harper). 1943—*The Conspirators.*
1936		
AGNES SLIGH TURNBULL *The Rolling Years* (Macmillan) Dependable popularity.	Bestseller.	1938—*Remember the End* (Macmillan). 1942—*The Day Must Dawn* (Macmillan).
TRYGVE GULBRANSSEN *Beyond Sing the Woods* (Putnam) Norwegian writer whose work was well received here in the '30's.	Up in the tens of thousands. Literary Guild selection.	1937—*The Wind from the Mountains* (Putnam).

First Novel and Comment	What It Did	Subsequent Work
MARGARET MITCHELL *Gone with the Wind* (Macmillan) Mrs. Mitchell says she will not write another book.	Sensational fiction success of this century, with rapidity and amount of sales reaching astronomical proportions for the literary world.	
MARCIA DAVENPORT *Of Lena Geyer* (Scribner) Her only other book is a biography, *Mozart*. All three are substantial contributions to the book world.	Extremely popular through many printings.	1942—*The Valley of Decision* (Scribner).
WINIFRED VAN ETTEN *I Am the Fox* (Little, Brown) Nothing more has been published by this Iowa writer whose first book won such a distinguished prize.	Winner of the Atlantic Novel Prize.	
E. P. O'DONNELL *Green Margins* (Houghton Mifflin) Regional novelist of the Louisiana country.	First Houghton Mifflin Fellowship Prize novel was also a Book-of-the-Month Club selection. Sold 86,000.	1941 — *Great Big Doorstep* (Houghton Mifflin).
1937		
CONRAD RICHTER *The Sea of Grass* (Knopf) Increasing stature.	15,000 sold.	1940 — *The Trees* (Knopf). 1942—*Tacey Cromwell* (Knopf). 1943—*The Free Man* (Knopf).
JOLAN FÖLDES *The Street of the Fishing Cat* (Farrar & Rinehart) A number of books of this Scandinavian novelist, including a juvenile, have been brought out over here but none has attained the prominence of her first.	Winner of the International Prize Novel competition.	1937—*I'm Getting Married* (Farrar & Rinehart). 1938—*Prelude to Love* (Farrar & Rinehart). 1939—*Egyptian Interlude* (Farrar & Rinehart).
MILLEN BRAND *The Outward Room* (Simon & Schuster) Has not followed up the success of her short novel.	Book-of-the-Month Club selection.	1939 — *The Heroes* (Simon & Schuster).
GWEN BRISTOW *Deep Summer* (Crowell) The first three formed a historical trilogy later bound together; the fourth is in a setting of wartime America. All bestsellers.	Surprise seller.	1938—*The Handsome Road* (Crowell). 1940 —*This Side of Glory* (Crowell). 1943—*Tomorrow Is Forever* (Crowell).
CLIFFORD DOWDEY *Bugles Blow No More* (Little, Brown) Consistently good in the magazines as well as the bookstores, he has repeated every two years.	Good historical fiction.	1939—*Gamble's Hundred* (Little, Brown). 1941—*Sing for a Penny* (Little, Brown). 1943 — *Tidewater* (Little, Brown.)

First Novel and Comment	What It Did	Subsequent Work	First Novel and Comment	What It Did	Subsequent Work
JEROME WEIDMAN *I Can Get It for You Wholesale* (Simon & Schuster) Modern short story writer, who specializes in unusual titles like *The Horse That Could Whistle Dixie*.	About 18,000 sold.	1938 — *What's In It for Me?* (Simon & Schuster). 1940—*Letter of Credit* (Simon & Schuster). 1941—*I'll Never Go There Any More* (Simon & Schuster). *Lights Around the Shore* (Simon & Schuster).	DOROTHY BAKER *Young Man with a Horn* (Houghton Mifflin) They still like *Young Man with a Horn* better, but *Trio* is not far behind.	Literary Fellowship Award. Literary success that its devotees have not stopped talking about.	1943 — *Trio* (Houghton Mifflin).
CLYDE BRION DAVIS *The Anointed* (Farrar & Rinehart) Several book club selections and critical approval for this new writer.	Discoverers Club, and Book-of-the-Month Club dual selection.	1938 — *The Great American Novel* (Farrar & Rinehart). 1939 — *Nebraska Coast* (Farrar & Rinehart). 1940—*Sullivan* (Farrar & Rinehart). 1942—*Follow the Leader* (Farrar & Rinehart).	TAYLOR CALDWELL *Dynasty of Death* (Scribner) A book a year, at least, and all successful.	Advance praise and interest gave it a big sendoff.	1940—*The Eagles Gather* (Scribner). 1941—*The Earth Is the Lord's* (Scribner). 1942 — *The Strong City* (Scribner). 1943—*The Arms and the Darkness* (Scribner). 1943—*The Turnbulls* (Scribner).
VAUGHAN WILKINS *And So—Victoria* (Macmillan) Historical novels that have hit the mark.	High praise. 149,000 plus reprint sale.	1942—*Seven Tempest* (Macmillan).	LAURA KREY *And Tell of Time* (Houghton Mifflin) Another historical novelist who got her readers both times.	Another first novel that got an effective hand from the publisher in advance.	1940—*On the Long Tide* (Houghton Mifflin).
LAWRENCE EDWARD WATKIN *On Borrowed Time* (Knopf) Versatile, worth watching.	Short novel that was talked about and later a hit on Broadway.	1940—*Geese and the Forum* (Knopf). 1941 —*Gentlemen from England* (Knopf).	WILLIAM BLAKE *The World Is Mine* (Simon & Schuster) Should be another coming along soon.	The dark horse that the publishers groomed paid off.	1939—*The Painter and the Lady* (Simon & Schuster).
STUART CLOETE *The Turning Wheels* (Houghton Mifflin) Novelist of South Africa who has rung the bell repeatedly.	Both critical and popular success. Book-of-the-Month Club selection.	1939—*Watch for the Dawn* (Houghton Mifflin). 1940 — *Yesterday Is Dead* (Smith & Durrell). 1941—*The Hill of Doves* (Houghton Mifflin). 1943—*Congo Song* (Houghton Mifflin).	EVAN JOHN *Crippled Splendour* (Dutton) Why no more?	A bestseller by a new English writer.	
			1939		
DAN WICKENDEN *The Running of the Deer* (Morrow) No repeats as yet.	First novel given critical attention.		PIETRO DI DONATO *Christ in Concrete* (Bobbs-Merrill) Success story—the bricklayer who wrote a great novel.	Co-selection of the Book-of-the-Month Club and great publicity breaks as well as praise from the critics.	
ELMER RICE *Imperial City* (Coward-McCann) His literary interests since then have been in the field of drama.	Best seller by a famous playwright.		JOHN JENNINGS *Next to Valour* (Macmillan) Established historical novelist.	"Almost an overnight bestseller," *Publishers' Weekly.*	1941—*Call the New World* (Macmillan). 1942 — *Gentleman Ranker* (Reynal & Hitchcock). 1943—*Shadow and the Glory* (Reynal & Hitchcock).
1938			BERNICE KELLY HARRIS *Purslane* (University of North Carolina Press) Interest aroused by the first, unheralded novel of this Southern writer.	An advance sale of under 400 copies grew into several thousand.	1941 — *Portulaca* (Doubleday, Doran). 1943—*Sweet Beulah Land* (Doubleday, Doran).
EDMUND GILLIGAN *Boundary Against Night* (Farrar & Rinehart) Has developed the popular magazine, sea-adventure touch.	Discoverers selection.	1939—*White Sails Crowding* (Scribner). 1941—*Strangers in the Vly* (Scribner). 1943—*The Gaunt Woman* (Scribner). 1943 —*Ringed Horizon* (Scribner).	AUGUSTA TUCKER *Miss Susie Slagle's* (Harper) Local Baltimore interest spread until it pushed this first novel and its sequel into the best seller class.	$20,000 paid for the film rights of this unknown author's book before publication. Sold over 50,000 copies.	1942—*The Man Miss Susie Loved* (Harper).
FRANK O. HOUGH *Renown* (Carrick & Evans) Skilful historical novelist.	Very successful.	1939—*If Not Victory* (Carrick & Evans). 1941 — *Neutral Ground* (Lippincott).	**1940**		
NEVIL SHUTE *Kindling* (Morrow) Out-of-the-ordinary plots have made each of his numerous novels outstanding.	Unknown English novelist whose first book with a difficult theme caught on.	1939—*Ordeal* (Morrow). 1940—*Landfall* (Morrow). 1940 — *An Old Captivity* (Morrow). 1942 — *Pied Piper* (Morrow).	ROBERT HENRIQUES *No Arms, No Armour* (Farrar & Rinehart) May repeat.	Winner of All Nations Prize Novel competition and Literary Guild selection bestseller.	1943—*Voice of the Trumpet* (Farrar & Rinehart).

Josephine Johnson

Gwen Bristow

Margaret Mitchell

—*Asasano*

First Novel and Comment	What It Did	Subsequent Work	First Novel and Comment	What It Did	Subsequent Work
RICHARD LLEWELLYN *How Green Was My Valley* (Macmillan) Two entirely different novels, both clicked.	Over 150,000 sold. Made into a great movie.	1943—*None But the Lonely Heart* (Macmillan).	1941		
JAMES STREET *Oh, Promised Land* (Dial Press) Historical novels go over in a big way, particularly in the South.	40,000 sold.	1941—*Biscuit Eater* (Dial). 1941—*My Father's House* (Dial). 1942 — *Tap Roots* (Dial).	INGLIS FLETCHER *Raleigh's Eden* (Bobbs-Merrill) History repeats itself.	Good sales.	1942—*Men of Albemarle* (Bobbs-Merrill).
IOLA FULLER *The Loon Feather* (Harcourt, Brace) Young novelist off to a good start on both historical books.	Hopwood Award winner that in its 6th printing was selling over 2000 a week.	1943—*Shining Trail* (Duell, Sloan & Pearce).	JAN STRUTHER *Mrs. Miniver* (Harcourt, Brace) May be unique. Has also written several books of verse.	One of the most famous of the decade, both in bookstores and on the screen. Book-of-the-Month Club selection.	
JESSE STUART *Trees of Heaven* (Dutton) Known as a poet and short story writer of Kentucky, before he hit the jackpot with his first novel.	Sold 20,000 copies.	1943—*Taps for Private Tussie* (Dutton). 1944—*Mongrel Mettle* (Dutton).	WALTER VAN TILBURY CLARK *The Ox-Bow Incident* (Random House) Watch for his next!	The critics liked both the book and the movie.	
			ISABEL SCOTT RORICK *Mr. and Mrs. Cugat* (Houghton Mifflin) Her public wants more.	"We've got a sleeper on our hands," said the publishers. The public liked it and they pushed it along.	
EVELYN EATON *Quietly My Captain Waits* (Harper) Another historical novelist, well established.	Literary Guild selection, Harper "Find" and bestseller. $40,000 paid for the unpublished manuscript of this unknown author.	1941—*Restless Are the Sails* (Harper). 1943—*Sea Is So Wide* (Harper).	NATHAN SCHACHNER *By the Dim Lamps* (Stokes) Probably many more to come.	Booksellers liked this historical novel by the author of two scholarly works, in advance of publication.	1942—*King's Passenger* (Lippincott). 1943 *Sun Shines West* (Appleton-Century).
CARSON McCULLERS *The Heart Is a Lonely Hunter* (Houghton Mifflin) More will be heard from her.	Critical acclaim for a "remarkable first novel."	1941—*Reflections in a Golden Eye* (Houghton Mifflin).	MARCUS GOODRICH *Delilah* (Farrar & Rinehart) Worth waiting for the next.	Selling in its 40th thousand, *Life* featured this sea story.	
LEILA WARREN *Foundation Stone* (Knopf) Excellent beginning along both literary and commercial lines.	Well up in the thousands.		MAURINE WHIPPLE *The Giant Joshua* (Houghton Mifflin) Specialized scene, so far.	Houghton Mifflin Fellowship Award novel that outsold any earlier ones of the series.	
			ERIGID KNIGHT *Walking the Whirlwind* (Crowell) Well established.	Sold over 10,000.	1942—*Westward the Sun* (Crowell). 1943 —*Covenant* (Crowell).
NINA FEDEROVA *The Family* (Little, Brown) Both biographical in theme. What next?	Atlantic Prize Novel. Over 60,000 sold.	1942—*The Children* (Little, Brown).	MARITTA M. WOLFF *Whistle Stop* (Random House) More to come.	Hopwood Award. Very well received.	1942—*Night Shift* (Random).

First Novel and Comment	What It Did	Subsequent Work	First Novel and Comment	What It Did	Subsequent Work
1942			BRADDA FIELD *Bride of Glory* (Greystone Press)	Literary Guild selection. 125,000 in first printing.	
BUDD SCHULBERG *What Makes Sammy Run?* (Random House) Made a hit the first time.	Bestseller.		AUSTIN TAPPAN WRIGHT *Islandia* (Farrar & Rinehart) Unusual literary history of this mammoth novel representing the life work of a writer who died 11 years before it was published.	A bestseller for many months.	
ALLIS MCKAY *They Came to a River* (Macmillan) Solid success the first time.	Sold way up in the thousands.				
MILDRED JORDAN *One Red Rose Forever* (Knopf) Specializes in the Pennsylvania region.	Over 30,000.	1942—*Apple in the Attic* (Knopf).	JAMES ALDRIDGE *Signed with Their Honour* (Little, Brown) 23-year-old Australian correspondent.	30,000 printed before publication. Serialized.	1944—*The Sea Eagle* (Little, Brown).
HELEN MACINNES *Above Suspicion* (Little, Brown) Her wartime spy stories are the rage today. Market is waiting for more.	Sold over 40,000.	1942—*Assignment in Brittany* (Little, Brown).	PHILIP VAN DOREN STERN *The Drums of Morning* (Doubleday, Doran) Widely known for literary work in other fields. Now occupied as head of the Armed Services Editions.	Bestseller, highly recommended.	
JOHN FAULKNER *Men Working* (Harcourt, Brace) Good critical reception.	Younger brother of William Faulkner.	1942—*Dollar Cotton* (Harcourt, Brace).			
MARY O'HARA *My Friend Flicka* (Lippincott) Her Western ranch stories have made a definite market.	Sold a 1000 a day. Top movie success as well.	1943 — *Thunderhead* (Lippincott).	DOROTHY MACARDLE *The Uninvited* (Doubleday, Doran) Terror story that calls for another.	Literary Guild selection. Over 125,-000 sold.	
JUDITH KELLY *Marriage Is a Private Affair* (Harper)	Bestseller.		STEFAN HEYM *Hostages* (Putnam) Successful war novel.	First printing, 25,000.	
ARTHUR MEEKER, JR. *The Ivory Mischief* (Houghton Mifflin)	Book-of-the-Month Club selection. About 275,-000.		HELEN HOWE *The Whole Heart* (Simon & Schuster)	Good sales and critical attention.	

First Novel and Comment	What It Did	First Novel and Comment	What It Did	First Novel and Comment	What It Did
1943		BETTY SMITH *A Tree Grows in Brooklyn* (Harper)	And everyone knows about Brooklyn now. Harper "Find" and Literary Guild selection, one of the big bestsellers of the year. Movie rights bought two months before publication.	BUCKLIN MOON *The Darker Brother* (Doubleday, Doran)	Young Negro author who came to the fore with his first novel, a story of his race today.
MARGARET CARPENTER *Experiment Perilous* (Little, Brown)	Psychological mystery that was a Literary Guild selection.			ELIZABETH JANEWAY *The Walsh Girls* (Doubleday, Doran)	The newest "first novel" sensation and a Walter Winchell enthusiasm.
KATHRYN FORBES *Mama's Bank Account* (Harcourt, Brace)	A portion ran in *Reader's Digest* before publication. Widespread liking in a quiet way.			ALEXANDER SAXTON *Grand Crossing* (Harper & Brothers)	The reviews were enthusiastic about this story of a young man of today.
XAVIER HERBERT *Capricornia* (Appleton-Century)	Won the Commonwealth Centenary Prize. An Australian novelist who sold close to 50,000 copies here.	CHRISTINE WESTON *Indigo* (Scribner)	Literary Guild selection. 230,000 copies printed in '43.	CLEO DAWSON *She Came to the Valley* (Morrow & Co.)	A courageous woman in a Texas border town in the early days of the century.
		ALAN SEAGER *Equinox* (Simon & Schuster)	Around 30,000 sold.		
AYN RAND *The Fountainhead* (Bobbs-Merrill)	A good word-of-mouth bestseller.	BEN FIELD *The Outside Leaf* (Reynal & Hitchcock)	Regional novel of tobacco farming in Connecticut.	LAURA Z. HOBSON *The Trespassers* (Simon & Schuster)	Fictional treatment of the refugee problem. *The Trespassers* sold over 30,000.

The Exploitation of Books by Broadcasting and Talking Machines
Geoffrey Faber

from

The Author, vol. 47, no. 1, 1936.

THE EXPLOITATION OF BOOKS BY BROADCASTING AND TALKING MACHINES

By GEOFFREY FABER

THE present paper falls into two parts. In the first part I attempt to anticipate and describe future developments; in the second I review the existing European situation. It may seem that this is an illogical order of treatment; but my main thesis is contained in the first part, to which the second part is in the nature of an appendix.

It may also seem that the views developed in the first part are too remote, and even improbable, to be of any practical importance. In most countries all that broadcasting does with books is to provide listeners with a limited amount of literary criticism, or to provide authors and publishers with an opportunity of advertising their wares. With these activities I am not directly concerned. My subject is the *exploitation* of books by broadcasting and talking machines. Of this there is, as yet, very little serious evidence. But the technique and practice of broadcasting are still in their infancy; and the commercial gramophone, though nearly sixty years old, is still hampered by the short-playing record, and is still mainly content to be a purveyor of music and light entertainment. In the field of the mechanical reproduction of sound a technical advance, amounting to a revolution, is long overdue.

The world does not stand still. Human habits change, and the rate of their change is being enormously accelerated by the transformation which science is effecting in the material conditions of civilised life. We have, therefore, as publishers, good reason to ask ourselves whether the habit of reading is in any danger of being weakened or supplanted by some new habit in direct competition with the old; whether any indications of such a process are observable to-day; and whether there are any steps which we can take to minimise the danger—if danger there be. It is precisely now, before our territory has been directly threatened, that we should set ourselves to foresee the future and to fortify our frontiers.

By "direct competition" I mean something more than an encroachment upon the habit of reading by different forms of entertainment or recreation or instruction. Encroachment of this general type I call indirect competition. A great variety of indirect competition has developed, on the horizon of the book-trade, during the last generation. The radio, the gramophone, the cinema are only three among many new distractions, which have all done their best to wean mankind from books. In their failure, perhaps, is our own chief danger. For it tempts us to say to ourselves that, if reading has survived thus far, we can rely upon it to the end of time.

That will not be a safe assumption to make, until reading has survived the direct attack, which has not yet been delivered.

How is it, then, that reading has so far held its own? Certainly in this island reading has not only held its own, but has become much more general than it used to be. The evidence for this statement is to be found, not in the bookshops, but in the so-called "twopenny libraries" which have sprung up and multiplied in every town with incredible rapidity and success during the last few years. These libraries cater for the masses—for the very people whose leisure, one would have imagined, was most easily surrendered to the wireless and the cinema. That is a remarkable and significant fact. It is quite true that the books supplied through the twopenny libraries are not, for the most part, the kind of literature which makes a high demand upon the reader's intelligence. They are, nevertheless, books.

It would seem that the ordinary human imagination, however unsophisticated, needs and will continue to need a field in which it is stimulated to exercise itself. The escape into a ready-made world, however glamorous or exciting, which the cinema provides, does not and cannot meet this need. The theatre, even, does not meet *this* need. Except for the few, music does not meet it. Broadcast news and talks and variety entertainments do not meet it. One might have supposed that broadcast plays, by providing the sound and withholding the visual scene, would meet the need of which I am speaking; yet it is not so: the sound of different voices, each giving its own individual interpretation to its share in the dramatic dialogue, prevents the listener from the free exercise of his own fancy; and in spite of the depressing invisibility of the actors, the illusion of their physical presence is so strong that it inhibits his visual imagination.

Nothing, indeed, can meet this universal human need so well as books. For it is the peculiar virtue of a book that it cannot be read at all, unless it compels the reader to exercise such imagination as he has. And so strong is the pleasure to be obtained from this stimulant—a pleasure not at present to be obtained by any other means than reading —that for the sake of it he performs, without consciousness of effort, an intellectual feat of almost indescribable complexity. The philosopher reading a metaphysical treatise is, if you consider the matter closely, a much less remarkable phenomenon than an errand-boy engrossed in a " penny dreadful."

I have said that this unique pleasure is only to be obtained by reading. In practice this is, broadly, true at the present day. But in theory, and in past and possibly in future practice, it is equally obtainable by listening. " Is that true ? " somebody may object. " Is it not much more difficult to *listen* than to read ? " The facts of history and anthropology disprove the objection. In the dawn of literature and in primitive societies the story is *told* or *sung*. Wheels have a way

of coming full circle. We lettered Western nations have largely forgotten how to listen. But only because of a great invention. It was the invention of printing which doomed the arts of story-telling, of ballad-making, of minstrelsy. And it was not until the use of printing had been developed to the point, when cheap reading-matter was universally obtainable, that the oldest of human arts— the art of the story-*teller* as distinct from the art of the story-*writer*—finally faded almost out of existence, together with the secondary arts of reciting or reading aloud.

Yet the art of reading aloud has never wholly perished. To what extent it persists in other countries I do not know. In this country it still lingers on in old-fashioned family circles, and was habitual only a generation or two ago. Mothers, aunts, and nurses are, no doubt, still reading aloud to children all the world over. In our English church services the reading of the " lessons " from the Old and the New Testaments is a prominent and popular feature. In most of our public schools these lessons are read by the boys, and their performance is critically listened to. At many schools there are prizes for " reading aloud." The habit of giving public readings, for an admission fee, has now decayed. But in the last century it was very popular ; and the great English novelist, Charles Dickens, used to tour the country, much as a *prima donna* might tour it to-day, giving readings from his own works.

To listen is, in fact, easier than to read. The spoken lecture is still the most universal and effective instrument of education ; the preacher is still the most influential persuader of men's consciences. Even more significant is the mastery of rhetoric which characterises our modern dictators, and the use which they make of the wireless to bring their speeches to the ears of the people. The art, the habit, of listening has undergone, through the invention of broadcasting, a gigantic renascence. And one of the most surprising features of this new listening age is the discovery that one can listen, without discomfort or difficulty, to the voice of an unseen man or woman.

Up to the present time, there has been no really systematic attempt by the broadcasting services (except, perhaps in the B.B.C. " children's hour ") to take full advantage of this revived habit by reviving also the arts either of story-telling or reading aloud.* The genuine art of story-telling is an extempore art ; and the conditions under which such an art can be effectively developed are long since departed. It is unlikely that it has a future even in broadcasting. Broadcast story-telling is only a variant of reading-aloud, using a script and aiming at an illusion of spontaneity. It is, in effect, a mode of first publication ; and in this respect it may be the forerunner of developments very menacing to publishers. It is, however, the broadcast reading of printed and published books which more immediately concerns us.

In this direction the broadcasting authorities in general, have, as yet, shown little understanding of the possibilities. Here, at least, such readings as have been given suffer from at least three crippling defects. First, they are usually very short ; and secondly, they are usually inserted between items of altogether different character. Now reading aloud, from the listener's point of view, is not a thing to which he is able, or wants, to adjust himself all of a sudden, and for a short space of time. It should be a leisurely business. Reading aloud is a very much slower process than silent reading ; if ground is to be covered, an hour is not too much for a prose reading. And the act of listening is an act to which the listener must compose himself with the comfortable certainty that his mood will not be quickly destroyed by some violent alteration of the programme.

Thirdly, the reader must known how to read. Most authors are thoroughly bad

readers.* But the worst reader of all is the trained elocutionist. Reading aloud is a *natural* art—you possess it, or you do not possess it, and there is little more to be said. Little, that is, to be said which can convert a bad reader into a good reader. But much to be said upon the differences between the bad and the good.

Something of what can so be said, I propose to say, for it bears closely upon the question we have to consider—whether reading aloud, by the aid of the wireless or the gramophone, is *capable* of competition with silent reading.

The voice of the reader must, to begin with, have certain qualities. It must not be monotonous. It must be capable, without effort, of natural variation in pitch and tone. It must have *timbre*—it must in itself be a pleasant noise. It must be sympathetic to the microphone. These are physical qualities, easily tested. Far more important are the mental qualities of the reader, and the technique which he employs. Perhaps the first essential is, that he should use his voice as if what he is saying were being said for the first time. The vast majority of public readers break down before this test ; they fail to manipulate their voices with the necessary naturalness—you know either that they have too carefully calculated the effects they wish to produce, or that they are being taken by surprise by the text before them.

The next rule is that, while monotony is Scylla, over-dramatic emphasis is Charybdis. The voice of the reader must follow the changes of thought, emotion, action and person. Yet it must not follow them too far. If it does so, the reader is attempting to do the listener's work. And the whole point of reading aloud is that the listener should be stimulated by the voice of the reader to reconstruct in his own imagination the scene

---

* But see page 11 *infra*. I am also informed that in Australia the practice of broadcasting novels, by daily instalments, is in contemplation, if it has not already begun.

* " During the autumn season," writes my Norwegian correspondent, " it is a general practice to let the authors read selections from their new books. Voices have been raised, however, to give professional readers preference, as the authors are not always good reciters."

or the argument of which he is being given the elements. The upper dramatic limit can, nevertheless, vary very greatly, according to the powers of the reader. The finest reader, to whom I have ever listened, was the eighty-year-old Chaplain of an Oxford College. It is beyond my power to describe the beautiful and moving and extraordinarily wide variations of tone which he used in his reading of the Psalms. For this reason I am shy to limit the dramatic possibilities of reading aloud. Yet, in the light of this experience, I am sure of one fact : namely, that this eloquent variation of pitch and tone must not attempt to mimic the persons of a tale ; it must, if it is to be warmly accepted by the listener, be the expression of the reader's *own* emotions.

A great deal, here, must evidently depend upon the *rapport* between the reader and listener. Nothing but experiment can show how far such a *rapport* can be established between an invisible reader and his hearers. But it is already clear that a sympathetic voice can create it to an extraordinary degree. In our English broadcasts, it is customary for the announcer to bid his listeners " Good-night." A few years ago a dying child in a hospital asked that she might hear a particular announcer bid her good-night before she died. So friendly and comforting can be the quality of a disembodied human voice.

Reading aloud, then is a delicate and complex social art. Executed by a reader gifted with the right sort of voice and with natural taste it is capable of giving unique pleasure. This pleasure differs in many respects from the pleasure which is to be had from silent reading. There will always be silent readers—people who dislike the intrusion, however tactful, of another personality between themselves and the author ; and there will always be, especially in the study of difficult matters, an overriding advantage possessed by the printed book over any other conceivable communication of facts and ideas—the silent reader can re-read sentences and paragraphs, if their meaning or their connection has escaped him at their first

reading ; he can turn back to relate one passage with another ; he can pause to reflect ; he can begin when he likes, go on as long as he likes, and leave off when he likes. Yet some of these advantages could belong almost as easily to the talking machine as to the book—already the dictaphone has solved the problem of repeating a desired passage. And for many not unintelligent readers the spoken book, like the spoken lecture, has this peculiar advantage, that it *compels the attention to move*. The conscientious silent reader is apt to get stuck over a particular passage, when it would be better for him to be moving on with the main argument ; the spoken book will not allow him so easily to fall into this trap. Again, the pace of the spoken book is a great deal slower than the pace of silent reading ; the listener has, therefore, more time to digest the general argument, and his gain from this slower movement may very well more than counterbalance the difficulty of absorbing the full content of a hard passage. Moreover, the really intelligent enunciation of a difficult argument may be an enormous assistance to the understanding of it ; to hear an obscure passage in, for example, one of St. Paul's epistles, read by a man who really understands what he is reading, is a revelation of the aid which intelligent reading aloud can give.

To the exceptional man, to the man of strong and independent mind, or to the natural solitary or to the man of extremely rapid perceptions, silent reading will always be the ideal means of enlarging his knowledge or refreshing his imagination. But the great majority of readers are not to be so characterised. Most readers are out to enjoy themselves, and they do not wish their enjoyment to be more difficult than it need be. They want to be " taken out of them-selves "—as our English idiom has it. They would, indeed, rather not be alone. The phenomenon of the " best seller " shows that clearly enough. They read the book that everybody else is reading, not simply because the voice of the people is the voice of God, but because they obtain, in that way, a feeling of companionship with their kind. If it were possible for them to *listen* to somebody reading the latest successful novel they would obtain that sense of companionship in a still higher degree, not because other people would be listening at the same time ; but because they would be hearing a sympathetic human voice—a concrete symbol of their unity with their fellow-men.

The characteristics of good reading aloud seem, then, to be peculiarly apt for broadcast transmission or mechanical reproduction. But what are the probabilities that either the broadcasting services or the gramophone companies will set out to conquer this new field ? The indications are so slight that scepticism is natural. In Germany, indeed, the evidence seems to point in the contrary direction ; since the early experiment of broadcasting longish books by instalments has now been abandoned.

After all, broadcasting is barely in its 'teens. Yet already it is beginning to encounter the saturation problem. There is a limit to the amount of music which people can endure to hear ; there is a limit to their tolerance of informative talks ; until television comes, there is a limit to wireless drama. Hitherto the broadcasting services have been handicapped by the impossible task of trying to please everybody all the time, with the result that they are in danger of pleasing more and more people for less and less time. But as stations multiply, financial resources increase, and receiving sets become more selective, the broadcasting companies will be able to approach their ideal and please nearly all their listeners nearly all the time. They will then be able to give their nationals not one or two, but several alternative programmes. And one of those programmes will be, if I am not a false prophet, largely devoted to reading aloud.

Such a programme will have quite unique advantages. First of all, it will be very cheap. Second, it will have a regular, faithful and appreciative public. Thirdly, it

will be easy to arrange. It will mean no cudgelling of exhausted brains ; no invention of new topics ; no tracking down of experts. There *are* the books, thousands and thousands of them, enough to last for ever, old and new.

That stage will not, of course, be reached in one bound. There will be previous stages of cautious experiment. In England I imagine that the first stage will be the reading aloud of a book like " The Pickwick Papers " on (say) a Regional programme by instalments of half-an-hour every day. Appreciative letters will reach Broadcasting House ; many of them will say " half-an-hour is too short." The British Broadcasting Corporation will sit up and take notice. Here, they will say in the Programmes Department, is something which is going to be popular and save us a tremendous lot of trouble.

At what point the gramophone companies will also sit up and take notice I do not presume to forecast. But the commercial " talking book " is bound to come. Already there are talking-books for the blind— ordinary gramophone records, each of which will run for twenty-five minutes. The time must arrive when it will be in the power of the ordinary citizen to put a record on his gramophone and sit down to listen to it for half-an-hour. Only—it may not be a gramophone at all. There are several other sound-reproducing mechanisms in the process of being invented or perfected. In ten, or twenty, or thirty years' time, the talking book may be a very real competitor with the printed book—and a far more serious competitor than the broadcast book. Its development will be enormously facilitated if the " optical " gramophone is perfected. This invention is at present in a rudimentary stage ; but there seems no reason why it should remain there. The record is merely a black line of varying thickness printed on a strip of paper wound upon a drum. A photoelectric cell receives light reflected from the record and translates the fluctuations of the light into fluctuations of electric current, which are converted into sound by a loudspeaker. When this, or some similar invention, is brought to maturity, we may live to see complete talking books sold in little bundles of paper tape, at the price of a cinema ticket.*

In this renaissance of the reciter's art, which I am imagining, it is not to be supposed that, with all the extraordinary and novel resources at their command, the broadcasting and gramophone studios will be content to rely solely on the human voice. There will, at first, be many dreadful offences committed. But, when the first orgies are over, how subtle and manifold will be the auxiliary devices employed to suggest the background of the story which is being read aloud. The sounds of breaking waves, and crying sea-gulls, would wonderfully heighten the colour of a great descriptive passage, now in my mind, in one of Sir Walter Scott's novels. It would be an easy exercise to multiply such examples ; and it will be an exciting new adventure for the experts to discover just how far they can go

---

* For a popular account of the " optical gramophone " see Dr. Hatfield's talk in *The Listener* of January 22, 1936.

without going too far. And television may come to their aid—in what degree I scarcely dare suggest . . .

In their first stages, the broadcast and the talking books are likely to be non-copyright books—partly because there will be no fees or royalties to pay, and partly because ordinary prudence will confine the experiment to the established popular favourites. Unless publishers combine, in different countries, to form record-producing companies, it is difficult to see what protection they can hope to devise or receive against this coming form of direct competition with popular reprints of non-copyright books. It will, however, not be long before the broadcasting and gramophone companies enter the copyright field. And it may be a matter of life or death for publishers—more especially for fiction publishers—to have previously established their firm right to exercise, jointly with the author, control over, and to have a substantial financial interest in, the broadcasting and mechanical sound-reproduction rights for all books that they publish.

[The second part of Mr. Faber's paper will appear in the Winter issue.—Ed. *The Author.*]

Post-Georgian Poet in Search of a Master
Douglas Goldring

from

Coterie, 4, 1920.

DOUGLAS GOLDRING

POST-GEORGIAN POET IN SEARCH OF
A MASTER

I HAD been well brought up: I liked the best.
    My prose was modelled on Rebecca West,
My "little things" erstwhile reflected tone,
My brother poets claimed me as their own.
In those blithe days, before the War began—
Ah me, I was a safe young Georgian!

Now all is chaos, all confusion.
Bolshes have cast E. M. from his high throne:
Wild women have rushed in, and savage Yanks
Blather of Booth and Heaven: and T. S. E.
Uses great words that are as Greek to me.
Tell me the Truth, and ah, forgo these pranks—
Whom must I imitate? Who's really *It*?
On whose embroidered footstool should I sit?

There's Podgrass now—*he* seems a coming man;
Writes unintelligible stuff, half French, half Erse.
He told me Philomela had technique
But not much feeling; Crashaw knew his trade,
But Keats had no idea of writing verse...
The thing to read (he said) had just come out,
His latest work, entitled "Bloody Shout."

And then there's Father Michael, Secker's pal,
Who's left dear Sylvia for the Clergy-house.
Michael lives sumptuously: silver, old oak,
Incunabula, the Yellow Book, Madonnas, Art;

Excited wobblings on the brink of Rome;
The " Inner Life," birettas, candles, Mass;
Fun with *Church Times* and Bishops; four hair shirts,
And Mr. Percy Dearmer's Parson's Book.
He talked to me of Antinomianism
And stirred the incense, while two candles burned,
Then read aloud his works, with eye upturned.
(Somehow I felt I'd heard it all before—
When I was " boat-boy," in a pinafore.)

Are Sitwells really *safe?* Is Iris Tree
A certain guide to higher poesy?
Can Nicholls be relied on, for a lead;
Or should I thump it with Sassoon and Read?
Or would it not be vastly better fun
To write of Nymphs, with Richard Aldington?
Or shall I train, and nervously aspire
To join with Edward Shanks and J. C. Squire
—A modest "chorus" in a well-paid choir?

I've thought of middling Murry and Sturge Moore,
I've thought of Yeats (I thought of him before).
I've toyed with Aldous Huxley and Monro—
I don't know where I am, or where to go.

Oh, mighty Mr. Gosse! Unbend, I pray!
Guide one poor poet who has lost his way . . .

The Proletarian Writer
George Orwell and Desmond Hawkins

from

Collected Essays, Journalism and Letters of
George Orwell, vol. II, Sonia Orwell and Ian Angus (eds.)
Secker and Warburg, London, 1968.

The Proletarian Writer

Discussion between George Orwell and Desmond Hawkins

HAWKINS: I have always doubted if there is such a thing as proletarian literature—or ever could be. The first question is what people mean by it. What do *you* mean by it? You would expect it to mean literature written specifically for the proletariat, and read by them, but does it?

ORWELL: No, obviously not. In that case the most definitely proletarian literature would be some of our morning papers. But you can see by the existence of publications like *New Writing*, or the Unity Theatre, for instance, that the term has a sort of meaning, though unfortunately there are several different ideas mixed up in it. What people mean by it, roughly speaking, is a literature in which the viewpoint of the working class, which is supposed to be completely different from that of the richer classes, gets a hearing. And that, of course, has got mixed up with Socialist propaganda. I don't think the people who throw this expression about mean literature written *by* proletarians. W.H. Davies was a proletarian, but he would not be called a proletarian writer. Paul Potts would be called a proletarian writer, but he is not a proletarian. The reason why I am doubtful of the whole conception is that I don't believe the proletariat can create an independent literature while they are not the dominant class. I believe that their literature is and must be bourgeois literature with a slightly different slant. After all, so much that is supposed to be new is simply the old standing on its head. The poems that were written about the Spanish civil war, for instance, were simply a deflated version of the stuff that Rupert Brooke and Co. were writing in 1914.

HAWKINS: Still, I think one must admit that the cult of proletarian literature—whether the theory is right or not—has had some effect. Look at writers like James Hanley, for instance, or Jack Hilton, or Jack Common. They have something new to say—something at any rate that could not quite be said by anyone who had had the ordinary middle-class upbringing. Of course there was a tremendous amount of cant about proletarian literature in the years after the Slump, when Bloomsbury went all Marxist, and Communism became fashionable. But the thing had really started earlier. I should say it started just before the last war, when Ford Madox Ford, the editor of the *English Review*, met D.H. Lawrence and saw in him the portent of a new class finding expression in literature. Lawrence's *Sons and Lovers* really did break new ground. It recorded a kind of experience that simply had not got into print before. And yet it was an experience that had been shared by millions of people. The question is why it had never been recorded earlier. Why would you say there had been no books like *Sons and Lovers* before that time?

ORWELL: I think it is simply a matter of education. After all, though Lawrence was the son of a coal miner he had had an education that was not very different from that of the middle class. He was a university graduate, remember. Before a certain date— roughly speaking, before the 'nineties, when the Education Act began to take effect—very few genuine proletarians could write: that is, write with enough facility to produce a book or a story. On the other hand the professional writers knew nothing about prole- tarian life. One feels this even with a really radical writer like Dickens. Dickens does not write about the working class; he does not know enough about them. He is *for* the working class, but he feels himself completely different from them—far more different than the average middle-class person would feel nowadays.

HAWKINS: Then, after all, the appearance of the proletariat as a class capable of producing books means a fresh development of literature—completely new subject-matter, and a new slant on life?

ORWELL: Yes, except in so far as the experience of all classes in society tends to become more and more alike. I maintain that the class distinctions in a country like England are now so unreal that they cannot last much longer. Fifty years ago or even twenty years ago a factory worker and a small professional man, for instance, were very different kinds of creature. Nowadays they are very much alike, though they may not realise it. They see the same films and listen to the same radio programmes, and they wear very similar clothes and live in very similar houses. What used to be called a proletarian—what Marx would have meant by a proletarian—only exists now in the heavy industries and on the land. All the same, there's no doubt that it was a big step forward when the *facts* of working-class life were first got on to paper. I think it has done something to push fiction back towards realities and away from the over-civilised stuff that Galsworthy and so forth used to write. I think possibly the first book that did this was *The Ragged-Trousered Philanthropists*, which has always seemed to me a wonderful book, although it is very clumsily written. It recorded things that were every-day experience but which simply had not been noticed before—just as, so it is said, no one before AD 1800 ever noticed that the sea was blue. And Jack London was another pioneer in the same line.

HAWKINS: And how about language and technique? Cyril Connolly, you may remember, said last week that the great innovations in literature have been made in technique rather than in content. As an example, he said that there is nothing new in Joyce except his technique. But surely these revolutionary proletarians have not shown much interest in technique? Some of them seem to be little different in manner from the pious moralising lady novelists of the last century. Their revolt is entirely in content, in theme—is that so?

ORWELL: I think in the main that's true. It's a fact that written English is much more colloquial now than it was twenty years ago, and that's all to the good. But we've borrowed much more from America than from the speech of the English working class. As for technique, one of the things that strikes one about the proletarian writers, or the people who are called proletarian writers, is how conservative they are. We might make an exception of Lionel Brittain's *Hunger and Love*. But if you look through a volume of *New Writing* or the *Left Review* you won't find many experiments.

HAWKINS: Then we come back to this: that what is called proletarian literature stands or falls by its subject-matter. The mystique behind these writers, I suppose, is the class-war, the hope of a better future, the struggle of the working class against miserable living conditions.

ORWELL: Yes, proletarian literature is mainly a literature of revolt. It can't help being so.

HAWKINS: And my quarrel with it has always been that it is too much dominated by political considerations. I believe politicians and artists do not go well together. The goal of a politician is always limited, partial, short-term, over-simplified. It has to be, to have any hope of realisation. As a principle of action, it cannot afford to consider its own imperfections and the possible virtues of its opponents. It cannot afford to dwell on the pathos and the tragedy of all human endeavour. In short, it must exclude the very things that are valuable in art Would you agree therefore that when proletarian literature becomes literature it ceases to be proletarian—in the political sense? Or that when it becomes propaganda it ceases to be literature?

ORWELL: I think that's putting it too crudely. I have always maintained that every artist is a propagandist. I don't mean a political propagandist. If he has any honesty or talent at all he cannot be that. Most political propaganda is a matter of telling lies, not only about the facts but about your own feelings. But every artist is a propagandist in the sense that he is trying, directly or indirectly, to impose a vision of life that seems to him desirable. I think we are broadly agreed about the vision of life that proletarian literature is trying to impose. As you said just now, the mystique behind it is the class-war. That is something real; at any rate, it is something that is believed in. People will die for it as well as write about it. Quite a lot of people died for it in Spain. My point about proletarian literature is that though it has been important and useful so far as it went, it isn't likely to be permanent or to be the beginning of a new age in literature. It is founded on the revolt against capitalism, and capitalism is disappearing. In a Socialist State, a lot of our left-wing writers—people like Edward Upward, Christopher Caudwell, Alec Brown, Arthur Calder-Marshall and all the rest of them—who have specialised in attacking the society they live in, would have nothing to attack. Just to revert for a moment to a book I mentioned above, Lionel Brittain's *Hunger and Love*. This was an outstanding book and I think in a way it is representative of proletarian literature. Well, what is it about? It is about a young proletarian who wishes he wasn't a proletarian. It simply goes on and on about the intolerable conditions of working-class life, the fact that the roof leaks and the sink smells and all the rest of it. Now, you couldn't found a literature on the fact that the sink smells. As a convention it isn't likely to last so long as the siege of Troy. And behind this book, and lots of others like it, you can see what is really the history of a proletarian writer nowadays. Through some accident—very often it is simply due to having a long period on the dole—a young man of the working class gets a chance to educate himself. Then he starts writing books, and naturally he makes use of his early experiences, his sufferings under poverty, his revolt against the existing system, and so forth. But he isn't really creating an independent literature. He writes in the bourgeois manner, in the middle-class dialect. He is simply the black sheep of the bourgeois family, using the old methods for slightly different purposes. Don't mistake me. I'm not saying that he can't be as good a writer as anyone else; but if he is, it won't be because he is a working man but because he is a talented person who has learnt to write well. So long as the bourgeoisie are the dominant class, literature must be bourgeois. But I don't believe that they will be dominant much longer, or any other class either. I believe we are passing into a classless period, and what we call proletarian literature is one of the signs of the change. But I don't deny for an instant the good that it has done—the vitalising effect of getting working-class experience and working-class values on to paper.

HAWKINS: And, of course, as a positive gain, it has left behind quite a lot of good books?

ORWELL: Oh yes, lots. Jack London's book *The Road*, Jack Hilton's *Caliban Shrieks*, Jim Phelan's prison books, George Garrett's sea stories, Private Richards's *Old Soldier Sahib*, James Hanley's *Grey Children*—to name just a few.

HAWKINS: All this time we have said nothing about the literature that the proletariat does read—not so much the daily papers, but the weeklies, the twopennies.

ORWELL: Yes, I should say that the small weekly press is much more representative. Papers like *Home Chat* or the *Exchange and Mart*, and *Cage-Birds*, for instance.

HAWKINS: And the literature that really comes out of the people themselves—we have said nothing about that. Take, for instance, the camp-fire ballads of the men who built the Canadian Pacific Railway; the sea shanties; negro poems like "Stagolee"; and the old street broadsheets—especially the ones about executions, the sort of thing that must have inspired Kipling's "Danny Deever". And epitaphs, limericks, advertisement jingles—sticking simply to poetry, those are the special literature of the proletariat, aren't they?

ORWELL: Yes, and don't forget the jokes on the comic coloured postcards, especially Donald McGill's. I'm particularly attached to those. And above all the songs that the soldiers made up and sang for themselves in the last war. And the Army songs for bugle calls and military marches—those are the real popular poetry of our time, like the ballads in the Middle Ages. It's a pity they are always unprintable.

HAWKINS: Yes, but I'm afraid now we are drifting into folk literature, and it seems to me that we must keep the two things distinct. From what you say I imagine that this word "proletarian" is going to be quite meaningless if you detach it from revolutionary politics.

ORWELL: Yes, the term "proletariat" is a political term belonging solely to the industrial age.

HAWKINS: Well, I think we are completely in agreement that the theory of a separate proletarian literature just doesn't work. For all its apparent difference it comes within the framework of what you call bourgeois writing.

ORWELL: By "bourgeois" and "bourgeoisie" I don't mean merely the people who buy and sell things. I mean the whole dominant culture of our time.

HAWKINS: If we agree about that, we have still got to assess the contribution that these so-called proletarian writers have made. Because it *is* a contribution and it would be absurd to pass that over in disposing of the theory.

ORWELL: I think they have made two kinds of contribution. One is that they have to some extent provided new subject-matter, which has also led other writers who are not of the working class to look at things which were under their noses, but not noticed, before. The other is that they have introduced a note of what you might call crudeness and vitality. They have been a sort of voice in the gallery, preventing people from becoming too toney and too civilised.

HAWKINS: And then there's another contribution, which you yourself mentioned earlier, and that is language. T. S. Eliot stressed the importance of constantly drawing newly minted words into the language, and in recent years it is pre-eminently from the working class that new words and phrases have come. It may be from the film or the street or through any channel, but the proletarian writer deserves credit for giving modern English much of its raciness and colour.

ORWELL: Well, of course, the question is whether it has got much colour! But the thing you can say for the typical prose of the last ten years is that it has not got many frills or unnecessary adjectives. It's plain. It is rather questionable whether the sort of prose that has developed in this way is suitable for expressing very subtle thoughts, but it is excellent for describing action, and it is a good antidote to the over-refined type of prose which used to be fashionable—very good in its way, of course, but tending to emasculate the language altogether.

HAWKINS: Well, to conclude—it looks as if the slogan of pro-letarian literature has made a nice rallying-point for some work that was well worth having and it has been a focus for working-class writers, whether they were revolutionary or not, either in technique or in politics or in subject. But the phrase itself as a critical term is virtually useless.

ORWELL: It has had a certain use as a label for a rather heterogeneous literature belonging to a transition period, but I do agree with you that for there to be what could really be called a proletarian literature the proletariat would have to be the dominant class.

HAWKINS: Yes, and in assuming that it would certainly have to change its character. And that still leaves open the question we have only just touched on—how far can politics be introduced into art without spoiling the art?

Broadcast in the Home Service of the BBC, 6 December 1940; printed in the *Listener* 19 December 1940.